Chasing the Eastern Star

CHASING THE EASTERN STAR

Adventures in Biblical Reader-Response Criticism

Mark Allan Powell

Westminster John Knox Press
Louisville, Kentucky

Scripture quotations from the New Revised Standard Version of the Bible are copyright © 1989 by the Division of Christian Education of the National Council of the Churches of Christ in the U.S.A. and are used by permission.

Book design by Sharon Adams
Cover design by designpointinc.com

First edition

Published by Westminster John Knox Press
Louisville, Kentucky

This book is printed on acid-free paper that meets the American National Standards Institute Z39.48 standard. ∞

PRINTED IN THE UNITED STATES OF AMERICA

01 02 03 04 05 06 07 08 09 10 — 10 9 8 7 6 5 4 3 2 1

Library of Congress Cataloging-in-Publication Data is on file at the Library of Congress, Washington, D.C.

ISBN 0-664-22278-1

Dedicated to
Robert and Phyllis Leatherman

Contents

Introduction

This book is about how people read the Bible. It starts with the rather obvious observation that different people read the Bible differently and inquires why this is so. It ends with what I hope are less-than-obvious conclusions regarding the significance and implications of such diversity. Significance for *what?* Well, mainly, for *reading* . . . but also for *interpretation* (especially biblical interpretation) . . . and for *theology.*

Just over a decade ago, Harold Bloom wrote a book called *Ruin the Sacred Truths* that dealt with the interrelationship of poetry and belief in the reception and criticism of Western literature.[1] This book is somewhat like that one insofar as it analyzes the phenomenon of reading, noting moves that readers may be expected to make when perusing a given work of literature (in this case, the Gospel of Matthew) and considering reasons why they sometimes do not actually make those moves. It is not impossible that students of literature will find some value in this book for that reason alone. The Bible in general and the Gospel of Matthew in particular offer textbook examples of literary works that have been read in different ways and from different perspectives by people with all sorts of different agendas. And, certainly, some of the conclusions I reach regarding the reading of Matthew's Gospel could apply to the reading of other literature as well.

But if *you* are such a student—a person with a general interest in literature and in reading—then I should warn you that you will have to tolerate a bit of sermonizing as these pages unfold. This book is also interested in the specific implications that understanding the phenomenon of reading might have for how religious people use the Bible in their private and public lives. Thus, eventually (and perhaps ultimately), it is interested in *theology,* in how people reflect on and converse about God. Such a move may be inevitable. Bloom's book was fully secular, but he knew its implications had significance not only for the phenomenon of reading but also for the very concept of "sacred truth."

The field of biblical studies presently seems to be divided into two general camps: author-oriented scholars who use historical criticism and reader-oriented scholars who use literary criticism. There is something of a cold war between these—not much outright hostility but not much interchange either. I remember a session of the Matthew Group at the Society of Biblical Literature where two of our country's top scholars were scheduled to engage in dialogue on a common theme. Dan Via presented a literary-critical study of an important text; Robert Gundry responded with his own redaction-critical analysis of the same passage. It was interesting to hear both papers but at their conclusion neither scholar had much to say to the other. To quote Gundry: "I don't really understand what he was doing." And to quote Via: "I just can't look at a text like that."

Are they from two different worlds? And if they are, is there any problem with that?

One significant difference between these two approaches is the way they address diversity in interpretation. Both acknowledge this existential fact: people can and do interpret texts in different ways. But how should we account for this? Is it because some people understand the text rightly while others misunderstand it? Or is it simply that different people understand in different ways? The former answer tends to be favored by historical critics; the latter by literary critics. In an extreme rendering—which is usually a caricature—historical critics may be depicted as claiming that a text has only one correct interpretation: the meaning that was intended by the author.[2] Or, again, in an extreme rendering—also a caricature—literary critics may be depicted as recognizing an infinite diversity of interpretations, none of which can be ruled out by any objective standard. Removing exaggeration, it is safe to say that scholars who favor *authors* maintain that some interpretations are right and others are clearly wrong, while scholars who favor *readers* think it is abusive to impose understandings that limit people's creativity or imagination.

A little autobiographical reflection: I have been both an author and a reader and have experienced frustration on both accounts.

Reflections as a Reader

I am generally associated with the literary-critical camp of biblical scholarship, and I admit that I often view the author-oriented obsessions of historical-critical scholars as myopic. This prejudice will no doubt come through in subtle and less-than-subtle ways in the pages that follow. For me, the issue cuts deeper than professional affiliations—it goes to the heart of matters related to piety and faith. This is the *Bible* we are talking about—the sacred Word of God. I readily admit that if we were talking about Homer or Virgil, my investment in how the book is to be interpreted would be considerably lessened. The latter works are important and meaningful, but I do not recognize them as authoritative for my life.[3]

I am not only a Bible scholar; I am also a pietistic Bible reader—and proud of it (in a humble way, of course; we pietists have to be careful about being "proud" of anything). I read the Bible as a living Word that speaks today—to me, to the church, to our society. The revelation of scripture is obviously grounded in history, but I don't think it is limited to history. If it were, then why would we need the Holy Spirit? Why didn't the Holy Spirit just fly back to heaven as soon as the Bible was written? Having inspired those biblical authors to write those historical texts, was the Spirit's work all done? I think not. I believe that there still is a Holy Spirit and that he, she, or it continues to lead us into all truth—just like Jesus said (John 16:12–15).

Over the years I have detected a tendency in historical criticism that directs people away from present-day meaning. I remember vividly one occasion that may serve as an example. A "Ladies' Circle" was meeting for Bible Study in the parlor of a church. The leader read the text for the day from Galatians 5:13–15. She then invited participants to take turns sharing what Paul's words meant to them. One woman gave a testimony about the years of conflict she had experienced with her sister and told how both of them, as Christians, had tried to take to heart Paul's admonition not to "bite and devour one another." Next, the pastor of the church was asked to share his interpretation of the passage. He related that Paul's words in these few verses were directed to a congregation that had wrestled with the problems of integrating converts from the Gentile world into a new religion that had its roots in law-observant Judaism. He explained to the woman who had shared her story, as tactfully as he could, that Paul did not care about her or her sister; Paul was concerned with the relations of diverse social/ethnic groups in the first century. If the church is to find an analogous message in the text for today, it should look to its involvements in cross-cultural evangelism programs.

As a literary critic, I have concerns about a hermeneutic (that is, an approach to interpretation) that privileges so exclusively the value of authorial intent. Any literature that is worth reading transcends the contextual interests specific to its production. Texts come to mean things that their authors did not consciously intend.[4] The very definition of a "classic" may be a work that continues to be valued in a time and place other than that in which it was composed. Does anyone want to contend that the Bible is not classic literature? We may regard it as more than that, to be sure—and this *more than* may be what justifies its subjection to a critical scrutiny unparalleled in the study of ancient literature. But the last time I checked, *more than* means "in addition to" not "instead of." Apart from any doctrine of scripture or divine inspiration—if the Bible is simply moderately good literature—its ability to convey meaning must not be equated with expositions of the immediate concerns of its writers. To be blunt, a method devoted solely to the latter does not concern itself with what the Bible *means* but, at best, with what it *meant*.[5] Of course, historical critics may appeal to the principle of *analogy* for drawing relevant lessons from the time-bound original meaning for the present day. But what is a proper analogy to Jew/Gentile relations in first-century Galatia? The pastor says cross-cultural evangelism is but sibling rivalry is not. Who gets to decide? Basically, he does because he's the pastor.

As a Christian, I have concerns about a hermeneutic that privileges an educated elite, empowering them to determine the meaning of scripture that is to be authoritative not only for them but for everyone else as well.[6] Partly this is due to my own experience—I have learned too much about the Bible over the years from students and pastors—and from ladies in Bible Study groups—to imagine that my Ph.D. grants me a monopoly of insight into these writings. But largely my concerns come from the self-testimony of scripture itself. Does not Paul claim to be writing for people among whom not many were wise, not many were powerful (1 Cor. 1:26)? Did not Jesus choose to disclose the mysteries of the kingdom of heaven in tales for fishermen, peasants, and children? Is not the entire New Testament written in koine Greek, the language of the uneducated common folk? Do not these scriptures disclose a God who hides the truth from the wise and intelligent and reveals it to infants (Matt. 11:25), a God who chooses what is foolish and weak in this world to shame the wise and the strong (1 Cor. 1:27)?

Reflections as an Author

I share the above reflections as a Bible reader who discovers that his own inter-pretations of scripture—even those fired in the crucible of critical scholarship—are often strikingly different but not necessarily superior to the interpretations of other readers. But I am also an author of books, and I have learned what it means to have my words interpreted in ways that I did not intend. I don't like it.

- In one of my books I quoted a scholar on a position with which I did not concur, then gave my reasons for disagreeing with that posi-tion. Later, I was basically accused of inconsistent backpedaling by another scholar who couldn't understand why I would state two dif-ferent positions in such brief compass. Apparently, he assumed that I agreed with the position I quoted, and he took the next few sen-tences as a contradiction of my own position rather than as a rebuttal of someone else's.[7]
- In the conclusion to my book on *Jesus as a Figure in History,* I indi-cated that the scholarly quest to understand Jesus as a historical per-son may be distinguished from the religious quest to relate to the spiritual person of Jesus revealed in Christian story. I claimed, never-theless, that these two quests should overlap—that the latter ought to include the former—and I bemoaned the fact that this is not always the case. For some readers, however, the mere assertion of a distinc-tion overshadowed the appeal for convergence. Thus, a review of my book in *Expository Times* declared that I give the impression that the quest for the historical Jesus (which I spend 182 pages describing) is "really pointless" because "academic study has little place in the Christian's devotional life."[8]
- In an article for *Christian Century* magazine I described the career of Marsha Stevens, the self-proclaimed "born again lesbian singer"

whose evangelical, contemporary Christian music strikes some as incompatible with her homosexual lifestyle. I suggested that since the only biblical reference to lesbian activity is to that practiced by pagan idol worshipers (Rom. 1:26), the presence in the modern church of lesbians who claim to be evangelical Christians raises questions not addressed as such in the Bible. I said that the very "existence of people like Stevens must be factored into the debate." Two issues later, a letter writer quoted this exact phrase and accused me of promoting the classic liberal elevation of "the revelatory authority of human experience as the final arbiter in the debate." This was perhaps the first time that I have ever been identified as a liberal, much less a classic one, but I was intrigued by how easily my suggestion that human experience should be considered as *one* factor in a debate was taken to mean that experience should be the *final arbitrating factor* in that debate.[9]

Alright, now it sounds like I'm whining. Let me quickly assert that I do not regard myself as exceptionally victimized in this area. I have written a lot of book reviews myself, and I suspect that I have done worse to others than has ever been done to me. All authors believe their work is misunderstood, and most can easily get defensive about how clear the intended meaning should have been. All of the persons responsible for the apparent misunderstandings of my writings cited above are intelligent people with a good deal of professional experience at reading texts—including theological texts similar to those that I was writing. So maybe . . . just maybe . . . I *wasn't* as clear as I thought I was.[10] But, then, what's the point? Do we just decide that since all texts are subject to variant interpretations, everyone should be allowed to make of them what they will? Hey, not if it's my text, we don't! Not if I'm the author!

Those are my mixed and somewhat confusing experiences as both reader and author of texts. Here's how I try to make sense of them. I think that most of us,[11] about the time we are college sophomores, have an Aha! experience when we come to realize that all statements of truth are perspectival and therefore relative.[12] Faced with this realization, we must either give in to anarchy or work to embrace methods for organizing perspectives on truth in ways that help us order our lives. Most of us choose the latter course and, though we sometimes forget that our organizational schemes are precisely that, we do indeed find that method is preferable to madness. With regard to understanding the Bible, historical criticism and literary criticism are two organizational schemes, two rather different methods for structuring interpretive processes. They have essentially different goals. Historical criticism attempts to discern the intention of authors; literary criticism seeks to account for the responses of readers.[13] Both methods, both schemes, both goals, are intrinsically legitimate. What bothers me is when either discipline does not pursue its goals with integrity or when one discipline seeks to impose its goals on the other.

In the Bible Study example previously described, the pastor seemed to be telling a woman that her response to a text was not legitimate because it was not in line with authorial intent. Basically, he was evaluating a reader-oriented, literary interpretation of a text in light of whether it fulfilled the goals of author-oriented, historical criticism. Literary criticism calls for readers to identify their responses to texts in ways that initially transcend questions of legitimacy. Identification of such a response always reveals something about the reader as well as something about the text. To discount a response because it does not match the author's intention not only misses the point but also implicitly denigrates the person who offers the reading—if the interpretation is "illegitimate," then so is the interpreter.

In biblical studies, the work of historical critics and literary critics often overlaps, and insights discovered through one approach sometimes prove valuable for application in the other. Still, the goals of the two schemes are distinct: to discern the intentions of ancient authors on the one hand and to account for the responses of modern readers on the other. So stated, one might assume the latter goal to be the more attainable, and the former to be more daunting. After all, if the intentions of modern, living authors are hard to discern, what chance do we have of recovering the intents of ancient authors—of *anonymous* ancient authors even? In practice, however, historical-critical methods are better developed and more effective than literary-critical ones. Historical scholars have been working on their puzzles for quite some time, and the combined resources of source, form, and redaction criticism have brought a reasonable degree of success. The literary-critical paradigm, with regard to biblical studies at least, lags far behind. There are many methods and approaches under the literary-critical umbrella, but none of them has proved especially effective at enabling disparate critics to account for varied responses to texts.[14] The most promising, I think, is one of the most recent: narrative criticism, developed specifically within the guild of biblical scholarship.[15] Though many of the first narrative critics had basic formalist interests at heart,[16] the approach soon evolved into a subset of reader-response studies where its greatest potential was to be realized. It became the first truly postmodern approach to biblical texts, a method that was self-conscious of its methodological assumptions and of the implications of these.

Now, I'll admit that I hate the overused word *postmodern*—and I hope that by now you do, too. It is not just lexically nonsensical and ironically passé (what's next? postfuture?). It smacks of academic snobbery, of a "trendier than thou" attitude intended to intimidate those who fear they might not be up-to-date (What? You're only up on *modern* scholarship? I'm *way* beyond that!).[17] Nevertheless, one way the term gets used is to describe a self-consciousness in art—for example, consider the "postmodern" architecture evident in some restaurants that have visible heat ducts and plumbing pipes everywhere. It is in this sense, at least, that narrative criticism is postmodern: it puts its methodological pipes and ducts on display; indeed they become part of the phenomenon to be interpreted.

The best book I know of on the topic of postmodern biblical criticism is by

A. K. M. Adam. Drawing on the work of Cornell West, Adam describes post-modernism as evincing three typical characteristics:

> Postmodernism is *antifoundational* in that it resolutely refuses to posit any one premise as the privileged and unassailable starting point for establishing claims to truth. It is *antitotalizing* because postmodern discourse suspects that any theory that claims to account for everything is suppressing counterexamples, or is applying warped criteria so that it can include recalcitrant cases. Postmodernism is also *demystifying:* it attends to claims that certain assumptions are "natural" and tries to show that these are in fact ideological projections. (emphasis mine)[18]

Of course, narrative criticism does not exhibit any of these characteristics in and of itself. The procedural strategies of the approach can be (and sometimes are) applied by persons who regard them as deriving from some unassailable starting point or as revelatory of some totality of meaning or as reflective of the "right" or natural way to understand texts. All I can say is that *I* do not understand narrative criticism in such a way, nor do most of the narrative critics with whom I regularly converse.[19]

Most narrative critics prefer to speak of their discipline not as a "method" at all but as a *reading strategy*.[20] They are fully aware that texts can be and often are read with other strategies (other *methods*) that produce different interpretations. In fact, the impetus for narrative criticism is often to establish a common language for discussion of variant interpretations. Narrative criticism has sought to be something of a "base method" for literary appreciation of the Bible, the program that most literary critics practice first, even if they also want to do something else. The claim to such a status might seem arrogant, but in practice it often becomes rather humbling: most narrative critics view employment of their method as a means to some other end rather than as an end in itself.

The paradigm that I use for literary-critical study of biblical texts involves steps such as the following:

1. I seek to *identify* the responses of real readers to the text. This is the task of reader-response criticism at its basic level—what I call *descriptive reader-response criticism*.[21] It is also the task that has been most neglected in the discipline. In the simplest form of my paradigm, I might begin by identifying my own personal response to a given text before I proceed through the next few stages that follow. But this only scratches the surface of what should ultimately interest the guild of scholarship. What I really want is data concerning how multitudes of readers respond to the text, broken down into what could be revealing subcategories: Do women tend to respond differently than men? Do churchgoers respond differently than the unchurched? etc. Accumulating such data does not require a lot of specialized theological training. It may be the sort of grunt work that most scholars would prefer to assign to their doctoral

students. Still, one way or another, this task of descriptive reader-response criticism—of describing how readers do in fact respond—ought not be ignored.[22]

2. I seek to *compare* these actual responses of real readers with what appear to be expected responses to the narrative. Here, the somewhat tired but still operative literary concept of "implied readers" comes into play. This is the most controversial step of my paradigm; many literary critics avoid speaking of "expected" or "implied" readings. I understand the reasons for that avoidance and will discuss them below, but I maintain that some sort of norm must be established if we are going to measure (and, indeed, appreciate) diversity. To facilitate conversation, we need a standard for comparison and the best available one at present is that offered through employment of the now-chastened formalism of narrative criticism. Using that approach, we may discover a range or continuum of expected responses within which the responses of real readers will often fall. But we may also be able to define parameters that mark certain responses as "unexpected readings."

3. I seek then to *account* for these readings, especially the unexpected ones. I want to determine why some readers do not respond to the narrative as anticipated. Is the narrative's rhetoric flawed, leaving too many (unintentional) gaps that allow readers to make surprising interpretive moves? Or are the readers themselves different from the implied readers in definitive ways? Do they, for instance, lack knowledge that the implied readers are expected to possess, or do they believe things that the implied readers were never expected to believe? I find that at this stage the data that were supposedly gathered in step 1 become especially useful—sometimes a particular sort of unexpected response may prove to be typical of a certain social grouping, making the factors that account for it easier to determine. Also, investigation into the history of a text's interpretation (what the Germans call *Wirkungsgeschichte*) can be useful. Sometimes we may be able to determine when and where the responses of real readers began to diverge into the realm of unexpected interpretation. If we know when and where, we are on our way to knowing why.

As a scholar, that's it. Those three steps accomplish my goal of understanding variant readings. But, as a Christian, I am interested in going further:

4. I may want to *evaluate* both expected and unexpected readings to determine whether they should be regarded positively or negatively. It is only at this stage that I break with postmodern resistance to "legitimation." Notably, the approach outlined in steps 1–3 may be descriptive of evaluative processes, but it is not itself evaluative. Expected readings are not necessarily "right," and unexpected readings are not necessarily "wrong." Still, I do believe that some interpretations *are* right and that others *are* wrong. I know that I can only believe this by imposing my value system on both the texts and those who interpret them. I do so anyway, for as arrogant as such imposition may seem, the only alternative is a bland ethical neutrality—which would itself reflect imposition of a value system, indeed of one that I reject. Interpretations *can* be wrong—not only stupidly wrong, but dangerously so. For example, both feminist interpretations and anti-Semitic interpretations of Matthew's Gospel may represent

unexpected readings of that ancient text, arrived at via imposition of an unanticipated ideology, but I think that the latter creates problems where the former creates possibilities. I embrace the former and reject the latter. I do this self-consciously and publicly *as a Christian,* and if postmodernists have trouble with what seems to be (at this final stage[23]) a totalizing appeal to some foundational truth . . . well, so be it! I'm a Christian. I believe in Jesus Christ. To believe in him *is* to believe in foundational Truth (see John 14:6).

Let's imagine how the steps might apply to a common reading experience, a simple one, treated simplistically for purpose of illustration. I'm even going to cheat a bit and take a motion picture as the exemplary text, rather than a book (I'm going to do that frequently, because there are more available examples of movies that most of you have seen than there are of books that most of you have read—an unfortunate sign of our times!). We don't even need to pick a specific movie—let's just imagine one of those old "Cowboy and Indian" westerns, one in which brave settlers move west only to encounter hostile savages whom they must kill in large numbers to secure family and farm. The motion picture industry made dozens of these—and any one will do for this example.

When I see such a film, I may *identify* my initial response as revulsion at what I regard as a glorification of genocide. I am disturbed by the negative stereotypical depiction of Native Americans (often played by white people in makeup) and by the unjustifiably positive depiction of self-interested entrepreneurs as heroic pioneers. Second, I may *compare* this response with that which the film is apparently expected to evoke. I may sense that I am expected to take pride in the indomitable courage of the American spirit presented here rather than feeling shame or guilt or pity. I may not even know who it is that expects this of me—it just seems like the film itself expects it. Every time an Indian gets shot off his horse, the audience is supposed to cheer. I can recognize that this is the expected response even though I don't respond that way myself. Next, I may be able to *account* for why the film is not affecting me in the anticipated manner: it's not because the film's devices are ineffective, but rather that I (and many Americans) have come to believe differently than audiences were assumed to believe when this film was made. If I did a little research, I might discover that such movies played better in the days before Wounded Knee or the sixties' Civil Rights movement. Finally, I can *evaluate* both myself and the movie in this light. I might decide that revulsion is the only valid response and swear off ever watching such movies again; or I might determine that the movie can now function in a surprisingly valuable way, as an educational tool that reveals the cultural mind-set of a previous generation; or I might discover that the movie can still be entertaining and even inspirational if it is viewed simply as a dramatic clash between good and evil, ignoring the unfortunate association of those phenomena with specific social groups.[24]

Note that all of these steps are made without an explicit appeal to "authorial intent." I don't need to know who made the movie or what the intentions of those people were. I don't need to do any research on the historical processes that were involved in the film's production. I don't have to recover the original script or trace its development through various revisions. I don't have to determine how the director or producer reinterpreted parts of the screenplay. I take my cues from what is before me—the movie itself. My goal is simply to understand how the movie affects me, why it affects me this way, and why it may affect others differently. The steps of my evolving paradigm are designed to achieve such goals.

By following such steps in our interpretation of the Bible, I believe we can do reader-response criticism with integrity. But from now on, our examples will not be so simple, and we will not treat them so simplistically. In application to actual biblical texts (primarily, the Gospel of Matthew), the steps of my paradigm must be developed, argued, amended, critiqued, and illustrated. I try to do all that in this book, which I offer as an inaugural study and dedicate fondly to Robert and Phyllis Leatherman whose generous behest to Trinity Lutheran Seminary has tied their names forever to mine. It was the lecture I prepared for the inauguration of the Leatherman Chair that formed the impetus for this project. The grand occasion was set for the Day of Epiphany (January 6, 1997), so I thought I would do a little reader-response study on the magi. But to do it with integrity I soon found I had at least to write this entire book and probably more besides.

Perhaps this is two or three books in one, bound only by common authorship and similar subject matter. If so, they may be evaluated separately—and, indeed, in prepublication they have been. Some tell me the first part introduces a good dose of common sense into a realm of theory run amok, yet the latter parts fail to apply these principles persuasively with regard to Matthew. Others say that I am quite the lightweight where theory is concerned but nevertheless manage to turn up some interesting insights regarding the magi in the final chapters.

Well, *I* think the different parts of the book go together, such that you should either like the whole thing or despise it. You should either be convinced everywhere or nowhere. That's what I intend, but then I am an author and you, a reader. The advantage is yours.

PART ONE
MEANING

Meaning is what we make of texts, not an ingredient in texts.
—A. K. M. Adam[25]

What does the story mean?

This is the question that most readers ask of most stories. Not everyone agrees that it is a good question. Some critics think that stories are by nature so complex and elusive as to be ultimately meaningless. Others consider stories to be so full of meaning that any attempt at defining what a story means will be inevitably restrictive and naive. The recent history of literary criticism has featured prominent works with titles like "Against Interpretation," "Criticism Without Boundaries," and "Resistance to Theory." This aversion to meaning has been predictably slow to catch on in biblical circles. Still, hermeneutical shockwaves from the upheavals in secular studies have been felt, and traditional conceptions regarding meaning and interpretation have been challenged.

The approach taken in this book is a practical one. Whatever epistemological debates may rage in learned academies concerning the existence and/or determinacy of meaning, most of the readers I know continue to think that the stories they read do mean something—even if meaning is construed in as basic a sense as "entertainment value." The people I know describe stories in ways that ascribe meaning to them ("It's funny"; "It's inspiring"; "It gives you hope"; "It's sexy"; "It's scary"; "It makes you think"). They do not, however, always agree on *what* a story means or on *why* it means this or on *how* we determine that it means one thing and not another.

We begin this section of the book with an introduction to what all interpreters must face—the inevitable plurality of interpretations. Whether this is viewed as a statement of the problem or as a description of possibilities reveals a great deal about the interpreter, but, in either case, recognition of the reality of polyvalence must be the starting point for contemporary hermeneutical reflection. Lest the discussion of theory get too stodgy, chapter 2 offers the results of two experiments I have conducted to illustrate some of the principles explained in the first chapter. Originally conceived as a sideline, this chapter turned out to be, perhaps, the most interesting part of the book, with significance that transcends its ostensibly illustrative function. Anyone who is or has a pastor or priest should be especially intrigued. Then, we will hunker down again for another chapter on literary theory, albeit one with an eminently practical goal. The question we want to answer by page 74 is, How can we continue to speak of texts as conveying meaning once we come to acknowledge our own role in conceiving and defining such meaning?

Chapter One
Polyvalence

Reader-response criticism begins with—in fact owes its existence to—the reality of *polyvalence*. Big word. What does it mean?

I like to tell people that "polyvalence" is when you have a lot of those little window blinds hanging in your house. I *like* to tell them that, but then they quit talking to me. When I don't want this to happen I go on to explain that in literary theory *polyvalence* refers to the multiplicity of potential meaning that seems to be present in any communication event.[26] Put simply, stories and other texts (essays, songs, movies, etc.) can mean different things to different people. They can even mean different things to the same person when they are read or experienced under diverse circumstances. The Bee Gees' song "How Can You Mend a Broken Heart?" seemed profound to me back in junior high school, but . . . let's just say that whatever meaning I once ascribed to the poem does not appear to have been universal or timeless.

Now, let me anticipate a common objection. The single greatest complaint against reader-response criticism is that it ratifies the sort of neutral relativism that runs rampant in our modern (and postmodern) times. The affirmation that "texts mean different things to different people" is taken to imply that "texts can mean anything to anyone." But of course the affirmation does not necessarily imply this. The mere fact that a slope is slippery does not mean that everyone will end up at the bottom.

I was at a meeting once where a scholar declared that a particular text "has many meanings." A critic across the table retorted, "Yeah. One right meaning and a lot of wrong ones." Laughter ensued, the mood of the group clearly favoring the latter don. Bible scholars expend a lot of energy advancing what they regard as correct interpretations of passages and assailing what they regard as incorrect interpretations. It's no wonder they get testy when they think that misinterpretations are henceforth to be regarded as "alternative readings."

The matter is really not that simple. Go stand outside your neighborhood cineplex some evening and ask the people exiting from a theater what they thought of the movie. Some liked it; some didn't. It affected some people differently than others. Ask, "What do you think the *message* of the film was?" and you'll probably still get different answers—especially if the movie was a bit more complex intellectually than, say, *Friday the 13th Part XVI* or *Backstreet Boys in Concert*. Now, if you compare all of these audience responses, you may indeed find a few nutty examples where you have to wonder if the persons were really in the same theater as everyone else. But would you really want to go to the opposite extreme and decide that only one of the several responses was legitimate and all the others wrong?

Polyvalence is a reality confirmed by daily experience. Most of us are quite accustomed to people responding differently to movies, jokes, stories, and songs. Sometimes we think that people respond differently than we do because "they don't get it"—they have misunderstood something that we understand properly. But other times, we just accept the differences as natural or even predictable. People make different connections. When someone begins telling us about a book he or she read with the words, "It really spoke to me . . . ," we don't assume it would speak to us in the same way. In fact, we may be glad it doesn't, yet equally glad that it speaks to the other person.

Eventually, we will have to explore the reasons for this discrepancy. Why do we sometimes celebrate variant reading experiences as reflective of human diversity and other times denounce them as dangerous or stupid misinterpretations? On what basis do we make such judgments? But, for now, let us just agree not to throw stones at messengers who tell us what we probably already know. Texts can and do mean different things to different people, and at least some of the time people can and do find multiple meanings of texts to be acceptable.

Reader-response critics often begin by noticing how many divergent meanings can be ascribed to a single text over the expanse of space and time. They catalog these, in much the same way you did, standing outside the movie theater and taking notes on people's comments (I know you didn't really do this; I'm just pretending that you did). When interpreting biblical materials, reader-response critics may check out commentaries, plow through scholarly journals, review Sunday school curricula, listen to an assortment of sermons, even (for some passages) look into secular sources to see how the text plays in the world at large (the magi story discussed in the third part of this book is a good example of a biblical narrative that has had a good run in the secular market). They may also review the history of a text's interpretation, reviewing how it has been used throughout our grand but sometimes ignoble Christian era. What did the "church fathers" say? The Reformers? The Crusaders? The saints? The heretics?

German scholars have come up with a word for this sort of research which, like most German words, is kind of scary: *Wirkungsgeschichte*. Basically, the term means "the study of the history of influence." The history of a text's influence may include much more than what traditionally passes for "interpretation." Not only what has been written about a text but also what it has inspired—artwork, hymns, popular traditions, and spin-off legends—all these may interest the reader-response critic. Certainly, the Sistine Chapel ceiling belongs to the biblical creation account's history of influence. The Passover custom of leaving an empty chair for Elijah probably belongs to Malachi's history of influence (Mal. 4:5). I've always wondered whether what happens to Pinocchio and Geppetto has anything to do with Jonah (but that may be why I am, at best, considered to be a *New* Testament scholar).

Cataloging such influences and interpretations is obviously a daunting prospect. When I began my work on the magi story I figured that even a modest accumulation of data necessary for responsible interpretation would take a few years off my life. But then, six months into the project, a wonderful man named Richard C. Trexler published a somewhat obscure treatise on this exact topic. I was describing my current research in casual conversation to Karen Barta at a meeting of the Catholic Biblical Association where I had just presented the first draft of what is now chapter 7 of this book. She said, "You know, I think I saw an announcement for some kind of a study on magi traditions." What sweet words those were, and how I hope that heaven holds special rewards for people like Prof. Trexler. His vast survey provided a wealth of information with a focus exactly on the areas where my own knowledge was most scant (art, architecture, drama). My initial conclusions (based only on the history of theological interpretation) could be appropriately expanded, confirmed, rejected, or revised. I was left with a lasting impression that reader-response studies, particularly *Wirkungsgeschichte*, must be an interdisciplinary exercise. Limits of time, energy, and intellect prevent most of us from acquiring knowledge in a multiplicity of fields.

Computers help. Word searches on the Internet turn up surprises, but the accessibility of historical (e.g., ancient or medieval) data there is still rather limited. Of course, reader-response criticism itself is still a recent field of study and, if it endures, the interest in cataloging and classifying historical and contemporary interpretations will no doubt lead to more refined methods for accumulating the data the discipline demands. Studies like this one, I hope, will someday appear very primitive indeed.

In any case, the cataloging of variant interpretations is only a first step. Eventually, we want to analyze such responses to explain the polyvalence, to determine *why* texts yield so many divergent meanings over the expanse of space and time. Literary critic Wolfgang Iser says that all stories contain "gaps" that must be filled in by their readers.[27] Recognizing gaps entails paying attention to what the text does *not* say. Information may be missing or it may be presented ambiguously such that it can be construed in more than one way. Inevitably, readers fill such gaps differently, yielding a generous supply of polyvalence.

Gaps are not mistakes. Of course, less-than-competent authors can be guilty of negligence—they may simply forget to tell us something or they may fail to explain a development because they have no explanation and hope we won't notice. Perhaps this is what critics mean when they say that a story has "holes" in it. But gaps are something different. They may exist by intention, as an appeal to our imagination, or they may simply owe their existence to the intrinsic limitations of narrative. No story, no matter how detailed, can be exhaustive in what it tells.[28] When we are reading, we always know that in the real world more events would have happened than are reported. We may wonder what the characters would have said and done in such instances. We may wonder, too, about unreported aspects of a character's demeanor or personality, desiring to round the figure out in our minds as a more complete human being. Or, perhaps, we may *not* wonder about such things but subtly fill in the missing information with data of our own contrivance. In other words, we may close the gaps without even noticing they were there.

In the Gospel stories, one obvious gap concerns the physical appearance of Jesus. None of the four Gospels ever describes Jesus, except that one gives a rough estimate as to his age (Luke 3:23).[29] Was he short or tall? Dark or light? Was he bald? Did he have a beard? Muscular? Effeminate? Most readers fill in this gap as they read these stories, positing their own portrait of Jesus derived from . . . well, a variety of sources but not from the stories themselves. History of interpretation (and art) reveals that different readers have imagined the physical appearance of Jesus quite differently in diverse times and places.

Here is another example of a narrative gap, which will become relevant to my exposition of the magi story: Matthew 2:2 says that magi came to Jerusalem to worship the newborn king of the Jews because they "observed his star." The narrative does not explain *how* the magi knew from this star that a Jewish king had been born in Jerusalem. Almost all modern readers assume that they knew this because they were either astrologers or astronomers and were able to interpret astral phenomena according to their particular religious or scientific views. Different theories abound as to which constellation or planetary conjunction or meteor or comet might have intrigued these magi but even at a popular level readers today assume the magi interpreted some kind of sign in the heavens in keeping with their magian lore (whatever that was). In other words, the magi were able to figure out something that would have been meaningless to non-magi who might have witnessed the same phenomenon. None of this is in the text, but the assumption is so strong that most readers today do not see how anybody could possibly think otherwise.

In fact, however, readers filled this gap very differently for hundreds of years. In the early and medieval church, it was usually assumed that the magi's specialized learning had nothing to do with their comprehension of the star (presumably because divine use of astrology was literally unthinkable). Some thought the star led the magi in the same way that the pillar of fire led the Israelites; some thought it spoke to them; some thought its manifestation was accompanied by angelic interpreters. The first of these suggestions, at least, is almost in keeping with what is relayed in Matthew 2:9 where the star is said to go ahead of the magi and to stop over the place where the child was, showing them the very house where he was to be found. Are we to imagine a star that is only fifty feet or so off the ground? One would not have to be much of an astrologer or astronomer to follow such a star as that. In any case, what is certain is that readers for centuries filled this gap in the magi story differently from how most readers would fill it today. Are we right, and were they wrong? Do we fill the gap correctly because we have somehow advanced in understanding? Or can the different readings be attributed to other factors?

Polyvalent interpretations result from readers filling gaps in divergent ways. I can think of at least four factors that influence how readers fill such gaps, factors that may influence some readers to fill gaps differently than others.

Social Location

Any survey of the history of a text's influence reveals diverse interpretations that have appeared over the expanse of space and time. But, actually, space and time are only two of the factors influencing interpretation. Other elements also come into play: age, race, gender, career, social class, income, education, personality, health, marital status, emotional stability, and so forth. Taken together, such factors all contribute to what we may call the *social location* of any reader.

Stories do not simply "mean different things to different people"; they tend to be interpreted in different ways by readers who have different social locations. We see this at a public level in America when a popular film polarizes audiences and reviewers. In 1989, Spike Lee's masterful *Do the Right Thing* had that effect with regard to race: blacks tended to applaud its liberal pieties while whites (even white liberals) condemned what they saw as an endorsement of militancy. Two years later, Ridley Scott's *Thelma and Louise* had the same effect with regard to gender. Many women thought it was a tale of liberation; many men (including me) thought it was a glorification of hate crimes. If you look up the latter movie on the Internet, you can find the following two synopses of the film:

- A pair of gutsy, independent women discover the strength of sisterhood during a hell-raising, joy-riding escape from the laws of men.[30]
- Female friends leave responsibilities and family behind to become criminals and fugitives.[31]

I regularly teach a course on Matthew's Gospel, and we devote a generous amount of time in that class to considering the three most read chapters of the Bible: Matthew 5, 6, and 7—also known as the Sermon on the Mount. I pay special attention to these immortal words of Jesus: "Do not resist an evildoer. But if anyone strikes you on the right cheek, turn [to him] the other also" (Matt. 5:40). How might social location affect the meaning people derive from these words? Of course, in a seminary classroom we discuss all this from a historical perspective. What did Jesus' words mean in the first-century context? Does the slap on the cheek refer to some specific ritual action, such as excommunication from a synagogue? Such considerations are significant, but, I tell my students, the bottom line remains: When these words are read aloud on any Sunday morning in almost any congregation in America, there will be people present—mostly women and children—who have recently been slapped or struck in the face. If this is not your recent or regular experience, then begin by recognizing that those for whom it is will hear the text with a poignancy you can scarcely imagine.

Reading Strategies

People receive and process literature in different ways. This is easy to demonstrate: if five people are videotaped separately reading the same text out loud they will inevitably make different choices with regard to vocal inflection. They will emphasize different words, interpret characters with different tones of voice, vary their pace, and so forth. Of course, we all do this when we read silently as well. Some people tend to search for consistency when they read, accenting points of repetition that contribute to an ongoing theme. Others are more attracted to contradiction, focusing on unresolved ambiguities. Most stories have elements of both order and chaos, but a preferred (even subconscious) reading strategy can emphasize the one and diminish the other. Thus, the same story affects different readers differently.

This is but one example of what is meant by "reading strategy." I now give two more that may at first seem extreme or bizarre—but that is, partly, the point.

I am honored to count myself as a friend of theologian Walter Bouman, who loves mystery novels. So do I; we are especially fond of P. D. James. But Bouman has an annoying habit—he always reads the ending of the book first. He likes to know how the book turns out before he reads it. I have tried to explain to him that the whole point of a good mystery is *not* knowing how it turns out . . . we're supposed to try to figure it out, solve the crime before the detective does. And, besides, these stories are supposed to be suspenseful. But Bouman stubbornly persists in reading the last chapters first. He even attaches significance to this act—*theological* significance. The joy of reading a story for one who knows the ending is discovering how we will get there. So, too, life is a mystery, but Christians know the ultimate future. The ultimacy of God's eschatological revelation impinges proleptically on . . . and, then, it all gets over my head.

Eschatology and proleptics aside, I think this is a really stupid way to read a mystery novel. Still, I would not go so far as to say Bouman is wrong to read this way. I wouldn't even say that he misunderstands the stories. He enjoys reading this way and finds that doing so renders the stories especially meaningful for him. He gets something out of them that is different from what I get out of them. I can accept that.

My second example features a Pentecostal woman. She tells me that every morning she reads a passage from the Bible, expecting God to speak to her. One day she read this passage from Isaiah: "Ho, every one that thirsteth, come ye to the waters, and he that hath no money; come ye, buy, and eat; yea, come, buy wine and milk without money and without price" (Isa. 55:1; KJV). She immediately discerned from this that God wanted her to go to the grocery store. She *did* have money, and she knew the store did not give food away for free, and she was quite certain that God would not want her actually to buy (much less drink) any alcoholic beverage. Still, the text spoke of buying food, so off to the store she went. When she got there, she ran into a member of her church who was strapped for cash and was prepared to write a bad check to cover the week's groceries. She bought the groceries instead, fulfilling for her friend the text's prophecy.

This person's interpretation of Isaiah 55:1 differs widely from my own. Is this because she is a woman and I am a man? Or is it because she is a Pentecostal and I am a Lutheran (albeit, a charismatic Lutheran who sometimes speaks in tongues)? Aside from our different social locations—though possibly, in part, because of them—she and I employ diverse reading strategies. In reading biblical texts, I am especially conscious of literary and historical contexts that she freely ignores. And she looks for direct existential engagement that I would be surprised to discover.

And now I must be frank: I am bothered by this person's reading of Isaiah in a way that I am not bothered by Bouman's reading of P. D. James. While his treatment of the text seems cavalier but harmless, hers strikes me as potentially dangerous. I think immediately of the old preacher's joke: A man opened his Bible one day to read the verse "Judas went out and hanged himself." Confused, he opened it again to find "Go thou and do likewise."

What's the difference? Is it simply a distinction between the authoritative value granted to the text? (Bouman, as far as I know, does not make life choices based on his understanding of P. D. James stories.) Or are there broader issues at play? Are there right and wrong ways to read texts? Or are there right and wrong ways to read texts *as scripture?* And if there are, who gets to decide which ways are right or wrong? Scholars? This has certainly been the case in much of Christian history. But, then, Jesus says,

> "I thank you, Father, Lord of heaven and earth, because you
> have hidden these things from the wise and the intelligent
> and have revealed them to infants; yes, Father, for such was
> your gracious will." (Matt. 11:25–26)

"These things"? What are "these things" hidden from the wise but revealed to babies? Well, now we are getting ahead of ourselves. I wax proleptic and Boumanesque, almost revealing insights that are to be uncovered later. For now let us note what seems to be indisputable: texts sometimes mean different things to different people because people read them in different ways.

Choice of Empathy

It is a common experience for readers to identify with one or more of the characters in a story and to experience the narrative in ways determined by these identifications. Literary critic M. H. Abrams describes empathy as an "involuntary projection"[32] according to which we imagine ourselves as inhabiting the narrative world and being affected by what happens there. This capacity for empathy is what enables us to cry at sad stories and to tremble at scary ones. We feel what we would feel if the story were real[33] and we were experiencing it as the characters do.

Empathy may be realistic or idealistic—the former is based on analogy; the latter on fantasy. Truth be known, I am not really very much like James Bond, but I always imagine I am when I watch those movies. By contrast, sometimes I am drawn to identify with a character I would never emulate on the basis of some similarity, even a superficial one. Be it Elmer Gantry or Owen Meany, I can't help but empathize at least initially with an ordained minister in a tale because, after all, I am one.

In short, choice of empathy may be based on any number of factors including the social location and/or reading strategy of a reader. But such choices are usually made unawares. Most readers are not cognizant while reading a story that they have chosen to empathize with certain characters rather than with other ones. Often, readers do not even consider the possibility of experiencing the story from alternative points of view—at least not until they compare notes with readers who have done so.

Studies in reader empathy can be intriguing. What do you think? Would women tend to empathize with female characters and men with male ones? Well, yes—all else being equal[34]—but to what effect? Feminist scholar Judith Fetterly notes that (until recently) almost all of the female characters in literature were created by male authors. Thus, for centuries, women have tended to identify themselves with women characters whose perspectives and values were actually defined by men. A masculine perspective is presented in literature as "the woman's point of view" and, through empathy, unsuspecting women identify themselves with this patriarchy in disguise.[35]

Of course, gender is not the only factor. The biblical story of the Good Samaritan provides a compelling example for empathy choices along other lines. I have heard, read, preached, and taught this tale for decades—mostly in mainline, middle-class Protestant churches. The details of interpretation and application have varied over time, but the general consensus has always been that "the moral of the story" is that we ought to be willing to help anyone in need. Our commitment to relieving human suffering ought to transcend political, ethnic, and other sorts of rivalries: Who is my neighbor? Anyone who needs my help. This seems to be the way the story is read even at a secular level in our society.

People who have little connection with religion will refer to the opportunity or obligation of helping the less fortunate as "being a good Samaritan." Our government has even instituted what it calls "a Good Samaritan Policy" in providing disaster relief to other nations.

So, I was a little surprised when I went to live in Tanzania and discovered that many people there understand the story differently. The "moral of the story," these Tanzanians told me, is that people who have been beaten, robbed, and left for dead cannot afford the luxury of prejudice. They will (and should) accept help from whoever offers it. When grain is brought to a famished village, parents of starving children do not much care whether the Moslems, the Roman Catholics, or the Jehovah's Witnesses bring it. This philosophy was even enacted at a national level, through a policy of "nonalignment" that allowed the country to accept aid from capitalist and communist governments alike. The Good Samaritan story in the Bible was specifically referenced to legitimate such policies, just as it is invoked in the United States to legitimate American policies. In short, the story was understood to answer the question "Who is my neighbor?" not with "Whoever needs my help" but with "Whoever helps me."

As I have shared this illustration in the United States, I have found that many American Christians smile at the Tanzanians' reading of the familiar tale, regarding it as a quaint misunderstanding. But who is to say which understanding is correct? The variant interpretations are obtained through empathy choice: Americans tend to identify with the men walking down the road (the priest, Levite, and Samaritan), who must ask themselves whether the injured person in the ditch is their neighbor. Tanzanians, however, tend to identify with the person in the ditch and consider the question from his perspective. Obviously, one can do either, but I think it is interesting to note the exact wording of the question that is posed in Luke's Gospel: Jesus concludes the story of the Good Samaritan by asking his interlocutor, "Which of these three, do you think, was a neighbor to the man who fell into the hands of the robbers?" (Luke 10:36). He does not ask, "Which of the three regarded the injured man as his neighbor?" but (in effect) "Which of the three would have been regarded as neighbor by the injured man?" In short, the story presents Jesus as encouraging the empathy choice (and resultant interpretation) that tends to be favored by Tanzanians.

Far from misunderstanding the story of the Good Samaritan, Tanzanians have either read it more carefully than Americans or for some other reason[36] have tended to hear the tale the way that Luke (and probably Jesus[37]) intended it to be heard. I do not think the parable was ever meant simply to present a moral tale about how people should be willing to help each other. That would be bland and obvious—people did not get crucified for holding such opinions. Rather, the main point of the story was that religious leaders (and by implication all religious people) need to evaluate their faith and life from the perspective of the marginalized people of the earth. An expert in religious law asks Jesus, "Who is my neighbor?" This was the sort of question that first-century religious scholars debated in first-century ivory towers: Who is my neighbor? Only Jews? Only law-observant Jews? Only Jews who belong to our party? Rather than answer the question, Jesus suggests a different way of asking it. In effect, he says, "What if you were beaten up, robbed, and left lying naked and half-dead in a ditch? *Then* how would you answer?" The main point of the story was not to provide an answer to one particular question but to suggest an orientation for the consideration of all questions. Jesus is presented as endorsing what some modern theologians call "the pedagogy of the oppressed." He views the suffering people of the earth not as "less fortunates" in need of help, but as teachers whose perspectives and experiences reveal truth that power and privilege quickly obscure.

The story of the Good Samaritan is somewhat exceptional in the explicit textual encouragement it offers for reader empathy. This is not usually the case. More often, stories simply develop in ways that allow (invite?) readers to try out various roles and obtain different meanings accordingly. What is intriguing about the Good Samaritan story is that here, even when there is explicit textual encouragement to identify with one character (the injured person), many readers have not done so. Most people in America have read the story in an unexpected way, stubbornly if subliminally ignoring what the text clearly says. I suspect that many Americans have tended to empathize with the potential helpers in the story rather than with the needy person because they do not view themselves as experiencing the sort of extreme dependence and vulnerability attributed to the latter character.

There are two points here that we do not want to miss. First, the influence of social location seems to have been strong enough in this instance to overpower textual signals in determination of reader empathy. If empathy choices produce variant readings even when there are such textual signals, how much more might this be the case when such signals are absent! Second, identifying the common American interpretation of the story as a product of contextualization does not imply that it is therefore an incorrect or inappropriate reading. If middle-class Americans readily identify with the persons walking down the road in this parable and are moved to evaluate the level of their concern for the needy . . . can that be a bad thing? . . . is it contrary to the intention of Jesus or Luke? . . . would it be wrong, even if it were? Surely, a story like this one can make several points simultaneously. I suspect the Tanzanian reading rather than the American one is closest to what the author would have regarded as "the main point" of the tale, but readers are not constrained by authorial intent. Readers can and will elevate minor points and sublimate major ones. This, in my view, does not constitute misinterpretation. If it does, we're all in trouble—and not just with this text.

Conceptions of Meaning

Yet another reason that texts mean different things to different people is that people differ in what they regard as constituting "meaning." This is the most difficult point to explain—without getting lost in all sorts of obscure conversation about philosophical constructions and hermeneutical categories. For the truly arduous and/or foolish, Paul Ricoeur, Jacques Derrida, and Michael Foucault have all written about this, and you may go to them for more nuanced discussion.[38] They are brilliant scholars, at least according to one common definition of brilliance, that is, "capable of writing things that nobody understands." My skills and, fortunately, my goals are more modest. I am content simply to note a reality: people do in fact conceive of meaning differently. For this immediate purpose, the attendant philosophical and hermeneutical implications do not much matter.

Simply to be illustrative (not exhaustive), here are two different conceptions of meaning:[39]

a. *Meaning as message.* The meaning of a text may be described in essentially *cognitive* terms. Understanding the meaning of the text entails identification of the point or points that are made therein.

b. *Meaning as effect.* The meaning of a text may be described in *emotive* or *affective* terms. Understanding the meaning of a text involves recognition of its impact on those who receive it.

Examples of the first construal of meaning can be found in most biblical commentaries. There, the goal of interpretation is usually to disclose the message of the text. That seemed to be the goal for both Americans and Tanzanians in our previous discussion of the Good Samaritan story. We saw some discrepancy as to just what the point of the story might be, or as to which point might be major and which minor. But the underlying assumption for all interpreters was that the goal of interpretation should be to discern the message of the story.

Examples of the second construal of meaning (effect) can be found in many popular movie reviews. Critics often try to predict how audiences will react to a film: Will they laugh or groan or weep? Will they be inspired or bored? They base these predictions not only on their own personal responses to the film in question, or on their general knowledge of films and film making, but also on suppositions that they have acquired regarding movie audiences. Indeed, their predictions are inevitably contextual, based on an assumed audience appropriate to the film's genre; they don't even try to predict how fans of "horny teenager movies" will react to highbrow period pieces (or vice versa). Our point, though, is that movie critics are usually more committed to depicting a film's impact than its message. This is because they recognize that most moviegoers are more concerned with how a film will affect them than they are with what point or points it seeks to make. Receiving the message, if there is one, is but part of a total experience.

Now, obviously these examples are not airtight. There are moviegoers (and critics) who are primarily interested in message. There are also Bible scholars (may their tribe increase!) who understand interpretation as a process of actualization and who tend to interpret passages by discerning their actual and potential impact on human lives. But let's go with the stereotype a while longer. I picked movie reviews rather than book reviews to illustrate meaning as effect because I find that the latter often *do* concentrate more on message. This is true not only in academia but also in popular reviews of novels—even novels that are then made into films. Why? I think there is a tendency in our society to associate "message" with words and "effect" with pictures: the wordier a medium, the more likely we are to focus on message.

Consider the following list of media ("texts"):

> essays
> stories
> narrative poems
> free verse
> photographs
> representational paintings
> impressionist paintings
> abstract paintings

The first four items use words; the last four typically do not. Also, the list reveals a general decrease in clarity of expression and increase in appeal to the imagination (or, to put it another way, an increase in the obvious function of "gaps").

I find that when I ask people, "What do you make of this essay?" they usually tell me what they perceive to be its message. They summarize the main points of the essay and tell me whether they agree with these or not. They also may comment on how effective the author is at establishing his or her argument. Evaluation of both content and style seem related to message. When I visit a museum of modern art, however, and stand in front of some cubist or surrealist masterpiece and ask, "What do you make of this?" I usually receive a response related to the work's impact. People will tell me whether they like the work or dislike it, often with strong emotional sentiment attached to the opinion. They may attribute these reactions either to the work's subject matter or to the artist's technique, but, in either case, evaluation of both content and style are related to effect.

Again, these experiences are far from absolute. I know people who read essays as they would poems or paintings, appreciating the beauty of images and savoring the word pictures. And then, of course, I have known persons who try to find messages in everything, including modern art. Indeed, as a bit of an aside, I suspect that this is one reason why some people do not appreciate such art—they have been so conditioned by our wordy society to define meaning as message that they are not able to shift gears. They equate "message-less" with "meaning-less." Spend a day in the art museum, and you will see people shake their heads and say, "I just don't get it" or (very telling) "What's the point?"

I think back now to days long ago when I took Art History at Texas Lutheran College. I remember that several of us students were stymied by the significance accorded to Jackson Pollock, who used to hang canvases on a wall and then shoot paint onto them from across the room with high-powered squirt guns. We thought that all of his so-called paintings pretty much looked alike and that they were just a mess. We thought it was pretty stupid that any museum would want to hang one of Pollock's pieces as "art" since we figured squirt-gun painting was something anybody could do. It may have been I who said out loud, "*I* could do this!" prompting our professor to respond, "Oh, could you? You can squirt paint on a canvas—sure. But do you think you can squirt paint onto a canvas in such a way that people all over the world will be able to look at it and know what you were *feeling* at the time?"

Uh, no, probably not. Then, the prof showed us three slides of Pollock's paintings and asked everyone in the class to write down one word to describe the emotion that the work aroused within them. Sure enough, with one painting virtually everybody in the room wrote "hope," for another, "despair," and for a third, "rage" (or reasonable synonyms). Then we went back to look at them again to ask "why?" Was it the colors, the textures, the lines of movement? We didn't even know. We couldn't say. But we realized that every one of these paintings conveyed a mood—not a message but a *mood*. Those paintings have been very meaningful (i.e., full of meaning) for me ever since.[40] There could be many other examples drawn from other forms of art. How would you describe the meaning of Mahler's fourth symphony (or, if you prefer, Hendrix's "Voodoo Child [Slight Return]")? Would you talk about the *message* of the work, or about how it *affects* you?

To begin summing up, one point we have made is that different construals of meaning contribute to the existential reality of polyvalence. We've probably beaten that one into the ground by now, but one reason I've been hitting it so hard is that I have been trying to sneak up on you while doing so and make another point as well. Reader-response criticism does not just *recognize* these different construals of meaning (message and effect); it also *advocates* for the latter, especially with regard to literature and most especially with regard to stories. The conception of meaning as message tends to be author-oriented: the message that is perceived is ultimately that which the author intended to convey, defined in terms of a point or points that the author wanted to get across. Meaning as effect tends to be more reader-oriented: the impact of a text on human lives is measured in terms of how it actually affects people who receive it in a variety of circumstances.

With regard to interpretation of biblical stories (or any stories for that matter), the author-oriented model seems unnecessarily reductionist in a way that does not do justice to the genre—which is to say that it ironically violates its own respect for authorial intention. If Matthew, Mark, Luke, or John had simply wanted to convey particular messages about Christian life and faith, they could have done so more effectively by writing essays (or epistles!). Stories are powerful in terms of overall impact, but their generic strength is not *cognitive* persuasion. Essays are better suited for persuading people to accept the correctness of an argument. Stories are effective at impacting people's lives, sometimes in subtle ways that they don't even realize.

Thus, the meaning of a story should not be simply equated with its message. Look at this example:

Story	Message
"In a certain city there was a judge who neither feared God nor had respect for people. In that city there was a widow who kept coming to him and saying, 'Grant me justice against my opponent.' For a while he refused; but later he said to himself, 'Though I have no fear of God and no respect for anyone, yet because this widow keeps bothering me, I will grant her justice, so that she may not wear me out by continually coming'" (Luke 18:2–5).	We need to pray always and not lose heart (see Luke 18:1).

Luke (or Jesus) tells us explicitly what the message of the story is, but the story must serve some greater purpose than simply conveying this message. Otherwise, it would be superfluous. Luke could have simply reported that Jesus said, "You need to pray always and not lose heart." We would have the message. What would we lose if he had not also reported the story?

I hope it is obvious that we would lose more than just an illustration of the message. The story has meaning that transcends its stated message. The mere fact that the recipient of prayer (God) is represented by an unrighteous judge will cause many readers to reflect on matters unrelated to praying always and not losing heart. The depiction of supplicants as a poor widow is likewise compelling. Such images will inevitably affect readers in ways that must be counted as part of the meaning of the story.

To drive this point home, let's compare the above tale to a different story that conveys essentially the same message:

Story One:	Story Two:
Suppose one of you has a friend, and you go to him at midnight and say to him, "Friend, lend me three loaves of bread; for a friend of mine has arrived, and I have nothing to set before him." And he answers from within, "Do not bother me;	"In a certain city there was a judge who neither feared God nor had respect for people. In that city there was a widow who kept coming to him and saying, 'Grant me justice against my opponent.' For a while he refused; but later he said to him-

the door has already been locked, and my children are with me in bed; I cannot get up and give you anything." I tell you, even though he will not get up and give him anything because he is his friend, at least because of his persistence he will get up and give him whatever he needs (Luke 11:5–11).

self, 'Though I have no fear of God and no respect for anyone, yet because this widow keeps bothering me, I will grant her justice, so that she may not wear me out by continually coming'" (Luke 18:2–5).

Many interpreters would claim that the message of these stories is essentially the same, but I do not know any interpreter who would persist in saying that the stories mean the same thing. To say this would imply that the differences— second-person narration vs. third-person narration; dialogue between social equals vs. dialogue between nonequals; concern for others (feeding a visitor, waking children) vs. concern for self—count for nothing. And to say that the stories mean the same thing would raise a serious question as to why Luke (or Jesus) bothered to tell them both.

Interpreters who define the meaning of a story in terms of its "message" alone sin gravely against Marshall McLuhan, who taught us that *the medium is the message*. The narrative form of a story—its characters, plot, settings, and rhetoric—are as integral to its meaning as any message(s) its author may hope it conveys. This point, I think, is so obviously valid that I should not have to keep repeating it—but *biblical* interpreters have been frustratingly slow to pick up on it. Granted, not many Bible scholars will argue with me (on this point), but then they go on to write commentaries on biblical books that simply do not take meaning as effect into account. I expect this is due to the legacy of the field— biblical interpretation has typically served the interests of dogmatic theology. So, again and again, biblical stories are interpreted in terms of a supposed, cognitive message (dogma) that the author intended to convey (and could have conveyed more effectively through some other genre). Rarely, does one find a commentary that says, "The meaning of this story is to inspire worship . . . to provoke repentance . . . to comfort . . . to antagonize. . . ."

Okay, off the soapbox for now. Let's conclude: the mere fact that people define meaning differently opens the door to polyvalence. And if meaning can (I would say *should*) sometimes be defined in terms of effect, that open door is thrown wide. Author-oriented meaning-as-message assumes a fairly restricted range of interpretation. Authors might intend to convey more than one point in a text, but there are limits to how many points can reasonably be attributed to such intention. Reader-oriented meaning-as-effect assumes a potentially unlimited range of meaning. Every individual reader may be affected differently.

Chapter Two
Two Experiments

This chapter offers a break from the theoretical orientation of the last one. I summarize the results of two experiments that I have conducted with regard to polyvalent reader responses to texts. Although I took these experiments very seriously, I realize that tighter controls and a broader sample would be needed to confirm my results.

Reader-response critics claim that social location affects interpretation and that, accordingly, interpretation sometimes reveals as much about a reader as it does about a text. Such factors as gender, ethnicity, and social-economic class supposedly influence the way that we understand literature. I have noticed, however, that while this claim is frequently offered as a self-evident observation, it is rarely substantiated or documented.[41] I am frankly amazed that so little data is available on this topic. It seems like a field ripe for research projects. Why not, for instance, explore the effect of gender on reading by giving a text to both men and women and documenting how they respond to it? Of course, such an experiment would have to account for other factors. A large sample of both men and women would have to be drawn from a diverse population to ensure that differences that appeared attributable to gender were not in fact attributable to some other combination of factors. Experts at statistics, especially those with a background in the social sciences, know how to conduct such studies.

I lack the expertise, the resources, and the inclination to do this sort of major research myself. Still, I have been curious as to whether such a project would yield meaningful results, so I conducted these two probes, which, though inconclusive, are nevertheless interesting and promising. One purpose of this chapter is to convince somebody somewhere that such research is worth pursuing at a more intense level. Another purpose is to provide illustrations of certain points made in the last chapter—the undeniable reality of polyvalence and its relationship to such factors as social location, reading strategy, empathy, and conception of meaning. A third purpose is to afford me a platform for waxing tentatively homiletical on points that my admittedly inconclusive research brings to the fore. And then, all these noble goals aside, I hope you will just find this break from theory to be engaging and fun. I do.

Both of my experiments focus on one fairly minor attribute of social location: the distinction between lay church members and ordained ministers. In each case, I used a relatively small sample of one hundred readers—fifty clergy and fifty laity. I made an effort to include a variety of denominations, and I selected clergy and lay representatives from the same congregations. In other words, I used a Baptist minister and a member of his church, a Roman Catholic priest and a member of his church, a Lutheran pastor and a member of her church, and so on. I also attempted in each instance to select persons who were similar in other obvious ways: the two Baptists (or Catholics or Lutherans) were the same gender and race; they were about the same age; and they had similar levels of income and education. I tried to get a 50/50 sample for which the major distinguishing characteristic would be lay/clergy status.[42]

After selecting two similar persons from a church, I made an appointment to meet with each individually. I explained to the subject that I was conducting a survey and gave him or her a sheet of paper with a Bible story and a single question (as in Tables 1 and 2, which follow). I did not set a time limit, but no one took over fifteen minutes to read the passage and provide an answer.[43]

Before reading the reports, stop and speculate for a moment as to what you would expect to find. Suppose you gave a Bible story to fifty pastors and fifty parishioners and asked them the questions that serve as subheads below. If you collected a hundred sheets and looked through their answers, do you think you would be able to tell which ones came from the clergy and which from the laity? On what basis?

My amateurish exploratory research revealed telltale signs that did link particular interpretations to these two types of interpreters. When sifting through these data, I very quickly got to the point where I could correctly identify a response as "clergy" or "lay" most of the time. And if you think that was just because the clergy used theological words the laity would never use, well . . . read on.

Mark 7:1–8: What Does This Story Mean to You?

I took the story found in Mark 7:1–8 and presented it under the heading "What Does This Story Mean to You?" (see Table 1).

TABLE 1

Mark 7:1–8: What Does This Story Mean to You?

Now when the Pharisees and some of the scribes who had come from Jerusalem gathered around [Jesus], they noticed that some of his disciples were eating with defiled hands, that is, without washing them. (For the Pharisees, and all the Jews, do not eat unless they thoroughly wash their hands, thus observing the tradition of the elders; and they do not eat anything from the market unless they wash it; and there are also many other traditions that they observe, the washing of cups, pots, and bronze kettles.) So the Pharisees and the scribes asked him, "Why do your disciples not live according to the tradition of the elders, but eat with defiled hands?" He said to them, "Isaiah prophesied rightly about you hypocrites, as it is written,
'This people honors me with their lips,
    but their hearts are far from me;
in vain do they worship me,
    teaching human precepts as doctrines.'
You abandon the commandment of God and hold to human tradition."

Each person was simply asked to read the story, reflect on it for a moment, and write an answer to the question. No one had access to commentaries or study aids that might influence his or her perception. Thus, these are not "studied" responses. Even so, I admit that as a New Testament professor I find it difficult to read them without evaluating them. I detect some glaring exegetical errors and also some rather creative insights, on the part of both clergy and laity. But, these are all beside the point. Let's agree, for a little while, not to think in terms of who got it right and who got it wrong.

Here are the clergy responses. Skim the list and see if you can detect points of continuity and discontinuity. My numbering of the responses is not entirely random. I tended to group items that I found to be similar in at least one aspect. But don't let that scheme override your own perceptions. There would be many other patterns that a different order of presentation might bring to the fore.

CLERGY RESPONSES TO QUESTION IN TABLE 1

C-1. The folks in my church always say, "We've never done it that way before." Jesus wants me to tell them, "Human traditions are less important than God's commandments."

C-2.   Scripture is more important than human traditions. People don't want to hear that but it's true (and it's my job to tell them).

C-3.   I need to be a prophet of mercy, not judgment. People hear enough condemnation already. Jesus affirms those whom the world calls "unclean."

C-4.   Jesus attacks the hypocrisy of religious legalism and expects us to do so as well.

C-5.   If I want to be a faithful servant or a good pastor, I need to do what Jesus did: a) denounce hypocrisy; b) insist on true worship (from the heart); c) teach divine commandments not human precepts.

C-6.   The disciples are my church. The Pharisees are the world, the flesh, and the devil. My job is to build the faith of those the Lord has entrusted to my care and defend them from the accusations these enemies bring against them.

C-7.   Traditions are from men, not God. True disciples trust in the Word not traditions. The Lord has called me as a minister of His Word to make disciples by teaching his commandments. Sometimes this means exposing the hypocrisy of those whose hearts are not right with God.

C-8.   I recognize these Pharisees—I think they joined my congregation! They worship with their lips and argue about things that are only "human"— precepts or traditions. I'm not going to thunder at them the way Jesus might ("You hypocrites!") but I do hope I can get through to them in time.

C-9.   I can easily relate to what Jesus faces here. The supposed inadequacies of his disciples are an implicit criticism of him. That's like saying I'm a bad pastor if the people in my church are sinners. If they weren't sinners, they wouldn't need me.

C-10. Jesus is able to recognize the hypocrisy of those who abandon God's Word because he knows the scriptures himself. I need to know the Word, memorize it, and live in it if I am to know what is of God as Jesus did.

C-11. Evil comes in many guises, as an angel of light, or here, in the form of those who worship with their lips and seem to be concerned about pious behavior. Jesus sees through their hypocrisy and exposes it. Lord, help me do the same.

C-12. Am I ready to do what Jesus did? Defend the guiltless and accuse the powerful? Comfort the afflicted and afflict the comfortable? That is the question the story raises for me.

C-13. How many of us have churches filled with people who worship with their lips but not their hearts? Ouch. That verse stings. But here, too, is the only solution. Teach "as doctrine" the word of the gospel—not just self-help psychobabble—and you may reach a few.

C-14. I heard it said once that "nothing touches the heart but what comes from the heart." If I am right with God myself, then I can preach his word as Jesus did and touch the hearts of those who have lost their way.

C-15. To *me*? To *me* the story says, if you want to be like Jesus, you need to be able to take the heat. Jesus isn't afraid to tell it like it is, even if that means knocking a few cherished traditions.

C-16. There is a real difference here between being religious and knowing God. I know that difference because I used to be "just religious" myself. Now that I am a pastor, people think I am a religious person, but my whole job as a pastor is to get religious people to see what a relationship with God is really all about. That is exactly what Jesus is doing here.

C-17. Jesus clarifies the true role of tradition. If it is to be more than empty ritual, people need to see how it is grounded in scripture and expressive of the heart. If we show people this, they will experience the liturgy (and other traditions) as something that draws them closer to God rather than as an obstacle to be overcome.

C-18. Any minister who is worth his or her salt must be prepared to confront hypocritical dependence on tradition ("the way we've always done it") when that conflicts with the leading of God's Holy Spirit or the testimony of scripture.

C-19. The best analogy I can think of right now is being "politically correct." Modern Pharisees get all over people for not using the right pronouns, which is like not washing your hands according to what somebody has decided is the "right" way to do it. Well, I'm with Jesus. It's what's in the heart that counts.

C-20. No matter how helpful or meaningful religious traditions can be, they do sometimes get in the way of hearing the will of God. Those of us who are religious leaders, in particular, need to be like Jesus in discerning whether a given tradition is helping or hurting the church to be what God wants it to be.

C-21. It is our job as pastors to constantly review the tradition of our elders, whatever that may be, to bind it or to loose it, whichever is necessary, to tell people as Jesus did, "this is God's commandment, this is just a human precept."[44]

C-22. Jesus tells "church leaders" that they don't have a clue what the real problems and needs of his disciples are. I've said the same thing to the bigwigs in our denomination.

C-23. Jesus says some pretty harsh things to his disciples sometimes, but he's not going to let the Pharisees attack them. Same here. I can rail against my sheep from the pulpit, but I'd lay down my life for them if the wolf came around.

C-24. Every Sunday I look out over my congregation and think, Are they getting this, or are they just going through the motions? Jesus seemed to have the same doubts about the religious people of his day. That's comforting, I guess.

C-25. I wish I had the courage to do what Jesus does—tell hypocrites to their face what God thinks of them. What does this mean to me? It convicts me for not being more like Christ.

C-26. Jesus models boldness in proclaiming the word, drawing on scripture and applying it to an existential situation. He's not trying to win any popularity contest.

C-27. How can we get people to quit worrying about what is wrong with everybody else and just look to God with thanksgiving and praise?

C-28. I tell people religion is not about getting cleaned up on Sunday morning for God. It's about getting our hands (and clothes) dirty out in the world, doing what God calls us to do.

C-29. We need to preach the Word, even if people would rather just hear homey stories and take part in religious rituals. What they need may not be what they want. They need to hear us preach the Word of God.

C-30. Our church has a tradition of potluck suppers and rummage sales that I think are more important to some than the law and the gospel combined. In seminary I thought I would be a prophet but now I feel like a guest speaker at a religious club. So I have to ask, if Jesus was the pastor here, what would he have to say?

C-31. I've felt like Jesus does here when outsiders disparage members of my church. They may have their problems, but they're my responsibility and if anyone's going to disparage them I want it to be me.

C-32. We need to distinguish between what is essential (the gospel) and what is nonessential (adiaphora).

C-33. People tend to prize what is familiar above what is necessary. Jesus challenges us to sacrifice tradition and follow God's will.

C-34. Some of our traditions are good, some are bad, but none are as important as the Word of God.

C-35. Jesus offers grace, to comfort those whom hypocrites assail with their legalism.

C-36. Jesus' last sentence here is explained in terms of what follows—condemnation of Corban.[45] He doesn't mean to say that tradition always voids commandments.

C-37. Some things are worth fighting about and others aren't. We should not trouble the faithful over meaningless details (like liturgical preferences or speaking in tongues). These things just divide the church. But God's commandments are eternal and people who are faithful to Jesus do not try to compromise them.

C-38. What would Jesus do? He would denounce shallow worship, false doctrines, and compromised ethics. So should we.

C-39. Jesus says that we are not called to live according to the tradition of the elders but according to the Word of God.

C-40. Pastoral ministry walks the fine line between affirming ritual and transcending it. We must be alert to the creeping presence of hypocrisy, when what should be matters of the heart become meaningless. Jesus affirms ritual that expresses the heart, denounces that which does not.

C-41. I find that people are always tempted to put tradition ahead of scripture. Tradition can be important, but we must find ways of evaluating the traditions of *our* elders to see if they are what God still wants us to do today. Scripture is timeless.

C-42. I always try to distinguish in my preaching between "Thus says the Lord" and "Thus says your pastor." I hope my words are good, but they are not God's.

C-43. We might ask, what is it that defiles our hands today? Is it failure to keep all the p's and q's that certain religious authorities think are so important, or is it failure to do justice and love mercy—the real commandments of God?[46] Jesus tells us what our priorities should be.

C-44. Jesus shows me the need to distinguish between what is of man and what is of God.

C-45. I don't think you can say what the story means without looking at Isaiah to see what it says.[47] Prophecy is being fulfilled in the obstinacy of Israel and their rejection of the Messiah.

C-46. The story presents Jews as petty and legalistic. This is not true.

C-47. The story suggests that Christians are superior to Jews because they don't keep kosher laws. Personally, I find that offensive.

C-48. I don't know why you chose this text.[48] It is one of many anti-Semitic passages in the Bible. The representation of Pharisees is historically inaccurate. They were not given to hypocrisy or casuistry. And, certainly, they did not *abandon* God's commandments in favor of human traditions.

C-49. The issue of whether Christians should keep the Jewish law was a big one in early Christianity. Mark is writing for Gentiles, and so of course he wants to make the point that the law is no longer valid, except certain moral precepts like the Ten Commandments. Of course, this is contradicted elsewhere in the Bible, and it's probably not what Jesus would have thought either. One hopes that in the next millennium we will get beyond this kind of squabbling over who is most faithful to God and that Christians and Jews will benefit from each other's strengths. They have a lot to teach us, especially about tradition and law—the very things this text rejects.

C-50. What do I think it means? Christians are good. Jews are bad. They don't really worship God. He won't hear their prayers, and they're all hypocrites. That's what it means. Do I believe it? No, I do not.

Perhaps the first thing you notice is that the last few responses stand out a bit from the rest. Five persons (C-46–50) protest against what they seem to think are anti-Semitic shadings in the text. It's not clear to me whether C-45 is protesting against such shadings, simply noting them, or even approving of them. In any case, my initial (defensive) reaction to these responses was dismissive: these people are not answering the question. They are telling me what the story does *not* mean instead of what it *does* mean. But, on further reflection, I must grant that distancing oneself from a text is as much an act of interpretation as embracing it. The distancing occurs not because the text is regarded as meaningless but because it is perceived as meaning-full, albeit in potentially dangerous or troubling ways.

Many other themes surface as well, but, despite recurring motifs, the diversity of responses is striking. The mere fact that so many matters come to the fore is interesting, as is the manner in which they are addressed. But now, let us look at responses received from laity.

LAY RESPONSES TO QUESTION IN TABLE 1

L-1. I can identify with Jesus' disciples. They don't seem to know what all the right religious traditions are, or maybe they just don't care. Jesus says it's what's in their heart that counts.

L-2. I was on our Altar Guild and the pastor fussed at me for not putting things in the right place on the right day. My God, why does it matter?

L-3. In Jesus' day the leaders of the church were the hypocrites and that is sometimes still true. Do they really worship with their hearts or is it just a bunch of head knowledge? I don't always know what to do, but I'm pretty sure I'm a disciple and not a Pharisee.

L-4. I try to follow Jesus but like his disciples I don't keep all the rules. Sometimes I don't know them and sometimes I just don't do them. This story offers hope to people like me.

L-5. If the church tried to tell me how to wash my hands, I wouldn't do it either.

L-6. We still hear two voices, one that accuses us and one that gives us grace. Will we listen to Jesus or the Pharisees?

L-7. We have one decision to make: follow Jesus or the Pharisees. The Pharisees offer us rules and Jesus offers us life.

L-8. It comforts me to know that I don't always have to get everything right to please Jesus.

L-9. This story encourages me and gives me hope. The disciples are not very religious in an outward way, but they are not hypocrites either. I think I can say that about myself, too.

L-10. It motivates me to reexamine my own choices regarding religious practice. Which are really important? The disciples forego empty rituals that don't count.

L-11. The story reassures me that Jesus accepts me because of who I am and not because of what I do (or don't do).

L-12. I must admit, it troubles me. Maybe the disciples don't need to keep the traditions of their elders, but maybe they'd be better off if they did. Those old traditions can have a lot of meaning if you take time to understand them. They didn't become traditions for nothing.

L-13. If I were one of Jesus' disciples, I would be pleased to hear him tell the Pharisees, "Back off, don't be so picky. Take the log out of your own eye first."[49]

L-14. There are so many Pharisees in our world today. Every time I turn on the T.V. or the radio I hear them trying to tell me how to live. Jesus says, "Enough already!"

L-15. It always amuses me to hear Jesus call religious leaders "hypocrites." They always think that *we* are hypocrites because we say we're Christians but don't keep all their rules. Well, now the shoe's on the other foot.

L-16. This happens to me, too. I get my hands dirty, just living in this world. (I mean, with sin.) I need to wash them but not like the Pharisees. I need to wash in the blood of the Lamb.

L-17. Being a disciple of Jesus means we keep *his* commandments, not the commandments of men (or women).

L-18. I know exactly how the disciples felt. They got in trouble for doing what Jesus thought was important instead of what their bosses thought was important. I could tell you stories about the place where I work.

L-19. Jesus accepts disciples even when their hands are defiled. Praise God! That's me. A "disciple with hands defiled."

L-20. The world tells us, "You can't eat until you wash your hands." In other words, you have to make yourself clean first before God will accept you. But Jesus accepts us the way we are.

L-21. Pastors and other church leaders are always criticizing everyday Christians for one thing or another. I hear Jesus saying, "Leave them alone. They're doing the best they can."

L-22. I am a Christian who doesn't like the tradition of the elders. I don't want to do things just because the church did it this way in the past. That's the main reason people don't come anymore. Get with the times.

L-23. You can wash everything in your house and you still won't be clean if you don't know Jesus. The Pharisees washed the outside and not the inside.[50] Disciples have Jesus in their heart and are clean within.

L-24. I am always amazed at the pettiness of organized religion—what happens when the heart is gone and just the outer shell remains. Jesus' disciples worship him with their *heart* and hands and voices.

L-25. I'm embarrassed to admit that I have a lot in common with the Pharisees. I worship with my lips but don't always mean it. I guess I'm a hypocrite, too.

L-26. The story convicts me of my own sin, judging others without first judging myself.

L-27. Shame. Guilt. When my heart is far from God, I don't admit it but just keep pretending, worshiping "in vain." This one really nails me.

L-28. I'm confused. Are we *not* supposed to do anything in church that comes from "humans"? What about the Bible itself? It's the word of God but people wrote it.

L-29. I find it frustrating that Jesus would be so quick to condemn people who are honoring God "with their lips." I don't feel spiritual all the time; nobody does. I think what's important is that you go and worship whether you feel like it or not.

L-30. Jesus sounds like a Pentecostal here who thinks that it doesn't matter what you say or do if your heart is in it. This is annoying, and I can't believe that it would be right if we had the whole story. Other places he tells people to keep traditions (every jot and tittle).[51] If this was all we had, I wouldn't like him very much.

L-31. The story is discouraging to those of us who value ritual and liturgy. "Human" tradition can come from God and help God's people. It is way too easy to label "hypocrisy" things that you don't appreciate but which might be very meaningful to others.

L-32. Do we abandon God's commandments and hold to human traditions? Do I? This verse is disturbing, one I need to think about.

L-33. The Bible is more important than anything else. Everything else is just the thoughts of humans. We need to make sure we are keeping the Word. That's what Jesus is saying to us.

L-34. Jesus says we are hypocrites if we go to church and keep all the human traditions but don't do what God commands.

L-35. I was raised Catholic and so I know about "human traditions." I visited a Greek Orthodox church and that's even worse. I used to be one of these people that Jesus says to them, "You hypocrites! Why don't you just do what God says?"

L-36. I worry that I will become one of the Pharisees. Church doesn't mean what it used to mean to me. The hymns I loved and the people I knew are all gone. Everything looks different. I still go and I still worship God but I mean it less and less.

L-37. This is the question I have been asking my pastor in this class he is teaching about what we believe. Most of the stuff about all the creeds and the sacraments and infant baptism isn't in the Bible. I don't say it's wrong, but Jesus says "in vain do they worship me teaching *human precepts* as doctrine." That's scary. Where is this passage, because I want to show it to him.

L-38. Well, I'm not the one to ask because I haven't done very good at pleasing God or humans either one. I'm probably the biggest hypocrite of all. If this grace stuff doesn't work then I am in big trouble.

L-39. I know I would be one of the Pharisees, not one of the disciples.

L-40. Hypocrisy is the cancer of Christianity. Here are two ways we get this sickness: a) worshiping in style without substance; b) teaching unbiblical doctrines. If we avoid these things, we might avoid becoming hypocrites (though there are other ways, too).

L-41. It makes me pray, "Lord Jesus, let me honor you with my heart and let me keep your word. And keep me from judging others."

L-42. The whole point seems to be that we should not judge other people like the Pharisees do. We've got enough to do worrying about ourselves.

L-43. I need more of Jesus not more religion.

L-44. What are our seminaries teaching? Preachers today don't know the Word but they know a lot of human ideas. They can tell you what this theologian said. I want to know what God thinks.

L-45. Love is what's important, not all these customs. Did the Pharisees act very lovingly? I don't think so. There are better ways to criticize people. Anyway, Jesus loves his disciples and they love him.

L-46. Well, I'm glad I'm not Jewish because I wouldn't want to have to worry about all those things. I don't know if they still do that today, but it's so much better to just be able to trust in Jesus and know that I am saved.

L-47. Praise the Lord! Before I got saved I tried to please God in lots of ways too, but now he lives in my heart, and I know that he is my Lord and Savior. The disciples must be already saved here (they have answered his call) because they seem to know what the Pharisees don't, that washing cups won't get you to heaven.

L-48. First, it reminds me that it is by grace alone that I am saved. Second, it gives me a heart of compassion for God's own people (the Jews) who are still trying to please him with their religion of rules instead of just believing in the Messiah that he sent to them.

L-49. It angers me to see how Jewish people are described. I know Jewish people who keep these rules—washing pots and things like that. I don't think they are hypocrites. It's just their way of worshiping God.

L-50. Why are the Pharisees always the bad guys? Don't Christians have enough hypocrites of their own?

The list concludes again with responses that focus on the explicitly Jewish element in the text, though this time only two are clearly opposed to what they see there. Many of the other themes noticed in the clergy responses can be seen in these lay responses as well. But how do the two lists compare?

The most compelling result of the study for me is the following: *Most of the clergy responses indicate reader empathy with the character of Jesus, while most of the lay responses indicate reader empathy either with Jesus' disciples or with his audience (the scribes and Pharisees).* Of course, this conclusion represents *my* reading of these hundred other readers. Another reader (you, for instance) might read these responses differently. But let me lay out the matter as I perceive it.

With regard to clergy, I believe the first forty responses (C-1–40) were probably derived through a reading strategy that sought alliance with the point of view of Jesus. In the first thirty-one responses (C-1–31) this is fairly explicit. The respondents actually state a connection with the character of Jesus. In some cases the identification is what I call *realistic empathy* (I think, do, or feel what Jesus thinks, does, or feels); in other cases it is what I call *idealistic empathy* (I *should* think, do, or feel what Jesus thinks, does, or feels). In nine more instances (C-32–40), I believe a similar connection is implicit. The respondent attempts to articulate the point of view of Jesus, probably on the assumption that he or she ought to emulate this. The last ten responses are the most ambiguous. With regard to C-41–44, I suspect the respondents are hearing the words of Jesus from the point of view of the scribes and Pharisees, and then stating their intention to distance themselves from the latter. In C-45–50, the respondents seem to be reacting to points of view that they attribute to the story's author or narrator rather than to any of the characters.

With regard to laity, I believe the first twenty-four responses (L-1–24) were probably derived through empathy with Jesus' disciples. In most of these (L-1–20) I think the connection is fairly explicit: the respondent states outright that he or she is or should be like these disciples. Even in L-12, the respondent seems to assume that emulation of the disciples is expected, and this is what troubles him or her. In eighteen more instances (L-25–42), respondents explicitly identify themselves with the Pharisees who serve as the audience for Jesus' words in the story. In some cases (L-28–31) they resist these words, but even then they appear to have assumed that the words addressed to the Pharisees are now addressed to them.[52] The final eight responses (L-43–50) are ambiguous— the respondents are interacting with certain themes in the narrative, but I don't see any clear indication that they have identified more closely with one character than with another.

So we may summarize these data as follows:

Empathy Choice	Clergy	Laity
Jesus	40	0
Disciples	0	24
Pharisees	4	18
Other	6	8

I find these data striking—especially the zeros. Is it not intriguing that while almost half of the laity would identify with the disciples in this story, *no* clergy-person would do so? That the great majority of clergy would identify with Jesus while *no* layperson would do so? Why would this be? At the time I did this study, "What Would Jesus Do?" bracelets were flying off the shelves at Christian bookstores and most of the folk I saw wearing them were laity. Why did only clergy apply that question to this story when I asked them to consider, "What does this mean to you?"

Of course, this is only one story, and we should be careful not to extrapolate too many general conclusions. Perhaps the choices of empathy are tied to the roles the characters play in this particular tale. This story presents Jesus as one who quotes scripture and evaluates religious doctrine, things that clergy do. But, then, by the same logic more clergy might have been expected to identify with the Pharisees. The profession of these Pharisees (leaders of religious institutions) is analogous to that of clergy today, yet laity were more than four times as likely to identify with them than modern pastors or priests. Indeed, I find it noteworthy and just a tad ironic that although only four clergy saw themselves as identifiable with the Pharisees in this story, six laypersons specifically identified clergy as such (L-2, L-3, L-15, L-21, L-37, L-44; cf. L-5–7, L-14).[53]

We are trying to be descriptive not evaluative, but now I am going to offer a bit of counsel for those who appreciate my occasional piety. Others may skip without (scholastic) penalty to the next subheading. In my own career, I have more opportunity to speak to clergy than to laity. After conducting this experiment, I began passing along two kinds of advice to them, which I will also offer to you:

First, be aware that the people in the pews may be hearing texts differently than you do. A sermon that seeks to build on what you assume to be the self-evident message of the lesson is likely to fail. Even parishioners who derive a similar message from the text may engage that message in profoundly different ways. For instance, in our example, laity who identified with the Pharisees were variously embarrassed (L-26), shamed (L-27), convicted (L-26), confused (L-28), frustrated (L-29), alienated (L-30), discouraged (L-31), affirmed (L-35), worried (L-36), scared (L-36), or provoked to further thought (L-32). That is quite a range of emotions to address, and we haven't begun to consider the responses of those who empathized with the disciples.

Second, I encourage you clergy (laity, too, actually) to reap the spiritual benefits of what I call "casting the scriptures" in your own devotional life (I encourage you, first—if necessary—to have a devotional life). I mean *casting* in the sense of dramatic production: casting a play. When you read a biblical story for private reflection, ask yourself what that story means and then consciously *identify* the character with whom you have naturally empathized. If the story were a play, this is the part that would be assigned to you. Next, *question* the casting. Read the story again, trying out for a different role. Force yourself to empathize with a different character and to experience the story world from that character's point of view. Inevitably, this leads to new perceptions, ones that you may have missed. Of course, you need not reject the part that your natural inclinations first chose. If you're a pastor and you discover that you always try out for the role of Jesus, well, so be it. I don't think that means you have a messianic complex—and even if you do, wanting to be like Jesus is not the worst trait a church leader can have. The point of the exercise is simply to expand horizons and add new perspectives. Plus . . . we *can't* be Jesus all the time—sometimes the lead is taken and we just need to settle for something else.[54]

Luke 3:3–17: What Does This Story Mean?

For my second experiment I took a story concerning John the Baptist from the Gospel of Luke. The text is given in Table 2. The conduct of the experiment was the same as that described previously for Mark 7:1–8, with one exception. When I prepared the handout for use in the study, I decided on the spur of the moment to delete the words *to you* from the question at the top. Instead of asking, "What does this story mean to you?" I asked simply, "What does this story mean?" In retrospect, this was a stroke of unwitting genius, for the most interesting revelation of the study came as a result of this minor change in wording.

Let us again look first at the clergy responses.

CLERGY RESPONSES TO QUESTION IN TABLE 2

CC-1.   Luke reports something that happened in the first century. Before Jesus began his ministry, John the Baptist called people to repentance. He attracted quite a bit of attention, drawing large crowds out in the wilderness, where he practiced a ritual baptism. The movement apparently took on messianic overtones, though Luke reports that John denied any identification of himself as the Messiah, speaking only of one who was still to come.

TABLE 2

Luke 3:3–17: What Does This Story Mean?

[John the Baptist] went into all the region around the Jordan, proclaiming a baptism of repentance for the forgiveness of sins, as it is written in the book of the words of the prophet Isaiah,

> "The voice of one crying out in the wilderness:
> 'Prepare the way of the Lord,
> make his paths straight.
> Every valley shall be filled,
> and every mountain and hill shall be made low,
> and the crooked shall be made straight,
> and the rough ways made smooth;
> and all flesh shall see the salvation of God.'"

John said to the crowds that came out to be baptized by him, "You brood of vipers! Who warned you to flee from the wrath to come? Bear fruits worthy of repentance. Do not begin to say to yourselves, 'We have Abraham as our ancestor'; for I tell you, God is able from these stones to raise up children to Abraham. Even now the ax is lying at the root of the trees; every tree therefore that does not bear good fruit is cut down and thrown into the fire."

And the crowds asked him, "What then should we do?" In reply he said to them, "Whoever has two coats must share with anyone who has none; and whoever has food must do likewise." Even tax collectors came to be baptized, and they asked him, "Teacher, what should we do?" He said to them, "Collect no more than the amount prescribed for you." Soldiers also asked him, "And we, what should we do?" He said to them, "Do not extort money from anyone by threats or false accusation, and be satisfied with your wages."

As the people were filled with expectation, and all were questioning in their hearts concerning John, whether he might be the Messiah, John answered all of them by saying, "I baptize you with water; but one who is more powerful than I is coming; I am not worthy to untie the thong of his sandals. He will baptize you with the Holy Spirit and fire. His winnowing fork is in his hand, to clear his threshing floor and to gather the wheat into his granary; but the chaff he will burn with unquenchable fire."

CC-2. John fulfilled the prophecies of the Old Testament regarding a forerunner, just as Jesus would fulfill the prophecies of a coming Messiah.

CC-3. The main point comes in the last paragraph. John may have been a prophet, but a greater one was coming.

CC-4. The point seems to be that knowledge of God's salvation caused people to take account of themselves. Even John's baptism brought the response "What shall we do?" How much more would the coming of Jesus bring people to ask this question.

CC-5. The emphasis is clearly on judgment. John promised that there would be a judgment and that Jesus would carry it out. Those who don't bear fruit get thrown into the fire.

CC-6. It means that God will have a people prepared, even if he has to make them from scratch. God is willing to start over and make children from stones if need be. He sent John to preach judgment and Jesus to clear the threshing floor. He stopped at nothing to get people ready.

CC-7. Why was it necessary for John to come first? Just to fulfill the scriptures? No, he had to put people's hearts right with God so they would be receptive to Jesus.

CC-8. Luke tells us that God sent John to prepare people for the coming of Christ. He did this by demanding fruit worthy of repentance. He also announced that Christ was about to arrive.

CC-9. Luke says that John came into a world filled with expectation because they were looking for their Messiah, but later when the Messiah came they did not recognize him and even John did not recognize him.[55]

CC-10. The picture we get is one of people who are spiritually hungry. They would do whatever it takes to please God, but they were so worked up that they confused the messenger with the message. John is pointing them to Jesus, not to himself.

CC-11. Luke describes the scene that stood as the threshold for the coming of Jesus. People were looking for salvation, but they still had to be prompted to act on it and to repent. So God sent John to help get them ready.

CC-12. When John came he fulfilled the prophets and preached God's Word faithfully—but he was really just the last of the Old Testament prophets himself. He himself said that Jesus would offer something new, something more powerful. The new covenant is one of spirit and fire.

CC-13. Perhaps the most obvious (and therefore overlooked) point here is that *baptism* is mentioned for the first time. Until now, the mark of belonging to God's people was circumcision, which automatically left out half of the human race. John deserves credit for being the one to see how foolish this was and to replace circumcision with baptism, a symbol of salvation for *all* flesh, male and female. Jesus may have been influenced by this.

CC-14. John understood Jesus to be the powerful new agent of God, but he was wrong about what Jesus would do. Jesus did not come to throw the chaff in the fire, but to become a friend of sinners and to welcome them.[56] John expected a Judge, not a Savior.

CC-15. John thinks religion is a matter of keeping the right rules. Won't he be surprised when Jesus does come and refuses to keep all those rules himself?

CC-16. John spoke of transformation—valleys being filled, rough ways made smooth, etc. He said this is what would happen when God came into the people's lives. There would be a moral transformation of who they were. Jesus is the one who would effect this through the baptism in the Holy Spirit.

CC-17. It talks about a "wrath to come" but also says that "all flesh" will see God's salvation. Luke is a universalist who uses metaphors of judgment existentially. The wrath is experienced now but eventually all will be saved.

CC-18. All of the things that John says to do have to do with money—sharing possessions and not taking from others. This sets up Luke's pronouncement that Jesus came to bring good news for the poor.[57]

CC-19. Luke wrote his Gospel to defend Christians against Roman persecution. He presents John as a prophet who encourages good citizenship (take care of yourselves, obey the laws, don't cause trouble).

CC-20. Luke is "preparing the way" himself for the transfer of salvation from Jews to Gentiles, which he will narrate in Acts.[58] Being a descendant of Abraham no longer counts, but receiving the coming Messiah.

CC-21. Luke shapes his account of John the Baptist's ministry to make clear that John is subordinate to Jesus. John's role is clearly that of a forerunner. His ministry is similar to that of Jesus, but only preparatory. John himself identifies Jesus as the more powerful one whose sandals he is unworthy to untie. Most likely, Luke is trying to forestall or combat subordinationist christology that may have regarded Jesus as a disciple of John the Baptist since, after all, Jesus *was* baptized by John (a historical fact Luke neglects to report!).

CC-22. Luke does not say that the *people* need to prepare the way for God to come to them. Rather, God sends John to prepare the way. This is an act of sheer grace. God says, I am going to come to my people and nothing will keep me from them. My servants (John, Jesus?) will do everything necessary for me to come to them.

CC-23. Luke seems to like the question "What then should we do?" The people ask it here, and if I am remembering right they ask it again on the day of Pentecost[59] (which may be referred to here also—in the reference to baptism with the Holy Spirit). I think it comes up other places too, but I would have to check. Luke really wants us to ask that question, in response to whatever it is that God has done.

CC-24. Luke knows the Parousia has been delayed, and he writes to people who may be troubled by this. Here he wants to emphasize that the judgment of God *will* come eventually, even if it seems to have been delayed. This judgment will establish justice in all the earth.

CC-25. The way Luke tells the story of John the Baptist, he can offer people salvation if they repent and live right, but Jesus will come and offer salvation by a cross.

CC-26. We read about John in all the Gospels, but only Luke shows him to be concerned with details, sharing your coat, etc. (the third paragraph). So he wants us to get down to the nitty gritty and ask, what difference does this really make?

CC-27. Luke's intent seems to be brought out in the phrase "*all flesh* shall see the salvation of God." In this story there are Jews and Romans and "even" tax collectors all coming to baptism and all being promised the Holy Spirit.

CC-28. Luke wants to say that salvation is (potentially) for all. God has no favorites and there are no "chosen people." But everyone alike must bear the fruit of repentance.

CC-29. Why does Luke try to connect the work of John the Baptist to the prophecy in Second Isaiah? I would need my library to study this, but it seems that he sees John as fulfilling the Isaianic vision of universal salvation. And of course he does this by speaking of judgment and wrath because judgment *brings* salvation.

CC-30. Luke takes the traditions of John the Baptist and uses these as a link between the eras. On the one hand, John fulfills the Old Testament prophecies; on the other, he himself prophesies of Jesus. In John, Luke shows us what he regards as the best of the old and the promise of the new. It is interesting that baptism becomes the symbol that unites these.

CC-31. The story is found in the first part of Luke's third chapter. It must be considered in light of chapters 1 and 2, where Luke presents the announcements and births of John and Jesus in ways that beg comparison. John is great but Jesus is greater. The same contrast is now made here with regard to their ministry. Luke's agenda is to promote Jesus over John with a view to first-century rivalries between disciples of the two leaders.

CC-32. Luke is interested in explaining repentance so that everyone could understand what it meant. There are no confusing ethical dilemmas here. Luke just told his church that God wants people to help the needy, be honest at business, and refrain from violence. People could either do these things or not do them. The church today could benefit from emulating this simple and direct approach.

CC-33. It is curious that Luke indicates that John's baptism brings forgiveness of sins. I think he also said this earlier when John was born.[60] If John brings forgiveness, why do we need Jesus? In Luke, Jesus seems to serve some other role, not bringing forgiveness but the kingdom of God. He brings liberation to captives and enacts social justice.

CC-34. Luke calls for action, with a sense of immediacy ("even now"). He wants people to believe that what they do has consequences both in the present and forever.

CC-35. Luke says that Jesus will baptize people in the Holy Sprit and then later shows how this is fulfilled (in the book of Acts).[61] So, from the very start, he's saying that Christians should be Pentecostals.

CC-36. Luke makes clear that neither John nor Abraham is the one the people need. Jesus is the mightier one who gives the spirit. Later, in Acts, people baptized by John have to get rebaptized in the name of Jesus in order to have the Holy Spirit.[62]

CC-37. Luke is trying to tell us that the grace of God is not cheap. It calls for a response, that is, for repentance and amendment of life.

CC-38. Luke wants us to tell people that God expects something from them. Faith ought to impact life and make a difference in how we live.

CC-39. The "way of the Lord" is a way of salvation, but that way needs to be prepared. Those who know Christ need to prepare the hearts of others so that the Lord Jesus can come to them.

CC-40. I think the message of the text for my church would concern the proper way to prepare for the coming of the Lord today—and I don't mean the apocalyptic second coming, but how does our society prepare to welcome Christ? If we knew he was coming to our home or town or congregation, what would we want to fix up before he got here?

CC-41. This text always comes up in Advent, a week or two before Christmas when no one wants to hear about judgment or repentance or "the wrath to come." I think it's misplaced, so I always preach on the Old Testament (messianic prophecies).

CC-42. I remember preaching on this one Christmas season, and I asked, "What do we do to get ready for Christmas?" (Buying presents, sending cards, baking cookies.) Then I asked, "What if we were as concerned about being ready for Christ (preparing the way) as we are for Christmas?"

CC-43. Amid all the harsh words are kernels of grace: all flesh will see salvation; God can raise up children from stones; the wheat will be gathered into the granary. I think we have to look for the gospel in a text like this one and not be swayed by all the fire and brimstone that may have worked better in another time and place.

CC-44. I think of that song by Aretha Franklin. There ain't no mountain too high or valley too low to keep God away from us.[63]

CC-45. The lesson is that God wants a people prepared. Perhaps this is why Jesus has waited so long to return. Can we hasten that day by living like God's people should?

CC-46. The message for people today is that the baptism Jesus offers is one of spirit *and* fire. He empowers us to live for him but also burns up everything that keeps us from doing that.

CC-47. The most striking part of the story to me is the sort of "anti-evangelism" in the second paragraph. Today, churches are so concerned about getting members or making converts that they lower standards to attract the masses. But John turns away people who ask to be baptized—until they bear fruit worthy of repentance.

CC-48. I think the message for today is that we need to preach law as well as gospel. We need to be bold as John and lay out the requirements of God. This is what "prepares the way" for people to hear the word of salvation through Christ Jesus.

CC-49. There are many verses but I am drawn to this one: "not worthy to untie the thong of his sandal." John was the one prophesied long ago and people had been waiting for him for hundreds of years. He was the greatest man ever born of woman[64] but even he was not worthy to untie the sandal of our Lord.

CC-50. To be honest, John sounds like some kind of TV evangelist, all law and no gospel. This text really can't be read on its own. It's part of a bigger story because John is only the forerunner to Jesus. I think I would tell people, "You see, if not for Jesus, this is what we would get." This is the Bible without Christ (which come to think of it is what we usually get from TV evangelists).

What do you notice in reviewing these responses? I was struck immediately by a different tone than seemed to be reflected in the clergy responses to the story from Mark 7. Still, once again, a variety of themes and motifs emerged, such that polyvalent interpretation is demonstrable, even among just the clergy.

Now, here are fifty responses to the same story offered by laity.

LAY RESPONSES TO QUESTION IN TABLE 2

LL-1.   John was trying to tell people that Jesus was coming just like many preachers today are trying to get us ready for his return, but people don't listen any more now than they did back then.

LL-2.   I am confused why, if the whole purpose of baptism is forgiveness of sins, people have to repent first and stop sinning. If you can do that, you don't need forgiveness of sins. Maybe this is the difference between Jesus and John the Baptist. Jesus offers forgiveness to people who are lost in their sins and really need it.

LL-3.   John is talking to Jews who thought that they could be saved just by being born that way. I actually heard a Christian preacher say this once too, that all the Jews got some kind of free ticket for salvation just because they're Jewish. Well, this verse definitely disagrees with that. The only way to the Father is through the Lord Jesus Christ.

LL-4.   When I read this story I am inspired by the portrait of what a biblical preacher really can be. John the Baptist proclaims the word in a way that deals with the everyday stuff of people's lives—how to serve God wherever you are, be it as a tax collector or as a soldier. It's a ministry of law and gospel. He talks about forgiveness and salvation but also about repentance and judgment. And most important, he points away from himself, directing people to Jesus. This is the type of witness I would like to be.

LL-5.   We need to warn people to get ready for the coming of the Lord. If we don't, who will?

LL-6.   It encourages me to be more forthright about sticking up for what I believe. John did this, and people respected him for it.

LL-7.   I am humbled by John's example because he was the greatest man ever born[65] and yet he says he is unworthy to tie the Lord's sandal. If he is unworthy, how much more are we? But we still think we are so important sometimes. It is all about the Lord and not about us.

LL-8.   I agree with John when he says, "You must bear *fruit* worthy of repentance." Too many people think that just being baptized or coming to church is enough, when there is no fruit of the Lord's presence in their lives.

LL-9.   I have felt like a voice crying in the wilderness before—like I was the only one who cared about what was *right* (not just what would *work* or make money). You do just want to think of everyone else as a brood of vipers, but we have to leave the judgment to God. Actually, it says that here, too.

LL-10. This story upsets me because the crowd that comes to be baptized gets lambasted, which is just like what happens when we go to church and the preacher tells us how bad we are. I want to say, "Hey, at least we're here. That should count for something." But then what he says about not depending on your ancestors really hits home, because I think sometimes we just think we can be baptized as babies and then ride to heaven on our parent's faith. Now he says we have to bear fruit worthy of repentance. So the crowd asks, "What then should we do?" which is exactly the question I'm asking now.

LL-11. It shocks us into asking if we are ready for our Lord to come.

LL-12. We have a choice of getting baptized with spirit or with fire, and how we live our lives now determines which it will be.

LL-13. It scares me, obviously, because even though we are told all the time that we are saved by grace, here the Bible says it depends on how you live.

LL-14. It is very "in your face." It's like, "The Lord is coming, and if you're not ready, you're really going to be sorry." It doesn't worry me, though, because I think that kind of religion is just exploitative.

LL-15. I actually find it very comforting, which may seem surprising, but with all the talk of judgment, the first paragraph says, "All flesh will be saved," so I don't think we have to be afraid.

LL-16. It warns us of the need to prepare a way for the Lord in our own individual lives. It's not enough that God chose Abraham and others in the Bible, but now he wants to come into our hearts, and we have to make room for him there.

LL-17. Not all of it applies to me, but the part about "whoever has two coats" does because I probably have five or six coats. I'm not a literalist, but it seems that almost everyone in America has more than they need of many things while people in other countries don't have enough. For us, "preparing the way of the Lord" probably means finding more equitable ways of distributing the earth's resources.

LL-18. It moves me to get serious about acting on faith. The time may be short. We know what is expected of us. Now, we just have to do it.

LL-19. I gotta say it provokes me, in more ways than one. It makes me think, what do I have to do to get ready for the Lord? And, it irks me somewhat, because just when I thought I was ready, something else comes up, and the Holy Ghost says, you aren't ready yet. So I get provoked a lot by this story and by other texts that tell me what I need to do.

LL-20. You probably showed us this text to try to scare us into getting more serious.[66] It is scary when I read it and think about whether or not I am ready to meet my maker, but to be honest with you I don't think about it that often and neither does anyone else I know. There's just too many other things to do in a day that there is no time to think about things like this.

LL-21. It simply challenges us to always be ready for the Lord to come, whenever that may be. Of course, there is no way we ever get it down perfect, but there is always room for self-examination and improvement.

LL-22. I think that if we are always worried about whether we are "prepared" for the Lord or not we will miss the bigger picture. None of us is ever worthy of Christ, not even John the Baptist himself. So being prepared means just opening our hearts to him to receive his forgiveness.

LL-23. What are the valleys, what are the mountains, what are the hills in my life that keep God away from me? What crooked things do I need to make straight, what rough ways need to become smooth for me to see his salvation?

LL-24. The story challenges us to put our words into action and live the way God wants us to live: helping the poor, being honest in our job, and not trying to push others around. This is all pretty simple, but how many people even do this much?

LL-25. I always look for promises in the Bible and here I find two—salvation and the baptism in the Holy Spirit. Many people in our world have not experienced either. Many people in churches have only the first. Why settle for just "avoiding hell" when Jesus offers so much more?

LL-26. The story shakes me out of my comfortable little world where everything seems okay as long as I don't ask too many questions. It forces the ultimate questions of judgment day upon me already, ahead of time, and asks for consideration of how I will fare in that balance. Even spiritualized as symbol or metaphor, such imagery commands a response.

LL-27. It gives me pause to consider something I don't plan to think about until I'm a lot older, unless I land in the hospital with some terminal disease. Am I ready? Well, I'm better than some, worse than others. I don't know, but if I don't make it, wherever I go will be awfully crowded.

LL-28. He sounds like "a Baptist," if you'll pardon the pun, in that all he talks about is condemnation. I'm not afraid of God, and no preacher will ever make me be. God is love. He doesn't throw people into fires to suffer forever and ever. Stories like this just make me sick. I'm sorry it's in the Bible, but there are a lot of things in the Bible that don't reveal the God of love.

LL-29. "Filled with expectation"—so am I. Not for John but for Jesus. Having been baptized, the way of the Lord is prepared for me, by faith, and I am ready for him to come, for me or for the whole world, anytime. I am ready.

LL-30. Our parents' faith does not save us. They can be saints; it doesn't matter. Everyone needs to be born again—PKs, everyone. We need to find the Lord ourselves, and he needs to make a difference in our lives—the fruit worthy of repentance.

LL-31. The ax and the winnowing fork are pretty scary. They terrify our conscience, and I can only respond like Luther: "I am baptized."

LL-32. Like these people, I keep looking for something that I can do to earn my salvation. The gospel tells us that Jesus has done it all.

LL-33. I find it intimidating. Anytime we are asked, "Are you ready for the Lord to come?" the answer will obviously have to be "No." I mean, who would claim that they are? That would be pretty arrogant. So, of course, we get intimidated and then dig in and try harder. We probably need to hear this now and then, but too much overkill and people just tune out. I think most people are doing the best they can, and encouragement works better than threats.

LL-34. What strikes me is the juxtaposition between social responsibility and messianic enthusiasm. The people are all worked up over someone who is going to come and deliver them from all their troubles—but John tells them to focus on the present and help each other right now. If we take care of the present, the future will take care of itself.

LL-35. Well, if I'd been there, I would have been one of the "brood of vipers," I guess, so I suppose the meaning is that I better clean up my act and fast before the wrath of God descends. But this was a long time ago, right? Hasn't happened yet.

LL-36. It just angers me. Stories like this perpetuate the image so many people have of Christianity, that it is a judgmental religion, all about rules and punishment. Forgiveness gets mentioned once here and then is quickly forgotten.

LL-37. It fills me with excitement. We live on the brink of the future—our Lord is coming, with threat and promise. We wait for his arrival with fear and joy.

LL-38. It tells me that, when all is said and done, there will be justice at last. I find this reassuring; it is the hope that lets us go on in a world where we do not see that justice now.

LL-39. It gives me hope for the future. I don't have much hope for the present. We're not doing a very good job of "preparing." But the Lord will come either way, whether we're ready or not.

LL-40. We cannot save ourselves, but God can save us. If God can make children out of stones, then he can make us into whatever he wants us to be. He can baptize us in the Holy Spirit and purify us in the fire, sanctify us in his image till we are "done."

LL-41. I think the Holy Spirit must have picked this one because I have to admit it convicted me where it says the tax collectors shouldn't take more than they are owed, because that probably means that we ought to give them everything that they are owed.[67]

LL-42. The ultimate question is, Are we chaff or are we wheat? There is going to be a day of reckoning, when everything is exposed.

LL-43. I find it a little threatening, like some of the stories in the Old Testament, but I think this was before Jesus died for us, and that changes everything. We are not going to get burned up just because we failed to do the things that these people get told to do. God is more merciful than that.

LL-44. I don't know what it all means, and I especially don't understand that one verse—"all flesh shall see the salvation of God"—because I thought that "flesh and blood cannot inherit the kingdom of God."[68] It is not our flesh that gets saved but our soul. Our bodies just rot or get eaten by worms. Our soul goes to heaven and inherits the kingdom. So I don't have any idea what it means.

LL-45. I find it so amusing that the people want to follow John rather than Jesus. They still do that now, when they act like their pastor or some other leader is the Messiah. They confuse the messenger with the one who really is the Message.

LL-46. I saw a button that said, "Jesus is coming—and is he *pissed!*" That about sums it up.

LL-47. I was baptized as a baby in a Catholic church and only later found out that the Bible says you must be baptized for repentance. People are not ready for the Lord if they have not repented and asked Jesus to come into their hearts as their personal Lord and Savior. Also, like it says here, they are not ready if they are still living in sin.

LL-48. It's hard to take such a story seriously in our world today because only crackpots believe this way: The end is coming soon! Prepare to meet thy doom! There must be a message somewhere for us, perhaps in the third paragraph with its counsel of wise and ethical behavior. I think we can all live that way whether we believe the end is coming soon or not.

LL-49. Stories like this make me mad. This is the kind of religion I was brought up with and there are too many bad memories associated with that kind of preaching. It's why I didn't go to church for years. If I went to church now and heard this one, I would just walk out.

LL-50. "People get ready . . . the Lord is coming!" Rod Stewart sang it. I hope he heeds it. It would be nice to have him in the choir in heaven.[69]

Now what do we make of all this?

Here is an initial observation:

- Twenty-six of the clergy responses refer to *Luke* (the author of the story). None of the lay responses do so.[70]

Why would this be? Is there something about the process of seminary education or the vocation of clergy that sensitizes people to identifying the titular author of a narrative? Is such sensitivity peculiar to biblical literature? What if I were to use one of Aesop's fables (say, "The Fox and the Grapes") in a similar study? Would half of the clergy mention *Aesop* in their response? Would none of the laity do so?

Another observation:

> • All fifty of the lay responses include a self-reference (that is, they use personal pronouns, such as "I/me" or "we/us"). Only twenty of the clergy responses do so.[71]

Why would this be? Is there something about seminary education or clergy vocation that desensitizes people to personal reference? Is this phenomenon peculiar to biblical interpretation? Or would it apply to other stories as well?

Before attempting an explanation, I thought I should check the above two observations against the only other data bank I possess—the clergy and lay responses to Mark 7:1–8 (Figure 1). In *that* instance,

> • Only one of the clergy responses (C-49) refers to *Mark* (the author of the story). Again, none of the lay responses do so.
> • All but four of the clergy responses (C-26, C-35, C-36, C-46) make a self-reference in answering the question "What does this story mean *to you?*" All but two of the laity (L-23, L-50) do so as well.[72]

Thus, there was no significant difference in the responses of clergy and laity with regard to these two points in the first experiment (Mark 7:1–8). But there was, I think, a very significant difference in those responses in the second experiment (Luke 3:3–17). For me, the different results of the two experiments is what is most impressive (see Table 3).

TABLE 3

	Mark 7:1–8: What Does This Story Mean to You?	Luke 3:3–17: What Does This Story Mean?
CLERGY: refer to author	1	26
LAITY: refer to author	0	0
CLERGY: self-reference	46	20
LAITY: self-reference	48	50

I do not think the divergent results can be accounted for by anything intrinsic to the stories themselves. I suspect, rather, that the difference accrued from the way in which the question was asked. The two words *to you* made a significant difference for clergy in determining how they responded to the story, but not for laity. The laity demonstrated a tendency to read stories as applicable to themselves with or without prompting; clergy demonstrated an ability to read stories as applicable to themselves when prompted to do so, but they often did not do this unless prompted. If you go back now and skim once more the clergy/lay responses to the second story (Luke 3:3–17), you may be struck by something that I do not know how to quantify in a table. When I asked a layperson, "What does this story mean?" he or she invariably assumed I was asking, "What does it mean *to you?*" But when I asked clergy the same question, they almost never assumed this—even in the responses where they made self-references, they usually interpreted the story in terms of what they thought it would have meant or should now mean to someone else (to the author, to their congregation, etc.).

This is explicable. Most clergy must read Bible stories on a weekly basis and ask themselves, "What does this mean for the people in my church (or my community)?" Most seminaries that train clergy include exegetical programs that teach them how to interpret biblical materials contextually—which often means how *not* to read their own situation or perspective into the text. They are taught to avoid *eisegesis* (reading their own ideas *into* a text) and to perform *exegesis* (reading the author's ideas *out* of a text).

With this in mind, I actually organized the clergy responses in our second study according to three contexts:

- I believe the first sixteen clergy respondents (CC-1–16) understood the question in a *historical* sense: "What did John the Baptist mean when he did and said the things reported of him in this text?" In these cases, Luke is referenced only as the one who reports or describes what John said and did. In a sense, John seems to be the real author, for it is his words (reported by Luke) that convey meaning. The message of the text is defined in terms of *John's* intention. Or, to put the matter differently, the primary hermeneutical context for meaning is understood as *the setting for the story,* that is, the time and place when the events narrated in the story took place. For these respondents, descriptions of "what the story means" are worded mainly in the past tense, though of course the meaningful event in the past may reveal lessons that are still relevant for the present. Thus, CC-6 seems to think that this description of God's past actions discloses something about God's typical nature.

- Twenty more clergy respondents (CC-17–36) seem to have understood the question in a *redactional* sense: "What did Luke mean to convey when he wrote this text or incorporated it into his Gospel?" In these cases, Luke himself is referenced as the author, as the conveyer of meaning. The message of the text is defined in terms of *Luke's* intention. The primary hermeneutical context for meaning is understood to be what I call *the discourse setting of the narrative,* the time and place in which the narrative was written. These clergy understood the question "What does this story mean?" as asking not "What did

John the Baptist mean to say to people when he preached to them?"
but "What did Luke mean to say to people when he told the story of
John the Baptist's preaching?" For these respondents, descriptions of
"what the story means" are also worded primarily in the past tense—
though, again, lessons for the present are sometimes appended.

- In fourteen cases (CC-37–50), respondents seem to have understood
  the question in an *existential* sense: "What does the story mean to us
  (or to me) today?" The author Luke is only mentioned in the first
  two of these (CC-37, CC-38) and even there is envisioned as speaking directly to the respondent's own context ("Luke is trying to tell
  us"; "Luke wants us to"). The link between author and reader is
  unmediated. In the next twelve responses (CC-39–50), the author
  drops out altogether. Now the *story* or the *text* seems to speak directly
  to the respondent. The primary hermeneutical context for meaning is
  no longer the setting of the narrative's story or that of its discourse
  but rather *the setting of its readers.* Of course, even in these instances,
  the historical or redactional mediation may simply be unmentioned.
  These respondents might be simply stating the "lesson for today"
  that they derive based on discernment of historical or redactional
  meanings similar to those offered in the earlier examples.

What should we conclude? Most seminaries train their clergy to interpret texts
in light of their historical context and in light of the apparent intentions of the
author. This seems to be working. Most, if not all, of the clergy demonstrate a
certain commitment to doing this. But when I have shown the results to groups
of laity they have invariably shaken their heads in dismay. Whatever benefits
clergy may derive from their studies, they moan, something has gone terribly
wrong when pastors need special prompting to regard scripture as applicable to
themselves. On the other hand, when I have shared these data with clergy
groups, there has been a fair amount of (defensive?) posturing to the effect that
laity must be naive and presumptuous and terribly narcissistic to assume that
everything in the Bible is there for them. Scripture, these clergy insist, records
God's word to various people at different times and places, and the circumstances and contexts in which it is given are always significant for interpretation.

I have some opinions about these matters, but first let me describe the distinction we have already noticed in slightly different terms. Laity always evinced
a *reader-oriented hermeneutic.* They answered the question "What does this
mean?" from the perspective of readers, usually themselves. Laity—that is, most
people in the world—simply assume that the question of what a story means
implies reflection on what it means to the people who read it. Clergy, however,
only thought this way when the question was explicit: what does this mean *to
you?* Otherwise, clergy tended to evince an *author-oriented hermeneutic.* They
usually assumed that the question "What does this mean?" was a question of
what meaning the author had intended to convey through his words. In our
example, there was some discrepancy as to whether the author was identified as

John the Baptist (author of the words spoken in the story) or as Luke (author of the story itself), but in more than two-thirds of the responses, an author's perspective was thought to be definitive for determining meaning. This was not true for any of the laity (in either study).

In our first chapter, I indicated that there is a link between reader-/author-oriented hermeneutics and *conceptions of meaning.* The reader-oriented perspective tends to regard meaning as *effect,* while the author-oriented perspective tends to regard meaning as *message.* With that in mind, look now at some of the language clergy and laity used to tell me what the story in Luke 3:3–17 means:

Responses to Table 2: Meaning as Message or Effect?

Clergy	Laity
Luke reports something (CC-1)	I am confused (LL-2)
The main point comes (CC-3)	I am inspired (LL-4)
The point seems to be (CC-4)	It encourages me (LL-6)
The emphasis is (CC-5)	I am humbled (LL-7)
Luke tells us that (CC-8)	I have felt like (LL-9)
Luke describes the scene (CC-11)	This story upsets me (LL-10)
The most obvious point is (CC-13)	It shocks us (LL-11)
It talks about (CC-17)	It scares me (LL-13)
Luke's pronouncement that (CC-18)	I find it very comforting (LL-15)
Luke wrote his Gospel to (CC-19)	It warns us (LL-16)
Luke shapes his account (CC-21)	It moves me to get serious (LL-18)
He wants to emphasize that (CC-24)	It provokes me (LL-19)
Luke's intent seems to be (CC-27)	It is scary (LL-20)
Luke wants to say that (CC-28)	It simply challenges us (LL-21)
Luke shows us what he regards (CC-30)	The story challenges us (LL-24)
Luke's agenda is to promote (CC-32)	The story shakes me (LL-26)
Luke indicates that (CC-33)	It gives me pause (LL-27)
He wants people to believe that (CC-34)	I find it intimidating (LL-33)
Luke says that (CC-35)	It just angers me (LL-36)
Luke makes clear that (CC-36)	It fills me with excitement (LL-37)
Luke is trying to tell us (CC-37)	It gives me hope (LL-39)
I think the message of the text (CC-40)	It convicted me (LL-41)
The lesson is that (CC-45)	I find it a little threatening (LL-43)
The message for people today (CC-46)	I find it so amusing (LL-45)
The message for today is (CC-48)	Stories like this make me mad (LL-50)

Do you see the difference? In these instances, at least, the clergy answer the question "What does this story mean?" in highly cognitive terms that attempt to identify the point or message that is conveyed. The laity, however, are much more inclined to answer that question in terms of the effect or impact that the story has on them.

Of course, this is not absolute. Clergy respondents occasionally allude to "meaning as effect" (CC-23 thinks it evokes a question; CC-32 says it provides an example to emulate). Laity sometimes look for a message in the text (LL-48) and in other ways show great interest in cognitive interpretation of certain points (LL-2, LL-3, LL-44). Obviously "message" and "effect" are not mutually exclusive concepts but can and often do coexist in what we might label *meaning*. Still, when one looks at these two lists side by side, the difference in orientation is remarkable.

Less impressive but also revealing is the language employed in the first study (Mark 7:1–8), where I explicitly asked, "What does this story mean *to you*?" Even when clergy were prompted to answer the question in this way, very few told me how the story *affected* them. The following list is different from the foregoing one. It does not present contrasting responses, but similar ones. I list here all the explicit comments indicating effect that I can find in both clergy and lay responses to the first story. The contrast comes, then, in the number of those remarks:

Responses to Figure 1: Meaning as Effect

Clergy	**Laity**
That verse stings (C-13)	This story offers hope (L-4)
That's comforting, I guess (C-24)	It comforts me (L-8)
It convicts me (C-25)	Encourages me and give me hope (L-9)
Jesus challenges us (C-33)	It motivates me to reexamine (L-10)
I find that offensive (C-47)	The story reassures me (L-11)
	It troubles me (L-12)
	It always amuses me (L-15)
	I'm always amazed (L-24)
	I'm embarrassed (L-25)
	The story convicts me (L-26)
	Shame. Guilt. (L-27)
	I'm confused (L-28)
	I find it frustrating (L-29)
	This is annoying (L-30)
	The story is discouraging (L-31)
	This verse is disturbing (L-32)
	I worry (L-36)
	It makes me pray (L-41)
	It gives me a heart of compassion (L-48)
	It angers me (L-49)

Again, simply pulling lines out of the responses like this may not provide a completely fair assessment. Certainly C-11 has been prompted to pray just as surely as L-41, though only the latter explicitly says that the text has affected him or her in this way. But I do think that this chart offers a graphic illustration of what is essentially true: the lay responses even to *this* question ("What does it mean *to you*?") are more oriented toward defining meaning in terms of an effect on readers than in terms of a message conveyed by an author.

It seems to me, then, that the author-oriented hermeneutic may be less natural. It must be taught or developed and the process through which it is learned seems to bring a subtle distancing from appreciation for the effect or impact that stories can have.[73] Is such a process really useful or necessary?

Actually, I think it is. The principles of contextual exegesis taught in seminaries and practiced in parishes are important and, indeed, essential for preservation of orthodox faith (which I regard as a good thing). I continue to believe that theological doctrine needs to be grounded in interpretation of scripture as understood in light of the historical intentions of the Bible's original authors. Christian dogma should be expressive of the message of scripture, and that message is best determined with exegetical methods derived from an author-oriented hermeneutic. The church needs clergy and scholars capable of studying the Bible in this fashion.

But Christianity is more than dogma, and preaching is more than exposition of doctrine. After conducting these studies, I am struck by the likelihood of what could be happening in many churches on a regular basis. In denominations that I frequent, one or more biblical texts (often stories) are read by the minister or a layperson. I now imagine that as the congregation hears such a text, those who are paying attention are probably responding to the passage emotionally and aesthetically in ways similar to what I have listed above. They are being comforted, inspired, confused, frustrated, angered, and so forth. Then, an ordained minister gets up in front of the church, refers to the story just read, and attempts 1) to tell everyone what message the author intended to convey to his original audience and 2) to identify (on the basis of this) a message that the story may now convey to us today. Of course, this all may be very important, and it may be very well done, but that does not disguise what is happening: the preacher is answering a question ("What is the message of the story?") that few people were asking. Meanwhile, the divergent effects that the story itself had on those listeners are gradually diluted as the sermon proceeds and perhaps forgotten by the time it reaches conclusion. At the end of the service, many will shake the minister's hand and say, "That was a good message." And it probably was—but are messages all that the Bible seeks to convey?[74]

Back to the Main Point

It would be easy to lose track of the point these studies have for the developing argument of this book.[75] I hope that the implications of my study for ministry and theological studies are not altogether neglected, but they are not relevant as such for what follows. The reason I conducted these studies in the first place was to try out suppositions about polyvalence. Whatever, ultimately, is made of my analysis of clergy/lay hermeneutics, these studies illustrate that people do in fact derive widely divergent meanings from the same text, and that such divergence can be attributable to such factors as social location, reading strategy, empathy choice, and conception of meaning. I think that this point—stated in the first chapter—has been established. Now, we can move on to other considerations.

Chapter Three
Expected and Unexpected Readings

Stories can and do mean different things to different people. So should they just be allowed to mean anything to anybody?

Allowed? What does that word imply? There are no Interpretation Police who will arrest you for misinterpreting a text—unless, for instance, the text in question is a traffic sign. Of course, we are *legally* free to make what we will of stories. But should we? Should there be "rules of interpretation" and what function should these serve?

In this chapter, I will argue that there are such rules and that their function is primarily social and descriptive—not ethical or prescriptive. The origin of such rules, furthermore, is democratic—they do not represent anything intrinsic to human understanding or to the nature of literature, but merely express the recognized habits of a large number of people.

Literary critics have often proposed rules for the interpretation of literature that are somewhat analogous to rules of grammar. It is not a sin to use language in ways that grammarians call incorrect. Sometimes it can be highly effective to do so—just try to imagine Bill Withers singing "There Isn't Any Sunshine When She's Gone." But ultimate recognition of basic language patterns is what facilitates communication. Ever since we tried to build that tower, we humans have realized that it just won't work to have every individual speak his or her own language (cf. Gen. 11:1–9).

Now, this is a touchy subject, in literary-criticism circles at least. Lots of my literary-critical colleagues think that what happened at the aforementioned tower building was actually kind of cool. If God's intention in confusing the tongues of humanity was to thwart mortal pride, then the laugh's on God. The beautiful diversity of human language that has developed since is itself a more fitting monument to human achievement than the dumb tower would have been.

Well, my favorite name for a rock band is the moniker Lanny Cordola bestowed on one of his Chicago incarnations: Chaos is the Poetry. I do like ambiguity, and I am all for diversity. But it seems to me that appreciating diversity means not just claiming the right to speak my own language but also making some effort toward understanding yours. To do that, we may both need to recognize what linguists call "rules of grammar." We don't have to agree with them; we might choose not to follow them. But we probably have to acknowledge them and know that they exist if we are ever to understand each other's different ways of speaking. The linguists, by the way, do not (usually) make up these rules—they just listen to how language is spoken and try to describe whatever apparent rules are observable.

We are using language as a metaphor for literature. I can, of course, interpret stories any way I please—and so can you. But if we want to talk to each other about a story—especially one that we interpret differently—we will probably end up referring to some generally recognized rules of interpretation. One example would be that interpretation is normally rendered by one who has read the work to be interpreted in its entirety. Let us suppose that you and I are arguing about a book that we have both read and that we have experienced quite differently. You say the book presented a wrenching but ultimately heartwarming tale. I claim that my heart was neither wrenched nor warmed. We argue for a while, dismayed by the contrast in each other's experience, and then I admit to you that I actually read only the first half of the book and never finished it. Would that not strike you as relevant information? Wouldn't you think it a bit ludicrous of me to put forth my reading experience as comparable to yours when I hadn't even read the entire book?

Most people would. Of course, there is nothing wrong with someone reading only half a book. But a common assumption for discussion about a book's meaning is that participants in the discussion have actually read the book to be discussed—in its entirety, unless otherwise stated. Such an assumption illustrates what I mean by "rules of interpretation": presuppositions that we tend to make regarding reading processes that affect interpretation. Really, that's *all* I mean—and yet this remains an incredibly touchy and controversial subject. Often, when I start talking about rules for interpretation, I get viewed as some kind of control freak—people assume that *I* want to make the rules and that *I* want to enforce them. Neither. I just want to recognize rules (though I prefer to call them "expectations") that seem to exist already. And I don't really care whether you follow them or not. I would just like for you to admit it when you don't so that I can take that into account when trying to discern why your reading experience is different from mine.[76]

In chapter 1, I told you about my friend Walter Bouman who always reads the last chapter of P. D. James's novels first. He loses some of the suspense factor that most readers find in those books, but he gains something else (a sense of eschatological prolepsis) that he cherishes. If I did not know that he reads this way, he and I might spend countless hours trying to figure out why I find the novels to be suspenseful and he does not. Is it just because he is smarter or more perceptive than I am? Is it our difference in age, or in our generational background and upbringing? No. It's because he reads the last chapter first! He chooses to break another basic rule of interpretation: readers are not only expected to read stories in their entirety but they are also expected to read them sequentially from beginning to end. I don't think that there are "right" and "wrong" ways to read P. D. James novels. But I do think that readers are expected to find these novels suspenseful and that this expected response is contingent on reading in a certain way. Bouman reads them in an unexpected way, and his unexpected response to them is explicable in light of this.

What I want is a hermeneutic that works in real life, that recognizes the reality of polyvalence and yet facilitates the kinds of conversations that people often have about stories. I know a theology professor, Don Luck, who asks students to explain the "existential cash value" of various philosophical dictums.[77] That's what I want—a hermeneutic that has *existential cash value,* one that helps to explains why my wife and I are affected differently by the same movie, or why clergy and laity assign different meanings to the same Bible story. A helpful step toward understanding those differences consists of establishing a common language for talking about how implied readers are expected to respond.

Labels

Some years ago, I tried to expand the lingo of biblical hermeneutics by introducing the new categories of *expected readings* and *unexpected readings.*[78] The field was already terminology heavy, and my suggestion was not universally appreciated. But prior to this, the dominant categories in biblical interpretation were "understanding" and "misunderstanding." Every Bible scholar, it seems, would claim to understand the meaning of the text that he or she was studying and, often, claim that others misunderstood it.

This concept of understanding and misunderstanding is still with us.[79] It seems to presume an author-oriented hermeneutic that construes meaning as message: the correct interpretation of a story's meaning is derived by understanding the message that the author intended to convey. Thus, the categories of understanding and misunderstanding are necessarily evaluative. To understand a story is to interpret it properly; to misunderstand it is to interpret it improperly. I do not reject this paradigm for interpretation. I agree with it. Indeed, I have written books on the disciplines of historical criticism (source criticism, form criticism, redaction criticism), and I regularly teach classes on these disciplines. But as we have seen, interpretation requires a broader field than this. We may speak not only of messages conveyed by authors but also of effects experienced by readers. Then, the categories of understanding and mis-understanding seem limited. I would be uneasy assuming that readers who are affected in one way by a text necessarily understand it or that readers affected another way necessarily misunderstand it.

Still, in my experience, a distinction can be made between responses that would be expected of readers and responses that would not be. Let us imagine four people reading the story of Jesus' crucifixion in the Gospel of Matthew:

- Reader One is *inspired* by the story because it presents Jesus as a man of integrity who is willing to die nobly for his convictions.
- Reader Two is *traumatized* by the story because it reveals the depth of human depravity on the part of those who denounce, betray, and torture an innocent man.
- Reader Three is *comforted* by the story because it portrays Jesus' death as an atoning sacrifice through which God offers forgiveness and mercy to the undeserving.
- Reader Four is *delighted* by the story because it reports the gruesome execution of a meddlesome busybody who tried to tell everyone else how they should live.

Although all four of these responses are very different, I would put the first three in a separate category from the fourth. I can account for the first three readings without knowing much about the readers. All three of these readings pick up on cues within the Matthean passion narrative. The story seems to solicit such responses. I cannot, however, account for the fourth reading on the basis of Matthew's narrative itself. I find nothing in the story that solicits or encourages such a response.

From this example, one might gather that categories of expectation are as value-laden as categories of understanding. Many would think that Reader Four produces an unexpected reading that is clearly wrong, while Readers One, Two, and Three produce diverse readings, any one of which may be regarded as expected and correct. But note that I do not charge the fourth reader with *mis-understanding* Matthew's story. The labels "expected" and "unexpected" need not carry the connotations of "right" and "wrong," as we shall see. The labels themselves are only descriptive, not evaluative.[80]

A Note in the Sanctuary

One Sunday afternoon years ago, back when I was pastor of a church in south-east Texas, I was flipping through the used bulletins from our morning service, separating the pages that could be recycled from the glossy inserts that could not. A slip from a notepad fell out, on which was scrawled the following:

What does Union Carbide have in common with Thom McAn?
About 2,000 black loafers.

I was immediately irritated, indeed angered by this note. Somebody—some member of my congregation or, at least, someone present with us for worship that morning—had written a racist joke and passed it to someone else right there in our sanctuary.

To "get" the joke, you may have to know certain things: that Union Carbide was a factory in the area that employed a large number of African Americans and that Thom McAn was a popular chain of shoe stores. Thus, the term "black loafer" is being used as a pun, referring both to a type of shoe sold by Thom McAn and to supposedly lazy African Americans employed by Union Carbide.

My response to the note was what I now call an unexpected reading. The expected response was amusement, but I was angered not amused. What happened when I picked up that scrap of paper? In the split second after I read it, I both *identified* the expected reading of the text and *rejected* it, choosing to distinguish myself from the text's implied audience by responding to it in an unexpected way. I want to use this somewhat crude example of a reading experience to illustrate several points about expected and unexpected readings:

1. My unexpected response to the text was not a result of misunderstanding. I understood the message that the author intended to convey, but my response to the text was not that which the text solicited. Thus, my response reveals as much about me as it does about the text. You could ply me with questions: To what extent was my response (anger) conditioned by the context in which the text was received (anonymous note, read alone, in my church)? What if a friend had told me the joke? What if I had simply overheard the joke in a bar? What if I'd heard an African American comic tell it on television? The genius and the challenge of reader-response criticism is that it attempts to deal with all of these factors: text, context, and audience. Reader-response critics may be said to interpret *reading experiences* rather than texts. And such a project necessarily includes interpreting the interpreter.

2. I was able to identify the expected response to this text even though my own response was at variance with it. This, for me, offers pragmatic proof for the existential reality of what I call expected and unexpected readings. We do not simply impose our own understandings on texts, assume that these are normative, and then equate our responses with what would be expected of readers. At least, we don't *always* do that. Sometimes, we are able to detect an expected, implied reading distinct from our own understanding.

3. I was able to identify the expected response to the note based on the text itself. I had little else to go on. I did not know the identity of the author or the intended recipient. The note did not say at the top "This is a joke" or "You are expected to find this amusing." I figured that out from cues within the text itself.

4. My identification of the expected response to the text was nevertheless dependent on knowledge and competence that I had obtained apart from this

reading experience. This is an important corollary to the point just made. Although I did figure out the expected response from cues within the text itself, I had to be able to interpret those cues. I had to know certain things that were simply assumed for this text—what Union Carbide and Thom McAn are. I also had to possess a degree of literary competence to recognize a rhetorical device employed in this text, namely, the pun. I needed the competence of genre recognition to know that a short text consisting of a question and an answer, where the answer constitutes a pun, is one instance of the genre *joke,* for which the anticipated response is amusement. Such assumed knowledge and competence belong to what narrative critics call "the readers' repertoire," a matter to be discussed in detail in chapters 5 and 6 of this book.

5. The reason I did not respond to this text in the expected manner was that, even though I did possess the knowledge and competence assumed for its readers, I did not *believe* the way its readers were assumed to believe. In literary terms, the *implied readers* of this note would be people who believe African Americans are lazy or who at least think it is humorous to insinuate that they are. I do not believe or think this, so I did not respond in the manner expected of the text's implied readers.

6. We have here an instance in which I think an unexpected response is morally and ethically superior to an expected one. I indicated previously that the categories of expected and unexpected readings are descriptive, not evaluative. When one takes the next step, however, and does evaluate an interpretation (theologically, ethically, or morally), we see that there is no necessary correlation between expected reading/positive evaluation and unexpected reading/negative evaluation. In this example (the racist joke) those simplistic correlations would be reversed.

Now, before we move on, let's take another one-paragraph break for those who may have specific concerns arising from Christian theology (or piety). One might rightly wonder whether lessons drawn from analysis of a racist joke can properly be applied to interpretation of texts that are to be regarded as sacred scripture. Does not acceptance of the authority of scripture compel us to accept what I call expected readings as divinely inspired and to reject what I call unexpected readings as human intrusions? This question is a valid one, but it is also inevitably connected to all kinds of doctrinal and confessional issues that wise scholars know to avoid. Shunning identification with the latter camp, I shall tread right in and take up this matter—but not until chapter 10. In the meantime, if *you* believe the Bible is in any sense a book of scripture, a book that reveals divine truth, then ask yourself, Can we (ever) yield to the authority of this book by responding to it in unexpected ways? I will tip my hand just enough to indicate that I think we can. I do hold, strongly, to a doctrine of the authority of scripture—but there are instances where I am convinced the *best* interpretation of scripture (the one that God wants us to adopt) is an unexpected reading. Certainly, Jesus often interpreted the Bible in unexpected ways.[81] Is hermeneutics the only area in which we are *not* to emulate him?

But we are getting ahead of ourselves again. For now, the question must be whether it is actually possible or desirable to distinguish expected readings from unexpected ones in the first place. And that takes us into what for me is safer territory, my old stomping grounds of narrative criticism.

Narrative Criticism

I now regard narrative criticism as a subset or variety of reader-response criticism. The latter is a broad field that encompasses several different systems of interpretation.

There is simply *descriptive reader-response,* which seeks to catalog the variety of interpretations offered for a given text and to understand what factors influence this diversity. I believe the experiments laid out in chapter 2 exemplify this approach. You will recall that I made no attempt there to evaluate the individual responses of clergy or laity. I did have some evaluative remarks regarding the need to recognize the diversity of such responses, but I did not attempt to evaluate the legitimacy of the responses themselves. Such initial neutrality is typical of descriptive reader-response criticism.

An important subset of descriptive reader-response criticism is *Wirkungsgeschichte,* the German approach that attempts to catalog the variety of interpretations that have been offered for any given text throughout history. Again, those who use this approach often have some evaluative comments to make regarding what they think the history of interpretations reveals, but the method itself is purely descriptive.

Reader response also encompasses many overtly *ideological approaches* that seek to read texts from the perspective of readers who are informed in particular ways. For instance, *womanist* reading attempts to read literature from the distinct perspective of African-American women.[82] Womanist scholars may not care whether the author of a text intended for it to be read from this perspective. They may not care whether they are expected to read from this perspective. They somewhat defiantly determine to read texts this way regardless—even if that means transforming or resisting intended or expected responses. Hypothetically, any ideology can serve to produce an ideological reading of any text. Approaches that have actually been applied to the New Testament include Marxist reading, Jungian reading, Mahāyāna Buddhist reading, Latin-American liberation theology reading, Japanese Feminist reading, and many more.[83] Proponents of ideological reading typically assert that *all* readings are ideological. The question is not whether to read texts from an ideological perspective, but whether to identify explicitly the perspective from which one reads. Thus, reader-response criticism in general and ideological approaches in particular often appeal to what is called *deconstruction,* that is, to the demonstrable inability of any text to sustain a single or dominant interpretation. Practitioners of deconstruction have been highly successful at critiquing all ideologies and methods from a postmodern perspective, demonstrating that the polyvalent potential in texts and in language is so great as to render all attempts at interpretation ambiguous, transient, and necessarily subjective.[84]

And then there is *narrative criticism,* a basic discipline that is practiced by almost all reader-response critics yet sometimes despised by them when it is not combined with other approaches. Reader-response advocates tend to think that narrative criticism should be a means to an end, not an end in itself. The same, of course, might be said for all the other disciplines just cited, but the sentiment is generally expressed most vigorously with regard to narrative criticism. For better or worse, narrative criticism is the field of my specialty. I was specifically trained in it as a doctoral student; I wrote a (literally) defining book on the practice and procedures of the discipline[85]; and I have worked with the approach in one way or another for about twenty years now. I do have many other interests, and I have done a lot of other things, but when my name comes up at academic conferences, if people know me at all, they usually know me as "that narrative-criticism guy."

Narrative criticism is unique among reader-response approaches in that it does not concern itself directly with the actual responses of real people.[86] Instead, narrative criticism seeks to determine a range of expected responses that might be attributed to a text's implied readers. The concept of *implied readers* has been defined differently by various scholars,[87] but it refers essentially to an imaginary set of people who may be assumed to read a given text in the way that they are expected to read it, bringing to their reading experience the knowledge, competence, beliefs, and values that appear to be presupposed for the text in question. In short, narrative criticism attempts to define agreed-on strategies for interpretation that will allow interpreters (at least, interpreters who agree on the strategies) to distinguish expected readings from unexpected ones.

Debate continues as to whether it is really possible or helpful to make these distinctions. Let's take the latter question first. If the descriptions (expected/unexpected) are not intrinsically evaluative, then of what use are they? They are valuable nonetheless because they aid us in understanding our role in the reading process.

I have become convinced that, ultimately, whether or not we regard these distinctions as helpful depends on the value that we place on self-consciousness in reading. I happen to think it is a good thing to be aware of what one is doing when reading a text, so I do find the distinctions between expected and unexpected readings to be useful. The opposite point of view was asserted explicitly by two of my literary-critical cohorts at a 1992 conference on reader-oriented approaches to the Bible. The three of us were on a panel at the Eastern Great Lakes Biblical Society, at which we were asked if we think it is useful for a reader to know whether the meaning that he or she derives from a text differs from that which was "probably intended by the author" or "expected of the implied readers." I said yes; they said no.

Let us be careful to see what is at stake (and what is not at stake) here. Many reader-response critics would respect or even advocate the practice of *resistant reading,* according to which readers intentionally interpret texts in accord with an ideology that would not be expected of its implied readers (see previous discussion, page 63). I have already indicated that I agree with them, as the example of the previously cited racist joke clearly indicates. Similarly, a story that presupposes an anti-Semitic perspective may be (I would say *should* be) interpreted from a perspective that defiantly rejects the orientation that was intended by its author and is expected of its readers. But the question put to the EGLBS panel was not whether the apparent intentions of authors or the presumed expectations of readers ought to be determinative for meaning. The question was whether readers who interpret texts in ways contrary to those intentions or expectations ought to be made aware that they are doing so. I suspect that my colleagues voted "no" on this one because they assume that any such imposition of awareness would implicitly curtail interpretive freedom. They imagine, for instance, a male professor informing a female student that her feminist reading of a text is not in keeping with what the author intended—or, for that matter, with any response that would be expected of the text's implied readers. I do hope that I am sensitive to the pedagogical dynamics of social power implied by such a scenario, but I still say that I favor self-awareness in the reading process. And such awareness, it seems to me, can only be assisted by recognition of interpretive moves that readers make. I approve of feminist interpreters reading patriarchal texts from a feminist perspective, but I believe this is done with greater integrity when the interpreters acknowledge that such reading may be defiantly unexpected.

My own observation is that unexpected readings can be unwittingly resistant. Readers may interpret stories in accord with an evaluative point of view different from that which is presupposed for the story without realizing that they are doing so.[88] The tendency to do this is heightened with texts that are regarded as authoritative. What is actually an unexpected reading is then mistaken for and even defended as "the message of the text." By seeking to establish a range of meaning definitive for what would be expected of a text's implied readers, narrative criticism attempts to bring a clarity and integrity to the interpretive task that can be lacking in reader-response approaches otherwise. I view the critically determined expected reading as having a function analogous to that of a control group in a scientific experiment.[89] It offers a base reading against which the responses of real readers might be compared and contrasted. Responses that are unexpected may be identified and possibly explained. This, indeed, is what I meant when I said that narrative criticism is practiced by almost all reader-response critics, though often in combination with some other approach. Proponents of *Wirkungsgeschichte* may do a little narrative criticism on the side to determine whether the history of interpretation has produced largely expected readings or unexpected ones. A womanist interpreter may check to see the extent to which an African-American woman's reading of a text is in line with what was expected of the text's implied readers. The gathering of such information is necessary for understanding interpretive processes apart from any question of which interpretations (if any) should be deemed authoritative or correct.[90]

I underscore what I said in the Introduction (pages 6–7). I personally understand narrative criticism to be a postmodern approach to biblical interpretation. An expected reading of a text is not to be described in a foundational, totalizing, or mystifying way. An interpretation that appears to be expected of a text's implied readers is simply *one* interpretation against which others may be measured. To borrow an example from A. K. M. Adam,[91] most literary critics would agree that implied readers of *King Lear* are expected to be moved by the king's folly and suffering. But what does this say about the person who is not so moved? Must we decide that there is something wrong with her, or that she has misread the play? No. All we need say is that she has not responded to the story in the manner that we believe would be expected of its implied readers. Narrative criticism (as a discipline) makes no judgments about the rightness or wrongness of actual interpretations evinced by real readers.[92]

This approach has nevertheless been greeted with suspicion by reader-oriented critics who fear the purpose of determining expected readings is to limit interpretive options. I must admit that their suspicions are sometimes well-grounded, for a number of biblical interpreters have in fact used narrative criticism to further that goal. Still, a hermeneutic that privileges the perspective of implied readers (like one that canonizes authorial intent) has to be grounded in confessional propositions, the defense of which is extrinsic to the program itself. The question of whether a hermeneutic of scripture ought to allow unexpected readings of texts to be accepted or expected readings of texts to be resisted is an intriguing one, but narrative criticism itself offers no insight for resolving this dilemma. Scholars who believe either way can (and do) make use of the approach. All the approach does is provide a fairly reliable means (i.e., an agreed-on strategy) for determining whether readings are expected or unexpected in the first place. Even if a favored reading is determined to be unexpected, readers remain free to embrace it. And even if an interpretation that readers find repugnant is deemed to be the expected reading, those who want to resist it may still do so.[93] Narrative criticism does not limit interpretive options; it allows choices to be made advisedly.[94]

Now for the question of possibility: Is it really *possible* to make a distinction between expected and unexpected readings?[95] First, we must consider a philosophical objection. A number of literary theorists have told me that these categories are epistemologically flawed because texts do not have expectations, nor can they convey them; all so-called expectations are imputed to texts by readers through some dynamic of psychological projection. This seems basically correct; I at least admit that I don't have the background or facility in philosophy to sustain any kind of debate with those who want to argue on such grounds. But, as I said near the outset of this chapter, I want a hermeneutic that has existential cash value. Human experience tells me that most of us do in fact *sense* that we are expected to respond to certain texts in certain ways. Furthermore, as we noted with the previous example of the racist joke, we are sometimes able to detect such expectations even when they are not fulfilled for us personally. People will argue as to whether or not *Nightmare on Elm Street* is a scary movie (i.e., whether it succeeds in scaring them), but I have never met anyone who does not think it is supposed to be a scary movie. People will argue as to whether pornographic films are sexy, but I've never met anyone who doesn't think that the

Narrative Criticism: The Emergence of a Prominent Reading Strategy

In the late 1970s, biblical scholars began to show renewed interest in a literary interpretation of the Old and New Testaments, and they turned for assistance to approaches that had been practiced in secular studies for some thirty years: narratology, Russian formalism, French structuralism, and American "New Criticism." Biblical critics were understandably more interested in drawing from the tried and true than in sampling what might just be the latest fads. Literary studies produced in this period focused heavily on conflict analysis, character development, and the interpretation of rhetorical devices such as symbolism and irony—all matters basic to first-year Literature 101 courses in the secular field. The name *narrative criticism* came to be applied to the eclectic discipline that developed from this somewhat haphazard borrowing. Narrative criticism was specifically designed for the interpretation of biblical literature; it ignored or modified concepts that did not seem relevant yet tended to favor insights originally applied to modern novels. The storylike quality of biblical accounts came to the fore in spite of the obvious historical grounding for these writings' content and influence.

Narrative criticism was defined as a text-oriented approach to scripture as opposed to the author-oriented mode of traditional historical study. Meaning could be determined by paying attention to the form, structure, and rhetorical dynamics of the work itself, without reference to background information regarding what the author may or may not have intended. Meanwhile, almost unbeknownst to these pioneers in biblical literary criticism, the secular academy had moved decisively again, away from what it regarded as traditional text-oriented approaches toward reader-oriented ones. The emphasis now was on studying the processes through which readers make sense of texts, the social and literary dynamics that interact when actual human beings produce or create meaning out of texts. Thus, in 1990, I defined narrative criticism as a text-oriented approach that could be distinguished from both author- and reader-oriented modes of criticism. At the same time, I averred that "of all the types of literary criticism (practiced in biblical studies), narrative criticism and reader response are the most similar and they may eventually become indistinguishable" (*What Is Narrative Criticism?*, p. 21). My editor, Dan Via, wrote in the margin of my manuscript, "They should!"

When biblical critics did discover the prominence of reader response in the academy at large, they sought to redress the situation in biblical scholarship but may have overreacted. The concern to be modern produced panic that missed an essential point. In the secular academy, the proliferation of reader-oriented approaches to literature did not consist of simultaneous competing claims to have discovered a "right approach" but rather sprung from a recognition that diverse approaches served different constituencies in various ways. Scholars who were quick to abandon the recently acquired narrative criticism as "outdated" (a *terrible* thing to be in scholarship) did not seem to realize that this approach itself might be an example of what so many secular scholars were working so hard to develop within their own guilds: a strategy for understanding a particular type of literature in a particular way for a particular constituency. Meanwhile, scholars who feared that secularization of biblical studies had gone too far adopted their own brand of foolishness, occasionally asserting that meaning derived through narrative criticism was somehow intrinsically or objectively true: meaning lay in the text itself just waiting to be discovered and extracted through dispassionate application of a method, the principles and procedures of which were themselves apparently beyond critique.

When things settled down, narrative criticism was seen to have endured but seemed transformed. On closer inspection, the approach itself may have changed little, but the rationale for its employment was altered. Indeed, I would now say that narrative criticism is *still* a text-oriented strategy, but it is employed in at least three different ways by interpreters who have diverse hermeneutical goals:

- *Author-oriented hermeneutic.* Interpreters who are primarily interested in determining the intention of a text's historical author have discovered that narrative criticism provides them with an "index" of authorial intent. Narrative criticism seeks to determine how readers are expected to respond to the story, but historically minded critics may assume that such expectations reflect the historical intentions of the author. Thus, narrative criticism may be used to supplement or confirm the insights of redaction criticism. This approach to interpretation is often, though not always, accompanied by a confessional posture that grants authoritative status to authorial intent: acceptance of the Bible as scripture means that we are called to believe whatever message the author intended to convey.
- *Text-oriented hermeneutic.* Some interpreters are interested in using narrative criticism for its own sake, as an end in itself. Determining how readers are expected to respond to biblical stories is viewed as a complete exegetical process. This perspective usually seems to be informed by a confessional posture that recognizes the expected response to scripture as the divinely ordained one. Thus, authoritative status is granted to the exegetically discerned anticipated response of implied readers rather than to the exegetically defined intention of a historical author.

> • *Reader-oriented hermeneutic.* Many interpreters use narrative criticism as a "base method" to guide them in discerning and understanding disparate and polyvalent responses. By gaining a general idea of how readers are expected to respond to a story, interpreters are able to identify more readily the points at which individuals or communities adopt variant reading strategies and so are able to probe the processes that determine these. Authoritative status may or may not be granted to what is deemed to be the expected reading. In either case, this reading strategy enables dialogical interpretation of the interpreters as well as of the text. In this instance, at least, Via's wish is fulfilled.

targeted audience for such films is expected to find them sexually arousing. I don't see why this should be controversial. Outside the ivory tower of academia, most people seem to think that books, movies, and other texts do in fact solicit expected responses. Granted, some of these people have not had any courses in epistemology, and if they did take such courses perhaps they would repent of their conceptions. But it seems to me that we have two options: enroll the world or learn to speak in terms that relate to how people actually think.

Still, I can appreciate the desire for clarification. If I am going to say that a particular interpretation is expected, I must realize that some people are going to ask, "Expected by whom?" By *the author?* Narrative criticism has not traditionally said that. Narrative criticism has traditionally said, "by the text itself."

There are no three words in the English language more annoying to many literary critics than those—*the text itself.*[96] The point is made, again, that texts do not have perspectives or ideologies—only authors or readers have perspectives and ideologies. Texts themselves cannot mean anything, for the conception or reception of meaning is a function of animate, intelligent beings (authors, readers). And I say, again, that this seems to be true, but it also misses the point. It's a bit like saying "guns don't kill people; people kill people."[97] There is a sense in which it is obviously, even pedantically, true and a sense in which it is nonsense. Personification of texts is common in everyday speech. At times, the strong presence of an author does intrude: we may hear someone say, "Shakespeare is so enigmatic" or "Stephen King scares the hell out of me." But more often, I think, people just talk about how a book or movie or play or television show affects them. Typically, the author recedes behind the story so that we do not even sense his or her presence.

In the example of the note found in the sanctuary, I labeled the text "a racist joke." But if texts cannot have ideologies, then technically the joke itself cannot be racist. So what do I mean when I use that kind of language? Do I mean that the *author* is a racist? I don't think it's that simple. When I found that note, I probably did assume that the author was a racist, but that wasn't all. I took the joke *itself* to be racist and offensive even apart from its author's motives.

When I found the note in the sanctuary I assumed that it had been written by some racist person who sought to amuse another racist person to whom he or she passed it. But, for a moment, let's imagine several other scenarios that could account for the origin of the note:

- Two women are sitting in the pew. One of them says, "You need to pray for my husband. I heard him tell the most disgusting joke to his friends the other day. I can't even say it out loud. . . ." Then she writes the words on the note and passes it to her companion.
- A disgruntled church member thinks to himself, "This pastor of ours thinks he's so smart, and he always acts like we're just a bunch of rednecks. Maybe if we really were as bad as he thinks, he'd get mad and leave. I know what'll piss him off. . . ." Then he writes the words on the note and tucks them inside a hymnal.
- A church council member thinks to herself, "I've tried to convince people that the issue we most need to address within our congregation is racism, but no one seems to realize how serious it is. This church needs a wake-up call. . . ." Then she writes the words on the note and leaves them lying on the pew.

Would it make any difference? Would the text not be a racist joke if it originated in one of these ways?

I don't actually think any of the above scenarios are very likely, but they would be possible. The point is that we can never know for certain what the intention of a text's author may have been—and such ignorance is exacerbated when the author is unknown or unavailable for comment. What we do, then, is extrapolate from what we have—the text itself. We personify texts, attributing to them the ideologies, perspectives, and motivations that they appear to espouse. Most people—given the necessary data to understand the note I found—would say, "This is a racist joke—regardless of who wrote it or why."[98]

Still, at the academic conventions I attend, there is one scholar who sees a part of his mission in life as being to remind me that texts themselves do not actually espouse (or mean) anything. I am (usually) grateful to him for these reminders because even while using the common parlance, I like to hold in the back of my mind the realization that our manner of speaking is not precisely descriptive of reality. Nevertheless, I have to wonder, When he and his wife come home from the theater and she says, "That was a funny movie," does he correct her? Does he say, "The movie *itself* was not funny, dear. What you really mean is that you believe the scriptwriter, the producer, the director, and the actors all collaborated to produce a film that they intended to be humorous and that for you this intention was fulfilled"? Does he say that?

In practice, many literary critics use the technical term *implied author,*[99] which means about the same thing as "the text itself" but makes the personification explicit. Either way, one essential point for biblical studies is that expectations are to be determined with reference to the perspective that now appears to inform the text of a document (say, Matthew's Gospel) when it is viewed as a narrative whole. Thus, narrative criticism is not interested in sorting out source strata to determine which material is most reflective of the final redactor's concerns. Even though ideas now expressed in Matthew's Gospel may derive from a variety of sources, the narrative may be read in its finished form as presenting a single (albeit complex) perspective—the perspective of the text or of the implied author.

I do think it is important to remember that the concept of implied readers is a construct and, therefore, is itself infected by the subjective input of those who do the constructing. Basically, what happens is this: every person who reads a story constructs his or her own concept of implied readers who would hypothetically respond to that story in what he or she assumes to be anticipated ways. When a hundred people read the same story, they probably come up with a hundred slightly different conceptions of the implied readers for that story. This does complicate the interpretive process, but I do not think it invalidates that process. It just means that the approach is not perfect and the results are not absolute. Every construction of a text's implied readers is always open to critique from other readers who construe the textual dynamics or rhetoric differently. Narrative criticism is no different from historical criticism or any other approach to interpretation in this regard.

The fact is that the New Testament Gospels have been read by Roman Catholics, Protestants, fundamentalists, atheists, and Jews, all of whom differ in their interpretations of these narratives. Indeed, a major impetus for applying historical criticism to such documents has been to transcend subjective disagreements by enabling consensus to be reached on at least one point: the historical intentions of the book's author(s). This has worked, at least some of the time. There are instances where Protestant scholars might agree with Roman Catholics that a particular interpretation is indeed what the Gospel author intended, while offering diverse evaluations of that intent.[100] At other times, however, supposedly objective historical-critical descriptions of authorial intent have tended to split along confessional lines in suspiciously revealing ways.[101] Such impasses do not invalidate the historical-critical method as such but merely illustrate the inevitable influence of human prejudice. Perhaps the twentieth century's most important proponent of using historical criticism to study the New Testament once gave an address titled "Is Exegesis Without Presuppositions Possible?" His answer was "No."[102]

So, narrative criticism posits a different but analogous reading strategy according to which some degree of consensus might be reached regarding responses that appear to be expected of a text's implied readers. The strategy is different from (not better than) historical criticism in that it emphasizes reader-oriented dynamics, such as the conception of meaning as effect. Accordingly, it is more open to polyvalence—to defining general parameters for expected readings rather than defining meaning with regard to one specific context. Of course, the approach is itself subjective, and of course an approach for discerning expected responses that used different principles and procedures would achieve different results. Almost everyone (I hope) who uses narrative criticism knows these things.

Because narrative criticism is a postmodern reading strategy, the following traits ascribed by A. K. M. Adam to postmodern thinkers may usually be ascribed to narrative critics:

- they do "not look for an absolute foundation but for a starting point suitable to their purposes";
- they do "not try to explain everything about a work" but try to "sketch a series of interesting relations among certain aspects of one or more topics";
- they do "not claim privileged access to the truth, but simply claim to have provided a provocative reading of the topics they engage"; and
- they acknowledge "that various forces that are ostensibly external to intellectual discourse nonetheless impinge on the entire process of perceiving, thinking, reaching, and communicating one's conclusions."[103]

Norms for Reading

I define expected readings as ones that concur with meaning that is conveyed by the implied author to the implied readers. Thus, the identification of expected and unexpected readings rests on discernment of the effects that the narrative would have on the readers who appear to be presupposed for the text, readers who receive the text in a manner that we deem normative on the basis of what we perceive to be its implicit assumptions. The question of whether we can or should speak of a "normative way of reading" is also controversial, but most literary critics recognize that some minimal assumptions must be made to facilitate rational discourse. I have already indicated two aspects of what would typically constitute a normative way of reading: readers are generally expected to read a work in its entirety and to read it sequentially from beginning to end. The assumption is certainly not that all readers actually do read in this way nor is any conclusion implied that those who read differently are wrong to do so. The point is simply to provide some guidance for readers who wish to compare and contrast their experiences with a given text.

As for more details of what constitutes "normative reading" most critics would include "linguistic competence," or knowledge of the language in which the text is written.[104] Less obvious but also necessary are minimal assumptions about what is called "literary competence," general awareness of how this type of literature is usually perceived. Implied readers are expected to be able to follow rhetorical moves made within a narrative and to interpret a story in ways consistent with its genre. Implied readers are also expected to know certain things, to believe certain things, and to espouse certain values. Assumptions regarding beliefs and values are especially significant, as they may be so subtle as to go undetected. For example, the notion that "whatever scripture says is true" is never taught in Matthew's Gospel but seems to be presupposed for Matthew's readers. Readers who do not believe this may respond to the story in unexpected ways.[105]

Definition of expected and unexpected readings with reference to *implied readers* rather than original *intended readers* suggests a literary orientation that transcends strictly historical concerns. The perspective of a narrative's implied readers is certainly informed by historical considerations—implied readers cannot be assumed, for instance, to have knowledge that would have been unavailable to the narrative's actual original readers. Still, when parameters for determining expected readings are set by what appears to be presupposed for the narrative they will typically be broader than if they were set with reference to the historical situation of the original readers. Jonathan Swift's satirical tale of the Lilliputian wars in *Gulliver's Travels* was originally intended to address the situation of Protestant/Catholic conflict in the author's homeland (Ireland). The specifics of that conflict are not, however, explicitly present in the narrative, and the story can certainly be understood as having a more general application regarding the foolishness of war and bigotry. We might say, then, that the original, intended readers of Swift's tale were expected to draw lessons from the story regarding a specific crisis while the implied readers of this story are expected to draw lessons appropriate to analogous crises in their own situations. Thus, we can see reason for Jack Dean Kingsbury's claim that readings expected of implied readers (as determined through narrative criticism) may serve as an *index* of the reading that would have been expected of the original, intended readers[106] and, accordingly, as an index of authorial intent.[107]

Nevertheless, I think it is important to maintain a distinction between implied readers and original or intended readers. For this reason, I do not use the term *authorial audience,* which some narrative critics have adopted as preferable to *implied readers.*[108] The former term was first suggested in the secular academy by Peter Rabinowitz to describe what he calls "the audience that the author appears to have had in mind."[109] Even this is a more generic concept than a literal "original audience" but it represents a subtle departure from the idea of readers "presupposed by the story." In practice, the distinction between a critically defined authorial audience and critically defined implied readers is not always apparent, but the hermeneutical implications of the definition are substantial and, indeed, reflective of the different interests narrative criticism can be made to serve. Scholars who now speak of an authorial audience often use narrative criticism to help understand better the rhetorical impact that the historical author intended for the text to have; thus they use the approach as a sort-of expanded redaction criticism in service to a basically author-oriented hermeneutic. Scholars who continue to speak of implied readers tend to use the approach as an aid for understanding the different expected and unexpected effects that a text may have on its diverse readers. As such, they use the approach in service to a basically reader-oriented hermeneutic. Of course, one need not choose between these options, for they are not mutually exclusive.[110]

To return to our example of Jonathan Swift's tale, an unexpected reading would be one that fails to regard it as a satire altogether and understands it instead as a literal historical report. Such a reading would not only have been unexpected for the original readers but also for the narrative's implied readers who are assumed to know enough about the real world (tribes of people a few inches tall do not actually exist) and about how stories work to recognize the piece as satirical.[111] It is not necessary to maintain that the audience the author had in mind would have known these things—though that would certainly be true. It is possible, based on what is found in the text of the narrative itself, to maintain that such information is presupposed for the story.

As an aside, we might note that Jonathan Swift's tale was not intended to be received as an entertaining children's story either. The fact that thousands of children have found it entertaining does not change the fact that this most popular of all interpretations of the story should probably be classed an unexpected reading. But who would want to say the children are *wrong* to enjoy the story as they do?

PART TWO: READING MATTHEW (A CASE STUDY)

The Gospel of Matthew is a story *of Jesus, a narrative, not an essay or a chronicle.*

—Richard A. Edwards[112]

We learn ways of reading (or hearing) stories at an early age. We recognize when a story is not affecting us in what we take to be the expected fashion. We perceive that the story is supposed to be humorous, even though we do not think it is funny. We realize that the story is supposed to be scary, even though we are not scared. What do we do when this happens? Sometimes, when we care about the story, we regret the distance between what we take to be its intended and actual effects and attempt to bridge this gap to make our reading experience more satisfactory.

If the fault lies with the narrative itself, little can be done. Perhaps the story is just not a very good one, at least in our estimation. Or, perhaps, the story itself is all right but is not told well. We think the story could be funny, or scary, or whatever, if only it were told by a more gifted author.

At other times, we may feel like the fault lies with us. The story may be a good one, well told, but we realize it is "over our heads." There are too many big words that we don't understand, too many obscure concepts or allusions that escape our grasp. We recognize that we are not appreciating the story as we would if we knew everything that we are expected to know. What do we do? If the story is important to us, we try to increase our knowledge in order to appreciate it more fully. We look up words in the dictionary, do some research on the period of history in which the story takes place, or do whatever else is necessary to gain the knowledge we are expected to have.

Then, again, stories sometimes fail to affect us as they might because we know *too much*. If we have seen a motion picture version of the same story or talked with a friend who has read the same book, we may find our reading experience compromised. Associations imported from the film or advance knowledge regarding how the story will turn out prevent us from appreciating it as intended. What do we do? If the story is important to us, we may pretend that we do not know what we are not expected to know. We may strive to approach the story on its own terms, pretending to forget whatever extraneous information we have acquired.

At first, this strategy of "pretending" sounds silly—but we do it all the time. My wife cries at movies a lot. We have the videotape for the film *E. T.: The Extra-Terrestrial,* and because we have raised four children we have seen it several times. Every time we get to the end, to that part where we are supposed to think that E. T. is dead, my wife cries. Sometimes, I want to say (but, of course, I know better), "We've seen this before. He's not really dead." But she hasn't actually forgotten this from the last time we watched the film. She is pretending to have forgotten it so that the movie can affect her the way it intends to affect her.

Narrative critics attempt to read the Gospel of Matthew as a story, as a work of literature that engages the imagination as well as the mind.[113] In doing this, they recognize the gap between the effects that this Gospel is expected to have on its readers and the effects that it actually does have on many real readers today. Narrative criticism attempts to bridge this gap by enabling readers to experience the story in the manner expected of its implied readers, that is, the readers presupposed for the narrative. Of course, as real readers, we remain free to approve or disapprove of whatever effects we decide the narrative is expected to have on us.

To define the implied readers of Matthew's Gospel more precisely, I suggest the following propositions:

- Matthew's implied readers are assumed to read the Gospel in a normative way—that is, (at least) to read the entire Gospel straight through, from beginning to end.
- Matthew's implied readers are assumed to know everything that the Gospel expects them to know, and they are assumed *not* to know anything that the Gospel does not expect them to know.
- Matthew's implied readers are assumed to believe everything that the Gospel expects them to believe, and they are assumed *not* to believe anything that the Gospel does not expect them to believe.

The next three chapters are devoted to exploratory and exemplary exposition of these three propositions.

Chapter Four

How Are Readers
Expected to Read?

This is a short chapter because it deals with a matter that is quite obvious and one that is simple enough to require little explanation. Obvious and simple, however, should not be equated with insignificant. What is most obvious is sometimes what is most easy to overlook.

In chapter 3, I chose as the most obvious example of an unexpected reading that I could think of the rather ludicrous instance of a person arguing over the interpretation of a book that he or she has not actually read in its entirety (see page 58). Over the years, I have found that this example evokes chuckles from seminary students and pastors, who tend to be quick to agree that a person cannot possibly identify the expected effect of a work of literature without actually reading the entire work. At that point in my presentation, I ask for a show of hands as to how many of these students or pastors have read the entire Gospel of Matthew—straight through, from beginning to end. Some hands go up, but certainly not all. And these seminarians and pastors are often in positions where they regularly (and even authoritatively) tell people what they believe the Gospel of Matthew means.

Let us imagine for a moment that we are *not* talking about the Gospel of

Matthew or any other book of the Bible. Let us just pick at random any classic work of literature—say, Dostoevsky's *Crime and Punishment*. Let us imagine that I am a college professor and that you sign up to take a course with me on that book. You notice that, curiously, the book itself is not a text for this course. Then you get my syllabus, which explains what we will do. We will meet once a week throughout the semester. Each time, I will open *Crime and Punishment* to some selected page and read a paragraph. I will then lecture on what point I think Dostoevsky was trying to make with those particular sentences. Would you not feel cheated? Okay, it might be an easy course and you might get some easy credit, but that's not the point. Let us assume that you are actually a motivated student who wants to learn something about the subject. Would you think that there is any possible way that you would come to understand the meaning of *Crime and Punishment* without actually reading the book itself—the entire book, all the way through, from beginning to end? Yet the experience I have described is precisely what most people have with the Gospel of Matthew. They hear selected passages—pericopes—read out loud on Sunday morning, one a week, in no discernible order, and yet somehow they come to believe that understanding the various points made in these various passages adds up to an understanding of the book as a whole.

No. If we want to understand the effect that Matthew's Gospel is expected to have, we must read the entire book, straight through, from beginning to end. This is not controversial—at least it should not be. The implications of this radical realization, however . . . well, they just might be terribly controversial. It just might mean—depending on circumstances, of course—that every interpretation of Matthew's Gospel that you have ever heard (or offered) is in fact an unexpected reading. This is because, first, the treatment that this book normally receives within the community that calls it scripture (namely, dissection into lectionary texts) does not favor such reading. It is also because, until fairly recently, the dominant scholarly approach to interpretation (historical criticism) has not even attempted to inquire into the matter of how readers are expected to respond to this book.[114] I must say that I find this incredible. I am open-minded enough to recognize the value of unexpected readings. I entertain a broad enough hermeneutic to recognize that the church might not want to limit its understanding of biblical texts to meanings that we are expected to derive there. Still, to confess that a book is divinely inspired, authoritative scripture and then *not even bother to find out* how readers are expected to respond to it . . . well, I find that to be simply amazing. Yet that is our legacy.

Matthew's implied readers are expected to read the entire story from beginning to end. Real readers who do not do this may interpret the story in unexpected ways. They may miss connections that they are expected to make or fail to discern themes that are developed throughout the narrative as a whole. Beyond this rather obvious observation, there is only one matter that requires further discussion.

The question that has arisen among literary critics is whether implied readers must always be thought of as people who are reading the narrative for the first time.[115] In other words, when we focus on any particular passage in Matthew's Gospel, should we assume that implied readers are expected to understand the passage in light of the entire Gospel? Or, should we assume that they are expected to know only that portion of the Gospel that precedes this passage? Different answers to these questions may yield different interpretations of what constitutes an expected reading.

We may illustrate these different interpretations with reference to Matthew 9:15. When Jesus is challenged to explain why his disciples do not fast, he responds, "Can the wedding guests fast as long as the bridegroom is with them? The days will come when the bridegroom is taken away from them, and then they will fast." Most interpreters recognize this saying as a prediction of Jesus' death, which will be narrated later in the Gospel. The question is, Are Matthew's implied readers expected to recognize this? If implied readers are assumed to be reading this narrative sequentially, for the first time, won't the passage simply be mysterious to them? Nothing in the narrative up to this point has told readers that Jesus is going to die. Some narrative critics, however, do not care to elucidate such moment-by-moment interpretations that readers might make while moving through the story. Rather, they simply emphasize that readers are expected to make connections between different parts of the book and so would affirm that the reader of Matthew's Gospel *is* expected to recognize Matthew 9:15 as a prediction of Jesus' death.

This question of how much to emphasize first-time reading remains unresolved among biblical-literary critics. For now, we may just need to specify which strategy we employ. For instance, I might say, "Assuming a first-time reader, this would be an unexpected reading." That allows narrative critics who do *not* assume a first-time reader to distance themselves appropriately from my conclusion. The whole purpose of this enterprise, let us recall, is to understand better the factors that produce variant readings. We define as unexpected readings those interpretations produced through a reading strategy that differs from what *we* regard as normative. Naturally, people who conceive *their* reading strategy to be normative might define *our* interpretations as "unexpected."

We can live with the counterdefinitions, of course, but this approach works best when we agree on a common basis for determining our "control group," that is, for determining the baseline reading against which all of our variant interpretations may be compared. For what it's worth, I favor defining the expected reading of any narrative as the reading of a first-time reader.[116] It makes sense to me to assume that stories unfold and develop in ways that do not anticipate prior acquaintance with the text. Of course, many stories use foreshadowing and prediction and other devices to entice their readers with clues of what is to come, but the whole point of such devices would be lost if the readers are assumed to have read the story before.[117]

I hear two closely related counterarguments for why Matthew's implied readers should not be construed as first-time readers and neither of them make sense to me (of course—in deference to my opponents—since the arguments do not make sense to me, it is possible that I am not now about to state them very well).

First, it is said that virtually no one actually does read Matthew's Gospel in this way and that, probably, few people ever did. This seems to be beside the point. The expected reading of a narrative is not the majority reading, and it makes little difference from a theoretical perspective whether people really do read a narrative the way that we assume implied readers are expected to read it. If unexpected readings outnumber expected ones, so be it—that may be one of the interesting facets of interpretation that narrative-critical study is bound to discover.

Second, it is said that most people today *cannot* read the narrative in the manner expected of a first-time reader even if they want to because almost everybody who has any interest in Matthew's Gospel already knows how that story develops and how it turns out. Specifically, with regard to Matthew 9:15, it is hard to imagine any reader of Matthew in the ancient or modern world who would not know that Jesus is going to be crucified. I agree with the latter part of this statement, but not with the objection inferred from it. Furthermore, I actually do think that Matthew's implied readers are expected to know even at this point (9:15) that Jesus is going to be crucified—but not because they are assumed to have read the story before. We'll get to that. But, first, the basic objection here fails because a) it is beside the point, in the same way as the previous objection—implied readers are a theoretical concept, not an existential reality[118]; and b) it denies the role of imagination in the reading process.

Some opponents of the first-time reader hermeneutic styled it at one academic conference as "the Martian hermeneutic." People like me, they claim, assume that implied readers would have to be from Mars—just arrived on Planet Earth, picking up a book of which they are totally ignorant and proceeding to read it.[119] No, they would just have to be normal earthlings equipped with normal human *imagination.* The objection is beside the point, in any case, but the fact is, most people *are* able to experience familiar stories *as though* they are receiving them for the first time. Otherwise, why does my wife cry every time E. T. appears to meet his demise?[120] For what it's worth, my own personal experience of Matthew's Gospel confirms the possibility of adopting this sort of imaginary first-time approach. Every three years, I read the Gospel of Matthew in its entirety once a month (the other two years I read Luke or both Mark and John). I find a setting that is very private and read the book slowly, out loud from beginning to end at a single sitting. A month later, I do this again, and so on for a year. Given the number of three-year cycles since I began this practice, I'd have to estimate that I've read Matthew in this fashion at least eighty times by now. But, always, I read the book as though I am reading it for the first time. The narrative seems to invite this, as certain themes develop and unfold as the story progresses. I have no trouble doing this, and—trust me—I am not a person who has been exceptionally gifted in the imagination department (Bible professors seldom are). I am probably not as interesting or as creative a person as, for instance, *you* are. Still, even a tedious little person like me has no trouble reading Matthew's story, experiencing it emotionally and aesthetically, over and over again, as though reading it for the first time.

Let's return to the example of Jesus' saying in Matthew 9:15, about the "bridegroom being taken away." Of course, I know that Jesus is going to be crucified, and so I "get" that this statement might be a veiled reference to his impending death. But in Matthew's narrative, Jesus speaks these words to his disciples, and I realize that, at this point in the story, *they* do not know Jesus is going to be crucified. I am able quite easily to empathize with them and to recognize that for them the statement is mysterious and ambiguous, even if I know things that they don't. Implied readers are expected to be able to understand the perspectives of the various characters in the narrative—and this forces an assumption of first-time reading. If we are to receive the story in the manner expected of its implied readers, we must be able to pretend that we do not know how the story is going to turn out—if for no other reason than to hear the words of Jesus the way the characters in the story would hear them.

Now, as an aside to this discussion, let me assert that I do not presume a Martian hermeneutic, for reasons that will become clear in the next chapter. Even first-time readers can be expected to interpret stories on the basis of knowledge that celestial visitors would presumably lack. Implied readers of Matthew are presumed to know that Jesus will be crucified not because they have read the end of the story, but because widespread knowledge of this fact was assumed in the world that produced this narrative. Readers of the book *Gone With the Wind* are not expected to be surprised when General Sherman burns Atlanta, although some of the characters in the story are certainly shocked and dismayed by what is, for them, an unexpected development. Readers of that novel are able to identify with the surprise that these characters experience at this development even though they (as readers) saw it coming and indeed were expected to see it coming. In an analogous fashion, I am able to identify with the wonder of the disciples at Jesus' mysterious saying even though *I* understand it, and indeed am expected to understand it, in ways that they cannot.

For readers of *Gone With the Wind* to know from the outset that Atlanta will be burned is a quite different matter than for readers of *A Taste of Death* (a P. D. James novel) to know from the outset the identity of the murderer. Even a first-time reader may be expected to possess knowledge of the first sort, for it is not internal to the world of the narrative. But when my friend Bouman reads the ending of the James novel first, he doesn't just read the book with information unknown to the characters. He reads it with information that readers are not expected to possess—and of course he realizes this (I suspect it is partly the awareness that he is "cheating" that drives him to adopt the rebellious practice).

In short, implied readers are generally expected to be able to recognize different levels of narration, to distinguish between what they (as readers) are expected to know or believe and what characters in the story are expected to know or believe. The ability to make such distinctions is often assumed for reception of irony: readers may be expected to understand a comment or action in ways that they simultaneously realize is lost on the characters. The charge that real readers are not able to fulfill such expectations is, I think, exaggerated, but even if absolutely true would not invalidate the theoretical principle. That principle is derived from the existential fact that most readers imagine that they are *supposed* to be able to read stories in this way regardless of whether or not they are actually able to do so.

Chapter Five

What Are Readers Expected to Know?

According to the model that I have suggested, interpretations of Matthew may be called unexpected readings if they a) fail to take into account knowledge that is assumed to be possessed by the implied readers, or b) depend on knowledge that is not assumed to be possessed by the implied readers.

But what can the implied readers be assumed to know? And how do we determine this? The latter question intrigues me because it seems rarely to be addressed. As I flip through commentaries on Matthew, peruse scholarly papers, review Sunday school curricula, and listen to sermons, I continually encounter the phrase "Matthew's readers know. . . ." I don't often disagree with what is said next, but I am impressed by the baldness of such an assertion. How do we know what Matthew's readers know?

Often, the persons using this phrase seem to mean it in a historical sense. By "Matthew's readers" they mean not implied readers but intended readers, that is, original, first-century readers. There is some overlap between these two concepts, but they are not identical. In chapter 3, I suggested that the implied readers of Jonathan Swift's *Gulliver's Travels* are not expected to know that the story is (at times) a fairly specific satire of Protestant and Catholic conflicts in Ireland.

I am willing to grant that Swift himself probably did expect his intended, eighteenth-century readers to know this, but there is nothing in the narrative that necessarily presupposes such knowledge for implied readers.

This distinction both simplifies and complicates our task. Many historical scholars think that Matthew's Gospel was written around 85 C.E. for a predominantly Jewish-Christian community somewhere in the vicinity of Antioch.[121] It may be worth asking what Matthew's Gospel would have meant to such people, but *our* goal is more generic. We want to ask how Matthew's Gospel is expected to affect implied readers, who are not so circumscribed by space and time. We are asking, "What does this story *mean?*" not "What did it *used to mean?*" Our task is simplified in that, to do this, we do not need to recover every bit of knowledge that would have been possessed by Antiochian Jewish-Christians in 85 C.E. Our task is complicated, however, by the need to identify *what* knowledge is expected of the implied readers. Of all the things that might have been known to those original, first-century readers, which items are essential for interpretation of this story anytime, anywhere?

As indicated previously (see pages 72–73), I agree with the majority of scholars that we must assume basic linguistic and literary competence as expectations of Matthew's implied readers. By *linguistic competence,* I mean that Matthew's implied readers are expected to know the language in which the story is told. A problem immediately arises, since Matthew's Gospel was written in koine Greek, a "dead language" that few people know today. There seem to be two ways of dealing with this problem.

We might recognize that, although Matthew was originally written in Greek, it has been translated into English. So, we could simply assert that we are going to interpret a modern English version of Matthew rather than the original Greek version. But then we must ask, Which version? King James? New International? The Living Bible? Whichever version we pick, our interpretation of the story will be somewhat different than if we had picked another one. For example, when we discuss Matthew 5:6, I might say, "The assumption of linguistic competence implies that Matthew's implied readers are expected to know what the word *righteousness* means." If, however, we were interpreting The New Living Translation of Matthew, I would have to alter that comment to insist that Matthew's readers are expected to know what the word *justice* means. These assertions are not the same—the English words *righteousness* and *justice* have rather different connotations.

My preferred course of action is to interpret the narrative of Matthew's Gospel in koine Greek, though, even then, the necessity of translation is not averted since I am currently writing in English. Accordingly, I want to contend that the assumption of linguistic competence implies that Matthew's readers are expected to know what the word δικαιοσυνη means. If real readers don't know what that word means, then they must recognize that they lack knowledge that would be expected of Matthew's implied readers. Indeed, we all need to recognize this, whether we've had courses in Greek or not. Simply to say that δικαιοσυνη means "righteousness" or "justice" is not enough—the word actually means something that these and other English terms only seek to approximate.

I hope that the preceding paragraph has caused a pall of disillusionment to fall on my more enthusiastic readers—it is necessary that we realize what is and is not possible. And this is a cold, hard fact: we cannot ultimately read Matthew's narrative in the manner expected of its implied readers. We cannot know everything that they would be expected to know, and no matter how good we are at pretending, we cannot really forget everything that they are not expected to know. If you do not know koine Greek, you will never be able to read Matthew or any other part of the New Testament the way that you are expected to read it. And even if you have learned some koine Greek at college or seminary, even if you have studied the language for years, you will at best know it only as a second language. We can never pick up the cadences of syntax and connotations of words that are expected to come naturally to Matthew's implied readers. That much is lost to us.

Why pursue the matter any further, then? The goal is *asymptotic*—a fancy word that comes into theological study from mathematics.[122] In math, the term describes a phenomenon that constantly approaches but never actually reaches its apparent goal. At least, that's what theologians (who usually haven't studied much math) say it means—and I have to trust them. For example, mathematicians might propose that we consider a set of numbers beginning with 128, progressively multiplied by one-half. That set would be (128, 64, 32, 16, 8, 4, 2, 1, 1/2, 1/4, 1/8 . . .), with the "dot dot dot" indicating infinity. Mathematicians claim that this set of numbers will grow ever smaller, constantly approaching zero, but that it will never actually reach zero. Now, not to stray too far from the subject, but when they told me things like this in high school, I used to think that if mathematicians are going to say things like this then at least one mathematician somewhere should have to spend his or her entire life listing these numbers just to check and see if it is really true. What if they *did* get to zero? Wouldn't *that* be a surprise?! But, anyway, mathematicians call such things asymptotic, and theologians—who are always on the lookout for words that ordinary people don't know—grabbed this one up right away. It's a pretty cool word, really. It refers to any unattainable goal that is deemed worthy of pursuit due to the intrinsic value of the approach itself. Narrative criticism enables us to come closer to identifying how stories are expected to be experienced by their implied readers than we would come otherwise. It brings us nearer to a goal that we know is ultimately unattainable. That has to be enough. If it's not, you've wasted your time and your money on this book and for that, I'm sorry.

I said that most scholars recognize that Matthew's implied readers must also be presumed to possess *literary competence*. This phrase derives from secular studies of modern literature, where it usually means, for starters, that they must be presumed to be able to read. Again, we have an immediate problem because most of Matthew's original recipients were probably illiterate. The common practice in the ancient world was for a crowd (in this case, a congregation) to gather and hear a text read aloud. Some Matthean scholars, therefore, reject the term "implied readers" in favor of some other designation such as "implied audience," or even "implied auditors" (which always strikes me as odd and even scary around tax time). I don't like to nitpick, but it seems to me that Matthew's Gospel is a *written* text and a written text by definition presupposes readers. Okay, I *do* like to nitpick. A tape recording or a motion picture or a concert performance may have an implied audience; a written text always has implied readers.

The issue, really, is analogous to that of translations. We might choose to interpret the New International Version narrative of Matthew's Gospel. I choose not to. I want to interpret the koine Greek version instead. Likewise, we might choose to interpret an oral performance of Matthew's Gospel given at some particular time and place. If I did choose to do that, I would try to interpret it from the perspective of the audience. But I choose to interpret the written text of Matthew's Gospel. Can I do this from the perspective of some hypothetical audience that *hears* the written words? Nonsense! If you want to do "audience-oriented criticism" then tape some performances and have at it! But if we are talking about a written text (and we are), then there is no "audience"; there are only readers.

So, regardless of whether or not the historical members of Matthew's original community could read, the implied readers of Matthew can. And *read* does not simply mean recognize words on a page. The assumption of literary competence also carries the notion that readers are expected to be able to follow the general rhetoric of the narrative and to recognize and accept principles basic to its perceived genre. Readers of *Gulliver's Travels* are expected to realize the story is fictional; only an unexpected reading would regard it as a factual account of an actual journey. The exact genre of Matthew's Gospel is debated, but certainly readers are expected to regard it as religious testimony, not as fiction but also not as a disinterested, objective historical account.

Another example of literary competence would be recognition of what critics call the device of a "reliable narrator."[123] Every narrative must be narrated; every story is told by someone or something, by a voice that may or may not be identified but that is referred to by literary critics as the voice of the narrator. In certain types of literature—in *most* types of literature, actually—this voice of the narrator is implicitly presented as reliable. Real readers are, of course, free to question what the narrator says—and many probably do—but implied readers are not expected to do so. In other words, when the narrator of Matthew's Gospel says that "Hezron was the father of Ram" (1:3), implied readers are not expected to wonder whether this is really so (perhaps Ram was actually the father of Hezron?!). If I question the validity of what the narrator says on such matters, I will end up producing a possibly interesting but certainly unexpected interpretation of the story. To determine the effect that the story is expected to have on its readers, we must ask how the story would affect readers who take whatever the narrator says to be reliable.

Other knowledge—not directly related to linguistic or literary competence—may also be assumed to belong to the repertoire[124] of Matthew's implied readers. I find it helpful to discuss this assumed knowledge in two broad categories, which relate to what literary critic Seymour Chatman describes as the two components of any narrative: story and discourse.[125] According to this model, *story* refers to the content component of a narrative (what the story is about) and *discourse* refers to the rhetorical component of the narrative (how the story is told). The distinction is somewhat artificial[126] but can prove useful. For our immediate purposes, the most important difference between story and discourse is temporal. The temporal setting for the story of Matthew's narrative is about 4 B.C.E. (when Jesus was born) to about 30 C.E. (when Jesus was crucified). But the temporal setting for the discourse of Matthew's narrative is about 85 C.E., when the narrative was actually written.

Knowledge Relevant to the Story Setting of Matthew's Narrative

With regard to the *story setting* of Matthew's narrative, I propose that implied readers are only expected to know *what is revealed within the narrative.* They are, however, expected to know almost everything that is revealed within the narrative. Thus, the implied readers of Matthew's Gospel not only know that Hezron was the father of Ram (1:3) but also that John the Baptist was beheaded at the command of Herod (14:9–10) and that the Sadducees say there is no resurrection (22:23). All of these points are stated or reported in the text that these imaginary implied readers are assumed to be reading. Real readers are typically less attentive to what is revealed within a narrative. Many people who have read Matthew's Gospel may find it difficult to recall whether Hezron was the father of Ram or vice versa—even if they *are* disposed to accept what the narrator says as reliable. The narrator states the information clearly in 1:3 but, unlike implied readers, real readers tend to forget.

One reason, then, that real readers arrive at unexpected interpretations is that they fail to notice or remember information provided within the story. Let's take a more significant example. In Matthew 25:31–46, Jesus identifies himself with needy people whom he describes as his "brothers." He says that deeds of mercy performed for these people are done for him. Real readers of Matthew's Gospel may interpret this to mean that, since all people throughout the world are Jesus' brothers (and sisters), any deed of mercy performed for the needy qualifies as ministry to Jesus himself. In fact, this has been a common interpretation of this passage, one that is often proclaimed in sermons and developed in devotional writings. Matthew's implied readers, however, would not be expected to interpret the passage in this way. Matthew's implied readers would be expected to recall that, earlier in the narrative, Jesus' "brothers" were defined as people who do the will of God (12:50). Accordingly, Matthew's implied readers understand Jesus' reference to "the least of these, my brothers" in 25:40 as applying not to all needy people everywhere but, specifically, to needy people who do the will of God.[127]

But now we must pause to consider another option: Is it possible, ever, for readers to interpret a narrative in unexpected ways because they are *more* attentive to what is revealed in the narrative than implied readers are expected to be? This can happen. In a recent film,[128] for example, the leading female character asks a doorman for the apartment number of a man she wishes to visit. The doorman replies, "2D." Later, we see the woman being admitted to the man's apartment, but the number on his door clearly reads, "2A." A host of questions might flood our minds: Was the doorman lying? Did the man change apartments? How did the woman find the right apartment when she had been given wrong information? Actually, all of these questions are irrelevant. The mix-up of numbers in the film is simply a mistake, a gaffe that the audience is not supposed to notice. When members of the audience do notice the numbers and try to read some significance into them, they are interpreting the film in a way that its implied audience would not.

In Matthew 12:40, Jesus tells the religious leaders of Israel that "as Jonah was three days and three nights in the belly of the whale, so will the Son of Man be three days and three nights in the heart of the earth." This saying is a prediction by Jesus of his own burial and resurrection, which is reported later in the narrative. If one reads very carefully, however, one may notice that Jesus does not actually spend "three days and three nights" in the heart of the earth, as he predicted. At most, he is in the tomb for portions of three days and *two* nights. Are the implied readers of Matthew expected to notice this discrepancy and wonder what it means? I don't think so. Implied readers are expected to hear this prediction as parallel to other statements Jesus makes, statements that indicate he will rise from the dead "on the third day" without bothering to enumerate the exact number of nights (16:21; 17:23; 20:19; cf. 27:63–64).

Such a decision seems reasonable to me and if you have been able to follow me in making it, then let us pause to reflect on the implications of what we have just done. Hermeneutically, we have just decided that implied readers of Matthew are not expected to regard the text as "inerrant."[129] If various Christian groups want to impose such an expectation on the text for confessional reasons, they are of course free to do so, but I would say that they are then reading the text in an unexpected way. Thus, I would tend to regard "fundamentalist interpretation" of the Bible as a variety of ideological criticism, analogous to feminist or Marxist criticism. In each case, an a priori decision is made to subordinate the text to a set of ideological principles (fundamentals), which are not themselves subject to critique by the text.[130]

In any case, we have noted that real readers may interpret texts in unexpected ways if they are either more or less observant than the implied readers are expected to be. This begs a practical question: How can we tell just what the implied readers are expected to notice? On what basis can I say that implied readers *are* expected to notice the connection between Matthew 12:50 and 25:40 (regarding the identification of Jesus' "brothers") but that they are *not* expected to notice the discrepancy between 12:40 and 27:57–28:10 (regarding the number of nights that Jesus was in the tomb)? Suppose you want to assert the vice versa? How can we test these suppositions to tell if they are accurate? Well, absolute certainty is simply not possible, and there may be times that we are just left to disagree, but I do suggest one criterion that we might agree to use to put such proposals to the test.[131]

- *Thematic coherence.*[132] Does the knowledge that readers are expected to notice yield a reading that seems reasonable within the context of the narrative as a whole? To presume that implied readers do notice the connection between 12:50 and 25:40 seems reasonable because for Jesus to identify himself with needy persons who do the will of the Father in heaven matches his identification elsewhere with a) missionaries who proclaim the advent of the kingdom of heaven (10:40; cf. 10:5–7); b) humble children who are the greatest in the kingdom of heaven (18:2–5); c) disciples who gather in his name to pray to the Father in heaven (18:19–20); and d) people who baptize in the name of the Father, Son, and Holy Spirit (28:19–20). In short, Jesus' claim to be present in and through "godly people" as opposed simply to "needy people" is a consistent theme in this Gospel. To presume, however, that implied readers are expected to notice a discrepancy between Jesus' prediction in 12:40 and what actually happens in 27:57–28:10 does not seem reasonable. Jesus is not elsewhere portrayed in this narrative as a person who fails to get his predictions right.[133]

As I have indicated, even professional readers[134] of Matthew's Gospel who accept this criterion will sometimes disagree in their conclusions regarding just what Matthew's implied readers are expected to know. The controversy over first-time reading discussed previously (pages 78–82) confirms this. Still, there is sufficient consensus to allow preliminary discussions about texts and their reception to proceed.

To summarize the main points of this section, readers who wish to determine the effect that Matthew's narrative is expected to have on its implied readers must a) be attentive to information within the narrative that implied readers are expected to notice and b) be willing to overlook certain things in the narrative that implied readers are not expected to notice. We should be extremely cautious in ascribing knowledge revealed within the narrative to the latter category, but we may find warrant for doing so when consideration of such knowledge leads to an interpretation inconsistent with what would hold for the narrative as a whole.

Knowledge Relevant to the
Discourse Setting of Matthew's Narrative

Almost all narrative critics recognize that the implied readers of a given narrative are expected to know certain things that are not explicitly revealed within the narrative.[135] But we are at once on shakier ground when we try to define such knowledge with any precision. This is, indeed, the hornet's nest of narrative criticism. On the one hand, narrative critics assert that implied readers are expected to know things that were generally known in the context (time and place) in which the narrative was written. On the other hand, narrative critics do not want simply to equate the implied readers of a narrative with its intended, historical audience.[136] Implied readers need not be assumed to know everything that people of the given time and place would have known—only those things that are presupposed by the narrative. But how do we tell which knowledge is presupposed by the narrative?

Consider an example that we will treat in great detail later on (chapter 7): In Matthew 2:1, the reader learns that magi came to Jerusalem. Since Matthew's Gospel does not tell us what magi are, we must be assumed to know what they are. But how much about magi are we assumed to know? It is possible today to find a good encyclopedia article on magi and to learn things about them that neither the author nor the original readers of the Gospel were likely to have known. Thus, it is one thing to say that knowledge of magi is presupposed by the narrative; it is quite another to decide just *what* knowledge is presupposed.

Another complicating factor lies in determining just how we should define the discourse setting of Matthew's narrative. When and where was this book written? Most scholars think the Gospel was composed around 85 C.E. for a Jewish-Christian community in a Roman city such as Antioch. But a few scholars disagree.[137] For what it's worth, I go with the majority view, but I also recognize that my decisions about what Matthew's implied readers are expected to know are more certain when they do not depend on too specific a definition of the discourse setting.

Having noted these problems, and with full acknowledgment of the challenge before us, we nevertheless proceed. I propose that the implied readers of Matthew's Gospel are assumed to possess *whatever knowledge concerning the spatial, temporal, and social setting of the story would have been regarded as common knowledge in the world that formed the discourse setting for the narrative.* Or, to put it differently, they are expected to possess knowledge that is assumed by all of the characters as well as by the narrator to be common knowledge.

Let's start with some easy examples. Matthew's implied readers are expected to know that five loaves and two fish would not normally be enough food for five thousand people (14:17); therefore, they are expected to regard what happens in 14:15–21 as extraordinary. Similarly, Matthew's implied readers are expected to know that a camel cannot really be swallowed by a human being; therefore, they are expected to recognize that Jesus' comment in 23:24 must be taken figuratively. This type of knowledge does not need to be spelled out within the narrative itself because it is regarded as common knowledge that can simply be taken for granted.[138]

Recognition that such knowledge must be attributed to implied readers is hardly controversial and seems to inspire argument only among the truly contentious. My point would be that such knowledge should be assumed for implied readers because it meets two criteria: a) it is relevant to (indeed, I would say *presupposed by*) the story; and b) it would have been regarded as common knowledge in the world that formed the discourse setting for the narrative. The juxtaposition of these two criteria has significant implications: assumed knowledge concerning the setting of the story must be defined in terms appropriate to the narrative's discourse setting.

That's not very clear, is it? Okay, to review, the setting of Matthew's *story* is about 4 B.C.E. to 30 C.E., mostly in Palestine; the setting of the *discourse* is (probably) about 85 C.E. in a Roman city outside of Palestine. Both settings—story and discourse—must be taken into account. On the one hand, Matthew's implied readers should not be assumed to know everything about early first-century Palestine that Jesus and his disciples would have known. To read the story in such a light is to read it as a historically referential account: if we do this, we will miss the literary effect that the story is expected to have on its implied readers. On the other hand, the assumed knowledge of Matthew's implied readers should not be simply equated with what would have been known by urban Roman Jewish-Christians around 85 C.E. To read the story in that light would be to read it from the redactional perspective of its intended, historical audience. This is closer to our mark but can also fail to discern the effect that the story is expected to have on its implied readers. Rather, we want to determine which aspects of that common knowledge appropriate to the discourse setting appear to be presupposed for the story. I know this is confusing. Examples will (probably) help.

Matthew's implied readers are expected to know some *geography.* They know what is meant by references to Judea (2:1), Galilee (2:23), Egypt (2:14), Israel (2:21), the Decapolis (4:25), Gennesaret (14:34), Magadan (15:39), and many other locales. These places are cited in the narrative with such brevity of detail that some familiarity must be assumed. But what are readers expected to know about these places? I see no reason to assume that they are expected to know everything that inhabitants of Palestine would have known in the early first century. Nor would I assume that they are expected to know everything that Christians in Antioch would have known in the latter part of that century. For instance, by 85 C.E. Christians in Antioch might have known that Pella (one of the cities of the Decapolis) became a refuge for members of the Jerusalem church who fled that city during the war with Rome. Accordingly, they might be prone to read the reference to crowds from the Decapolis following Jesus in a way that symbolized the later Christian presence there. But I find nothing in the narrative that presupposes such knowledge (indeed, the city of Pella itself is never named). So I have to conclude that, whatever Matthew's original readers might have thought, implied readers are not expected to think of the Decapolis as a haven for later Christian refugees.[139]

We must ask, What knowledge from the discourse setting of Matthew's narrative is presupposed by these geographical references in the story? I would answer, Not much—but at the very least, readers are probably expected to know which place names refer to nations and which to cities. Beyond this, readers are probably expected to have some inkling of the distances traversed as the characters move from place to place, and to know, for instance, that Egypt was not a part of Herod's jurisdiction (2:13–14). Occasionally, the narrative also seems to assume particular associations regarding locations. Matthew's readers are probably expected to associate "the district of Tyre and Sidon" (15:21) with Gentile territory and to know that "the holy city" (4:5; 27:53) refers to Jerusalem.

Matthew's implied readers are also expected to know some *history.* They know what happened to Sodom and Gomorrah (10:15; 11:24), and they understand what is meant by the expression "deportation to Babylon" (1:11, 12, 17). This information, of course, is contained within the Jewish scriptures, with which (as I will argue below) Matthew's readers are expected to be familiar. But Matthew's readers are also expected to know who Caesar is (22:17, 21) and to recognize what time period is meant by the phrase "in the days of Herod the king" (2:1). It is even possible that Matthew's readers are expected to know some early Christian history: characters such as Simon the leper (26:6) and Mary Magdalene (27:56) are introduced so casually that their names alone may be expected to strike a familiar chord.

Matthew's implied readers are expected to have some knowledge concerning the *social and cultural realities* of life in Palestine. They know what synagogues are (4:23), and they understand what it means for a person to be crucified (20:19), or for a man and woman to be betrothed (1:18). They are expected to know the difference between broad and narrow phylacteries (23:5) and to understand why someone would whitewash a tomb (23:27) or pour ointment over another person's head (26:9). Surely they can be counted on to know that ten thousand talents are worth more than one hundred denarii (18:23–35). Indeed, when our English Bibles report that Peter was accosted by collectors of "the temple tax" (17:24; NEB, NRSV, REB, TEV), they are being generous to modern-day readers. The koine Greek text of Matthew's story refers only to those who collect the *didrachma* (literally, "the two drachma"). The implied readers of Matthew's Gospel are apparently assumed to know that two drachma was the amount charged for the temple tax. In the same way, implied readers of Matthew's Gospel are expected to know something about many other areas of life: sowing (13:3–9), harvesting (13:3–9), winnowing (3:12), fishing (4:18–21; 13:47–50), shepherding (25:32), tenant farming (21:33–46), court proceedings (5:25–26, 40–41), and customs associated with weddings (25:1–13) and funerals (9:23).

Matthew's implied readers are also expected to understand *symbolic language* that is used throughout the narrative, even though the meaning of such language is often culturally determined. Matthew's readers know that being called "the salt of the earth" (5:13) is a compliment, while being called a "brood of vipers" (3:7) is not. This much, of course, might be determined from narrative context, but the fuller sense in which such metaphors and epithets[140] are to be understood derives from the social context of the narrative's discourse setting. The same is true for euphemisms: Matthew's readers are expected to know that the saints who have "fallen asleep" (27:52) are actually dead.[141]

Symbolic speech also includes *religious words and phrases.* Matthew's narrative often makes reference to abstract religious concepts without providing any precise definition of what is meant. A partial list of such concepts would include blasphemy (9:3), forgiveness (26:28), gospel (4:23), hypocrisy (6:2), judgment

(10:15), law (5:17), piety (6:1), repentance (3:1), righteousness (5:20), salvation (1:21), sin (1:21), wisdom (11:9), and witness (10:18). Matthew's readers are expected to understand these concepts in a manner appropriate to the social and cultural setting in which the narrative was produced. When Jesus says, "Do not give dogs what is holy" (7:6), implied readers are not just expected to know what dogs are and to recognize that the reference to dogs here is metaphorical rather than literal. Implied readers are also expected to know what is meant by the phrase "what is holy."

What is said of symbolic speech holds also for *symbolic actions*. When Jesus falls on his face in Gethsemane (26:39), implied readers are not expected to think he is clumsy but to realize that he has assumed an appropriate posture for prayer. When the high priest tears his robes (26:65), or when Jesus' disciples are instructed to salute a house (10:12) or to shake off the dust from their feet (10:14), Matthew's implied readers are expected to understand the symbolic meaning that attends such gestures. One can easily imagine how unexpected readings could result when real readers of Matthew lack such knowledge.

What happens, then, if information that is assumed to be common knowledge for Matthew's narrative is no longer available to us today? We may find that it is impossible for us to receive the text in the manner expected of its implied readers. If this is the case, our most honest response should be an admission of this deficiency in our method. Such an admission, I suggest, is more responsible than adoption of a hermeneutic that regards ignorant interpretations as encouraged by textual ambiguity.

I want to dwell on the latter point for another paragraph, but we have to switch Gospels momentarily to do so. In the Gospel of Mark, Jesus says that one should not put new wine into old wineskins (Mark 2:21–22). The best of interpreters will admit that the exact meaning of this metaphorical proverb is ambiguous. So reader-response critic Robert Fowler suggests that we are "encouraged to launch out on our own" in making sense of the saying.[142] I have no problem with Fowler launching out on his own and producing whatever interesting interpretations appeal to him, though I would label these as unexpected readings, admittedly divergent from what implied readers are expected to produce. But if I understand Fowler's point correctly, he is saying that the ambiguity of the metaphor is apparently deliberate, functioning within the narrative to deconstruct attempts at defining what is expected or unexpected. Ambiguous, unresolvable metaphors serve to advance a sort of hermeneutical anarchy that revels in its own interpretive chaos and prevents control freaks (like me) from deciding how passages are supposed to be read. Well, for what it's worth, I suspect that the only reason this metaphor is not defined is that Mark's readers are expected to be able to understand it without any explanation. In other words, the metaphor may appear ambiguous to Fowler and to me (real readers today), but it would not be ambiguous to Mark's implied readers. If we are unable to achieve the goal of reading Mark's narrative in the manner expected of its implied readers, so be it. Let us at least admit this, and not take the easy way out by claiming that readers are *supposed* to find the text ambiguous.[143]

But so far we have only identified one source of unexpected readings with regard to knowledge relevant to a narrative's discourse setting: the lack of such knowledge when it is presupposed. Unexpected readings may also result when a real reader possesses knowledge relevant to the discourse setting that is not presupposed, that is, knowledge that the implied readers are not expected to have. I can think of three ways that readers might be "overinformed" in this regard.

First, readers can possess false knowledge. They may think that they know things that are actually wrong. In Matthew 19:24, Jesus says, "[I]t is easier for a camel to go through the eye of a needle than for someone who is rich to enter the kingdom of God." Over the years, I have heard any number of persons interpret this saying by explaining that there was a narrow gate in the walls of Jerusalem called "the needle's eye," through which a camel could conceivably pass, albeit with difficulty.[144] Thus, they continue, Matthew's Gospel indicates only the difficulty of the rich finding salvation, not the impossibility of such an occurrence. Matthew's implied readers, however, would not be expected to know about this gate, because, in fact, it never existed. The comment in 19:24 is expected to be read as hyperbolic speech stressing the complete impossibility of rich persons entering the reign of heaven without divine intervention (19:26). The overinformed (falsely informed) reader arrives at an unexpected interpretation.

Second, readers may know things that, while accurate, would not have been known (or, at least widely known) in the world that provides the discourse setting for the narrative. Modern readers may know that salt cannot actually lose its flavor (5:13) or that mustard seeds are not really the smallest of all seeds (13:32). But the implied readers of Matthew's Gospel would never be expected to evaluate Jesus' words regarding salt and mustard seeds in light of such knowledge.

Third, readers can possess knowledge that would be appropriate for the discourse setting of the narrative but is simply not pertinent to the setting of the story. This is the vice versa of what was just stated (modern knowledge regarding salt and mustard seeds is pertinent to the setting of the story, but inappropriate for the discourse setting of the narrative). One example of this third sort of unexpected reading was given earlier: reading Matthew's reference to the Decapolis in light of the Christian exodus to Pella. Another would be the common historical interpretation of Matthew's Gospel as a response to Paul. Many scholars think that Matthew intends for the conservative statements Jesus makes in this Gospel regarding the eternal validity of the law (e.g., 5:17–20) to be read as a rebuttal of the more liberal view that Paul seems at times to present in his letters (e.g., Rom. 10:4; Gal. 3:23–25). We can certainly assume that Matthew's intended, historical audience knew of Paul's teachings—if the Gospel was written in Antioch, then it actually derives from the very community where Paul pressed his views on the law quite strongly (Gal. 2:11–14). Still, there are no references to Paul or his teachings in Matthew's story. Even if Matthew's first readers were expected (by the historical author) to read certain comments as allusions to Pauline doctrine, Matthew's implied readers are not expected (by the implied author) to do so. There is nothing in the text itself to indicate such an expectation.[145]

But now I want to make a potentially confusing distinction: implied readers may be expected to know things that would have been common knowledge in the world in which the story was written (the narrative's discourse setting) even though these things would not have been known in the world that forms the setting of the story itself.[146] This point does not contradict what was just said in the preceding paragraph: the assertion there was that knowledge basic to the discourse setting of a narrative is not *automatically* pertinent for understanding the story that the narrative relates. Still, a story may *presuppose* pertinent information from the time and place of its discourse setting. A good example of such a seeming anomaly is found in secular literary criticism of a recent novel by William Demby.[147] The book is set in the early 1960s and has John F. Kennedy as one of its characters. Readers of Demby's book say they experience a sense of impending doom as the story progresses because they know that Kennedy is going to be assassinated when the events of the novel reach November 22, 1963. One may ask whether this response of real readers is at variance with the anticipated response of Demby's implied readers. Critics such as Peter Rabinowitz and Wayne Booth have concluded that it is not.[148] Because the book was written at a time when the fact of Kennedy's assassination was well known, knowledge of this event may be regarded as presupposed by the discourse setting for the narrative. Similarly, I indicated previously (pages 81–82) that implied readers of *Gone With the Wind* are expected to know from the outset that Atlanta will be burned and that implied readers of Matthew's Gospel are expected to know from the outset that Jesus will be crucified. Such information was not only generally known in the world that produced these narratives but also is directly pertinent to the stories (unlike awareness of the flight to Pella or of the teaching of Paul).

Obviously, it is sometimes difficult to determine precisely which information implied readers should be assumed to possess. Let's take two examples of difficult cases and then apply what I think are reasonable criteria to them.

- *Which Caesar is on the coin?* In Matthew 22:17–21, Jesus is asked whether it is lawful to pay taxes to Caesar. He asks to see a coin used for paying such taxes and then asks, "Whose likeness and inscription is this?" He is told that it is Caesar's, and he responds, "Render therefore to Caesar the things that are Caesar's, and to God the things that are God's" (RSV). Interpretations of this passage vary, but Jesus' pronouncement is usually taken as endorsing only a token allegiance to Caesar: "Give the emperor his ultimately worthless coins, but reserve for God what truly counts." If this is correct, then Jesus is not so much endorsing separation of church and state as he is trivializing the ultimate significance of what appears to be the world's mightiest power. Such an interpretation assumes that Matthew's implied readers are expected to know who Caesar is—the emperor. They are expected to know something about the power and glory associated with that name and are also expected to realize that, with regard to

Palestine, such power has been imposed oppressively on a subjugated and resentful populace. But some scholars would go further. Commentaries often ask *which* Caesar had his image and inscription on the coin that Jesus saw. It was probably Tiberius. Some interpreters, then, attempt to define the implicit political critique more precisely, with specific reference to Tiberian policies. The question for us is whether such an interpretation would constitute an expected reading. Are Matthew's implied readers expected to know which Caesar had his image and inscription on the coin? I think not, though I am less sure here than I am with regard to presumed knowledge of a flight to Pella or of the teaching of Paul.

- *Will the temple be destroyed in 70 C.E.?* Jesus predicts in Matthew's story that the temple will be destroyed (24:2), but the narrative ends without this prediction having been fulfilled. As real readers, of course, we know that the temple was destroyed in 70 C.E. Knowledge of this event, furthermore, would have been widespread in the world that provided the discourse setting for Matthew's narrative. So are Matthew's implied readers expected to know that Jesus' prediction will be fulfilled when the temple is destroyed forty years after his death? The characters in Matthew's story do not know this will happen, but we may still ask whether Matthew's implied readers are expected to know something that the characters would not know. I believe they are—but not simply because the book's intended, historical audience would have known it. Implied readers should not automatically be assumed to know whatever intended readers would have known. The task is more complicated than that.

To determine the effect that the narrative is expected to have on its implied readers, we must struggle to define which information relevant to a narrative's discourse setting implied readers should be assumed to possess. Certain criteria may guide us in making these determinations.

1. *Availability.* Was the knowledge that appears to be presupposed generally available for the time and place in which the narrative was produced? Is the presumed knowledge *appropriate* for the discourse setting of the narrative and would it have constituted *common knowledge* for that setting? It makes sense to assume that readers are expected to know that ten thousand talents are worth more than one hundred denarii, because this probably was common knowledge in the world where Matthew's Gospel was produced. But I do not think it would make sense to assume that Matthew's readers would know that orchid seeds are smaller than mustard seeds; this would not have been common knowledge in that world (or even in ours!). Readers who have this latter knowledge need to feign ignorance on that point if they wish to determine the effect the narrative is expected to have on its implied readers.

On the image of Caesar, I can't say with any certainty that whose image was on the Roman denarius fifty years previous would have qualified as common knowledge in Matthew's world. But I can't say that this wouldn't have qualified as common knowledge either. There just isn't enough data to determine this with confidence. As for the temple destruction, as previously indicated, we can say with absolute confidence that the circumstances of the temple's destruction would have constituted common knowledge in the world in which Matthew's Gospel was produced, assuming that most scholars are right in dating the work later than 70 C.E.[149]

2. *Reference.* Does this knowledge relate to anything that is actually referenced in the text? If we are to say the knowledge is presupposed, then we should be able to point to something in the text that calls for readers to have this knowledge.[150] I am willing to grant that such references might be implicit, but I think that explicit references and strong allusions carry the most weight for determining that knowledge regarding this matter is assumed. Matthew's narrative explicitly refers to talents and denarii in a way that assumes readers know their relative worth (18:23–35), but it does not explicitly refer to the Christian flight to Pella or to the teachings of Paul.[151]

The text does explicitly mention that an image and inscription of a Caesar is on the coin, but it does not explicitly mention which Caesar this is. Thus, the suggestion that implied readers are expected to know which Caesar is on the coin receives only moderate support from this criterion. If the text did not emphasize that the coin contained a specific image and inscription, I would dismiss the suggestion that implied readers are expected to know Tiberius's image was on the coin outright. But I would be more inclined to accept the implied critique of Tiberian politics if, when Jesus asked, "Whose image is this?" his interlocutors had responded, "Tiberius" instead of simply "Caesar."

The text never explicitly refers to the temple being destroyed in 70 C.E., though it does make reference to the temple being destroyed at some indefinite time in the future (24:2). As in the previous example, then, the suggestion that the reader is supposed to know specifically that the temple would be destroyed in 70 C.E. receives only moderate support from textual references. There is, however, another passage that might tip the scales a bit. In Matthew 24:15, Jesus offers what is probably a further reference to the temple's violation[152] and, this time, the narrative exhibits a direct appeal to the reader. The narrator interrupts Jesus' speech to say, "Let the reader understand." Rather than being invited to hear Jesus' words in the way that they are heard by characters in the story (who know nothing of the destruction in 70 C.E.), Matthew's implied readers are explicitly invited to hear these words with some sort of special understanding that transcends what is available to those characters. Thus, the narrative does seem to presuppose that readers know about something that has happened to the temple in the time period between the setting of the story and the writing of the narrative. In my view, the narrator's comment in 24:15 increases the likelihood that implied readers are expected to understand that verse as well as 24:2 as direct allusions to the events of 70 C.E.

3. *Thematic Coherence.* Is the interpretation gained by assuming that readers possess certain knowledge consistent with interpretation of the narrative as a whole? As far as the image of Caesar is concerned, nowhere else in this narrative

is Jesus presented as a critic or supporter of any individual ruler or authority. When he does speak of oppressive rulers, he does so generically: "You know that the rulers of the Gentiles lord it over them, and their great ones are tyrants over them" (20:25). It is consistent with this perspective for Matthew's implied readers to be expected to take Jesus' comment in 22:21 as applicable to any Caesar, not just (or primarily) a specific one.[153]

As for the temple destruction, the supposition that implied readers have this knowledge yields an interpretation that regards Jesus as a reliable prophet whose predictions are fulfilled, an interpretation that coheres well with the presentation of Jesus elsewhere in the narrative.

The main points of this section can be summarized as follows: To determine the effect that Matthew's Gospel is expected to have on its implied readers, we must seek a) to possess or obtain knowledge concerning the spatial, temporal, and social setting of the story that readers are expected to have; and we must seek b) to amend or pretend not to possess knowledge concerning the story's setting that readers are not expected to have. To define which knowledge implied readers are expected to have, we must consider what would have constituted common knowledge in the world that formed the narrative's discourse setting and then determine whether this knowledge is actually presupposed for the story. The question becomes, "What pertinent knowledge concerning the story's setting was basic for the time and place that the narrative was written?" We may consider such criteria as reference, availability, and thematic coherence when making these deliberations.

Intertextual Knowledge

The implied readers of Matthew's Gospel are expected to have knowledge of other literature that is cited (by reference or allusion) within the narrative. Such knowledge is referred to as *intertextual*.[154]

Before we go any further, however, allow me to address the "high J" Meyers-Briggs types among my readers who might be troubled by the fact that I said earlier (page 86) that I would introduce *two* categories of knowledge that can be attributed to implied readers and now appear to be sneaking in a third one. Not to fear! I stick by my two categories: a) knowledge of the story setting revealed within the narrative, and b) knowledge presupposed for the story but derived from the discourse setting of the narrative. Intertextual knowledge is simply a subset of the latter category—it is one instance of what may have been regarded as common knowledge in the world that produced Matthew's Gospel, of knowledge that implied readers would be assumed to possess. It gets its own subheading because, in literary criticism, intertextuality has become a significant field in its own right. Both secular and biblical literary critics have been fascinated by the dynamics involved in interdependence of texts, by the apparent or even explicit presumption that readers of some texts are acquainted with others. Roland Barthes used to refer to the phenomenon playfully as *déjà lu*, an experience in which the reader senses that he or she has read this somewhere before.[155]

The most obvious instances of intertextuality in Matthew's Gospel are references or allusions to the Jewish scriptures, that is, to the several writings that Christians now refer to as the Old Testament. Occasionally, these citations are explicit, such as when the writings of David (22:43–44), Isaiah (3:3), or Jeremiah (2:17–18) are referred to by name. More often, however, the reader's ability to make this connection is simply assumed. When Jesus responds to Satan three times by declaring, "It is written . . ." (4:4, 7, 10), implied readers are not expected to wonder *where* these statements might be written (on a placemat at some Galilean restaurant perhaps?). They are expected to realize that what follows are quotations from scripture. Other phrases used to introduce scriptural quotations include "Have you not read . . . ?" (12:3, 5; 19:4; 22:31) and "Have you never read . . . ?" (21:16, 42). The use of the latter two phrases is ironic, playing off the assumption that the implied readers have indeed read the texts that characters within the story have neglected to consider. Furthermore, Matthew's implied readers are expected to be able to recognize scriptural citations even when no such phrase is used. When John the Baptist sends his disciples to ask Jesus whether he is "the one who is to come," Jesus replies, "Go and tell John what you hear and see: the blind receive their sight and the lame walk, lepers are cleansed and the deaf hear and the dead are raised up, and the poor have good news preached to them" (11:3–5). Jesus does not specify here that he is quoting scripture, nor for that matter that he is quoting anything at all, but Matthew's implied readers are expected to recognize that he is responding to John's question with words drawn from Isaiah (35:5–6; 61:1). Similarly, when Jesus tells the religious leaders to "go and learn what this means: I desire mercy and not sacrifice" (9:13), the implied readers are expected to recognize that he is quoting Hosea (6:6) and that the referent for the first-person pronoun "I" is therefore God. Jesus' point is that *God* prefers mercy to sacrifice and that God says this in scripture.

Matthew's implied readers are expected to know these scriptures well enough to recognize subtle allusions to them. When Jesus is offered vinegar to drink on the cross, implied readers are expected to notice the connection to Psalm 69:21. The description of John the Baptist as dressed in camel's hair with a leather belt around his waist (3:4) is expected to summon images of Elijah (2 Kings 1:8). When Judas is paid thirty pieces of silver to betray Jesus (26:15), implied readers are expected to think of Zechariah 11:12, and when Joseph of Arimathea places Jesus in his tomb (27:57–60), implied readers are expected to think of Isaiah 53:9.

Unexpected readings may result, then, if real readers of Matthew's Gospel do not know the scriptures as well as is assumed for the Gospel's implied readers. A real reader who is not familiar with Deuteronomy may have trouble making sense of Jesus' conversation with the Sadducees in Matthew 22:23–32. In the latter passage, the Sadducees, who do not believe in resurrection (v. 23), try to stump Jesus with a trick question. Drawing on Deuteronomy 25:5–6, they describe a scenario through which a woman follows the teaching of Moses to become the wife, successively, of seven different men. Then they ask Jesus,

"Whose wife will she be in the resurrection?" When Jesus says the Sadducees do not know the scriptures (v. 29), an uninformed reader might conclude that he thinks their understanding of Moses' teaching regarding successive marriage is incorrect. Implied readers are expected to know that this is not the case. Moses really did say that a childless widow should marry her late husband's brother, in the very fashion that the Sadducees have described. The Sadducees' error lies elsewhere, in their failure to understand that the scriptures teach a resurrection of the dead.

Or, again, when Jesus cries out from the cross, "My God, my God, why have you forsaken me?" (27:46), readers who do not know the scriptures might just think that he has lost hope or abandoned trust in God. Implied readers are expected to recognize that this is a scriptural quotation (Ps. 22:1). This does not remove the shock of Jesus' citing such a verse, but it does indicate in some sense that, even in his hour of desolation, he understands his destiny in terms of the scriptures he must fulfill (cf. Matt. 26:53–54).

In light of these observations, we must again ask whether it is possible for unexpected readings to result from real readers being overinformed, from knowing the scriptures too well, or knowing them in ways not expected of implied readers. This can certainly happen when readers bring a modern critical understanding of the Old Testament to bear on Matthew's narrative. Real readers, for instance, might question whether David was really the author of the words ascribed to him in Matthew 22:43–44. They might attribute laws concerning successive (levirate) marriage (22:24) to the "P" strata of the Pentateuch rather than to Moses. But Matthew's implied readers are expected to regard David as the author of Psalm 110 and Moses as the author of the legal material in Deuteronomy. Critically informed real readers just have to go with the flow and pretend they don't know these things if they want to discern expected responses to Matthew's narrative.

Unexpected readings may also result when real readers scrutinize the texts cited in Matthew in a manner not expected of the Gospel's implied readers. Matthew says that Jesus' birth in Bethlehem fulfills a prophetic saying: "And you, Bethlehem, in the land of Judah, are by no means least among the rulers of Judah" (2:5–6). Modern readers of Matthew often discover that the words "by no means" are not actually found in Micah 5:2. Implied readers are not expected to notice this. Again, Matthew 27:9–10 quotes the prophet Jeremiah as saying, "They took the thirty pieces of silver, the price of the one on whom a price had been set, on whom some of the people of Israel had set a price, and they gave them for the potter's field, as the Lord commanded me." Real readers have not been able to find this quotation anywhere in the writings of Jeremiah—or anywhere else for that matter. Instead, the citation appears to be a composite quote, based primarily on Zechariah 11:13, with some assistance from Jeremiah 18:1–12 and 32:6–15 and, possibly, some phraseology drawn from the Pentateuch.[156] But Matthew's implied readers would never be expected to argue with the narrator over such details. If real readers want to read the Gospel of Matthew in the manner expected of its implied readers, they will sometimes have to set aside their own knowledge concerning the scriptures and simply take what is said about the scriptures in Matthew's narrative at face value.

We move on now to the question of whether Matthew's implied readers are expected to have knowledge of texts other than the Jewish scriptures. The best candidate for such consideration would be the Gospel of Mark, which most scholars believe was written prior to the Gospel of Matthew and used as a source for the composition of that work. The problem is that this indebtedness is never acknowledged. In other words, Matthew's readers are never told that some of the material in the narrative is derived from Mark's Gospel, or even that the latter work exists. Furthermore, the material drawn from Mark is often presented in radically altered form without defense. As an example, let us consider the account in Matthew 22:34–40, which is derived from Mark 12:28–34. The story in Mark's narrative tells of a scribe who asks Jesus an apparently sincere question, agrees with the answer that Jesus gives, and is commended by Jesus for his insight. In Matthew's story, however, the scribe is presented as an opponent of Jesus who attempts to put him to the test (22:35). Readers familiar with Mark's Gospel would find it difficult to accept the new version of this encounter without explanation, but no explanation is provided. The assumption seems to be that Matthew's implied readers are not expected to know the Gospel of Mark and will not wonder why such changes have been made.

Since many real readers of Matthew today are familiar with Mark's Gospel, we must recognize that this familiarity may result in unexpected readings. In fact, much of the work of redaction criticism, which has dominated biblical studies for four decades now, produces unexpected readings in the sense in which we are employing that term. Redaction critics typically compare Matthew's Gospel to that of Mark and attempt to explain the reasoning behind the changes that have been made. This approach has enhanced modern understanding of the Bible in significant ways but has not managed to read Matthew's narrative in the manner expected of its implied readers.[157]

Unexpected readings result from what I call *extratextuality*, reading a narrative in light of texts that its implied readers are not expected to know.[158] Matthew's implied readers are not expected to know the identity of the disciple who cuts off the ear of the high priest's slave in Gethsemane (26:51; cf. John 18:10) or the fact that the slave was subsequently healed by Jesus (cf. Luke 22:51). Matthew's implied readers are not expected to know that one of the two robbers crucified with Jesus rebuked the other and appealed to Jesus for mercy (27:38; cf. Luke 23:39–42). Real readers who are familiar with the entire New Testament must pretend that they do not know these things if they wish to identify the effect that Matthew's narrative is intended to have on its implied readers.

We recognize, then, that unexpected readings may occur when real readers have either too little or too much knowledge of other texts. Accordingly, real readers must struggle to discern which texts implied readers are expected to know and how well implied readers are expected to know them. As with other types of knowledge discussed previously, this struggle is not always an easy one. Three criteria are significant for determining whether the implied readers of Matthew's Gospel are expected to recognize a proposed intertextual connection:[159]

- *Availability.* Was knowledge of the alleged precursor text available in the discourse setting of the successor text (in the time and place that it was written)? There is no question that the Jewish scriptures were widely known in the world that produced Matthew's Gospel—a given, since they are often referred to explicitly. It would be ludicrous, however, to infer from Matthew 12:25 that Matthew's implied readers are expected to be familiar with the speeches of Abraham Lincoln, for those texts did not exist at the time when Matthew's Gospel was written. Lincoln's claim that "a house divided against itself cannot stand" should be regarded as an intertextual allusion to Matthew's Gospel rather than the other way around.
- *Degree of repetition.* To what extent are features of the alleged precursor text repeated in the successor text? Jesus' citation of Hosea 6:6 in Matthew 9:13 rates high in this regard because the words "I desire mercy and not sacrifice" are repeated verbatim. The allusion to Psalm 22:18 in Matthew 27:35 is less direct, although the reference to dividing garments and casting lots in both passages suggests a possible connection.[160] Our suggestion that Matthew 3:4 alludes to 2 Kings 1:8 is also tenuous, but the descriptions of both Elijah and John the Baptist as persons who wore hairy garments and leather girdles is noteworthy.
- *Thematic coherence.* Is the meaning or effect suggested by the proposed connection consistent with that produced by the narrative as a whole? The proposal that Matthew 3:4 alludes to 2 Kings 1:8 is likely (in spite of the low degree of repetition) because John the Baptist is identified with Elijah elsewhere in the narrative (17:11–13).

With such criteria in mind, we may examine three potentially difficult cases:

Essene Writings?

What are implied readers expected to make of Jesus' comment in Matthew 5:43, "You have heard that it was said, 'You shall love your neighbor and hate your enemy'"? The introductory phrase "You have heard that it was said . . ." implies that what follows is a familiar citation. Matthew's implied readers are expected to know, furthermore, that the phrase "you shall love your neighbor" is a quotation from scripture (Lev. 19:18; the degree of repetition here is almost exact).[161] But what of the phrase "hate your enemy"? It has been suggested that this derives from Essene writings, where children of light are directed to hate children of darkness (1QS 1:4, 9–11).[162] But it seems unlikely that Matthew's implied readers are expected to know these texts. The writings did exist by the time Matthew was written, but we have no evidence that they were available or known where this Gospel was produced (or even in the area where Jesus had conducted his ministry). The degree of repetition between 1QS 1:4, 9–11 and Matthew 5:43 is slight, consisting more of parallel ideas than of similar wording. Nor would the criterion of thematic coherence be satisfied by this connection, for Jesus is not elsewhere presented in Matthew's narrative as a critic of Essene doctrine. Asked whether Matthew's implied readers are expected to know Qumran writings, based on this one alleged allusion, we would have to conclude "not impossible, but not likely."

Another suggestion makes more sense: implied readers regard the entire phrase "you shall love your neighbor and hate your enemy" as deriving from the scriptures. The only problem with this proposal is that the degree of repetition for the full phrase is low. The words "hate your enemy" cannot be found explicitly in Leviticus or anywhere else in the scriptures. The basic thought, however, is present. Psalm 139:21–22 reads, "Do I not hate those who hate you, O Lord? And do I not loathe those who rise up against you? I hate them with perfect hatred. I count them as my enemies." The degree of repetition here is at least as great as for the Qumran passage, but now other criteria are met as well. In terms of availability, there is no question that the book of Psalms was widely known in the narrative's discourse setting, since obvious quotations and allusions to Psalms are found throughout Matthew. And in terms of thematic coherence, the presentation of Jesus as one who supplements what has been revealed in the scriptures with new insight is consistent with his characterization throughout the narrative (5:17). In fact, the very phrase used to introduce this citation, "You have heard it said . . . ," occurs several times in the narrative material immediately preceding this passage (5:21, 27, 33, 38; cf. 5:31) and in every instance is used to introduce a citation from the scriptures. For these reasons, we may conclude that Matthew 5:43 offers no warrant for concluding that Matthew's implied readers are expected to know the Essene writings of Qumran. The verse can be understood in terms of the readers' presumed knowledge of the Jewish scriptures.

Tradition of the Elders?

Another potentially difficult case involves the reference to the "tradition of the elders" in Matthew 15:2. Pharisees and scribes who come to Jesus from Jerusalem ask him, "Why do your disciples transgress the tradition of the elders? For they do not wash their hands when they eat." Since no further explanation is given (cf. Mark 7:3–4), we should assume that Matthew's readers are expected to know what the tradition of the elders says about washing hands before eating. The content of this tradition would probably have been available knowledge in the world that formed the narrative's discourse setting[163] and some knowledge of what is contained in this tradition of the elders is necessary for a thematically coherent interpretation of the passage. Implied readers are at least expected to know that the scribal concern is for ritual purity rather than, say, hygiene; this much is necessary for them to see the connection to Jesus' comments on defilement in 15:10–20. The problem, this time, is not *whether* Matthew's readers are expected to know what the tradition of the elders said about the washing of hands—the problem is *what* Matthew's readers are expected to know in this regard. We do not possess any definitive copy of this tradition of the elders today.[164] Reading this text in the manner expected of its implied readers may be impossible because the implied readers are expected to have knowledge of a precursor text no longer available to us. The significance of this lapse is difficult to determine. Perhaps readers are expected to know no more than that the issue was one of ritual purity. If this is the case, we may be missing nothing. But perhaps readers are expected to have more detailed knowledge concerning the tradition of the elders, knowledge that would introduce nuances of meaning real readers can no longer discern today.

Oral Christian Tradition?

A third difficult case involving questions of intertextuality concerns references to Jesus' claim that he is able to destroy the temple and rebuild it in three days. In John's Gospel, Jesus does in fact make such a claim (John 2:19), but the Gospel of Matthew never quotes him as saying this. In Matthew 26:61, however, witnesses at Jesus' trial accuse him of having made such a claim, and in 27:40 the charge is taken up by mockers who deride Jesus as he hangs on the cross. Since the implied readers of Matthew's Gospel are not expected to know the Gospel of John, how will they regard the charge that Jesus made a claim that Matthew never depicts him as making? Are implied readers expected to regard this charge as a false accusation, since Jesus is never represented in this narrative as saying what he is accused of having said?[165]

Another possibility exists. Perhaps Matthew's implied readers are expected to be familiar with a body of oral tradition that attributes this saying to Jesus. This body of oral tradition would then be regarded as the precursor text to which an intertextual connection is now drawn. Such tradition may certainly have been available. The high degree of repetition between what Jesus is alleged to have said in Matthew 26:61 and 27:40 and what he is actually quoted as saying in John 2:19 argues for the likelihood of such a saying being known in contexts independent of either Gospel. And the assumption that readers are expected to know Jesus made such a claim coheres thematically with other information in the narrative. Jesus does, after all, claim that his ministry represents "something greater than the temple" (12:6), and he does predict an eventual destruction of the temple (24:1–2). We have previously noted instances in which Matthew's readers might be expected to have prior knowledge of Christian tradition: implied readers may be expected to understand Jesus' reference to the bridegroom being taken away (9:15) as an allusion to his impending death, and they may be expected to have already heard of such persons as Simon the leper (26:6) and Mary Magdalene (27:56), who are introduced without description. They are apparently expected to know what the "church" is (16:18; 18:17). Is it too far-fetched, then, to assume that Matthew's readers might also be expected to know that Jesus claimed he could destroy and rebuild the Temple in three days—even though that claim is never mentioned specifically in the narrative?

Thematic coherence, however, can also be ascribed to interpretations that do not assume the reader has intertextual knowledge of Jesus making this claim. Readers may simply be expected to regard the charge in 26:61 as a mangled version of what Jesus has said previously in this narrative: he has claimed that the temple would be destroyed (24:1–2), that he would rise from the dead in three days (16:21; 17:23; 20:19; cf. 12:40), and that he would build a church (16:18). In light of sayings such as these, readers might be expected to take the charge that Jesus said he was able to destroy the temple and rebuild it in three days as the witnesses' misconstrual of what Jesus actually said.[166] They would thus regard the charge as false in a literal sense (Jesus did not really say this), but ironically true in its representation of what will now take place. Jesus' death will in fact signal the demise of the temple cult (27:51), and his resurrection after three days will grant him the authority to begin a new community of disciples from all nations (28:18–20). Such an interpretation does not require knowledge of traditions about Jesus that are not reported within this particular narrative.

Having considered these options, I offer my own unsatisfactory conclusion: I do not think that the question of whether Matthew's implied readers are expected to interpret 26:61 and 27:40 in light of intertextual allusions to a body of oral tradition can be answered with any certainty. Personally, I believe that it is best not to presume intertextual connections to a body of material that is not clearly cited or referenced, when a meaningful and consistent interpretation can be obtained apart from such connections. But the possibility that knowledge of traditions not preserved within Matthew's narrative may be presupposed cannot be entirely discounted and may provide a viable explanation for these particular verses. Richard Hays says,

> [W]e must reckon with varying degrees of certainty in our efforts to identify and interpret intertextual echoes. Sometimes the echo will be so loud that only the dullest or most ignorant reader could miss it; other times there will be room for serious differences of opinion about whether a particular phrase should be heard as an echo of a prior text and, if so, how it should be understood. Precision in such judgment calls is unattainable.[167]

Still, I note as before a distinction between admitting unresolved ambiguity due to the ignorance of modern readers and supposing intentional ambiguity as the expected perception of implied readers. I am unsure here of what connection the text is making not because I have succeeded in exposing its inherent openness to indeterminacy but because I have failed to identify what it is that implied readers are assumed to know. Admission of such failures is necessary for hermeneutical integrity.

To summarize the main points of this section, real readers who wish to determine the effect that the Gospel of Matthew is expected to have on its implied readers must 1) have the knowledge of texts cited through quotation or allusion that implied readers are expected to have, and 2) be willing to set aside knowledge concerning these texts that implied readers are not expected to have, as well as knowledge concerning other texts that implied readers are not expected to know. Criteria such as availability, degree of repetition, and thematic coherence help real readers determine which intertextual connections implied readers would be expected to make. Even so, detection and interpretation of intertextuality can be a struggle, and determination cannot always be made with certainty.

Determining what implied readers are or are not expected to know is not an exact science, but neither are such determinations made arbitrarily. By monitoring the expectations of what implied readers appear to be expected to know, we gain the opportunity to increase or limit the knowledge through which we interpret the narrative. Thus, we come closer to determining the effect that the Gospel is expected to have on its implied readers than we would be able to come otherwise. By pursuing such an asymptotic goal, furthermore, we may discover why our responses are sometimes at variance with what the text expects.

Chapter Six
What Are Readers Expected to Believe?

In the first chapter of Matthew's Gospel, a Jewish man named Joseph learns that his betrothed spouse, Mary, is pregnant. Since he has not had sexual relations with her himself and since he does not know that the Holy Spirit is responsible for her condition, he naturally assumes that she has been with another man. The narrator of Matthew then tells us, "Joseph, being a righteous man and unwilling to expose her to public disgrace, planned to dismiss her quietly" (1:19).

Matthew's implied readers are expected to regard whatever the narrator says as reliable, so surely they are expected to believe that Joseph really is "a righteous man." But what exactly makes him righteous in this instance? At least two interpretations present themselves: a) he is righteous because he plans to dismiss (divorce) his adulterous spouse; in addition, he is merciful and plans to do so quietly; or b) he is righteous because he plans to carry out the necessary divorce of his spouse in as merciful a fashion as possible. The first interpretation equates righteousness with obedience to a moral code, which may or may not be observed mercifully; the second implies that righteousness can only be achieved through merciful action. Commentators choose up sides as to which interpretation is most likely. I don't think we can tell with absolute certainty, but my guess is that we are not expected to find the passage ambiguous. My guess is that Matthew's readers are assumed to have very clear beliefs regarding what a righteous man would do in such a circumstance.

Whichever option is preferred, some modern readers may have trouble regarding Joseph as righteous at all. Should he not at least have gotten her side of the story before deciding to divorce her (quietly or not)? Would it make any difference, for instance, if she had been the victim of rape? Or is the point simply that she is now "damaged goods" that no so-called righteous man would want to possess? Ah, but these are unanticipated questions. It is not wrong to ask them, but when our immediate goal is to discern how implied readers are expected to respond to the story we must, for the moment, set them aside. Matthew's implied readers are expected to regard Joseph as a righteous man and, accordingly, to view his actions as definitive of what constitutes righteousness *in this story.*

Literary critics sometimes say that readers enter into an implicit contract with an author (or implied author).[168] They agree to accept whatever dynamics the narrative establishes as determinative for the world in which the story takes place. Readers of George Orwell's *Animal Farm* are not shocked to find that the animals in the story can talk to each other, though they would be amazed to discover such a thing happening in the real world of their everyday lives. If a story is set in Middle Earth or "a long time ago, in a galaxy far away," we don't debate the physical realities of those locations; we just say, "Okay, tell me what rules apply for such a setting." If there are hobbits and elves, or wookies and ewoks, we accept that.

I am trying to cite obvious examples of stories that create worlds completely different from our own—but, actually, every story does this in subtle and perhaps undetected ways. Every story creates its own world with operative rules different from what we experience in the real world. For instance, most of us (I hope) do not live in a world where an interpretive voice (a narrator) keeps us informed of the activities and inner thoughts of others. Samuel Coleridge coined a memorable term to describe what is required of us: a "willing suspension of disbelief."[169] We enter into the world of a story while reading it and pretend to believe whatever is appropriate for that world. When we quit reading, we reassume whatever beliefs seem appropriate in our own world.[170] But this does not mean that we escape our experience with the alternative reality unscathed (that is, unaffected)—nor should we assume that stories that are the most "realistic" will necessarily be the ones that affect us most deeply. The analogy of a contract is apt, furthermore, for most readers will hold the narrative (the implied author) accountable for sticking to whatever vision of reality is established for the story. James Bond can do a lot of remarkable things, but he cannot fly like Superman. And Superman cannot just suddenly turn invisible when he's never been able to do that before (he has to get hit with some kind of radiation or something first).

In the Gospel of Matthew, God speaks audibly from heaven, fantastic miracles occur, and Jesus interacts freely with supernatural beings such as angels and demons—even with Satan himself. This is definitely a world different from that in which we live. Even those who believe these stories are literal-historical reports will usually concede that day-to-day life in the present world is different from what is described in Matthew's narrative, where such events are commonplace. In any case, all readers who wish to determine the expected effect of Matthew's Gospel will have to bracket out of consideration their own presuppositions about such things and accept (or pretend to accept) whatever constitutes reality in the world of Matthew's story.[171]

My favorite demon story in Matthew is the one where Jesus casts a whole passel of the nasty spirits into a herd of pigs (8:28–34). I like to call it the story of "deviled ham," and it may be my favorite for that reason alone (an old joke, always in search of a new audience). My second favorite demon story is the tale of the moonstruck child in Matthew 17:14–21. A man brings his son to Jesus claiming that the boy has been cursed or, literally, struck by the moon. Matthew's implied readers are probably expected to believe that the moon can and sometimes does behave in such a fashion. In the cultural context that formed the discourse setting for Matthew's narrative, the moon was usually thought to be a god, and in Jewish circles this had to mean that it would be a lesser god or spirit. Further, since this "god" known as the Moon was worshiped by pagans, it pretty much had to be an evil god or spirit, usurping glory from the one and only true God, who had in fact created it. Evil gods do not have limitless power, but they can wreak havoc on human beings. Thus, Matthew's readers are expected to believe that the cavalier and sometimes evil spirit known as the Moon has struck or cursed this poor child, causing him to "suffer terribly." This is confirmed when Jesus cures the child not by healing the disease as such but by driving a demon out of him. Jesus: 1, Moon: 0.

Many English Bible translations try to help readers out by simply saying that the child brought to Jesus was an epileptic.[172] They do this on the assumption that the effects of the Moon's curse on the child (as described in 17:15 and in Mark 9:18 and 20) resemble what modern medicine would diagnose as an epileptic seizure. Modern readers might not understand the more bizarre assumptions of Matthew's story world, but they can get the main point of the story: a child had epilepsy, and Jesus cured him by performing an exorcism. Hmmmm. But what if I am not so interested in getting the *point* of the story as I am in determining its impact? What if we conceive of meaning as *effect* rather than merely as *message?* To discern impact or effect, I may choose to empathize with one of the characters in the story, possibly the father who comes to Jesus. Personally, I think I would react quite differently if I believed my son suffered from a medically diagnosed condition than I would if I believed he had been struck by a capricious heavenly power. The effect of the story on me, emotionally as well as cognitively, will differ depending on whether I believe what I am expected to believe. At the very least, this will influence whether I regard the temporal and earthly deliverance that Jesus accomplishes as evidence of a more cosmic triumph.[173]

But so far we are only scratching the surface of what we really need to discuss. The belief that God can speak from heaven or that demons can possess small children is not too different from the examples of knowledge presupposed for Matthew's readers that we discussed in the last chapter. The existence of demons is as much a part of reality for Matthew's story world as the existence of Caesar. Believing in demons does not require an act of faith; it only requires awareness of how things are. Perhaps we should not even say, "Matthew's readers are expected to *believe* in the reality of demons." More accurately, Matthew's readers are expected to *know* that demons are real. They are expected to know that God can and does speak from heaven and that fantastic miracles are sometimes performed by God's agents. So far, everything mentioned in this chapter properly belongs in the last one. Matters of "assumed knowledge" only appear to be matters of "assumed belief" to people whose vision of reality refuses them the former status—and this refusal in and of itself testifies to our failure to meet the expectations of Matthew's implied readers.

When we speak of believing what readers are expected to believe, we need to go deep enough to uncover the core value systems that govern the standards of judgment that are operative within this story's world. David Rhoads equates such standards of judgment with "the narrator's ideological view," which may be constructed from various clues in the story.[174] Such evaluative standards are often so subtle, so basic, that they are unstated and easily go undetected. But are they the same values that we, the real readers, bring to the text?

Perhaps we must first identify an underlying assumption that allows us to speak of values at all: things *can be evaluated*. Some qualities are "good" and others are "bad." The very use of such words as good and bad implies this—and words like these are used often in Matthew's Gospel. Check a concordance for the occurrence of these evaluative adjectives: *adikos* (unrighteous), *agathos* (good), *akeraios* (innocent), *dikaios* (righteous), *kakos* (wicked), *megas* (mighty), *mōros* (foolish), *oknēros* (lazy), *phronimos* (prudent), *pistos* (faithful), *ponēros* (evil), *praos* (meek), *sophos* (wise), *synetos* (intelligent), *tapeinos* (humble).

Let us return to the example with which this chapter opened. I would now want to say that Matthew's implied readers are expected to know that Joseph is a righteous man (the narrator tells them this) and that they are also expected to know what constitutes righteousness in this world (the world of Matthew's story). Beyond this, however, they are expected to *believe* that being righteous is a good thing; they are expected to *value* righteousness. Now, you may think that such a belief is so basic, so obvious, that we need not spend any time on it. After all, can we imagine any reader—real or implied—who wouldn't think this? Alright, then, but what will these readers make of Matthew 9:13, when Jesus declares that he has not come to call the righteous, but sinners? If Matthew's readers are expected to regard "being righteous" positively, then won't they be thrown for a loop when Jesus claims to prefer the company of sinners to that of persons who are righteous? Is there maybe some sense in which "being righteous" is not a good thing?[175]

Thus, I organize this chapter on beliefs or values in two broad categories: those that are assumed by the narrative as part of the implied readers' *repertoire* and those that are presented within the narrative as part of the implied readers' *education.* The assumption is that Matthew's readers are expected to come to the narrative with certain beliefs and values, but that they are also expected to derive beliefs and values *from* the narrative. Matthew's readers are expected to have their beliefs and values shaped by the experience of reading this narrative, but such an expectation necessarily entails assumptions about what their beliefs and values were to begin with.

The Readers' Repertoire of Beliefs and Values

The story world of Matthew's Gospel assumes a system of beliefs and values that are shared by its implied author and implied readers. These matters are not taught within the narrative but are simply a part of its "infrastructure." For example, Matthew's implied readers are expected to believe that scripture reveals truth. It is easy to imagine modern readers who do not believe this today but rather difficult to imagine modern readers who would not recognize that they are *expected* to believe this. When Jesus quotes the scriptures, as he does frequently, we are not supposed to think he is just citing relevant or interesting passages of cherished literature. We are expected to regard what scripture says as revelatory of God's way of thinking: scripture is "the word of God" (15:6).

Likewise, when the narrator of Matthew's story says that Jesus taught the crowds "as one having authority and not as their scribes" (7:29), readers are expected to interpret this report as reflecting positively on Jesus vis-á-vis the scribes. The assumption—never stated in the text—is that teaching with authority is better than teaching without authority. Real readers do not always share the values assumed for this (or any other) narrative. In the real world, some people regard authoritative pronouncements as indicative of ineffective or irresponsible pedagogy. They might, accordingly, read Matthew 7:29 as describing Jesus' teaching in a way that sounds unappealing and inferior to that of the scribes. But such a reading diverges from what would be expected of Matthew's implied readers, interpreting the text in light of values inconsistent with those of the world that provided the discourse setting for the narrative.

Matthew's readers are assumed to believe that it would normally be shameful for a woman to become pregnant without having had relations with her husband. Readers who do not believe this are likely to miss the point of the potential scandal in Matthew 1:18–20. Likewise, Matthew's readers are expected to believe it is wrong for a man to take his own brother's wife and make her his own—while the brother is still alive, that is (cf. 22:23–28). A reader who does not believe this is wrong might not view John the Baptist's complaint against Herod as just (14:3). Such examples assume acceptance of commonly held views regarding kinship, marriage, and sexuality. These mores are not so much taught within the narrative as they are presupposed by it.

Unexpected readings result when real readers do not share the same values as those assumed for the narrative's implied readers. There are two common reasons for such a lack of continuity: 1) the real-life setting of readers is distinct from the discourse setting of the narrative (that is, the time and place in which it was composed); and 2) the real-life setting of readers is distinct from the story setting of the narrative (that is, from the nonreferential world composed of characters, events, places, and things that only approximate reality but are never quite real).

Beliefs and Values Implied by the Discourse Setting

By definition, values and beliefs are always contextual—they are assumed or affirmed within a particular culture. Narratives naturally embody elements of the value system for the cultural context in which they are produced. They may do so knowingly—even defensively—or unwittingly.

Sometimes values are *regarded as universal,* but even then the contextual aspect may be recognized. The Second Book of Samuel relates a scandalous tale in which Amnon, the eldest son of King David, rapes his half sister Tamar. When he seizes her for this purpose, she protests, "No, my brother, do not force me; for such a thing is not done in Israel; do not do anything so vile!" (2 Sam. 13:12). The latter part of this response implies that the action would violate some absolute standard of right and wrong: to do such a thing would be intrinsically vile. But the preceding comment takes a different tack, emphasizing that the action contradicts the value system of one particular culture. I can think of a good many reasons Tamar might give her brother as to why he should not rape her. It is interesting that this is the reason she does give: "such a thing is not done in Israel." What I think this illustrates is that the values of a cultural group can be affirmed in a way that indicates "what should be recognized by all is especially true for us." We see this in America when a news story surfaces about police violating a prisoner's civil rights in egregious ways. The public revulsion seems to say, "This is not only wrong, it's un-American"—and indeed the latter thought almost carries more weight than the first.

Values can also be *regarded as absolute* even when there is acknowledgment that they are not universally recognized. In the musical play *Fiddler on the Roof,* the practice of arranged marriages is portrayed as oppressive and a Western concept of romantic love is celebrated. To use our terminology, values that derive from the discourse setting of the play's composition (modern Western society) are imposed on the setting of the story (czarist Russia). The assumption behind the play, I think, is that the Western way of romance is better: it may not be universally practiced, but it should be.

In Matthew's Gospel, Jesus criticizes Gentile rulers as tyrants who lord over others (20:25). This criticism assumes a defensive cultural value. Matthew's implied readers are expected to assess tyranny negatively and to realize that in so doing, they profess a different value system than is associated with Gentiles. In other words, the readers are expected to regard this value as absolute (or, universally true) even while realizing that it is not universally recognized. Matthew's readers are not expected to believe that it is okay for Gentiles to lord over people but not for us to do so. No. It is wrong for the Gentiles also, although they don't seem to know this; we must take care not to become like them. Thus, despising tyranny becomes a defining value for the contextual group to which Matthew's implied readers are presumed to belong. We have said that Matthew's implied readers are expected to evince values that are intrinsic to the world that formed the discourse setting for this narrative. In this case, that discourse setting was apparently a cultural (or countercultural) group that despised the Gentile system of government, which it regarded as inherently tyrannical.

Unexpected readings result when we impose values on the narrative that would have been foreign perspectives for the world that provided its discourse setting. A modern vegetarian reader who thinks that the killing of the oxen and fat calves in Matthew 22:4 is shameful will be prone to interpreting this text in unexpected ways.[176] Matthew's narrative does not anticipate that its readers might believe that the killing of animals for food is wrong.

Of course we may not always be able to determine just which contextual values or beliefs appropriate to the discourse setting are expected. Here are two test cases to consider:

1. Are Matthew's readers expected to believe in ghosts? In one part of the story, Jesus' disciples are in a boat on the lake when Jesus comes to them at night, walking on the water. They see him and cry out in fear, "It is a ghost!" (14:22–27). Perhaps Matthew's readers are expected to think the disciples are foolish and superstitious for responding in such a way. But I don't think so. I think that Matthew's implied readers are probably expected to consider this a sensible initial reaction: since ghosts do in fact exist, a man walking on water might understandably appear to be one.

2. Are Matthew's readers expected to regard slavery as an acceptable social institution? In Matthew 8:5–13, a centurion appeals to Jesus to heal his servant (or possibly, his son), who suffers from paralysis.[177] In the conversation that follows, he speaks to Jesus of the authority he exercises over his slaves, likening their willingness to do his bidding to the certainty that Jesus' word of healing will be obeyed. Are Matthew's readers expected to be shocked by this analogy? Should they think it shameful that this Roman soldier keeps human beings as slaves and brags about his ability to boss them around? I don't think so. I think Matthew's readers are expected to consider this to be a perfectly normal situation, the morality of which they would never think to challenge. The mentality that objects to one person keeping another as a slave is as foreign to this narrative as that which objects to killing a fatted calf for a banquet.[178]

Admitting to uncertainty, I list three criteria (familiar from the last chapter) as helpful in making such determinations:

- *Availability.* Were the values or beliefs that we want to assume on behalf of the implied readers widely held in the world that formed the discourse setting for this narrative? Application of this criterion requires that we have knowledge of that world, which can sometimes be limited. Still, as near as I can tell, belief in the existence of ghosts was widespread throughout the ancient Near East; I do not know of any writings from this time or place by persons who deny the existence of such spirits. Likewise, acceptance of slavery as an inevitable (if not necessarily commendable) social reality appears to have been the rule for this context; I do not know of any writings that denounce the institution as such. On the other hand, ideologically motivated vegetarianism, while not unknown (1 Cor. 8:13?), was certainly not a dominant value for this context, nowhere near prominent enough to be simply assumed for a narrative's readers without explicit indication.

• *Relevance.* Are the presumed beliefs or values that we propose for this narrative actually relevant to what is related in the story? This criterion enables us once again to distinguish between what appears to be expected of Matthew's implied readers and what might have been expected for the original, intended readers. I think it is a waste of time to ask whether Matthew's implied readers are expected to believe the earth is flat. The intended readers probably believed this, and we could argue on the basis of the availability criterion that the belief was so prominent within the discourse setting as to be presupposed for all narratives composed in that context. Still, if such a belief is in no way determinative for how this narrative affects its readers, then I would argue that it is not presupposed for readers implied by the narrative. But either a presumed belief in ghosts or a presumed acceptance of slavery would be relevant. In both cases, these beliefs relate to phenomena explicitly mentioned in the story and what one believes concerning these phenomena will determine how one regards the characters in the story. Are Jesus' disciples to be characterized as foolish and superstitious? Is the centurion to be characterized as tyrannical and oppressive?

• *Thematic coherence.* Is the interpretation obtained by assuming that readers are expected to evince these beliefs or values consistent with what appears to be true for the narrative as a whole? The disciples of Jesus evince a number of faults in this story, but nowhere are they depicted as foolish or superstitious, as wont to believing things about the nature of the world that are actually false. Accordingly, I suspect that a reader who regards their reaction to Jesus' appearance on the water in such a light would be prone to understanding their role in the story in unexpected ways. Similarly, Jesus is never depicted in this narrative as working miracles for oppressive people, much less as pointing to them as examples of great faith (8:10). To assume that the centurion is an oppressive and tyrannical man because he owns slaves would lead to an interpretation that presents Jesus as acting here in ways that are inconsistent with how he acts elsewhere in the narrative.

Such criteria, then, may help us to engage specific questions regarding beliefs or values that implied readers may be expected to hold. On a deeper level, however, cultural values often take the form of transcendent systems that undergird all the specific discussions of what is right or wrong. For instance, in modern

Western society personal liberty is highly esteemed, while in the world that produced Matthew's Gospel, ritual purity was highly esteemed. There are very few people in our modern world (from which real readers of Matthew's Gospel are currently drawn) who are willing to give up their individual freedoms (their civil rights) in exchange for some authoritative assurance that they will be regarded as pure. In fact, we tend to regard people who are willing to make such an exchange as abnormal and possibly defective—they've been "brainwashed" or become members of "a cult." I suspect that the relative values assigned to these matters (personal liberty and ritual purity) would have been reversed for the world that produced Matthew's Gospel and that Matthew's readers are therefore expected to read this narrative with a higher regard for the latter than for the former. Note that in Jesus' discussions with the Pharisees about purity and defilement (15:1–20; 23:23–28), the only disagreements are over the means to the end; the importance of the end itself—purity—is never questioned. But where does Jesus ever champion an individual's right to life, liberty, or the pursuit of happiness?

Our understanding of the value systems that are implicit for Matthew's narrative has been greatly advanced in the past two decades through the application of cultural anthropology. Scholars such as Bruce Malina and Jerome Neyrey have revolutionized our understanding of the Bible by uncovering the often unstated cultural scripts that informed life in the worlds that produced these writings.[179] The interests of cultural anthropologists are more historical than literary, but the results of their investigations are nevertheless critical for determining how a story is expected to affect its implied readers. As it turns out, the Gospel of Matthew has become one of the favorite documents for "case study" applications of this method.[180]

Perhaps the single, most pervasive cultural value that has been determined for the discourse setting of Matthew's narrative is the intrinsic significance of honor and shame. In that setting a person's honor would be construed in terms of his or her publicly recognized value or worth. Such honor could be ascribed to one at birth by virtue of heritage or station in life or it could be acquired through success at various endeavors that enhanced one's reputation. Increasing one's honor was generally considered to be the highest goal in life—more important, for instance, than acquiring wealth or worldly possessions. Indeed, wealth was sought precisely because its acquisition was likely to increase one's public status. Becoming wealthy was a means to an end, and that end was not so much the enjoyment of creature comforts as the acquisition of honor. The quest to increase honor was complicated, furthermore, by the cultural assumption that honor was "a limited good," one that could only be obtained at the expense of someone else. In other words, it was thought that there was only so much honor to go around, so that if one person gained honor, someone else would have to lose it. Such an understanding seems strange to the Western mind, for we are not socialized to think of something like honor as a product that has to be divided among the community. But in the world that provided the discourse setting for Matthew's narrative, people were prone to view not only honor but also such things as friendship, love, respect, security, and safety as items that "exist in finite quantity and are always in short supply."[181] Of course, this made for an intensely competitive environment, one in which display and recognition of honor were expected, as were repeated challenges to that honor by claimants who hoped to better their own position. So, Matthew's Gospel is filled with stories in which Jesus is put to the test by persons who demand a sign from him (12:38; 16:1), challenge his authority (21:23), or try to trap him into saying or doing the wrong thing (12:10; 22:15, 23, 35). Basically, Jesus bests his opponents at every turn, shaming them and earning even more honor (public acclaim) for himself. By the end of the story, it has become obvious that those who claim to oppose him for a variety of reasons are simply jealous of him (27:18).

To summarize this section, values pertinent to the discourse setting of Matthew's Gospel (that is, pertinent to the time and place in which the Gospel was written) are often assumed within the narrative. Readers may be expected to espouse such values even when they are not stated or explicitly referenced in the story. The contextual aspect of such values may be acknowledged, defended, emphasized, or ignored, but in any case the values themselves are usually assumed to be absolutely valid. If we want to discern the expected effect of the narrative on its implied readers, we must read it in light of these assumed values, which may differ from our own. Such criteria as availability, relevance, and thematic coherence help in discerning which beliefs and values implied by the discourse setting must be assumed to belong to the implied readers' repertoire.

Beliefs and Values Implied by the Story Setting

Readers may be expected to accept values as applicable within a narrative that are only generally indicative of what they espouse in real life. In the world in which I live, I do not easily class others into categories of "good people" and "bad people"; I know the world is more complicated than that. But when I used to watch television with my six-year-old daughter (she's older now), and she would ask me, "Is he a good guy or a bad guy?" I could usually answer without a lot of equivocation—in the shows we watched, characters tended to be one or the other.

Literary critics speak of "flat characters" who tend to embody a single trait, as opposed to "round characters" who may evince multiple or even conflicting traits.[182] An example of the latter would be the character Clint Eastwood plays in the movie *Unforgiven*—is he a good guy or a bad guy? It is not so easy to determine. But flat characters are usually unconflicted: the coyote just wants to catch the road runner; the wicked witch of the west just wants to "get" Dorothy—and her little dog, too!

Sophisticated readers often assume that stories populated with flat characters are less profound than those with round characters. This assumption is arrogant—and incorrect. They are not less profound; they are just more abstract. Round characters allow a story to explore the intricacies of human psychology, but flat characters allow a story to examine *values*. A character or group of characters may be presented as personifying a particular trait or value: lust, loyalty, kindness, greed. The story, then, is not so much about actual human beings as it is about values.

In Matthew's Gospel, Jesus says, "[Y]our Father in heaven . . . makes his sun rise on the evil and on the good, and sends rain on the righteous and on the unrighteous" (5:45). The verse does not tell us who or what is "evil" or "good," or who or what is "righteous" or "unrighteous," but it certainly does assume that such evaluative polarities exist. Does it really mean to suggest that *people in the real world* may be classed as good or evil, as righteous or unrighteous? Or does it mean that *characters in the story* may be classed as good or evil, as righteous or unrighteous? How we answer those questions depends on the perspective from which we are asking them. If we mean to ask how the historical author(s) of Matthew intended for the references to be understood, I must confess frankly that I do not know, nor do I think there is any sure way for us ever to find out. But, if we are asking how the implied readers are expected to understand the references, then I can confidently answer, "In the latter sense—as applicable only to characters in the story, not to people in the real world." Implied readers, we must keep telling ourselves, are only a theoretical concept constructed out of what is in the narrative. They do not have any opinions about real people or about anything else in the world outside the story. Matthew's implied readers are not expected to believe that some people in the real world are good and others bad, but they are definitely expected to believe that some characters in this story are good and others bad.

So we see another major reason that unexpected readings of Matthew's narrative may occur. Many modern readers receive the story in a directly referential sense, assuming that what it says about characters in the story applies to real people outside the story. Indeed, many people would say that this is why they read Matthew's Gospel, to learn about Jesus—and along the way about his disciples, and about the Pharisees, and about Pilate and Herod and other historical people who are portrayed as characters in this story. Such interpretations may be judged valid or invalid from a historical perspective, but in either case must be deemed unexpected from a literary perspective. Narrative criticism does not seek to determine what the story teaches about the world that produced it but rather uses knowledge about that world to determine the effect that the story is expected to have on its implied readers.

A vision of Matthew's story world may be offered in a parable that Jesus tells in 13:24–30 and then explains in 13:36–43. Jesus says the world is like a field in which the Son of Man (that's Jesus himself) has sown good seed and the devil has sown bad seed. As a result, "children of the kingdom" and "children of the evil one" live side by side, like wheat and tares growing in a field. Ultimately the point of the parable is that Jesus' disciples are not to assume it is their job to rid the world of weeds (evil people)—the angels will take care of that at the end of the age. But what seems most striking is the vision of reality this story offers—a world in which people are either wheat or weeds. People owe their place in this world either to Jesus or to the devil, both of whom appear to be credited with the power of creation. This is a very different vision than is offered by the book of Genesis, according to which all people in the world owe their existence to God and the evil one's role is limited to tempting them.

The more dualistic vision of the parable really does seem to apply to Matthew's narrative as a whole. There are good guys and bad guys in this story. We have mentioned an example of the former, Jesus' father, who is called a "righteous man" (1:19). The most obvious example of the bad guys are the scribes and Pharisees, whom Jesus explicitly regards as "evil" (9:4; 12:34, 39; 16:4; 22:18) and whom he calls "children of serpents" (12:34; 23:33) and "children of hell" (23:15). Such language implies rather strongly that they belong to the devil—that they are among the "children of the evil one" Jesus described in his parable. Surely, they are flat characters—in this Gospel (unlike the others), they are never once depicted as saying, doing, thinking, or believing anything that the implied readers are expected to regard as right.[183] Further, Jesus does not attempt to minister to them anymore than he would to the demons that he exorcizes. They are just bad people—destined for hell (23:33). In one terribly revealing passage, he counsels his disciples to leave them alone as well (15:14), reminding them explicitly of the parable he told earlier: "Every plant that my heavenly Father has not planted will be uprooted" (15:13). His disciples should simply go about their work as best they can, trusting that when the time is right, God's angels will take care of the scribes and Pharisees—and any other tares sown by the devil.

What are we expected to make of all this? Did the historical author of this Gospel really believe that the scribes and Pharisees who interacted with Jesus were put on the earth by the devil? That they were irredeemably evil and thus not candidates for conversion (didn't he know about Paul?)? Was he motivated in such beliefs by some virulent anti-Semitism, or at least anti-Pharisaism, that stereotyped an entire class of people in relentlessly negative ways? Well, personally, I doubt that the author of Matthew's Gospel thought this way, but we can never know for sure what his intentions or motives might have been. What we *can* know is what kind of an effect a story that works this way is expected to have on its implied readers. As I have indicated, flat characters personify values, enabling the story to comment less on actual human beings in the real world whom the characters might appear to represent than on the values that these characters embody and hence actually do represent. In Matthew's narrative, the scribes and Pharisees personify the primal value, "evil"; once readers get this, they realize that what the scribes and Pharisees do in this story is what evil does: it condemns the guiltless (12:7), blasphemes the Holy Spirit (12:31), neglects the weightier matters of the law (23:23), and so forth. Matthew's implied readers are not expected to draw historical conclusions about scribes and Pharisees from this story, but they are expected to come to an understanding of the nature of evil. They are expected to recognize that evil tends to be hypocritical, masquerading as good (23:27–28); that evil involves unwitting self-deception, failing to recognize its own duplicity (15:14; 23:16–22); that evil perverts what otherwise would be good, ignoring motives or outcomes (6:2, 5, 16).

Since we have touched on the topic of anti-Semitism in Matthew, let me acknowledge that this Gospel has in fact been interpreted throughout history in ways that denigrate Jewish people and their ancestors. It is largely because of Matthew's Gospel that most modern dictionaries list one definition of *Pharisee* as "a hypocrite." Simply to identify such interpretations as unexpected readings does not solve the problems they engender nor does it absolve the narrative of responsibility for them. The anti-Semitic readings, unfortunately, are not necessarily misinterpretations. Even if the main point of the author's negative characterization of Jewish leaders was to reflect on the quality of evil, the fact that the characters who personify this quality are Jewish leaders does carry interpretive baggage. An analogy may be drawn to the cowboy and Indian movies discussed previously (pages 9–10). Personally, I doubt that the folks who made these movies intended in any primary sense to disparage Native Americans; they probably just wanted to have good guys and bad guys for their tale and, since cowboys were the former, Indians seemed a logical choice for the latter. Nevertheless, the incredible insensitivity involved in that simple decision had far-reaching ethical consequences. Whatever the intentions of their producers, the movies may justly be blamed for employing stereotypes that easily lent themselves to referential interpretations. Likewise, Matthew's narrative does display an inherent prejudice against Jewish leaders, one that has lent itself easily to referential inferences about Jewish people in the real world.[184] Thus, by explicating the expected effect of such characterization on the narrative's implied readers, I do not in any way intend to let the real author (or his real readers) off the hook for what they have done. I do, however, think that recognizing the expected effect of the story on implied readers may help to redeem it for some real readers who would otherwise have to reject it outright.

To continue on a tangent (albeit a different one) for just a bit longer, this seems to be the best place to discuss a recent work by Petri Merenlahti and Raimo Hakola that uses my narrative-critical analysis of the Jewish leaders in Matthew as an example par excellence of what is wrong with narrative criticism:[185]

> [Powell thinks that] the fact that Matthew's Gospel has aroused hostility towards Jewish religious leaders, and toward the Jews in general, is based on a misreading. . . . Powell's suggestion that the function of Matthew's portrayal of the Jewish leaders is exclusively rhetorical calls forth serious questions: Is this a natural way to read such narratives as the Gospel? Are readers supposed to think that the Jewish religious leaders, as well as other characters in the Gospel, including Jesus, do not "stand for" any real people? Have all those who have connected Matthew's portrait of the leaders to some Jewish groups outside the story . . . indeed been misreading the narrative? The answer to all these questions is obvious enough: Powell is grossly misreading Matthew by reading the Gospel as he would read a fictional narrative. The natural way to read a Gospel. . . .[186]

I don't think these good people really understand what narrative criticism is or what it seeks to do; at least, I don't think they understand what *I* mean by narrative criticism when I present this example as an illustration of the reading strategy.[187] First, I do *not* think that (referential) readings that view Matthew's Gospel as arousing anti-Semitism are misreadings or misinterpretations. Indeed, it is possible that such readings are absolutely correct. I certainly do not think that the function of Matthew's portrayal of these leaders is "exclusively rhetorical." I am sure that Matthew's original, intended readers (historical people in the first century) were supposed to regard the characters in the story as representative of real people, and I am just as certain that most readers today also do so. I have never proposed and do not now think that people who connect the Jewish leaders in Matthew's story with Jewish groups outside the story are misreading the narrative. Rather, I proposed and still do propose that while it is possible and legitimate to read Matthew's Gospel as a referential narrative (from the perspective of its original, intended readers), it is also possible to read it as a nonreferential story (from the perspective of its implied readers)—and I think that it is at least aesthetically interesting and perhaps theologically relevant to do so. Reading a text in one way does not have to invalidate reading it in all other ways.[188]

But what is all this about "the natural way to read a Gospel"? And why is "Powell grossly misreading Matthew" when he does not read the book according to the acceptable strategy that Merenlahti and Hakola think they have discerned? The (slightly) implicit assumption is that there is only one worthwhile goal that all readers of a text such as Matthew's Gospel ought to pursue: discernment of the message that the author wished to convey to his or her original audience. Anything else would be unnatural.[189]

We have returned to a point that I raised in the Introduction: historical criticism and literary criticism pursue diverse goals. Indeed, different varieties of historical and literary criticism pursue different subgoals. There is no integrity in condemning one approach because it does not meet the goals of a different approach.[190] A long time ago—in the very book that Merenlahti and Hakola are critiquing—I suggested that different approaches to biblical interpretation may be likened to keys on a ring: "The various keys open different doors and grant access to different types of insight. Narrative criticism has been able to open some doors . . . but it will not open all the doors."[191] The example's a bit simplistic, I suppose, but it works. Merenlahti and Hakola are only interested in one set of doors—historical, referential, author-oriented ones. They want to "reconceive narrative criticism" so that it will better fit the locks that open those doors. I've certainly got no problem with that, and I just might add their RNC (reconceived narrative criticism) to my own key ring as well.[192] I'm just not willing to hand over my old NC key to get it. Truth is, it still fits very nicely in those doors that they either don't care about or don't even know exist.

Now, we have been off on a tangent. To come back to task, let me affirm that the immediately relevant point arising from my description of the Jewish leaders in Matthew is not the ethical question of whom Matthew chose to represent good and evil in his story or whether those representations can or should also be read referentially. Rather, the immediately relevant point is that Matthew's narrative *assumes an evaluative infrastructure according to which orientations may be identified as basically positive or negative.* Thoughts, actions, ideas, beliefs, traits, perspectives . . . all may be viewed as "good" or "bad." This evaluative system, furthermore, is presented as applicable for the world of the story and in that sense is not regarded as cultural but almost literally as "universal." If such a standard is contextual at all, it is such only insofar as it is limited to a literary context rather than to a spatial or temporal one—it holds true for the entire universe that forms the setting of this particular story.

We can be more specific about this universal, transcendent evaluative system that undergirds Matthew's story. It is grounded in divine standards that are not subject to human inquiry. In Matthew's narrative, whatever is of God is to be evaluated positively and whatever is not of God is to be evaluated negatively.[193] This is, ultimately, the only necessary determining factor for what is good or right or true. Consider Jesus' famous rebuke of Peter: "Get behind me Satan! You are a stumbling block to me; for you are setting your mind not on divine things, but on human things" (16:23). Readers are expected to evaluate Peter negatively in this instance because, whatever his intent, he is not oriented toward God. There is no middle ground. To think "human things" (as opposed to divine things) is to be identified with Satan. The universal value system undergirding Matthew's narrative assumes that God defines what is true and what is good and what is right. Readers are expected to evaluate positively only that which is of God.

Many modern readers may have difficulty submitting to such a rhetorical construct, to accepting the point of view ascribed to God as normative and, therefore, beyond debate. Critical readers may suspect that the author is presenting his own ideas as the perspective of God, and they may be right. Resistant readers may object that such a rhetorical move amounts to a power play according to which the author can avoid accountability—whatever opinions are ascribed to God must be accepted for no other reason than that they are ascribed to God. Again, they may be right. We can object to the narrative's rhetoric all we want, and we can reject its message or denounce the effect that it is expected to have on us, once we determine what that effect is. We cannot do this, however—we cannot determine the meaning of the story in terms of its expected effect on its implied readers—without first willingly suspending our disbeliefs and accepting that the point of view of God is definitive for all truth. All truth within this story, that is.

If we want to determine the effect that Matthew's narrative is expected to have on its implied readers we may need to pretend to believe differently than we actually do. We need to ask, "How would a reader who does *not* think there is anything wrong with slavery respond to this story?" "How does a reader who accepts that these scribes and Pharisees are children of the evil one respond to this story?" "How does a reader who evaluates everything in light of the point of view that is here ascribed to God respond to this story?" Such a reading strategy does not protect the narrative from our evaluative critique—it only delays such critique until we have dealt fully with the narrative on its own terms and determined the effect that it is ultimately expected to have. Sometimes, at least, such a determination might help to shape our critique, allowing us to offer it in terms of "the big picture" rather than simply harping on what turn out to be minor (though perhaps not insignificant) points.

The Reader's Education with Regard to Beliefs and Values

Matthew's narrative is obviously interested in shaping and affecting the values and beliefs of its readers. This is probably true for all narratives, but it is overtly true of Matthew's Gospel, where the protagonist's principal activity is offering moral instruction and the plot's principal conflict developments concern debates over ethical conduct. We may distinguish, then, between values that readers are assumed to have and those that they are expected to acquire. In literary categories, this may be expressed in terms of a tension between the implied author and the implied readers,[194] between how the narrative suggests readers *ought to think* (the perspective of the implied author) and how the narrative seems to assume readers *actually do think* (the perspective of the implied readers).

The belief that Jesus is the Messiah is not necessarily part of the repertoire of what Matthew's implied readers are assumed to bring to this story. Those readers are, however, expected to come to believe this after reading the first line. Why? Because the narrator says that Jesus is the Messiah, and the narrator is assumed to be reliable.[195] Matthew's readers are also expected to come to believe that Jesus is the Son of God. Why? Because God speaks directly from heaven and says, "This is my Son" (3:17). God's point of view is normative for this story, and whatever God says is by definition true. Readers are not expected to wonder whether God might be mistaken or lying. If God says Jesus is God's Son, then readers are expected to believe that he is.[196]

These are basic examples of how Matthew's implied readers are educated by the narrative, instructed to believe certain things that they are not necessarily assumed to believe otherwise. The beliefs that Jesus is the Messiah and Son of God are not intrinsic to the context that produced this narrative (as is the preference of honor to shame), nor are they assumed by the narrative's rhetoric (as is the reliability of the narrator and the reliability of God). Rather, they are dictated by that rhetoric; they are truths that the readers must be told apply for this story.

Once Jesus is established as a reliable character, he is able to function almost at the same level as God or the narrator. Matthew's implied readers come to accept what Jesus says as true also, and they are expected to accept the legitimacy of the values that Jesus evinces. When Jesus says that the poor in spirit are blessed (5:3) or that no one can serve both God and mammon (6:24), Matthew's implied readers are expected to believe these revelations are true. Thus, the readers' repertoire is expanded through the act of reading—beliefs and values taught within the narrative are added to those that are presupposed for it.

Things get interesting when the two categories conflict, when the narrative teaches values that are not simply intended to supplement what implied readers are expected to believe but to correct or challenge what they are expected to believe. So, when Peter asks Jesus how many times he should forgive someone who sins against him—"as many as seven times?"—implied readers are probably expected to regard this as generous. They are expected to be a bit shocked when Jesus responds, "Not seven times, but I tell you, seventy-seven times" (18:21–22). The rhetorical effectiveness of the story depends on such shock value. The story presupposes readers who are not already clued in to Jesus' radical ethic of unlimited forgiveness and who might therefore regard Peter's offer as stingy.

There is an analogy between the rhetoric of value formation used in this example and the rhetoric of suspense used in mystery stories. The latter is spoiled for readers who already know how the story is going to turn out. In the same way, readers who already believe what the narrative intends to reveal are not likely to be affected by the story the way that implied readers are expected to be affected by it. They may "get the point" but they do not "experience the impact." What real readers can do in both cases is use their imaginations to simulate the expected effect as closely as possible. They pretend they don't know how the mystery is going to turn out, and they pretend they believe, like Peter, that offering to forgive someone seven times is incredibly generous. That way, they are surprised anew each time the killer is revealed or each time they hear Jesus declare that their best offer falls far short of what God requires.

I indicated previously that many scholars believe a primary value (perhaps *the* primary value) for the world that produced Matthew's Gospel was the positive assessment of honor: acquisition of honor was a worthy goal, while loss of honor (acquisition of shame) was to be avoided at all costs. Jerome Neyrey has demonstrated the extent to which this cultural value from the discourse setting of Matthew's narrative is assumed within the world of the story. On one level, all of the characters, the narrator, the implied author, and the implied readers are all assumed to think this way. On the other hand, Neyrey also notes the peculiar way in which Matthew's narrative deconstructs its own assumed value system. In the Beatitudes (5:3–12), Jesus honors the dishonored. In the Antitheses (5:21–48), he summons his disciples to "call off the honor game," to forswear the pivotal cultural value of their social world. And in his teaching on the hypocritical practice of piety (6:1–8), Jesus calls on his followers to withdraw completely from the field of public approval and to gain favor with God by performing their honorable acts in secret.[197] Jesus, who is shown to be an eminently honorable figure, who repeatedly bests his opponents in matches to determine who will acquire more honor, is ironically portrayed as an individual who does not ultimately value the honor he obtains. In this sense, the readers' assumed value system is not so much rejected as it is critiqued "from within," that is, critiqued in a way that can perhaps only be understood by those who possess such a value system in the first place. The narrative both presupposes and challenges the readers' evaluation of honor and shame.

This rhetoric of value formation often uses characters in a narrative as foils for reader identification. Certain characters voice opinions that implied readers are assumed to harbor, which gives occasion for these to be challenged by a more reliable character. Essentially, a dialogue is set up between the implied author and the implied readers. In Matthew, the disciples of Jesus may sometimes become the voice for the implied readers, and Jesus, the voice of the implied author. The dialogue, however, is certainly not between equal partners; instruction in appropriate beliefs and values typically goes in only one direction. But the narrative rhetoric of Matthew does not always work this way, and we should not assume that readers are always expected to empathize with the disciples. At times, implied readers are clearly expected to distance themselves from the disciples.[198] For instance, when people are bringing children to Jesus and the disciples try to prevent it, readers are certainly expected to remember that Jesus told these same disciples, "whoever welcomes one such child in my name, welcomes me" (18:5; 19:13–14). In such an instance, I think Matthew's implied readers are expected to be aghast at the disciples' stupidity and wonder how they could get things so wrong. The rhetorical function of such an incident is confirmation. The implied readers are pleased to discover that they learned the lesson better than the disciples did, and the self-commendation they experience on this account rewards them in a way that is expected to establish the value even more firmly.

Let us now consider an episode in Matthew's story that is often considered "a difficult text" for modern audiences—the encounter of Jesus and the Canaanite woman in 15:21–29:

> [Jesus] went away to the district of Tyre and Sidon. Just then a Canaanite woman from that region came out and started shouting, "Have mercy on me, Lord, Son of David; my daughter is tormented by a demon." But he did not answer her at all. And his disciples came and urged him, saying, "Send her away, for she keeps shouting after us." He answered, "I was sent only to the lost sheep of the house of Israel." But she came and knelt before him, saying, "Lord, help me." He answered, "It is not fair to take the children's food and throw it to the dogs." She said, "Yes, Lord, yet even the dogs eat the crumbs that fall from their masters' table." Then Jesus answered her, "Woman, great is your faith! Let it be done for you as you wish." And her daughter was healed instantly.

Practically every line of this passage is subject to some sort of interpretive dispute, and this is not the place to entertain all the notions that have been advanced.[199] Still, we can probably say without controversy that the passage troubles modern readers because it seems to depict Jesus as reluctant to help a person in need. Indeed, Jesus seems to humiliate the poor woman, comparing her to a dog that does not deserve to get what is intended for children. It helps only a little that he eventually relents, after she accepts his humiliating analogy and claims indeed to be just a dog looking for crumbs of mercy that might fall on the floor.

I suspect that Matthew's implied readers are expected to find this story troubling as well—but for different reasons. I suspect that the story is supposed to be shocking not because Jesus initially refuses to help this woman, but because he eventually *does* help her—and even praises her as a person of great faith. The woman is a Canaanite, a representative of people whom the implied readers are assumed to despise, of people whom, according to the scriptures, God once apportioned for genocide in the world's first divinely sponsored ethnic-cleansing campaign. If God's will had been done, such people would not even exist. They *should* not exist; they have no right to be here, in the land that God gave to Israel (see Josh. 3:9–10; 12:7–8; 17:17–18; Judg. 1:1–10, 27–33; 3:1–4).

Can this really be the case? Does Matthew's narrative presuppose anti-Canaanite prejudice? Well, the word *Canaanite* is not used elsewhere in this narrative, but the umbrella term *Gentile* is (a Canaanite is one type of Gentile). Let's look at how that word is used:

- In 5:47, Jesus tells his disciples, "If you greet only your brothers and sisters, what more are you doing than others? Do not even the Gentiles do the same?" The word *Gentiles* is used in parallel structure to the word *tax collectors* in the preceding verse ("Do not even the tax collectors do the same?")
- In 6:7, Jesus tells his disciples, "When you are praying, do not heap up empty phrases as the Gentiles do; for they think they will be heard because of their many words." The word *Gentiles* is used in parallel structure to the word *hypocrites* in the preceding verse ("whenever you pray, do not be like the hypocrites").
- In 6:25–32, Jesus tells his disciples, "Do not worry about your life, what you will eat or what you will drink, or about your body, what you will wear . . . for it is the Gentiles who strive for all these things; and indeed your heavenly Father knows that you need all these things."
- In 10:5–6, Jesus sends his disciples out on a healing mission to "cure the sick, raise the dead, cleanse the lepers, cast out demons" (10:8). He tells them, "Go nowhere among the Gentiles, and enter no town of the Samaritans, but go rather to the lost sheep of the house of Israel." Here, the word *Gentiles* is in parallel structure to *Samaritans*.
- In 10:18, Jesus warns his disciples, "[Y]ou will be dragged before governors and kings because of me, as a testimony to them and the Gentiles." Here, Gentiles (along with "governors and kings") are cited as one example of wolves into whose midst Jesus' disciples are sent as sheep (10:16).
- In 18:17, Jesus concludes his instructions to the disciples on how to deal with unrepentant sinners by saying, "[I]f the offender refuses to listen even to the church, let such a one be to you as a Gentile and a tax collector." Again *Gentile* is parallel to *tax collector.* Notably, the only other word with which *tax collector* is sometimes paired is *prostitute* (21:31–32).
- In 20:25–26, Jesus tells his disciples, "You know that the rulers of the Gentiles lord it over them, and that their great ones are tyrants over them. It will not be so among you."

Gentiles are associated with vanity, tyranny, and sin. Even their best behavior is self-serving. God does not want to hear their long-winded prayers or heal their diseases. They can pretty much be put in the same class with hypocrites, traitors, and whores—people who implied readers are expected to despise.

So, yes, I do think that Matthew's Gospel presupposes an anti-Gentile bias.[200] The implied readers are expected to regard Gentiles in general as disgusting and disgraceful, as people whose beliefs, values, and especially behavior are condemned by God and abominable to all godly people. If we want to be more specific, we might recognize that there are different types of Gentiles (Romans, Greeks, Ethiopians, etc.) but, then, I would have to guess that Canaanites would be the worst of the lot. These, as I have indicated, are ones that God has decreed in scripture have no right or reason to live.

Let me be clear on this. I am not simply saying that Matthew's implied readers are expected to think that Canaanites are awful people; I am saying that they are expected to believe that Jesus also thought this way and that he was right to do so. Are we expected to regard Jesus as a bigot? No, because within the perspective of this narrative, knowing the truth about Canaanites does not qualify as bigotry. Canaanites *are* awful people and knowing this simply makes one knowledgeable, not prejudiced. The abominable character of Gentiles in general and of Canaanites in particular is part of the reality of Matthew's story world. If we don't want to think of Gentiles or Canaanites that way when we are not reading the story, we don't have to, but if we want to determine how this narrative is expected to affect its implied readers, then we need to accept its perspective on Gentiles and Canaanites as the way things are in the world of this story.

Assuming, then, that we accept this perspective, how will the story affect us? When this woman starts "shouting" at Jesus and his disciples in what appears to be a most annoying fashion, will we not regard her as terribly presumptuous? She even dares to address him as "the Son of David"! What right has she to do this? By what wild stretch of the imagination can God's promises to David be construed as applying to Canaanites? What arrogance! But, then, isn't it just like Canaanites to try to usurp for themselves what God has promised to Israel? They are like dogs hovering around the table—if you don't watch them, they'll dart right in and steal the children's food. Jesus puts her in her place, as well as he should. But, then, we discover that she accepts this status. She is not arrogant. She regards Canaanites the same way we do, the same way Jesus does. She knows she's just a dog, but she isn't after the children's food at all. She's just looking for crumbs that might fall her way. She wants to be an *exception*—like the Canaanite prostitute Rahab, who ended up being the great-great grandmother of David (1:5–6).

This seems to fit with a bigger picture. Earlier in Matthew's narrative, Gentile pagans from the East were brought by God to worship Jesus at his birth (2:1–12). A Roman centurion sought and received healing from Jesus for his servant (8:5–13). In those instances—like this one—the humiliation of the Gentiles was stressed. I can hardly imagine a more humiliating image (given the assumed cultural values) than that of men prostrating themselves—lying face down in the dirt—before a woman and a child (2:11; English translations some-times soften this with "knelt down" or "paid homage"). Or that of a Roman mil-itary officer telling a Jewish peasant, "I am not worthy to have you come under my roof" (8:8). These are scenes of exceptional Gentiles who recognize their lowly place in God's scheme.

But something else is going on here as well. The Gentile pagans who worship this Jewish Messiah are directly contrasted with Jewish leaders who do not (2:3–6). The Gentile centurion's faith is said to surpass what is found in Israel (8:10). And now, this Canaanite woman is said to have "great faith," a sure con-trast to the "little faith" evinced by Jesus' own disciples (6:30; 8:26; 14:31; 16:8; 17:20). As the reign of heaven draws near (4:17), signs of godliness—repen-tance, faith, and worship—seem to be popping up in the oddest places. God's rule is touching tax-collectors, prostitutes, and other sinners (9:10–13; 21:31–32). It is even touching Gentiles, even Canaanite Gentiles. This is not evidence that Canaanites aren't really so bad after all, but, rather, it is evidence that God's power and mercy surpass all human expectations. John the Baptist said that God could create children of Abraham out of stones (3:9). Jesus will testify that God can bring praise from the mouths of nursing babies (21:16, quoting Ps. 8:2). Is it any greater miracle, then, for God to put faith in the heart of a Canaanite? Perhaps it is—since even Jesus seems surprised[201]—but, in any case, Matthew's implied readers are expected to realize that such a miracle has occurred, one that expands their concept of God, of faith, of mercy . . . and, ultimately, inevitably, of Gentiles, too.

The implied readers are expected to be *educated* by what happens here. The narrative presupposes a strong anti-Gentile bias but then challenges and cri-tiques its own presuppositions. It does not, in my mind, eliminate the bias. It does not question the accuracy of what readers are assumed to believe about Gentiles; in fact, it seems to accept all of this without question. But, the implied readers discover that God seems to care for these Gentiles, disgusting though they may be, and God's mercy and power apparently extends to them in almost unanticipated ways. I say, "almost," because, after all, the scriptures did speak of God's servant, the Messiah, as one who would "proclaim justice to the Gentiles" and as one in whose name "the Gentiles will hope" (Matt. 12:18, 21; cf. Isa. 42:1–4). But now, in some instances, the faith of Gentiles is actually surpassing that of God's chosen people Israel. "How can this be?" implied readers are expected to ask, and they get no answer. But it is happening all the same. And what does it mean? Neither the implied author nor the implied readers seem to have figured that out yet—beyond the obvious conclusion that from now on disciples will have to be made from *all* nations (28:19).

This may not be what we would want. Personally, I would like to discover that the apparent anti-Gentile perspective in Matthew was just a ruse. I'd like to think that the implied author was playing with readers' prejudices only to deconstruct and denounce them completely. It would be so nice if by the end of this story readers were led to repent of their former biases and embrace all peo-ples of the earth with some twenty-first-century ideal of egalitarianism. I don't think the implied readers are expected to do that. But, I do think they are expected to realize that God's reach transcends their prejudices—even the legitimate ones! The implied readers are expected to conclude, "God chooses people we would reject and does not pause to get our approval first. The seed that is sown sometimes bears fruit where it shouldn't. Faith, worship, repentance . . . all crop up in the unlikeliest of places and all we can do is be surprised."

We are talking about the rhetoric of value formation, about the ways in which a narrative presupposes certain values on the part of its readers and then seeks to shape these through the reading process. Almost by definition, the formative process will be moderate. The implied author's appeal to the readers must assume a common value base. To recognize how implied readers' values are supposed to be shaped, then, we must first recognize what the pre-shaped values are assumed to be.

Let us move on to a brief discussion of gender in Matthew. The story of the Canaanite woman allows a convenient segue, for she is not only a Gentile but also a woman. Is the readers' antipathy for her expected to be intensified by this fact? I suspect that it is. In the world that formed the discourse setting for this narrative, it was not considered proper for women to initiate conversations with men in public. In Matthew's Gospel, in fact, this woman is the only one ever to do so: compare her "shouting" at Jesus and his disciples to the demure approach of Mrs. Zebeddee, who comes to Jesus, prostrates herself before him, and refrains from speaking until he asks, "What do you want?" (20:20–21; and she was accompanied by her sons—his disciples—at the time!). The Canaanite woman is also the only woman ever to request healing from Jesus. Her story makes an interesting comparison to those of the other two women involved in healing narratives.[202] First, there is the healing of Peter's mother-in-law (8:14–15). Jesus sees her lying in bed with a fever and touches her hand, and the fever leaves her; then she gets up and begins to serve him. Notice that she is not so bold as to ask him to heal her (nor is Peter). She is completely passive and, one might add, submissive. Second, there is the healing of the woman with hemorrhages (9:20–22). She doesn't ask for healing either but obtains it by sneaking up behind Jesus and touching the tassels of his prayer shawl. She is not passive but proactive. Still, her surreptitious approach reveals an awareness of (and respect for) convention. She knows better than to ask a favor of this man, and she cleverly seeks a way to obtain what she wants from him without having to do so. Her plan works, we are told, because of her extraordinary faith.

Against such a background, how are readers expected to regard this shouting Canaanite woman? She easily becomes a hero to modern readers, an exemplar of women who will not be denied. But I suspect that Matthew's implied readers are expected to think otherwise. This story presupposes a patriarchal mindset, a view that understands the social superiority of men over women not as the result of unfortunate prejudices but as (divinely ordained?) reality. Men have power and women do not: that is just the way things are. The implied author as well as the implied readers accept such roles without questioning their essential legitimacy, without imagining that something so basic could or should ever be different. Still, the shouting Canaanite woman does end up getting what she wants, and Jesus does praise her as a person of "great faith." The implied readers, not the least surprised by Jesus' initial reaction to her, are expected now to be shocked. And whatever we said before about God transcending ethnicity must also be affirmed with regard to gender. Without challenging the basic patriarchal perspective of its implied readers, Matthew's narrative does introduce parasitic doubts into that mind-set that just might begin to devour it from the inside out.

Feminism remains a foreign perspective, completely unanticipated by the implied author (or real author) of this narrative.[203] Feminist readings of Matthew, accordingly, are by definition unexpected readings (which does not make them wrong). But, I contend, Matthew's implied readers are expected to have their evaluation of gender roles critiqued and challenged within the basic patriarchal mind-set that is presumed for this story world. The critique comes generally through the claim that *God prefers the powerless to the powerful.* The first will be last, and the last first (19:36; 20:16). The one who is least is the greatest of all (20:26–27). At the beginning of the story, Matthew's implied readers are assumed to believe that men are greater than women because men are more powerful than women. By the end of the story, Matthew's implied readers are expected to have come to believe that women are greater than men because men are more powerful than women. Women are greater than men in the same sense that children are greater than adults (18:1–4). This is not feminism, which normally seeks to empower women and often seeks to debunk stereotypical gender roles. But it is a critique of patriarchy from within, a critique that the implied author foists on the implied readers without any sure resolution of where it might lead or what could happen as a result.

In another book, I have contended that Matthew's narrative depicts the church as ultimately being founded by women and grounded in their testimony.[204] In 27:55–56, we learn belatedly that some of Jesus' followers were present to witness the events of his crucifixion. Although his male disciples had deserted him (26:56), many women were present, including the mother of the sons of Zebedee (cf. 20:20) and two women named Mary, neither of whom have been mentioned before. These two Mary's are especially important to Matthew's story because they serve as the primary witnesses to three key events: the death (27:56), burial (27:61), and resurrection (28:1) of Jesus (cf. 1 Cor. 15:3–4). Sure enough, on Easter morning, they come to the tomb early on the third day to see what will happen (28:1). We are apparently expected to assume that they remember Jesus' predictions of a resurrection (16:21; 17:23; 20:19; they do *not* come to anoint the body as in Mark 16:1).[205] Their hopes are fulfilled. A shining angel appears. The women are shown the empty tomb. And then the women are commissioned to regain Jesus' disciples for him, reminding them of what Jesus himself had told them (v. 7; cf. 26:32). In fact, they are commissioned *twice,* first by the angel, then by Jesus himself.

These women are the first to worship the risen Lord and the first to be commissioned by him. Such primacy in worship and mission gives them the role in the church that had originally been offered to Peter (16:18–19). The apostasy of Jesus' male disciples is forgiven, but it costs them the legacy that they might have had. Jesus wills, instead, for his church to be founded by women, established on their faith and experience, and grounded in their proclamation of the gospel. The so-called "Great Commission" is a secondary commission. The unfaithful men cannot be sent to make disciples of all nations until after the faithful women first make disciples of them. Indeed, their calling to preach the gospel is made conditional on their ability to receive the gospel as proclaimed by women. To put it bluntly: if men are not able to accept women's proclamation of the gospel and submit themselves to it, there will be no mission to the nations (at least none carried out by men) and there will be no church (at least no church that includes male believers). The church of Jesus Christ is founded by women, but it may also include men—if the women follow Christ's direction to include men and if the men are willing to accept their inclusion on precisely those terms.[206]

This, again, is not a modern feminist reading of Matthew. It is, I think, the reading expected of Matthew's implied readers, for whom modern feminism is literally unthinkable. Women are not exalted as founders of the church and exemplars of faith because they should be considered "equals." They are so exalted precisely because they are not equals. Women may be the greatest in the kingdom of heaven even if, there, men are still the ones on thrones (19:28).[207] In terms of *repertoire,* Matthew's readers are assumed to evince a patriarchal mind-set that regards men as intrinsically more powerful than women. In terms of *education,* Matthew's implied readers are not brought to question this assumption but to question something even more fundamental: the positive evaluation of power. Men are more powerful than women, but *power is not necessarily a good thing.*

PART THREE
MATTHEW'S MAGI
(AN EXTENDED CASE STUDY)

*But as we mix in with the first devotees at the crib of Bethlehem,
we enter the realm of social and political experience.*
—Richard C. Trexler[208]

Here is what we've done so far: In Part One of this book, I suggested that a) biblical texts may legitimately mean different things to different people but that
b) these diverse interpretations may be identified as expected or unexpected
readings, based on an analysis of textual dynamics as understood through the
reading strategy called *narrative criticism.* In Part Two, I gave a fairly detailed
account of what such a reading strategy may entail. I asked, "How can we identify the expected responses of implied readers to a text such as the Gospel of
Matthew?" My answer focused on discerning what appear to be presuppositions
of the text. My analysis of these allowed me to reformulate the above question
more precisely: "How might (imaginary) readers be expected to respond to this
text if they read it completely, from beginning to end, knowing what they are
expected to know and believing what they are expected to believe?" I tried to
provide several examples of how such readers might be expected to respond. The
time has come now for a more extensive and detailed illustration, one that I
hope will clarify some matters that remain obscure and one that will also bring
us closer to answering that very important question: "So what?"

For those who care, what I have been offering in this volume is a somewhat
amateurish *postmodern phenomenology of reading.* If I had used that phrase on
page one, I suspect I would have lost a few of you, but let's use it now and
unpack it. A phenomenology of reading is simply a scholarly analysis of what
happens when people read: what sort of interpretive moves do they make—and
why? My presentation of narrative criticism in the foregoing chapters (or in my
prior book on the subject[209]) was not offered as a description of how people
should read but as a tool that may enable us to understand better how people
actually *do* read. My presentation is postmodern in that it does not envision that

there is any intrinsically correct way to read texts or that there is any ideologically neutral way of analyzing them. It is also somewhat amateurish in that I am not trying to establish any solid philosophical underpinnings for what I do, nor am I interested in trying to account for everything involved in the reading process. Aware of my limitations, I am content to account for *some* things, for matters that are of concern to me and to the people with whom I converse. I also admit that these concerns may ultimately be driven by theological interests. I am not just interested in the Gospel of Matthew as literature, and it would be deceptive to pretend that I am. I guess that I am ultimately interested in developing a postmodern phenomenology of reading texts *as scripture.* This book will not get us all the way there, but it makes a good start—and I hope it will be of partial use even to those who do not share my interest in theology.

So why does any of this matter? I know people who will probably like much of this book because they believe that the reading expected of the implied readers is the hermeneutically correct understanding of the text. Thus, to the extent that I have enhanced our ability to discern that reading, I have contributed to the exegetical goal of determining what texts mean. Likewise, I know people who believe that the meaning intended by the author represents the hermeneutically correct understanding of any text and yet, since a reading expected of implied readers may be an index of authorial intent, they too may feel that I have contributed to the exegetical task in an indirect way. Well, if you are one of these people and you have bought and/or read my book (thus far), I am grateful to you, but I do not agree with you regarding the significance of my work. As I have indicated previously, I think the boon of such analysis lies primarily in increased self-awareness of our role in the reading process. This point, I hope, will become increasingly clear in the chapters that follow. We will now witness how unexpected readings of a popular text have developed and observe how these are revelatory not only of exegetical dynamics regarding the text itself but also of social dynamics regarding the world(s) that has (have) interpreted it.

With all this as background, let us turn to Matthew's story of the magi. In the first volume of his magisterial commentary on the Gospel of Matthew, Ulrich Luz discovers that the interpretive scheme he calls *Wirkungsgeschichte* yields a particularly interesting result in his analysis of 2:1–12, the story of the magi. Typically, Luz believes that contemporary understanding of texts is aided through attention to their "history of influence" (which is what the word *Wirkungsgeschichte* means). Such attention furnishes correctives that may remind us of the full potential for meaning, aid in ecumenical understanding, and broaden our horizons.[210] But with regard to this passage, he admits, the history of the influence of the text turns out to be a "history of its lack of influence."[211]

Perhaps no other passage in Matthew has been subject to as much interpretive growth as this one. Legends concerning the magi abound, providing them with names, making them kings, designating their countries of origin, describing their physical appearance, and reporting on such extrabiblical occurrences as their return journey, their conversions, and their deaths. In the Middle Ages, a cult of relics concerning the magi arose. As saints, they were also assigned protective functions, some of which survive in popular piety today. In Spain, Argentina, Venezuela, Puerto Rico, and most areas of Mexico, the magi fill the role elsewhere assumed by St. Nicholas, giving gifts to children in honor of Jesus' birth.[212]

Besides invading the secular realm, the magi managed early to intrude on Lukan ground, securing a place for themselves at the manger in traditional art and music.[213] Matthean scholars may insist that this is blatantly unscriptural—the first evangelist indicates that the magi find the baby Jesus in a house (2:11)—and Lukan scholars may object that the magi are not only absent from the third Gospel but would have been quite unwelcome there. It makes no difference. What church would present a Christmas pageant or display a creche without "the three wise men"? Though, of course, Matthew does not say that they are three,[214] or that they are wise, or even that they are men.[215]

Luz observes that "the discrepancy between the biblical text and popular piety is thought-provoking."[216] I agree, and I believe the thoughts that it provokes may contribute to another benefit of *Wirkungsgeschichte* that Luz articulates in the introduction to his commentary. He suggests that, in addition to the advantages mentioned above, the history of influence may "clarify what we have become on the basis of the texts" and "help us understand *how* each interpreter is influenced by the texts" (emphasis his).[217] In this regard, the interests of *Wirkungsgeschichte* concur with those of reader-response criticism. Matthew's story of the magi provides a stellar example for testing this thesis.[218]

I am going to limit our discussion to two sample perceptions, namely the identification of the magi as kings and as wise men. Although Matthew does not explicitly attribute royalty or wisdom to the magi, the history of interpretation has often done so. Taken together, the two perceptions are revealing, furthermore, because the first is almost unanimously rejected by modern biblical scholars while the second has been (almost) unanimously accepted by them.

In keeping with the strategy laid out in the first two parts of this book, I now intend to offer what I call a *third-level critique* of these traditions, that is, a critique that engages them at the level of reception. Both traditions have typically been evaluated only at levels of history and redaction and, as such, the critiques that have been offered have been limited.[219]

What I call a *first-level critique* proceeds from the perspective of historical research and seeks only to determine whether an interpretation is historically accurate. For example, the popular tradition that the magi mentioned in Matthew 2 are kings might be judged inaccurate because a wealth of historical data indicates that magi in the ancient world were not in fact kings. Such an evaluation identifies attribution of royalty to the magi as erroneous without addressing the question of whether author or readers are responsible for the error. Thus, a critique at this level is concerned only with getting the facts straight; it offers no insight into the thinking of either Matthew or his readers.

What I call a *second-level critique* proceeds from the perspective of what biblical scholars call redaction criticism and seeks to evaluate an interpretation in terms of authorial intent. In this instance, redaction critics usually claim that neither the evangelist nor his original audience would have attributed royalty to the magi, but that this attribution is a mistake of later Christian tradition. Thus, the identification of magi as kings is still regarded as an error but not simply on factual grounds. The assumption here is that "an erroneous interpretation" is definitively one that violates the intent or understanding of the historical author. An evaluation of this order does decide who is responsible for the mistake (readers, not author) but still offers no real insight into the thinking of Matthew's readers—beyond the superficial observation that they have not understood the story properly.

What I call a *third-level critique* proceeds from the perspective of reader-response analysis, with particular reliance on the approaches of narrative criticism and *Wirkungsgeschichte*. Reader-response critics set aside (at least initially) the question of whether an interpretation is right or wrong and seek instead to discover what the existence of the interpretation reveals—about the text and about those who interpret the text. In this case, reader-response critics will acknowledge that the story of the magi can be read in ways that regard the principal characters as kings (or as wise men). This is an existential fact evident from the history of interpretation. The goals of a third-level critique are not to determine whether a tradition is right or wrong but whether it represents an expected or unexpected reading of the text and to articulate what such a reading reveals about the thinking of the text's readers. The process involved in conducting such a critique may indeed yield interesting insights about the text—even historical insights regarding its author and original audience—but the goal is to determine the extent to which readers who offer a particular interpretation resemble the text's implied readers.

Reader-response critics recognize that interpretation is not ideologically neutral.[220] When a persistent and widespread interpretation of a text can be identified as an unexpected reading, discussion is invited as to why real readers have not received the text in the manner expected of its implied readers. This question is worth considering because, right or wrong, unexpected readings are revelatory, especially when they derive from ideological differences between implied readers and real readers. Richard Trexler concludes from his study of magian traditions that "Christians have historically built into the nativity scene, as they have into other powerful sacred images, their own social and political experiences."[221] We will agree with this conclusion, though on different grounds than the ones he considers.

I propose, in short, an as yet unrecognized corollary to the axiom that expected readings provide an index to the intents of authors. I suggest that *unexpected readings provide an index to the intents of readers*. They provide a mirror that reflects the priorities of readers. So, regardless of whether such readings help us to discover anything about the text, they will often help us to discover something about ourselves. If attention to the history of influence helps us to understand what we have become because of certain texts, then attention to the "lack of influence" may help us to understand what certain texts have become because of us.

In the Introduction, I laid out a four-stage paradigm for engaging varied responses of readers to biblical texts:

- *Identify* the responses of real readers to the text;
- *Compare* these responses of real readers with what appear to be the responses expected of implied readers;
- *Account* for unexpected readings by identifying ambiguities in the narrative and variables in the reading process; and,
- *Evaluate* both expected and unexpected readings to determine whether they should be regarded positively or negatively.

In chapter 7, I will begin to illustrate this paradigm by applying step 1 (very briefly) and step 2 to one prevalent interpretation of Matthew's magi story, namely, that which regards the magi as kings. I will repeat this process in chapter 8, applying the same two steps to a different tradition, that which identifies the magi as wise persons. We will then apply step 3 to both traditions in chapter 9 and step 4 (briefly) to both traditions in chapter 10.[222]

Chapter Seven
The Magi as Kings

The identification of the magi in Matthew 2 as kings is taken for granted in the writings of Caesarius of Arles (d. 542)[223] and in a Syriac work called *Cave of Treasures*.[224] Thus, attribution of royalty to the magi appears to have been established by the onset of the sixth century. Apparently unchallenged for centuries, the tradition finally came in for an ecumenical critique around the time of the Reformation.[225] Luther polemically dismissed the magi's alleged royalty[226]; Calvin labeled the tradition "dubious"[227]; and Maldonado discreetly admitted that it was "less than certain."[228] Thus, even in what is called the pre-critical period, scholars of the Evangelical, Reformed, and Roman churches were united in their skepticism with regard to the identification of the magi as kings. Such misgivings have continued to the present day in which virtually all scholars reject attribution of royalty to the magi.[229] Still, four hundred years of suspicious scholarship have done little to offset the preceding millennium of piety, legend, and tradition. Creches, mosaics, and stained glass windows frequently portray the magi with crowns.[230] Menotti's *Amahl and the Night Visitors* is performed; "We Three Kings of Orient Are" appears in hymnals; and the Epiphany festival is still known in many churches throughout the world as "the Festival of the Three Kings."

The historical fact that magi were not kings (at least in the first century C.E.) seems secure. Our best research indicates that the word *magi* (in Greek *magoi*) was used in the first century with four general meanings.[231] *Magoi* could refer to a) members of a Persian priestly class[232]; b) possessors of supernatural knowledge and power; c) magicians; and d) deceivers or seducers. The first of these probably provides the "technically correct" definition while the latter three represent popular associations that derived from it. We cannot be certain which sense Matthew's implied readers would be expected to assign to the term or, indeed, whether the term might simply be expected to evoke a general sense of foreign culture and religion that encompasses all of these potential meanings. But for our immediate purposes we need only note that *royalty* is not even an option. Historically, at least, magi were not kings.

This is not, however, the end of the matter for a literary study. It would be possible for the magi who are characters in this story to be kings even if magi were not typically kings in the real world. Matthew's narrative does develop in ways that allow readers to identify the magi as kings and still make sense of the story.[233] The question, then, is whether such an identification is actually expected of the implied readers.

Readers who have made such an identification may find implicit warrant for doing so through intertextual connections with the following verses from the Old Testament:

> Nations shall come to your light,
>> and kings to the brightness of your dawn [*anatolē*[234]].
>>> (Isa. 60:3)

> May the kings of Tarshish and of the isles
>> render him tribute [*dōra*],
> may the kings of Sheba and Seba bring gifts [*dōra*].
> May all kings fall down before [*proskyneō*] him,
>> all nations give him service.
>> (Ps. 72:10–11 [LXX Ps. 71:10–11])

Matthew's narrative does not call attention to either of these verses with a formula citation; the narrator does not tell us that the magi are fulfilling these words from scripture. But, as we have noted before (page 99), Matthew's implied readers may be expected to know the Jewish scriptures so well that they can make such connections without explicit prompting—see the allusions to Psalm 69:21 in 27:48 and to Isaiah 53:9 in 27:57–60. But is such a connection expected here?

In chapter 5, we listed three criteria for evaluating whether readers are expected to recognize a proposed intertextual connection (pages 101–02). With regard to *availability*, there is no question that these passages from Isaiah and Psalms were widely known in the world that formed the discourse setting for Matthew's narrative. With regard to *degree of repetition*, the verbal similarities between the text of Matthew and that of the Old Testament are fairly close: the Isaiah passage goes on to say, "They shall bring gold and frankincense" (60:6), and Psalm 72 also says, "May gold of Sheba be given to him" (v. 15). Thus, Isaiah names two of the gifts (gold and frankincense) in a context where those who offer them are drawn by a brightness or luminance that was possibly described by the very word (*anatolē*) used for the star in Matthew's story. The Psalms text mentions one of the gifts (gold) being offered by people who fall prostrate, exactly as the magi do here.[235] Further correspondence might be detected at a basic level of content in that, like Matthew 2, Isaiah 60 and Psalm 72 both describe Gentiles paying homage to God's chosen ruler.

The third criterion I suggested earlier was *thematic coherence*: Is the interpretation gained by presuming that readers notice a proposed intertextual connection consistent with what seems to apply for the narrative as a whole? We must delay discussion of this question, however, until we figure out just what the interpretation obtained by presuming the connection would be. Eventually (pages 146–47), I will propose that three possibilities present themselves, but that only one of these is coherent thematically with Matthew's overall story. That one match will be enough, however, to confirm the likelihood that Matthew's readers are expected to recognize an intertextual allusion to the Jewish scriptures in this story of the magi.

What is significant is that the texts to which the story alludes—both Isaiah 60 and Psalm 72—describe homage and gifts offered by kings. So, if my reasoning is sound, we should assume that Matthew's implied readers are expected to notice that the magi in this story fulfill roles ascribed to kings in the scriptures. Even so, this does not necessarily mean that Matthew's implied readers are expected to regard these magi as persons who literally *are* kings. Intertextual connections in Matthew rarely depend on literal identifications but, more often, establish general similarities between current and prior stories. For instance, the narration concerning the payment of thirty pieces of silver by the chief priests and elders (Matt. 26:15; 27:5) clearly alludes to another story of the payment of a like amount by sheep merchants in Zechariah 11:10–13. Nevertheless, Matthew's implied readers are not thereby expected to regard these chief priests and elders as persons who are literally sheep merchants.

Still, the intertextual allusions in the magi story do present a potential for readers to identify the magi as kings, and this potential has often been realized in the history of interpretation. The attribution of royalty to the magi can be justified as an understandable construal of the narrative rhetoric of this Gospel. But, would the narrative's implied readers be expected to construe it this way? Would readers be likely to actualize the ambiguity in this way apart from the imposition of foreign knowledge or beliefs? To answer these questions, we must consider Matthew's characterization of the magi in light of what the implied readers are expected to know and believe.

What Are Matthew's Implied Readers Expected to Know?

Matthew's implied readers are not only expected to know things that are revealed in the story but are also expected to know some things that would have been considered basic knowledge in the world in which the story was produced. They are presumed to have knowledge relevant to what I call the discourse setting of the narrative (see pages 89–98). This explains why Matthew's implied readers would not take the intertextual allusion to Zechariah 11:10–13 in an overly literal fashion. Matthew's story presupposes readers who know that the chief priests and scribes who governed the temple in Jerusalem were not sheep merchants. By analogy, we may argue that Matthew's implied readers would not identify the magi as kings on the basis of the intertextual allusions previously listed because they are assumed to know that magi are not literally kings and would therefore understand that the allusions suggest a different association.[236] The so-called ambiguity introduced by the comparison between magi and kings is only ambiguous to readers who do not know what they are expected to know.

But we can go further. The intertextual connection does trigger for Matthew's implied readers *some* association of magi with monarchy. If Matthew's implied readers are assumed to know that the connection is not simply one of identification (magi = kings), then what other connection between magi and monarchy might they be expected to make? As background for answering this, we may consider three tiers of information, beginning with the least relevant and moving to the extremely relevant.

Greco-Roman Literature

A comprehensive survey of references to magi in Greco-Roman literature reveals that magi were typically associated with royal courts in the ancient world—but not as kings. Rather, they are almost invariably depicted as *servants of kings*. For instance, Strabo says that they "attend the Persian kings . . . guiding them in their relations with the gods" (15.1.68), and others indicate they had responsibility for educating royal children.[237] Xenophon claims "the college of the magi was instituted (by Cyrus) . . . and has continued in force with each successive king to this day."[238] Indeed, modern historians tend to view this political connection as typical, if not definitive. The particulars of magian religion may have varied with time and place,[239] but magi normally practiced their arts (whatever these were) for the benefit of the monarchs they served. Horsley states outright, "In the Persian empire . . . Magi were the royal priestly assistants of the Great King."[240] Eddy actually hypothesizes that magi were once a royal class whose role had been reduced by conquest. Hence, they hated their servile state, resented their masters, and became the principal proponents of a Persian movement that looked forward to the destruction of Hellenistic rule.[241]

In this regard, we may consider two stories that were well-known in the Greco-Roman world and that connect magi with royalty:

- *The story of Tiridates* is reported by Dio Cassius, Suetonius, and Pliny.[242] Tiridates was the king of Armenia who in 66 C.E. traveled from the east with the sons of three neighboring Parthian rulers to pay homage to Caesar in a manner indicative of worship. In Pliny's account he says, "I have come to you, my god, to pay homage, as I do to Mithras." At one point, Pliny refers to Tiridates and his group as magi, and he goes on to relate how they initiate Nero into their magical rites. Thus, we do have here an exception to the general observation that magi are not identified with kings, but it may be the exception that proves the rule. The point seems to be that King Tiridates and his princes are magi *in relation to Nero*. Even though Tiridates is a king in Armenia, when he comes to Rome he becomes (while there) a court servant of Nero.

- *The story of Gaumata* is reported by Herodotus, Justin, Strabo, and Ctesias and is referred to by many other writers including Josephus.[243] Gaumata was a magus who with the aid of his fellow magi revolted against the Achaemenid king Cambyses in the fifth century B.C.E. and for a time successfully established a government. Gaumata was subsequently killed by Darius I and the anniversary of his death became the occasion for a festival known as "The Slaughter of the Magi." Observance of this festival kept alive the tradition, such that even in the first century C.E. the story of Gaumata probably remained the best-known narrative concerning magi in the Roman empire.

The first of these tales concerns a king who becomes a magus and the second, a magus who for a short time becomes a king. Still, the lasting impression these stories convey is not identification of magi and monarchy, but disassociation of the concepts. One cannot be magus and king simultaneously. Tiridates realizes this; Gaumata does not and—precisely because of his aspirations and fate—becomes a symbol of magi as the antithesis of royal power. The Roman historian Herodotus tells us that Gaumata's death was mourned by all Asia and that when the Slaughter of the Magi festival was observed, no magus was allowed to show his face.[244] Such a prohibition reveals awareness of a popular identification of magi as opponents and ultimately victims of royal oppression. This story of magi as victims of tyranny, furthermore, is by no means unique. Aristobulus and Strabo report how Alexander had the magian attendants of Cyrus's tomb put under torture during a trial of a Persian satrap falsely accused of having rifled that tomb.[245] Indeed, casual references to such treatment of magi by their overlords abound in the relatively sparse body of literature that mentions them.

But how does this serve our purposes? I do not think we can assume that Matthew's implied readers are expected to have read Strabo or Aristobulus or Pliny or Herodotus. We cannot even say for certain that Matthew's implied readers would be expected to know the stories they report (though this would be more likely). Still, the stories do reveal how magi were viewed in the broad social context that forms the discourse setting for this narrative and what it reveals seems worthy of note. There is not a single story to be found anywhere in that broad context that depicts magi as powerful figures, much less as kings. There are only stories that depict them as servants of powerful figures and often as victims of abuse on account of their servile status. This, I think, is interesting.

Jewish Midrash

The perception that magi were typically thought of as servants of kings is confirmed when we turn to stories that derive from the more narrow discourse setting for the narrative—the world of Judaism. Jewish midrash[246] on the story of the exodus and on the story of Balaam both introduce magi into the biblical tradition. Both stories, furthermore, display remarkable parallels to Matthew's narrative:

- *The exodus midrash* identifies the sorcerers in Pharaoh's court as magi.[247] Biblical references to these sorcerers may be found in Exodus 7:11, 22; 8:6, 18–19; 9:11. In the midrash, then, magi are once more portrayed as servants of an earthly ruler. In fact, they are portrayed as servants of an *evil* ruler who, like Herod in Matthew's story, orders a massacre of male children (Exod. 1:22; Matt. 2:16).
- *The Balaam midrash* identifies the hapless prophet by that name as a magus.[248] In Numbers 22–24, Balaam is summoned by an evil king who seeks to elicit his aid in destroying God's chosen ones. As such, Balaam's position seems to parallel that of the magi in Matthew's story and, in both cases, the royal figure's exploitation of the magi is thwarted through divine intervention.

Again, we see that the two concepts "magi" and "kings" are related in these stories but that the connection is not one of identification. The people referred to as magi in these tales are not kings but servants. Indeed, the magi in these stories are emphatically people who lack political power or even personal power for self-determination.[249]

We cannot say for certain that Matthew's implied readers are expected to know these stories.[250] Nevertheless, insofar as they reflect thinking typical of the discourse setting of Matthew's narrative, they offer general impressions of how Matthew's readers might be expected to view the relationship between magi and kings. The witness of Jewish midrash is that magi were indeed typically associated with royal courts but that they were regarded as rather lowly servants of those who ruled. This is compatible with the witness from the Gentile world, which indicates that magi were sometimes viewed as victims of tyranny, as persons whose status as servants was dictated to them by powerful figures who used fear and intimidation to keep them in their place. Both of these impressions are confirmed in another very important source, the Septuagint text of Daniel 2.

The Jewish Scriptures

There is only one text that refers to magi that we can be certain Matthew's readers are expected to know. In the second chapter of the book of Daniel, we find the only references to magi in the Jewish scriptures themselves (the word *magoi* is used in vss. 2, 10).[251] I argued in chapter 5 that Matthew's implied readers are expected to know the Jewish scriptures (pages 98–100), and I do not think this point is controversial. I'm yet to meet anyone who disagrees with it. But, just to be on the safe side: even if someone does want to contend that Matthew's readers should not be expected to know all of the Jewish scriptures, we are on unbelievably sure ground in assuming that they are expected to know the book of Daniel. In Matthew 24:15, the narrator of Matthew's story actually addresses the reader directly, imploring him or her to understand the relevance of the book of Daniel to future events described by Jesus.[252]

So what have we here? We encounter magi who are summoned by King Nebuchadnezzar and commanded to interpret the king's dreams. As in the exodus midrash, these magi are depicted as ineffectual sycophants of the powerful ruler. But there is more. The narrative makes clear that the king's command is an unreasonable order (Dan. 2:10, 27) while also revealing that the consequences associated with it are dire. The king continues, "If you do not tell me both the dream and its interpretation, you shall be torn limb from limb, and your houses shall be laid in ruins" (2:5). The narrative continues by eliciting our sympathy for these magi and their colleagues, as Daniel himself makes intercession for them (2:12–17, 24). Even if we are not expected to approve of the magi's art, we (like Daniel) are to regard them as victims of injustice, specifically at the hand of the king they serve. Far from presenting magi as figures possessing royal power, this narrative (known to Matthew's implied readers!) presents them as servants of a monarch who exercises capricious and total control over their fortunes.[253]

Taken together, all of these stories present a general pattern that allows three conclusions: 1) magi were often associated with royalty in the discourse setting of Matthew's narrative; 2) when magi were associated with royalty in this setting, they were invariably cast in the role of servants to the royal powers; and 3) as servants, magi tended to be represented as relatively powerless individuals whose lowly stature became the subject of sympathy or ridicule. Thus, while I do suspect that Matthew's implied readers are expected to notice an intertextual connection between Matthew 2 and certain scriptural passages that refer to kings, I doubt that they would be expected to conclude that the magi in this story actually are kings. The connection merely allows for some kind of an association with monarchs, and the primary association suggested by the discourse setting of the narrative is that of royal servants, as persons whom the readers are expected to regard as lacking in political or personal power.

Before going further, I want to respond to one objection that I anticipate could be forming already in the mind of my own (real) readers. It may seem that in identifying magi as servants I overemphasize the lowly aspect of their stature. If magi were *royal* servants, they would nevertheless live in palaces and enjoy a lifestyle far above that of the common people. It would then seem better to regard the magi as *retainers,* as persons who possessed limited power and whose social position was ambiguous.[254] I do not dispute the historicity of such an identification. My interest, however, is in how Matthew's implied readers are expected to regard magi, and we are taking as one clue to this the manner in which magi are presented in other literature. The fact is, there are no stories in

which magi are contrasted with commoners in ways that make them appear relatively power*ful.* There are only stories in which they are contrasted with tyrants
in ways that make them appear relatively power*less.* So, if the "lowly" dimension
of their ambiguous status is being overemphasized, I am not the one who is
overemphasizing it; I am merely the reporter of what emphasis is evident in this
literature. To be blunt, when determining how Matthew's readers are expected
to regard magi, perception is more important than reality. We may know from
modern social-historical analysis that magi belonged to the retainer class, but
this does not change the fact that the literature most relevant to the discourse
setting of Matthew's narrative reveals a popular perception of magi as more
oppressed *by* royal power than possessed *of* it.[255] Of course, this dichotomy of
options (if not powerful, then victimized) derives from a dualism that we might
regard as simplistic, but it is nevertheless a dualism that is intrinsic to Matthew's
story world—a matter to which we must now turn.

What Are Matthew's Implied Readers Expected to Believe?

We need to consider how the relationship of magi to kings previously described
would be evaluated in light of the ideological point of view concerning royalty
that Matthew's readers are assumed to espouse. Put simply, Matthew's narrative
presents an apocalyptic vision of reality that does not invite favorable characterization of kings or earthly rulers.

The story world of Matthew's Gospel is a battlefield for conflict between the
Son of Man and the devil (13:24–30; 36–43). In Matthew's story Jesus is one
who embodies the very presence of God (1:23) in a world that has fallen under
the control of Satan (4:8–9). He proclaims the nearness of the reign of the heavens (4:17) while acknowledging the reality of the current reign of Satan (12:26).
He plunders the devil's house, enacting God's reign proleptically (12:28–29)
until, at last, he is able to claim that all authority in heaven and on earth has
been given to him (28:18). Still, the benefits of this victory are somewhat
deferred, for the reign of the heavens will not be manifest in its fullness until the
Parousia, when the devil and his minions are removed, cast into the fires prepared for them (13:40–42; 25:41). In the interim, the world will get worse not
better (24:21), as Jesus' followers continue to seek God's reign (6:33) and to
pray for its advent (6:10).

All references to royalty in this Gospel must be understood in light of this
fundamental opposition between the "reign of the heavens" and the reign of
Satan. Two texts are especially significant. In a scene of initial conflict, Satan is
able to offer Jesus "all the kingdoms of the world" because, apparently, they are
under his authority (4:8–9). Although this claim is made even more explicitly
in Luke (4:6), Matthew's readers also are expected to assume the offer is valid,
or else no real temptation would be involved.[256] If Satan really is held to rule all
the kingdoms of the world, then the clear implication is that the apparent rulers
of worldly kingdoms are his underlings. A second text presents a vision of
royalty congruent with this implication. In Matthew 20:25, Jesus says to his

disciples, "You know that the rulers of the Gentiles lord it over them, and their great ones are tyrants over them." This sweeping characterization seemingly typifies political rulers as embodying the qualities most antithetical to those that epitomize the reign of God (20:26–27).[257]

This generalization holds within Matthew's story, for we do not encounter here a single political ruler who exhibits positive traits. King Herod (2:16) callously slaughters children in a manner that recalls evil tyrants of old: the Pharaoh in the days of Moses (Exod. 1:15–22) and Nebuchadnezzar at the time of Jeremiah (compare Matt. 2:17–18 to Jer. 31:15; 39:1–9). His son Archelaus is as much to be feared as he (2:21). Herod the tetrarch murders God's prophet (14:3) and is perceived as a threat to Jesus as well (14:13). Pilate the governor reneges on his responsibility for administering justice by ordering the execution of a man he knows to be innocent (27:15–26).[258]

Though this portrayal of political rulers is the most significant for our present consideration, we should recall in passing that religious leaders fare no better in Matthew's narrative (see pages 117–18). The root character trait for all the various groups of religious leaders in this story is "evil," which identifies them with Satan, the "evil one" (13:19).[259] Plants that the heavenly Father did not plant (15:13), they owe their place in this world to the devil (13:24–26, 37–39).[260]

In Matthew's narrative, exponents of worldly power, be they political or religious, are invariably aligned with Satan, while the powerless are presented as ones with whom Jesus' disciples must identify. In contrast to political rulers, the followers of Jesus will be slaves, seeking not to be served but to serve (20:25–28). In contrast to religious leaders, they will be siblings, refusing positions of leadership in a community of equals (23:1–12). The antipathy for worldly power in this narrative is so great that Jesus himself is portrayed as a person who "has nowhere to lay his head" (8:20) and his disciples are required to renounce their possessions and go out into the world with no apparent means of support (10:9–10), helpless as sheep in the midst of wolves (10:16). As such, they will be dragged before governors and kings to give testimony (10:18). Thus the narrative offers an ideological vision of the world beyond that portrayed within the temporal boundaries of Matthew's story, and the only picture of royalty that vision offers is one of power exercised oppressively against the agents of God.[261]

In sum, Matthew's narrative depicts a world in which the rule of Satan and the rule of God coexist (13:24–30, 36–43). Consistently aligned with the rule of Satan are all representatives of worldly power: Gentile rulers, Jewish leaders, "great ones" (20:25)—all who are currently first but who are destined ultimately to be last (19:30; 20:16). God's rule is associated with those who lack power in this world: servants (10:24–25; 20:27; 24:45–46), the meek (5:5), children (18:1–4; 19:13–15; 23:15–16; cf. 11:25), little ones (10:42; 18:6, 10, 14), the "least" (25:40, 45)—all who are currently last but who are destined ultimately to be first (19:30; 20:16).

We have, then, a second reason for saying that Matthew's implied readers are not expected to do what many real readers have done: identify the magi as kings on the basis of an ambiguous intertextual connection. The implied readers of Matthew's Gospel share its ideological point of view. Such readers would not be expected to resolve the ambiguities in Matthew's narrative of the magi by identifying these characters as rulers of the earth who submit to Christ and so align themselves with the reign of God. No earthly ruler ever does such a thing in this story and the possibility of any earthly ruler ever doing this before the Parousia is never envisioned. Readers who believe that all kings are tyrants and all kingdoms ruled by Satan would not be quick to make exceptions of the magi simply because the story presents them as doing what scripture says kings ought to do.

But what if, as suggested earlier, Matthew's implied readers are expected to regard the magi not as kings but as royal servants? A connection with the royal court is maintained that makes the Old Testament allusion sensible while the servant status accorded to the magi allows readers to be favorably disposed to them. Thus, regarding the magi as servants of kings is compatible with both the knowledge presupposed by the discourse setting of this narrative and the ideological point of view assumed for readers of the narrative.

Characterization

All that has been said thus far concerns what we have called the readers' repertoire of assumed knowledge, beliefs, and values. Sometimes, though, a narrative may challenge the assumed knowledge or beliefs of its readers in an attempt to subvert or refine these. Hypothetically, it would be possible for Matthew's narrative to present the magi in such a way as to educate readers to a new way of thinking. The story could present magi as acting in ways that belie the readers' assumption that they are relatively lowly servants. This *could* be the case, but is it? No. The depiction of the magi in Matthew's narrative is consistent with what we have identified as the readers' presuppositions. The characterization of the magi is more in keeping with what would be appropriate for servants than for kings.

A close reading of the story reveals that the magi do not approach Herod or take any initiative in their relationship with him. Instead, Herod summons the magi (just as Nebuchadnezzar did in Daniel 2:2), sends them to Bethlehem, and gives them orders (2:7–8). He does not appear to regard the magi as visiting dignitaries but as menial underlings, whom he assumes (mistakenly) will do as they are told. Indeed, the impression gained from 2:12 is that they did *intend* to do as they had been told until they (like Balaam) received alternative instructions from a higher power.

The magi's worship of Jesus also conveys a notion of subservience. Their prostration (*pesontēs*, 2:11) conveys humiliation, especially in the presence of a woman and a child. While not uncommon in the ancient Near East, such an action would be inappropriate for kings from foreign lands who were merely recognizing the birth of a new "king of the Jews" (2:2). It would, however, be entirely fitting for servants, persons whose status requires demonstrative recognition of the preeminence of royalty.

Finally, we have the presentation of gifts, which the magi offer to Jesus out of their treasures. Some have suggested that the mere fact that they are able to offer such gifts characterizes them as wealthy and hence at least powerful if not kingly.[262] Yet Matthew's narrative does not emphasize the value of these gifts (as is frequently done in such stories) in a way that would present the magi as inordinately wealthy.[263] The story gives no indication of the amount of gold, frankincense, or myrrh that is proffered, and the economic status of Jesus and his family does not appear to be altered by the presentation.[264] Elsewhere in the narrative, gold is referenced casually as a typical possession of common people (10:9).[265] Within the context of Matthew's narrative, the relevant point is not how much the magi's possessions were worth but that they gave them up to Jesus, so that where their treasure was, their hearts might be also (6:21).[266]

Significantly, Matthew's story describes no exchange of gifts as would be customary in the ancient world.[267] Nor does the story allude to promised or eventual reciprocation, so that the reader may think the gifts have placed Jesus and his family in the magi's debt. Matthew's implied readers are expected to recognize that a unilateral presentation such as this represents payment of tribute. The transfer of valuables without expectation of benefit demonstrates acknowledgment of status differential. An exchange of gifts would be appropriate between royal figures. The payment of tribute that occurs here presents the magi in effect as saying, "You are a king; we are servants."

In sum, Matthew's narrative portrays the magi as obedient, humble, and submissive. Such traits are not associated with earthly kings in this narrative but with servants. The portrayal is therefore consistent with what Matthew's readers are expected to know about magi and to believe about royalty.

Conclusion

The potential for identifying the magi as kings is created by the narrative rhetoric of Matthew's story, which connects magi and kings intertextually without explicating the nature of the connection. This connection has typically been interpreted in one of two ways. For centuries, the preferred interpretation was to take the intertextual connection as implying *identification* (magi = kings). Though this persists at a popular level, more recent interpretations have taken the connection to be one of *representation:* while not literally kings, the magi may come to Jesus as the representatives of monarchs, such that their activity counts as though it were performed by their royal masters. The latter strategy admittedly yields only an indirect, partial fulfillment of scripture, but some might maintain that for Matthew's readers "near fulfillment" is close enough to count.[268]

I think we have established that Matthew's implied readers would not be expected to make either of these two connections. The first, identification, fails on three points: Matthew's readers are expected to know that people referred to by the term *magoi* are not kings; they are expected to believe that the rule of Christ is diametrically opposed to all earthly powers such that kings and other rulers of the earth will resist rather than welcome his reign; and they are expected to observe that the magi who do welcome Christ's reign in this story do not behave as kings but as servants. The second connection, representation, is slightly more viable because it fails on only the latter two points. Nevertheless, it fails. Such an interpretation fits with the readers' assumed knowledge that magi were servants of royal courts, but is still incompatible with the narrative's ideological point of view concerning royalty and lacks support from a careful reading of the narrative. Nothing in the text indicates that the magi are acting on behalf of others. The kings whom the magi supposedly represent have to be read into the story as unnamed background characters. Can Matthew's implied readers really be expected to read such characters into the story—kings who espouse values inconsistent with those attributed to rulers everywhere else in the narrative? And to do this with no greater motivation than to facilitate a connection with scripture that is at best weak and unsatisfying?

A more likely alternative is that Matthew's implied readers are expected to regard the connection between magi and kings as one of *contrast*. Knowing that magi are typically royal servants, these readers may be expected to regard the position of royal servant as antithetical to royal power. The intertextual connection becomes ironic, accenting reversal rather than fulfillment of expectations. This, of course, may be one reason that Matthew does not introduce the intertextual reference with a fulfillment citation. The scriptures are *not* fulfilled, and that is the point. Matthew's readers are expected to know that the scriptures speak of kings honoring God's chosen one, but now, when that one arrives, the kings of the earth do not respond. The gifts and the worship that scripture says kings would offer are brought by magi instead. It is as though, to use a medieval analogy, the time for the king to appear has come, and a court jester shows up in his place. "Magi?" Matthew's implied readers are expected to ask. "Where are the kings?" The point of the story, then, is that when Jesus came into the world he was not worshiped by kings but by servants. Part of the irony, of course, is that there *is* a king in the story, and he even speaks of worshiping Jesus . . . but it is not to be.

This reading makes sense of the intertextual allusion in a way that is consistent with the knowledge of magi relevant to the discourse setting of Matthew's narrative and with the ideological point of view concerning royalty presupposed for Matthew's readers. It is also consistent with what is actually presented in the text of Matthew's story, accepting the portrait there of magi who behave as servants. Far from identifying the magi as kings or as representatives of royal power, Matthew's implied readers are expected to regard these magi as symbolizing servants of earthly tyrants, servants who recognize in Christ their true and just ruler.

Still, the history of tradition reveals that readers whose knowledge or beliefs have differed from those expected of Matthew's implied readers have resolved the ambiguity of this intertextual connection differently. They have resolved it in a way that would not be expected of Matthew's implied readers nor, for what it's worth, intended by this Gospel's historical author. In fact, they have resolved it in a way that the first evangelist probably would have found appalling.

Chapter Eight
The Magi as Wise Persons

I should start this chapter by indicating that I was surprised by the results of the last one. I initially chose to examine the tradition of the magi as kings because I thought it offered an example of what just about everyone (scholars, that is) would regard as a popular but obvious unexpected reading. The whole point in choosing that example was that I thought the results of my study would be non-controversial. Well, leave it to me to find (or make) controversy where it never was before. Almost all scholars would agree with me in saying that Matthew's readers are not expected to regard the magi as kings, but almost no scholar would agree with me in saying that Matthew's readers are expected to regard the magi as servants.[269] Why do I have to go so far?

Well, the answer is that I am committed to reporting what my approach turns up. This book, after all, is primarily about a reading strategy, and if that strategy doesn't work, if it only sounded good in the first part of the book but now points up conclusions that are unconvincing . . . well, I owe it to you to report those conclusions and let you decide what they mean. I could have slanted things by simply saying my approach leads me to identify readings that regard Matthew's magi as powerful kings as unexpected readings. That would be true, and it would keep (almost) everyone happy. But my approach did in fact indicate more than this—it indicated that the expected reading of Matthew's story is one that regards Matthew's magi as powerless servants. I was surprised to discover that, and perhaps you were, too. But, then, what good is an approach that only tells us what we already know?

Well, if you don't like surprises, things are going to get worse. I had originally intended to study only the one tradition—the obvious unexpected reading that identifies the magi as kings—but while investigating this I accidentally stumbled on a considerable amount of data relevant to another tradition as well, namely, that which identifies the magi as "wise men," or "wise *persons*," as I prefer to say (see chapter 12). I was surprised (again) to discover that there have actually been a couple of scholars in the last century who doubted this tradition, though both made their arguments in contexts that did not earn much of a hearing for their views. A work from 1936 by W. K. Lowther Clarke tried to interpret the magi's adoration as representing conversion from an *unwise* way of life. His real interest was in developing a polemic against the Roman Catholic Church's endorsement of gambling (which he thought represented the modern equivalent of astrology, insofar as both involve yielding to determinism). At least he had a sense of humor. The article was called "The Rout of the Magi," invoking a prepoststructuralist pun that could make Derrida proud.[270] Better known today is the 1958 article by C. S. Mann, whose ideas are largely derived from Lowther Clarke, and who ends up suggesting that Matthew's magi were not Gentiles but Babylonian Jews.[271] No one, to my knowledge, has followed him in acceptance of this conclusion.

Amused, I grabbed on to these interpretations of "the magi as fools" as yet another example of a fairly far-fetched unexpected reading, worthy perhaps of mention in one of my jocose endnotes (you have been reading those, haven't you?). But the more rigorously I applied the same approach used in the last chapter, the more strenuously the data resisted being bent to my wishes. I wanted simply to survey the same three tiers of literature expressive of Matthew's discourse setting in order to show how the readers would know magi were not foolish but wise. I wanted to expose the underlying ideological perspective of the narrative in order to show how the readers would be expected to value wisdom and despise foolishness. It seemed an easy task . . . and yet . . . now I am left with the prospect that my name may some day end up on a short list with Lowther Clarke and Mann. I am convinced—though surprised—that the popular identification of the magi as wise persons is as unexpected as that of kings.

Let's begin by stating what should be obvious: an identification of magi as wise persons cannot be affirmed or denied as a historical fact in the same way as their identification as kings. The problem lies in the subjective sense given to the label *wise,* clearly an evaluative term. We may grant as a historical fact the assertion that magi were "learned," that is, that they possessed knowledge of certain subjects beyond that of their peers. At issue is the question of whether Matthew's implied readers would be expected to identify such knowledge with "wisdom."

We must beware of confusion related to the English word *wise,* which can carry different meanings. English Bibles often translate three different Greek words that are used in Matthew with the single word *wise.* These are *sophos* (11:25; 23:34), *phronimos* (7:24; 10:16; 24:45; 25:2, 4, 8, 9) and *syniēmi* (13:13, 14, 15, 19, 23, 51; 15:10; 16:12; 17:13). Only the first word means "wise" with respect to learning or expertise. The goal of scholarship is to make one wise in this sense: if one studies much and is *not* wise (*sophos*), then something has gone wrong. In Matthew, *phronimos* refers to a quality of character, not to something that is acquired through learning: to be "wise as serpents" does not mean to be well-educated; the "wise maidens" are not necessarily better instructed than the foolish ones. Similarly, *syniēmi* refers to a gift of God, to insight akin to faith rather than to knowledge acquired through education. Now, I think that when most people refer to the magi as wise persons they mean the word *wise* in the sense in which Matthew uses *sophos.* So that is what we will investigate. When we ask, "Are Matthew's implied readers expected to regard the magi as wise?" we mean, "Are they expected to regard the magi as persons who are learned in matters of significance?"

For most readers today, the answer to that question seems obvious. Magi were students of the stars, and their knowledge of the heavens was obviously worthwhile since it enabled them to interpret the sign that they saw in the heavens and thus come to Jerusalem in search of the Christ. But Matthew says nothing of this. The magi merely arrive in Jerusalem, saying, "Where is he who has been born king of the Jews? For we have seen his star in the East [or, 'at its rising,' depending on how one translates the Greek] and have come to worship him" (2:2). Matthew does not narrate the magi's perception or interpretation of the star. The narrative leaves a gap where this part of the story is concerned, and modern readers have bridged that gap with the suggestion that the magi's specialized knowledge allowed them to interpret the divine revelation. This suggestion has not gone unchallenged. Rosenberg, for example, has claimed that the magi would have been acting only on "common knowledge" in attributing the birth of great men to heavenly phenomena.[272] There are examples of such manifestations in rabbinic stories of Abraham, Isaac, and Moses, where the revelation does not require any special knowledge on the part of the recipient.[273] In any case, the history of reception (discussed in our next chapter) reveals that assumptions attributing valuable knowledge to the magi do not by any means offer the only way of bridging Matthew's gap concerning the nonnarrated revelation. We want to determine how the implied readers might have been *expected* to bridge it. Again, we will try to determine this by paying careful attention to Matthew's characterization of the magi, considered in light of what the implied readers are expected to know and of what they are expected to believe.

What Are Matthew's Implied Readers Expected to Know?

Since Matthew's narrative itself provides no information regarding magian knowledge, we must look elsewhere, to literature most relevant to the context in which the story was composed. What awareness of magian knowledge is presupposed by the discourse setting of Matthew's narrative? Was this story written in a context where readers would be expected to assume that magi possessed worthwhile knowledge?

As in the last chapter, we will look at three progressively relevant tiers of information—texts from Matthew's discourse setting that may provide some indication of what was "known" about magi.

Greco-Roman World

This time the witness of the Greco-Roman literature is mixed. Cicero refers to magi as "wise and learned among the Persians," but Tacitus denounces their arts as "absurdities."[274] The story of Tiridates described previously (page 139) presents Nero as an emperor who thought the magi's knowledge so valuable that he wanted to acquire it himself. Suetonius, however, says that Tiberius banished all astrologers from Rome in 19 C.E.[275] We do not know whether Matthew's readers would be expected to know these specifics, but the broad context of this narrative's discourse setting suggests that magi were considered to be persons who possessed special knowledge, the value of which was controversial.

Jewish Midrash

When we turn to the Jewish milieu, the verdict is decidedly negative. Not a single story or text presents magi as wise or indicates that the knowledge they possessed could ever be viewed as worthy of acquisition.[276] For convenience, we may simply consider the impact of the two midrashim (that's the plural of midrash) mentioned in the last chapter—the ones that identify Pharaoh's sorcerers and the prophet Balaam as magi. In the Exodus midrash, as in the Exodus story itself, the sorcerers who serve Pharaoh are essentially bunglers who provide the story with an element of comic relief. They are able to throw down staffs that become snakes but their snakes are swallowed by Aaron's (Exod. 7:10–12). They are sometimes able to duplicate the actions of Moses and Aaron that bring plagues upon the land (Exod. 7:22; 8:7), but by doing so they only make the situation worse (in the midst of a plague of frogs, magicians who can produce *more* frogs are not what the Pharaoh needs). At other times, they fail completely (Exod. 8:18), and eventually they themselves become plague victims (Exod. 9:11). Wise? No. They are fools.

Does this seem an overstatement? Well, then, let us look again at the Balaam midrash, as presented by Philo in his *Vita Moysis I* (XLVIII). Here is a story that identifies its principal character as a magus and then delights in exposing him as the "most foolish of all men" (293). Philo introduces Balaam as one who was "far-famed as a soothsayer" and "particularly admired" in that regard (264). Thus, he pays homage to the view held by some in the Greco-Roman world that respected the knowledge of magi. But then Philo proceeds to reveal how undeserving Balaam was of such respect. The incident with the donkey and the angel is telling. Balaam's inability to see the angel "was a proof of his insensibility," since "the unreasoning animal was shown to be superior in sight to him who claimed to see" divine things (272). Balaam characterizes himself as "ignorant" (273) and this description is readily confirmed in his subsequent inquiry as to whether he should turn back, for "why should he ask about a matter so evident, which in itself provided its own demonstration and needed no confirmation" (274)? When the time comes for Balaam to curse Israel, a genuine prophetic spirit does fall upon him, but the result is that it banishes "utterly from his soul his art of wizardry—for the craft of the sorcerer and the inspiration of the Holiest might not live together" (277). Still, when Balaam speaks the words of God (blessing Israel), he does so unwittingly, "understanding nothing" (283). Eventually, he comes to despise his old art, realizing how worthless it was (287). The short narrative comes full circle with a concluding comment on his ironic celebrity, as Balak calls the magus "most foolish of all men," and remarks that he must now return home with "deep disgrace, having brought ridicule upon the lore of knowledge upon which he had once prided himself" (292). On the lips of Balak, the former comment is clearly ironic: the king regards Balaam as "foolish" because he has lost out on rewards that would have come if had cursed Israel as commanded, but Philo presents the magus as foolish in a broader sense: he is a ridiculous figure whose useless art is easily thwarted by God and exposed for the nonsense that it really is.

I have treated the Philo citations in some detail because, of all Jewish writers relevant to the discourse setting of Matthew's narrative, Philo is typically regarded as the most quintessentially Hellenistic. If the Greco-Roman world provided mixed reviews as to how the knowledge of magi ought to be evaluated while the Jewish world typically rendered a negative judgment on this issue, we might have thought Philo would be a bridge figure. If any Jewish writings roughly contemporary with Matthew's Gospel were to view the knowledge of magi positively, wouldn't they be his? But, no! Even Philo thinks that magi are fools and that their knowledge—celebrated by the ignorant—is but an artificial system (*sophisteian*, 277). They are experts at nonsense—learned perhaps, but certainly not wise.

Jewish Scriptures

Even more important than Philo or other Jewish literature is the passage from Daniel 2, the only text dealing with magi that we can confidently ascribe to the repertoire of Matthew's implied readers. And here, also, the magi are presented as ineffectual. Their learning and their art does not enable them to know what needs to be known. Their role in the story is to serve as foils to Daniel, who receives true knowledge from God. Daniel is presented as the bearer of true wisdom; magi and other so-called "wise men" (*sophoi*, 2:27) are exposed as fools.

Taken together, these three tiers of information indicate that Matthew's implied readers are probably expected to regard magi as learned only in matters that the readers would regard as nonsense.[277] Matthew's implied readers are expected to "know" that magi are not wise persons but fools.[278]

What Are Matthew's Implied Readers Expected to Believe?

We may also ask whether an identification of the magi in Matthew's story as "wise persons" would be consistent with this narrative's ideological point of view concerning the relationship between wisdom and divine revelation.[279] A key text is Matthew 11:25. Jesus says, "I thank you, Father, Lord of heaven and earth, because you have hidden these things from the wise [*sophōn*] and the intelligent [*synetōn*] and have revealed them to infants." In short, God hides divine truth from the wise and reveals divine truth to those who lack wisdom. This perspective—stated so well in this single verse—is prevalent throughout the narrative. John the Baptist claims that God is able to raise children of Abraham from stones (3:9). Jesus says (quoting scripture) that God brings forth praise from the mouths of nursing babies (21:16). Infants, stones, sucklings . . . all are images of those who have nothing to offer, nothing to commend themselves. God creates or reveals what is needed, preferring apparently to write the divine will on almost blank slates.

The point is illustrated in the very selection and education of Jesus' disciples. He does not call scribes who, at least, would already know the scriptures and need only to be instructed in their proper interpretation. He calls fishermen (4:18–22) and tax collectors (9:9) who don't appear to know anything of relevance to their mission. Not once anywhere in this Gospel are Jesus' disciples ever depicted as knowing the scriptures or the will of God. The only time that they come close is especially revealing. They know that "Elijah must come first" (17:10), but they do not know that this teaching comes from scripture. It is only something that "the scribes say." The disciples are depicted as ignorant "blank slates" whom Jesus continually teaches, revealing to them what they need to know. As the story unfolds, we witness some progress. Sometimes, at least, they do understand (13:51; 16:12; 17:13).

The religious leaders of Israel not only know "that Elijah must come first" but a great many other things as well: that the Christ is to be born in Bethlehem (2:4–6), that Moses commanded the giving of divorce certificates (19:7), that the scriptures commend levirate marriage (22:24), that the Christ is to be the son of David (22:42), that it is unlawful to place blood money in the temple treasury (27:6), and so on. I submit that Matthew's implied readers are expected to regard such knowledge (as opposed to the astrological arts of the magi) as true wisdom. Knowledge of scripture . . . knowledge of the law . . . knowledge of the will of God—*these* are what mark people as truly wise. People who have such knowledge may genuinely be regarded as "wise and intelligent" in contrast to people like the foolish magi who know nothing worth knowing.

But—here is the surprise!—Matthew's story depicts a world in which God chooses to reveal divine things to those who don't know anything of value and to hide the truth from those who are wise and intelligent. So, in his ministry, Jesus not only teaches his know-nothing disciples but also refuses to teach the scribes, Pharisees, and other religious leaders of Israel. He insists that they are wrong about various things but does not try to correct them in a way that would bring them (like his disciples) to a renewed understanding. He condemns them without bothering to call them to repentance.[280] His philosophy concerning them can be summarized in the following directions to his disciples: "Leave them alone" (15:14).

In short, Matthew's evaluation of those who are deemed "wise" in the social world of this story is analogous to the evaluation of those who are deemed "royal." Wisdom and royalty are likewise rejected by God. The common denominator, I suspect, is that both are forms of power. In this story people who are powerful are rejected for no other reason than that they are powerful. Accordingly, Jesus' shocking words in 11:25 really do seem to represent an underlying evaluation of wisdom that is fundamental to this narrative: those who are wise and intelligent are rejected by God for no other reason than that they are wise and intelligent. Wise men like kings exemplify those who are first in this world: they will be last. Fools, like slaves, represent those who are last: they will be first.[281]

Matthew's implied readers are expected to share this ideological point of view regarding wisdom and its antithetical relationship to divine revelation. For this reason alone, they would not be likely to regard the magi as people who are wise. Indeed, if Matthew's *magoi* are to be equated with the *sophoi* of 11:25—as many Bible translators apparently think—then we are left with a story in which the Father reveals the Son to the wise and intelligent, a story that depicts God as doing the very thing that Jesus says God does not do. But if, as previously suggested, Matthew's readers are assumed to regard magi as fools, as people who know nothing about anything that is worth knowing, then the story in Matthew 2 fits well with the Gospel's ideological point of view. The presentation of the Christ child to ignorant fools is in line with the creation of children of Abraham from stones, with the evocation of praise from sucklings, with the theological education of fishermen, and with the revelation of divine truth to infants (11:25).

Characterization

We need to check these suppositions against a close reading of the magi story itself. We discover that, indeed, one of the chief character traits ascribed to the magi in Matthew's narrative is "ignorance."[282]

Readers are introduced to the magi as characters who have come from the East to ask, "Where is the child who has been born king of the Jews?" The fact that they are introduced as characters asking a question is significant: such narrative rhetoric emphasizes what they *don't* know (the location of the child) over what they *do* know (that a significant child has been born). The wording of their question indicates further that they do not really know the significance of this child. They think he is "king of the Jews," a political identification that in Matthew's narrative reflects the point of view of those who do not understand who Jesus is or what he is about (27:11, 29, 37).[283] Even Herod is able to perceive that what the star they saw really portended was the birth of "the Messiah" (2:4).

The magi get their answer and are sent off to Bethlehem to search diligently for the child but, as it turns out, they do not have to do this. The star now directs them, going before them and stopping over the very house where the child is. There is no thought here of learned astrologers computing the location based on a confluence of planets or constellations. As presented in Matthew's narrative, the leading of this star is like that of the pillars of cloud and fire during the exodus (Exod. 13:21), so obvious that it requires no scholarly interpretation. It points out the very house where Jesus has been born. It is a sign, a divine portent so blatant that any fool could follow it.

Finally, the narrative suggests that Herod initially dupes the magi with regard to his plans to kill Jesus. Matthew's readers are expected to regard Herod's stated intention of worshiping Jesus (2:8) with suspicion—especially since the narrator has offered them the inside information that Herod was troubled by news of Jesus' birth (2:3). But the magi give no indication that *they* are suspicious. The plot is averted not through their wisdom or cunning, but because God intervenes and warns them in a dream not to return to Herod.[284]

We may say, then, that Matthew's narrative presents the magi as ignorant in comparison to Herod (who knows the star portends a messianic rather than a normal political figure), in comparison to the chief priests (who know the Messiah is to be born in Bethlehem), and in comparison to the readers (who know that Herod is up to no good). The magi are, in fact, the most ignorant characters in the story. They seem to know less about what has happened or about what it may signify than anyone else. Still, God brings them to the Christ, while Herod—despite his government intelligence—is unable to find the Christ, and the chief priests—despite their scholarship—do not even care to try.

In short, the narrative does not portray the magi as wise men whose learning leads them to Christ but as ignorant people to whom God reveals the Christ. This characterization is consistent with the reader's assumed knowledge (which regards the so-called learning of magi as insignificant) and with the reader's assumed ideology (which holds that God offers revelation to the ignorant and withholds it from the wise).

Conclusion

The potential for identifying the magi as wise men is created by a narrative gap when Matthew presents these magi as having somehow concluded from a star that they should come to Jerusalem and worship the one born king of the Jews. We hear nothing at all about the magi's ability to interpret omens or about their scientific understanding of the heavens. Still, many readers have taken the text as implying that the magi used their learning (which did have something to do with stars) to figure out the meaning of a phenomenon that would have been lost on less educated people. Matthew's implied readers, however, would probably not be expected to fill the narrative gap in this way. For one thing, the discourse setting for this narrative suggests that its readers are probably expected to regard magian learning as consisting of nonsense, not potentially useful information. Beyond this, the ideological perspective of this narrative—shared by its implied readers—would be predisposed to resist any linkage of divine revelation to erudition.

Readers who know what this narrative seems to presuppose and who believe what they are apparently expected to believe would be inclined to bridge the narrative gap involving the manifestation of the star in other ways. The later behavior of this star would likely suggest to such readers that the initial revelation, like the latter one, involved a portent so obvious that anyone could have understood it. This would be consistent with the overall characterization of the magi as ignorant people who need to have everything made plain to them. The irony, as before, is that there *are* "wise men" in this story, but they are not the magi. They are the chief priests and scribes of Israel, who don't need to be told anything.

I am suggesting that Matthew's implied readers are probably not expected to read this story and conclude, "These magi are wiser than the chief priests and the scribes of Israel—I guess studying Persian astrology is more important than learning the scriptures." Nor are they expected to conclude, "Jesus was wrong when he said that God hides divine truth from the wise and intelligent. Actually, God prefers scholars to peasants." No, I think the implied readers are expected to respond, "God revealed the truth about the Christ to a bunch of pagan fools while those who were wise enough to figure it out for themselves missed it." Just like Jesus said.

Chapter Nine

Matthew's Magi in the History of Interpretation

I am proposing that millions of readers have read and still do read Matthew's story of the magi in a way that is almost the opposite of what is expected. Readers who are expected to see the tale as a story of God's rejection of the wise and powerful have come to view it as an almost definitive paradigm for God's blessing of the wise and powerful. Without (yet) evaluating these developments as positive or negative, we may at least be moved to ask, "How could this happen?"

For those who are keeping track, we have now reached step 3 in my four-stage process for understanding polyvalent interpretations of texts. Thus far, I have 1) used descriptive reader-response criticism to *identify* two prevalent interpretations of the magi story, and 2) used narrative criticism to *compare* each of these traditional interpretations with the manner in which the implied readers of the narrative are expected to receive the story. The third step of my paradigm calls for me to *account* for these unexpected readings. Why would readers take the magi to be kings when they are expected to take them to be servants? Why would they view the magi as wise when they are expected to view them as fools? We may come closer to being able to answer these questions if we can discover *which* readers have read the story in these ways and determine *when* and *where* they have done so. To do that, we will use yet another variety of reader-response criticism, *Wirkungsgeschichte,* which attends to the history of the text's influence.

On a small scale, we can sometimes account for an individual unexpected reading simply by asking the person to explain his or her response. This can be enlightening. I remember one of my early and embarrassing attempts at doing a Children's Sermon in some unfortunate congregation that drew my name out of the "supply preacher" bucket. I used the story of Zacchaeus, figuring that was a good one for kids. I said, "Now, Zacchaeus wanted to see Jesus, but he couldn't. Does anybody know why?"

Silence.

"Well, was it because he was too short?"

"No," one child responded, which surprised me because that's why *I* thought it was.

"Uh, it wasn't?"

"He wasn't too short," the child continued. "Everyone was standing in his way."

Well, for me, that was an unexpected reading of the story—and a fairly understandable one. This child, being small of stature himself, knew that there was no direct connection between height and vision. His eyes worked fine. The problem was other people getting in the way.

I thought that this was an excellent example—cute, even—of how social location affects interpretation. Imagine my surprise, then, when sometime later I actually read the Zacchaeus story in Luke 19 (which I had thought I knew well enough to tell from memory) and discovered that it says, "He was trying to see who Jesus was, but on account of the crowd he could not, because he was short of stature" (19:3). The text actually cites *both* reasons for the inability to see: "on account of the crowd" and "short of stature." Either factor alone would not have necessitated the sycamore climb. So, in retrospect, I think the child's answer was only unexpected to *me;* it was probably very much in keeping with what would be expected of Luke's implied readers.

In any case, accounting for unexpected readings on a larger scale is more difficult. We are now looking at interpretations that have been held by millions of people for hundreds of years. Personal idiosyncracies are not likely to explain them. The interpretations that ascribe either royalty or wisdom to the magi in this story have been so pervasive that they may be due to general social-historical phenomena that affected large numbers of the reading public; they may be attributable to what Kuhn calls "paradigm shifts," or Shakespeare, "sea changes."

We begin, however, with gaps. As indicated previously (page 16), the word *gap* is actually something of a technical term in literary criticism, referring to "what the narrative leaves out." In this instance, for example, Matthew's narrative does not tell us what magi are. The narrative simply says "magi came from the East." *What magi are* is a gap that must be filled with knowledge that is presupposed for the narrative's readers. Readers who lack this presupposed knowledge may fill the gap in unexpected ways.

Let us suppose, for instance, that Matthew's narrative contained either of the following as an additional sentence:

- "These magi were slaves of the royal court, often oppressed by their cruel masters."
- "These magi had foolishly spent their lives accumulating worthless knowledge."

I suspect that if Matthew's narrative contained the first of these sentences, readers would not have been likely to decide that the magi are kings, or if it contained the second sentence, they would not likely have decided that the magi are wise persons. But it is impossible for a narrative to ward off every unexpected reading by explaining everything. Every sentence of every narrative contains gaps, and every gap creates potential for unexpected readings.

To account for an unexpected reading, then, we might begin by detecting the gaps that give rise to it. I have already done this with regard to the traditions regarding the magi. In addition to the lack of any explicit identification of what magi are, Matthew's story of the magi contains at least two other gaps that have been filled in unexpected ways by readers.

First, the story alludes intertextually to scripture passages that speak of kings bringing gifts to a promised one, but the narrative does not explicate *how the magi are to be related to the kings in the scripture texts to which the story alludes.* I have suggested that readers are expected to see the magi in contrast to these kings, as servants performing what the Bible says kings should do. But the text does not explicitly state this. It leaves a gap that is open to other interpretations: perhaps the magi represent kings and offer gifts on their behalf; perhaps the magi actually are kings themselves. I think that, over the centuries, readers have pervasively and persistently filled the gap with unexpected interpretations. The question, now, is why?

Second, the story says that the magi came to Jerusalem seeking a newborn king as a result of observing his star, but the narrative does not tell us *what the magi saw in the star* or *how they knew what this meant.* I have suggested that readers are expected to regard the star as an obvious portent that required no specialized learning to interpret. But, again, the text does not state this outright, and readers have pervasively and persistently filled this gap with the assumption that the magi's scholarship allowed them to recognize what would have been lost on common people. Again, the question now becomes, why would readers fill the gap this way and not as they were expected?

In addition to identifying gaps or ambiguities in the narrative, we need to pay attention to variables in the reading process. The observable fact that readers resolve ambiguities (fill gaps) in ways that are unexpected is often explicable in light of differences between these (real) readers and the narrative's implied readers. This is especially true when the discourse setting of a narrative is distant in time and space from that of its current readers. Persistent and pervasive unexpected readings are usually an indication that readers no longer know what they are expected to know or no longer believe what they are expected to believe. This all makes sense on a theoretical level, but to ground the theory in experience we must survey how the story has in fact been understood in various times and places. Our great ally in such an enterprise is *Wirkungsgeschichte,* the study of a narrative's history of influence.

Servants Become Kings

Scholars typically regard the attribution of royalty to the magi as a mistake of later Christian tradition. A remark by David Hill is typical: "There is nothing to indicate that (the magi) were kings, but under the influence of such passages as Ps. 72:11 and Isa. 49:7; 60:1–6 . . . later Christian tradition pictured the wise men as kings."[285] The assumption here is that the Old Testament passages cited had an effect on later Christian tradition that they would not have had on Matthew's original readers, probably because at some point Christians had lost historical information about what magi really were and then interpreted the intertextual allusions more literally than a first-century reader would have done. In other words, once Matthew's real readers no longer knew what Matthew's implied readers are expected to know, they began reading the narrative in an unexpected way. This, of course, would be possible, but my own analysis of the tradition points in a different direction. My research indicates that shifts regarding *what readers believe* have played a greater role in turning Matthew's magi into kings than simple changes in *what readers know.* The crowning of the magi has been ideologically driven and has ideological implications.

We will examine two early texts that provide glimpses of the tradition in process, look briefly at the tradition during its heyday of acceptance in the medieval period, and then conclude with some observations about our own day. Anyone who finds this exciting really should obtain Richard Trexler's book, *Journey of the Magi,* which is mentioned often in the notes.

Tertullian

The first clue comes in one of the earliest references to the magi story.[286] In his tract against Marcion, written about a century after the composition of Matthew's Gospel, Tertullian notes in an almost cavalier, offhand remark that "the East considers the Magi almost as kings" and so, he argues, their offerings to Christ fulfill the Old Testament prophecies found in Psalm 72:10.[287]

We should note that Tertullian has no interest in ascribing royalty to the magi as such. His concern, actually, is to further the cause of pacifism. By means of a rather complex and convoluted argument, he hopes to strike down a favorite proof text against pacifism, and to do this he must show that the magi are allegorical symbols for certain Old Testament kings.[288] Notably, they are symbols of hostile kings from the past who were conquered by Christ rather than images of pious or present kings who worship him. Magi do not actually have to be kings for this allegory to work. They don't even have to be "almost kings," but apparently Tertullian thought the latter appellation would help his argument along.

At first, Tertullian's comment does seem to reflect the sort of trajectory of misunderstanding that scholars have usually projected for the development of this tradition. The mere fact that Tertullian considers an identifying comment regarding magi to be necessary presumes a degree of historical ignorance.[289] The Gospel of Matthew is scarcely a century old and already Christian readers need instruction as to what magi are. Matthew could use the term *magoi* without further elaboration, but Tertullian cannot. Furthermore, Tertullian's comment is generally regarded as inaccurate: magi were not considered to be "almost kings" in the East or anywhere else. It would be easy to understand how, by the sixth century, this gap of ignorance could widen and those whom Tertullian called "almost kings" could be promoted to become actual kings.

But the "almost" is significant.[290] What keeps Tertullian from crowning the magi altogether? Perhaps he is constrained by what historical knowledge he does possess, but—as patristic scholars will readily grant—such considerations do not usually hold Tertullian back. More likely, he is constrained by resistance to the ideological implications of such a move. Tertullian himself has an apocalyptic view of history not too dissimilar from that of Matthew, except in one respect. In his *Apology,* Tertullian insists repeatedly that the Roman government and all governments are instituted and maintained by God (not Satan). God is "the dispenser of kingdoms" (XXVI). Thus Tertullian assures the Romans of "the reverence and sacred respect of Christians to the emperor, whom we cannot but look up to as called by our Lord to his office" (XXXIII). This less dualistic accounting for world affairs would seem to create a possibility for righteous government, but that potential is not to be realized existentially. Rather, Tertullian appears to regard the emperor and all earthly rulers as playing roles in the divine drama similar to that assigned to Pharaoh in the exodus. God has so hardened their hearts that repentance remains hypothetical. Tertullian's *Apology* makes its case without illusion of success: "Go zealously on, good presidents . . . kill us, torture us, condemn us, grind us to dust; your injustice is proof that we are innocent" (L).

Tertullian's agenda is to further the cause of pacifism, to discredit exegesis that would present Christ as endorsing warfare or violence. But Tertullian does not believe that pacifism will bring about the conversion of worldly powers. More likely, it will bring Christians to terrible persecution and suffering, as it did Christ. Kings do not worship Christ—Tertullian knows this. So the magi must remain "almost" kings, symbols at best of hostile kings who in a bygone era were conquered by Christ "without fighting or armament." Even then, the story must be explicitly identified as figurative. It illustrates the manner of Christ rather than describing an actual conversion of earthly rulers, something neither Tertullian nor Matthew could envision. We turn now to one who could envision it—quite clearly.

Augustine

By the end of the fourth century, Augustine was able to regard the magi as models for earthly kings.[291] In an Epiphany sermon preached in Hippo Regius sometime between 393 and 405, we find the essential link that would complete the process of turning the magi into kings[292]:

> King Herod, you see, was afraid, when the Magi told him about the child. . . . How dread must be his judgment seat, when his infant's cradle could so terrify the pride of kings! How much more prudently do kings nowadays, not seek like Herod to kill, but rather delight like the Magi to worship him (Sermon 200).[293]

What was impossible for Matthew and hypothetical for Tertullian is assumed reality in the post-Constantinian world of Augustine. The magi are not just models for what kings of the earth ought to be. They are images of what certain kings actually are. If Augustine's reference is specific, he no doubt means to affirm the reigns of the joint emperors at this time, Arcadia at Constantinople in the East and Honorius at Ravenna in the West. But to some extent, the reference must be generic, as he goes on to exhort all earthly rulers to "have a pious and filial fear of him, seated at the right hand of his Father, whom that impious king feared while he was still nuzzling the breasts of his mother."[294]

If by the time of Tertullian readers of Matthew's Gospel could no longer be assumed to know what the implied readers are expected to know, by the time of Augustine these readers can no longer be assumed to believe the way Matthew's implied readers are expected to believe. Augustine in particular stands out as the architect of a vision of the political world drastically different from that presupposed in Matthew's story.[295] Rosemary Reuther says, "Augustine . . . discovers for the first time in theological history a principle of secularity in a way which recognizes the political order as fully legitimate in its own terms."[296] Augustine's presentation of the magi as images of pious kings subverts Matthew's apocalyptic vision of the political world by providing readers with positive images of royalty alongside the negative.

Now here is a telling point: Augustine's presentation of the magi as models of kings is completely independent of exegetical treatment that would require historical identification. In his ten Epiphany sermons,[297] he never once refers to the intertextual allusions that we have discussed[298] or indicates in any way that he believes magi were royal figures *historically*. Instead, they are depicted always as magicians or astrologers, as representatives of the masses of pagan Gentiles. The magi are allowed to symbolize royalty regardless of whether such symbolism has any basis in history. In short, Augustine does not represent a consummation of the trajectory we observed in Tertullian. He does not move from "almost kings" to "actual kings" in order to strengthen a proposed fulfillment of scripture. Augustine is unconcerned with whether the magi in Matthew's story were actual kings or with whether their actions fulfill Old Testament prophecies. Rather, the magi become symbols of kings for one reason only: to allow a reading of the story that will support a political perspective it otherwise would challenge.

Tertullian and Augustine make for an interesting comparison. Tertullian evinces both ignorance of what magi are and awareness of the intertextual allusions that might connect the concepts of magi and kings. Still, he does *not* identify the magi as kings and will not even allow them to stand symbolically for modern kings. Augustine blatantly presents them as images for such kings without evincing either the historical ignorance or the intertextual awareness that would seem necessary to sustain such an interpretation. Thus, the scholarly suggestion that later (ignorant) Christian tradition turned the magi into kings to facilitate a literal fulfillment of Old Testament passages is simplistic if not false. What seems more likely is that the historical ignorance and the literalistic reading of the intertextual allusions functioned together to facilitate the sort of interpretation that Augustine was advancing even without such support.[299] This conclusion is borne out by the history of artistic representation. As Richard Trexler has demonstrated, after 312—but not before—the star that the magi are depicted as beholding often takes the shape of a chi-rho, the very sign that the emperor saw in the heavens. Thus, says Trexler, "the magi are in a sense made to see the coming of Constantine as much as of Jesus."[300] These magi are not depicted in any way that obviously fulfills the relevant Old Testament texts; still, they are stand-ins for Christian emperors.

That interpretations which regard the magi as kings do not depend on historical ignorance is demonstrated by another major trajectory in the tradition of interpretation, one that we have mentioned previously (page 146). Even those who know that magi were royal servants, not kings, often persist in regarding them as *representatives* (virtually, ciphers) for rulers who are not referred to in the text. Julian the Apostate (d. 363) thought this, and John Chrysostom (d. 407?) regularly referred to the magi as "legates."[301] Such a strategy produces an unexpected reading, but of an interesting sort: the historical knowledge assumed for the narrative is respected, while the narrative's ideology concerning royalty is blatantly ignored.

In any case, the concern to demonstrate literal fulfillment of Old Testament passages has rarely been an end in itself. It was not such even for Tertullian, as we have seen. Since Constantine, the demonstration of such a literal fulfillment has typically served as a means to another end, namely the promotion of interpretations that address contemporary political situations from an ideological perspective different from that presupposed for Matthew's implied readers.

The Medieval Period

Throughout the medieval period, this narrative was read as presenting a contrast between godly and ungodly rulers, the former represented by the magi and the latter by Herod. This is widely attested in art, drama, politics, and homiletics[302]:

- *Art*. A common theme in art became the representation of additional figures joining the magi's train. Before Constantine the extra figures were not royal persons but deceased Christians (on sarcophagi), generous donors, or others thought worthy of honor. After the magi came to be identified with kings, this changed. The mid sixth-century nave of Sant' Apollinaire Nuovo at Ravenna depicts a heavenly procession to Jesus at his second coming (!) with the magi leading the procession and the Roman emperor Justinian concluding it. The famous shrine to the magi in Cologne depicts Otto IV as "the fourth magus" in a more traditional nativity scene that nevertheless is particularly interesting. The *four* figures occupy *three* successive arches. Otto IV is in the third arch and two magi are crowded together into the second. The clear impression is that the original plan had been to depict only the three traditional magi (one in each arch) and that the addition of the monarch was an afterthought. There, a story could no doubt be told.[303]

- *Drama.* The adoration of the magi became one of the most popular biblical events for presentation both in liturgical drama and in large outdoor festivals staged throughout Europe. Trexler finds the earliest evidence of magi theater to be in 814. It continued on a wide scale throughout the Renaissance. The history of these productions is varied and complex, but at least two different trajectories can be seen: 1) Official, state-sponsored festivals often featured monarchs themselves as the magi, processing through the streets in gala affairs enhanced by theatrical special effects (one such event in Florence in 1428 is described as featuring "700 costumed men on horseback, among whom were the magi and their retinue, honorably dressed"). 2) Popular festivals allowed commoners or children to be chosen as magi ("kings") and appropriately lauded for a temporary period. The so-called "Feast of Fools" sometimes featured a magian drama of this sort. These popular festivals were usually tolerated, although their subtext of revolutionary fervor was often none too subtle. Thus, both types of festivals recognized the magi as kings and used that symbol for diverse political ends.[304]

- *Politics.* The date designated by liturgical lectionaries as "the Festival of the Magi" became the traditional occasion for coronations. These coronations were held in Aachen (the burial site of Charlemagne), but it soon became standard practice for all monarchs to undertake an immediate pilgrimage to Cologne to pay homage to the magi's remains, which had supposedly been installed at a cathedral there in 1164. Indeed, the archbishop of Cologne would regularly preside over the coronations, such that the subsequent pilgrimage could be viewed as a mandatory extension of the liturgical rite. *Mandatory* is not too strong a word. All rulers would remember that a late twelfth-century dispute between two contestants for the German throne was in part resolved because one of the claimants had been installed "legitimately" by the archbishop of Cologne.[305] Henry VII and others made a point of recording their visits to the shrine with pictorial representations.

- *Homiletics.* The Christian lectionary chose January 6 (twelve days after Jesus' birth) to mark the arrival of the magi and sometimes accorded this day the added status of Epiphany (which otherwise could celebrate Jesus' baptism or Transfiguration). In any event, this was the one day a year when all temporal rulers were expected to be in church, prepared to hear public sermons addressed specifically to them. The tradition allowed the most humble priest to scold or praise the most powerful monarch, supposedly without fear of reprisal. One wonders how well this worked in practice, but at least theoretically the "loss of face" a ruler might suffer by submitting to such humiliation was nothing compared to what would be incurred by his refusal to submit to it. So it is that on the Feast of Kings in 1286 we find the poor friar Giles of Rome exhorting Philip the Fair to emulate the magi's good behavior in his own conduct of royal duties.[306] An Augustinian, Giles was faithful to the namesake of his Order.

The Modern Era

Even when historical knowledge was regained and the inaccuracy of the identification of magi as kings asserted, scholars tended to interpret the story along what had become traditional lines. We have seen, for instance, that Luther explicitly denounced such identifications as erroneous. Still, he occasionally refers to the magi as "the three kings" himself, notably in an exposition of Psalm 101 that sets forth his "two kingdom" theory of how God rules both temporal and spiritual realms through secular and ecclesial governments.[307]

For a contemporary example, we may turn to the work of Richard Horsley, the only modern scholar to maintain that "it may not have been subsequent Christian imagination that elevated (the magi) into kings."[308] Horsley knows that magi were royal servants, but he regards this position as implying that they were Median rulers whose legitimate rule had been undermined by imperialism. Matthew's favorable depiction of them is intended as an endorsement of their right to rule in defiance of the claims of Hellenistic conquerors.

Horsley, like Augustine, finds that regarding the magi as kings produces a reading that legitimates earthly rulers. Also like Augustine, he make no reference to the intertextual allusions. He displays no interest in establishing that the visit of the magi fulfilled Old Testament prophecies or in demonstrating why such fulfillment would be significant for Matthew. His only apparent motivation for identifying the magi with kings is ideological. For Augustine, the magi represent kings who acknowledge Christ, and for Horsley they represent rightful rulers of vanquished lands. In either case, they represent "good kings" who serve as foils to the "bad king" exemplified by Herod. Augustine's interpretation allows him to draw lessons from the story applicable to a society ruled by Christian emperors. Horsley also believes that his interpretation has contemporary political relevance, finding in the story a situation analogous to U.S. foreign policy in Latin America. The hopes for liberation embodied by the magi continue to be expressed by Nicaraguans and others who suffer under client dictators supported by the United States.[309]

The irony of readings such as those produced by Augustine and Horsley must not be missed. Matthew's implied readers are expected to find in this story affirmation that there can be no godly rulers in a world enslaved by Satan, which is why servants must now fill the roles ascribed to kings in scripture. For Matthew's implied readers, the line of opposition that defines whom God favors is drawn in terms of the acquisition of worldly power. God's reign favors the powerless and opposes the powerful. The unexpected readings that regard Matthew's magi as kings redefine this line of opposition such that now God's favor rests on the powerful, on legitimate (native) rulers, or on rulers who pay appropriate homage to Christ. In either case, the story no longer illustrates God's preference for the powerless but, rather, God's support of the powerful.[310]

Fools Become Wise

We have seen that the tendency for Christian readers to regard the magi as royal, powerful figures can be correlated closely with the Christian church's acquisition of worldly power. This might just make us suspicious as to whether acquisition of worldly wisdom did not have a similar effect. The fact is, the magi were not viewed as wise persons for a long time in the history of tradition. They did not really come to be thought of as such until the time of the Renaissance and, especially, the Enlightenment. It was the church's scholars (its own "wise men" of the day) who first decided the magi story was about "wise men," not kings.

I have suggested that the expected reading of Matthew's narrative views the magi not as wise persons but as pitiful or ridiculous characters who were learned only in matters of foolishness. This not only parallels the perception of magi offered by other Jewish stories from this period but was in fact the dominant reading of the text for centuries.

In the patristic and medieval periods, the magi's learning was often simply ignored. They were depicted as foreigners, as pious saints, and—after Constantine—as models of godly rulers. When their learning was addressed, however, it was almost universally denounced. Their so-called science or art was regarded as false knowledge, even as a false religion. It did not aid them in coming to the Christ but rather was rejected after they came to the Christ.[311]

We see this Christian evaluation of magian learning in the depiction of Elymas in Acts 13:6–11 as well as in the *Didache,* which commands Christians not to act the part of a *magos* (*Did.* 2.2). But let us focus on specific interpretations of Matthew's text. Justin reads Matthew 2 as a story that depicts magi as "turning from superstition to the adoration of the true God."[312] He does not think the magi were wise people whose study of the stars enabled them to decipher a heavenly portent revealing the secret of Christ's birth. He thinks they were superstitious people brought by God to abandon the nonsense they once called knowledge.

Among early witnesses, the reading of Ignatius is even more intriguing than that of Justin. Ignatius provides us with a response that is close (as close as we can get) to that of Matthew's original audience. He writes within a single generation of the narrative's composition in a social location similar to that in which it was composed.[313] He says,

A star shone in heaven beyond all the stars, and its light was unspeakable, and its newness caused astonishment, and all the other stars, with the sun and the moon, gathered in chorus round this star, and it far exceeded them all in its light; and there was perplexity, whence came this new thing, so unlike them. By this, all magic was dissolved and . . . ignorance was removed.[314]

This description of the star and its effects amounts to a midrash, going well beyond what is in Matthew's text. Two facets of Ignatius's interpretation, however, are especially interesting. First, he assumes on the basis of Matthew's narrative that what the magi saw in the east was indeed a heavenly portent so astonishing that it might potentially attract the attention of anyone, not just those with specialized knowledge. Second, he thinks the specific effect of this star's appearance was a dissolution of all magic (*mageias*), which in context must refer (at least) to the so-called science of the magi—a science that he explicitly identifies not as *wisdom* but as *ignorance*. In short, Ignatius appears to have read the Matthew story as describing an event in which God took pity on the magi and by means of a supernatural revelation dissolved their ridiculous "science" and removed their ignorance. The fact that this revelation involved a star, a sign in the heavens, is seen as wonderfully ironic—what better way to expose the foolishness of star worshipers!

Augustine also considers in some detail how the magi discerned from a star the insight that Matthew attributes to them. It was not a deduction based on their so-called knowledge of stars. He decides, like Ignatius, that what the magi saw in the heavens was something "new and unprecedented," something their science did not take into account. This prompted them to ask themselves what such a sign might mean. "They certainly heard the answer," the bishop of Hippo concludes, "evidently from angels." That's right—angels are introduced into Matthew's narrative gap, angels who tell the magi, "The star you saw is the Christ's; go and worship him where he has been born."[315] Given this interpretation, Augustine quite easily adopts Ignatius's second point as well, viewing the magi's adoration of Christ as an implicit renunciation of their former beliefs. About a decade after the sermon just quoted, he proclaimed that the "star confounded the futile calculations and divinations of the astrologers, when it pointed out to star-worshipers the creator of heaven and earth as the proper object of worship."[316]

This sort of reading appears to have been almost unanimous in the early and medieval church.[317] The assumption that the revelation to the magi took the form of some unprecedented spectacle is ubiquitous. Augustine's contemporary in the East, Ephraem, thought the magi saw an angel *in* the star. The Book of Seth said the star was "almost in the form of a little child, with a picture of the cross above him." And we have already seen that after Constantine, the "star" sometimes became a chi-rho in artistic representations.[318] One searches in vain for any interpretation that corresponds to what is so popular today, namely, one that views the learning of the magi as an asset that enabled them to interpret the revelation and so helped them to find the Christ. Rather, that so-called learning typically represents a false understanding from which they must be converted. The gifts of the magi are often understood as tokens of such a conversion. Frankincense and myrrh, it is asserted, were the instruments of their trade, and the gold presented to Christ was specifically that which they had received for the practice of that trade. Thus, their presentation of these items is a token of repentance equivalent to the burning of magic books in Acts 19:19.[319]

I do not want to contend that all these elaborations are in line with the reading of the text expected of Matthew's implied readers.[320] Dramatic descriptions of the celestial manifestation, appeals to angelic interpreters, identification of the meaning of the gifts . . . all these elements of reception history represent attempts at filling narrative gaps and resolving ambiguities. At present, I only want to note that for a long time readers filled these gaps and resolved these ambiguities in ways that regarded magi as persons devoid of useful knowledge. Matthew's magi seem almost universally to have been regarded as ignorant. Ignatius uses the very word *ignorance* to describe the state from which God called them. Augustine even applies Isaiah 1:3 to them: "In the Magi, the ox began to recognize its owner, and the donkey its master's manger."[321] The reference is reminiscent of Philo's ironic comment (see page 152) that the magus Balaam was less keen than the beast he rode. To use the modern idiom, these magi were "dumb as an ox (ass)." That's how most readers viewed them for centuries.

So when did this change? There are hints in the tradition of subversive counterreadings all along. The strongest of these comes from John Chrysostom, who complains in a fourth-century sermon that some Christians infer from Matthew 2 that astrology can be trusted.[322] He clearly regards this as a misunderstanding of the text, but his notation of it serves as a reminder of the fluidity of interpretation and, perhaps, the inevitability of deconstruction. Some scoundrels, from the golden-throated preacher's point of view, were taking the most clear proof text against astrology anywhere in the New Testament and twisting it so as to make it appear to support what it actually denounced.[323]

Still, the earliest reference I can find that extolls Matthew's magi as wise men is in the writings of the Venerable Bede in the eighth century. For him, they were paradigmatic theologians, searchers after truth whose quest brings them to Christ. Notably, Bede does not endorse astrology. He extols the magi as symbols of the knowledgeable while ignoring what, historically, would have been the specific content of their knowledge. For example, he offers a new, rationalist interpretation of the gifts. Instead of occult wares that must be surrendered, the items become practical offerings that the alert magi knew would be needed to supply understandable, if somewhat worldly, needs: gold to relieve the poverty of the peasant parents; incense to sweeten the odor of the stable; and myrrh to kill the worms in Jesus and strengthen his body.[324] Bede also stressed the magi's ecumenical character, identifying them as symbols of the three sons of Noah and, hence, as representatives of the three continents of the earth (Asia, Europe, and Africa). Together, they signify the wisdom of the whole earth.[325] Bede, of course, is recognized as the forbear of a major intellectual movement. He not only wrote his definitive *Ecclesiastical History of the English Nation* but also numerous books on natural phenomena. He was, truly, a Renaissance man before the time; how interesting, then, that his interpretation of the magi does not seem to surface again until the Renaissance proper, and then it flourishes. Let us consider the work of two otherwise diverse figures.

- *Roger Bacon* (c. 1214–c. 1292) was an English philosopher and scientist who specialized in mathematics and physics, especially optics. He considers the magi in a special section of his major scientific work *Opus Maius* under the heading "Application of Mathematics to Sacred Subjects."[326] Bacon rejects any astrological doctrine of determinism but holds that in this instance the heavens contained signs of God's work that could be recognized by ancient astronomers. Thus, God "willed to arrange his affairs in such a way as to show to rational souls by means of the planets certain things which he foresaw or predestined" (1.288). This has a double significance. On the one hand, divine approval of science is expressed; on the other, independent corroboration of Christian mystery is obtained: "we truly have great solace in our faith, when the philosophers who have been led only by the exercise of their reason agree with us" (1.276). The latter quote is a shocking revelation. Suddenly, the magi are "philosophers." They are led not by a miracle but "only [!] by the exercise of their reason." Exemplars of all "rational souls," their successful quest illustrates the facility of scholarship to uncover divine truth, which is attested in nature. Notably, the church did not take "great solace" in Bacon's disclosures but imprisoned him for the last fifteen years of his life.

- *Marsilio Ficino* (1433–1499) was an Italian priest whose translations and commentaries on classical authors are usually credited with generating Florentine Platonism, which had an enormous impact on subsequent European thought. His sermon on the magi, *De stella magorum,* was extremely influential, for it was taken up by his contemporaries Philippe de Mornay, Robert Parsons, and Sir Walter Raleigh and was frequently cited throughout the sixteenth and seventeenth centuries. According to Ficino, the magi demonstrate the existence of "a Gentile revelation" parallel to that of the Jewish scriptures.[327] The magi appear to have possessed a body of knowledge that must have its origin in God and that was able to lead them to some apprehension of divine truth. In fact, Ficino declares, the star of Bethlehem was a comet, which explains its curious behavior—its movement across the skies and its disappearance and reappearance as it coursed through the elemental sublunar spheres. The magi themselves were "oriental astronomers" capable of discerning this comet and of interpreting its movements. Of course, the comet was "non causa Christi, sed signum," that is, only a sign and not a cause of the divine events. Ficino, like Bacon, rejects astral determinism, but does allow that God sent these primal scientists a message in their own language. The story provides divine validation for the acquisition of pagan learning.[328]

We may pause to recognize how slim the exegetical evidence would be for these claims. On what textual grounds can the magi's response to the star be credited to the exercise of reason or science? Are not these introductions as tendentious as Augustine's importation of angels? What prompted such then-novel interpretations? Trexler notes,

> [T]his new imagination of the magi occurred not only in the wake of early modern hermeticism but also at about the time when the first court-sponsored academies of intellectuals were taking form in western Europe, bodies which later centuries would describe as scientific priesthoods also able to calculate the future.[329]

The magi came to be regarded as generic representatives of secular learning. The story actually became a favorite biblical paradigm for demonstrating how education leads to truth. The magi became astronomers or scientists. Like the heretical Copernicus, they were representatives of those who through secular science were able to see truth that eluded religious authorities. As such, they could be regarded as academicians or scholars by interpreters who would have denounced the tenets of actual magian lore as superstition. From the example of the magi, the seventeenth-century Bishop Lancelot Andrewes deduced, "There is no starre, or beame of it; there is no truth at all, in human learning or Philosophie, that thwarteth any truth in Divinite; but sorteth well with it, and serveth it."[330]

These magi were less representatives of Persia than of ancient Rome, which the Renaissance sought to recapture. This is pictured explicitly in the well-known painting of Domenico Ghirandaio called *Adoration of the Shepherds*. While the focus of the work is on its titular heroes, one corner of the painting reveals the magi en route to Bethlehem, passing under a Roman triumphal arch inscribed to Pompey. Likewise, an anonymous woodcut from about 1500 sets the adoration itself in Rome and presents at least one of the magi as dressed in the armor of a Roman soldier.[331] Botticelli's famous *Adoration* actually portrays members of the Medici family as the magi.

In the period of the Enlightenment, readings that viewed the magi as wise men came to be regarded as the only "academically correct" way of understanding this story. This does not mean that such readings prevailed. The populace continued to emulate royalty rather than learning, to the distress of Voltaire, who griped that "everywhere, the feast of the Kings is celebrated, nowhere that of the Magi."[332] It is highly unlikely that the Deist Voltaire thought people should be celebrating a feast devoted to observance of the Zodiac. Rather, in suggesting that magi are more worthy of honor than kings, he was using the word *magi* as a generic symbol for scholars, that is, for people like him.[333]

Such an interpretation served well the ideological interests of intellectual renewal but, as we have seen, ignored any consideration of the discourse setting of Matthew's narrative and stressed construction of what is not in the text (the magi's ability to interpret the star) over what is present (the magi's inability to find the Christ without explicit direction). Still, the reading has persisted[334] and survived to the present day where, in one form or another, it is endorsed by almost all modern scholars:

- Raymond Brown thought the magi "represent the best of pagan lore and religious receptivity that has come to seek Jesus through nature."[335]
- W. D. Davies and Dale C. Allison see the magi as "eastern intellectuals." Indeed, "it is readily apparent that the magi in the First Gospel play a favourite, well-attested role, one they played often in the Graeco-Roman world. They are the mysterious wise foreigners who, having mastered secret lore, are able to recognize who it is that will be king."[336]
- Richard Horsley describes them as "*the* figures in the East" (emphasis his) who would have the necessary wisdom to know what the sign in the heavens meant.[337]
- Martin Hengel and Helmut Merkel identify Matthew's magi as "the intellectually elite of the Gentile world" and understand the point of the story as being to offer a redemption of Hellenistic wisdom through its subjection to Christ.[338]

Such examples can be multiplied. Most telling, perhaps, is the simple fact that many modern versions of the Bible consider "wise men" to be a suitable translation of *magoi* in Matthew 2:1, 7, 16 (making the term an identical synonym for sophoi in 11:26; 23:34).[339]

So scholars discover in the story a blessing of scholarship. This is not surprising—I for one agree with the previously cited sentiments expressed by Bishop Andrewes. But would Matthew? I think not. Nor do I think that a blessing of scholarship is what Matthew's implied readers are expected to find in this text. The ideological evaluation of wisdom presumed for Matthew's narrative is not friendly to scholarship. Readers who believe the way Matthew's implied readers are expected to believe would not be motivated to find such a message. But post-Renaissance, post-Enlightenment readers *are* motivated to do so—in the same way that post-Constantinian readers were motivated to find a blessing of royalty. The reading of Matthew's narrative that regards the magi as wise men whose learning enables or at least assists them in finding the Christ is as unexpected as that which regards them as kings. Like the latter, it is a reading that developed through the exploitation of narrative gaps via imposition of ideology foreign to the world of the story and to the discourse setting of the narrative.

Chapter Ten

The Magi and the Gospel

It is risky business to try to trace the history of reception for any text, especially one that is nineteen hundred years old and that has been read as widely as Matthew's Gospel. Only a slim minority of the actual readings this text has received are recorded anywhere, and I do not pretend to have been comprehensive in my canvass of these. Still, I think that general trajectories in interpretation are discernible, just as I think that some implicit expectations about how such a text is expected to be received are discernible. Both presumptions are controversial, I know, and if my thesis is bold I am at least sufficiently modest to present it as a guess, as a hypothetical reconstruction of what appears (to me of course) to have happened.

Let me summarize briefly the findings of our last three chapters:

I think that Matthew's Gospel evinces an implicit hostility toward both wisdom and royalty, both of which are regarded as forms of worldly power. Matthew's implied readers, then, would be expected to interpret the story of the magi within this ideological framework. I think, furthermore, that Matthew's Gospel was written with the assumption that its readers would regard magi the way they were regarded in other Jewish literature of this period—as people lacking in the two forms of worldly power just cited. Specifically, Matthew's implied readers are expected to think of magi as ignorant servants, as people marginalized with respect to political power and with respect to true wisdom. Still, Matthew's narrative—like all narratives—contains gaps and ambiguities that allow even careful and compliant readers some fluidity of interpretation. Two such gaps were important for our study: 1) Matthew's description of the magi's actions seems to allude in some undefined way to actions ascribed to kings in the Old Testament; 2) Matthew's indication that the magi came to Jerusalem because they saw a star leaves open to the imagination what the exact nature of this revelation was and how the magi were able to interpret it. I have argued that a) these gaps created potential for Matthew's narrative to be read in unexpected ways and that b) the likelihood of this potential finding fulfillment was enhanced by a growing resistance to the narrative's ideological assumptions.

The history of reception seems to bear this out. As long as readers thought the way that Matthew's implied readers are expected to think, the gaps caused no problems. Readers noticed the intertextual connection between magi and kings without thereby identifying the magi *as* kings. Readers understood the revelation of the star in ways that did not attribute the magi's perception to their specialized knowledge. Instead, the most dramatic changes in the history of interpretation corresponded to changes in ideology. The post-Constantinian Christianization of the empire established a climate in which the magi came to be identified as kings by readers who had developed a new positive evaluation of royal power. Likewise, the Renaissance and especially the Enlightenment established a climate in which the magi came to be identified as wise persons by readers who had developed a new positive evaluation of secular scholarship. Both identifications are unexpected, and both are ideological readings. They impose foreign perspectives on the story, reading it through lenses that its readers would not be expected to possess.

Now, how do we evaluate such processes? That is the fourth step in my paradigm, the one that I have said is not really a part of my reading strategy as such. Any friendly use of first-person plural pronouns must now cease. I don't know how *you* might evaluate any of this. I can only tell you how I do: *I regard both the reading that identifies the magi as kings and that which identifies the magi as wise persons as spurious readings that are to be rejected.* But why?

I do not think they are to be rejected simply because they are unexpected readings. I will, however, acknowledge a certain prejudice in this regard. I admit to a default preference for expected readings; acceptance of biblical authority seems to imply that much. I guess that is one reason why I think the kind of work laid out in Part Two is worthwhile. I have said repeatedly that my main interest is not to determine a "correct" reading but to understand the reading process. Yes, but all else being equal, I would rather embrace an interpretation of scripture that falls within the parameters of expected readings than one that does not. Still, as we shall see, "all else" is not always equal.

I have found in my own use of the Bible that unexpected readings sometimes add dimensions of insight that I applaud. My understanding of scripture as a *living* Word requires that I acknowledge fluidity of interpretation, that I allow static texts to address changing contexts. I know Christian interpreters who want to deny the potential legitimacy of any unexpected reading of scripture, but I think they inevitably paint themselves into an untenable hermeneutical corner. For one thing, if one accepts the writings of the New Testament as scripture, then one endorses the legitimacy of numerous unexpected readings of Old Testament passages.[340] Does any interpreter seriously think that the implied readers of Exodus or Numbers are expected to regard the manna in the wilderness and the water from the rock as eucharistic symbols? If not, then Paul produces a strikingly unexpected reading of those texts in 1 Corinthians 10:1–5 (cf. Exod. 16:4–35; 17:7; Num. 20:7–11). Or, again, the Revised Common Lectionary used in most Christian denominations designates Isaiah 52:13—53:12 as an appointed lesson for Good Friday. I do not believe that the implied readers of that text are expected to identify the suffering servant of the Lord described there with Jesus—but I do identify that figure with Jesus when I hear that text read. In fact, I tend to view the Isaianic poem as commentary on the crucifixion.[341]

Likewise, I have no problem with interpreters differentiating themselves from Matthew's implied readers and deliberately interpreting the text from an ideological perspective that those implied readers would not be expected to espouse (e.g., feminism). Indeed, *I* do not personally view the world the way Matthew's implied readers are expected to view it, and I do not think that appreciation for the authority of scripture compels me to do so. I would be more charitable in my own assessment of political power than Matthew's Gospel is, and I would be much more generous in my evaluation of learning (secular and otherwise). If the only problem with the readings that regard Matthew's magi as royal or wise figures were that such readings are unexpected, that would not be much of a problem. I could easily contend that Matthew's apocalyptic vision of reality is appropriate only for the world of the story, that the narrative needs to be read from different (unexpected) viewpoints if its meaning is to be appropriated in our (real) world.

Nor do I think these readings are to be rejected simply because they legitimize political structures that the text was actually intended to subvert. Again, I admit to a prejudice in this regard, but I don't think this is definitive for my rejection of these readings. I like to think of myself as supportive of the marginalized, and I admit that what I have presented as the expected readings of Matthew's narrative are more appealing to me than the unexpected ones for this reason alone. But for me there is also something else at stake: *theology.*

The expected reading of Matthew's narrative presents the magi not only as lacking in power or wisdom but, generically, as devoid of anything to commend them to God. The unexpected readings that regard Matthew's magi as kings or as wise persons developed understandably as attempts to renegotiate the story for different political ends. Those ends—suspect in themselves—were achieved at a theological cost. In either case, the story is reconstrued so that God's selection of the magi now becomes understandable, and I submit that, to the extent that such an incomprehensible act is understood, the theology of the text is lost. The theological message must be removed from the story in order for a new political message concerning the blessing of power to be heard. I'm not politically inclined to favor this new message anyway, but when I discover that we must give up theology in exchange for it, then I must absolutely reject such readings.

Unexpected readings, when they are persistent, teach us one thing for certain: the expected meaning has been difficult to receive. Earlier, I suggested that some resistant readings can be "unwitting" (see page 65). If readers find the ideology of a text—particularly an authoritative text—to be offensive, they may be tempted to read that text from a different ideological perspective without even knowing that they are doing so. Perhaps readers have done this with Matthew, resisting the text's apocalyptic perspective or ideological evaluation of power in order to read the story through a lens that is more congruent with their own way of thinking. But I think they have done more than this, for I think Matthew's Gospel is more deeply offensive than such a scenario indicates. Ultimately, I think that I can identify by name the ideology that the history of tradition has so strenuously resisted in this text. It is not, this time, patriarchalism or anti-Semitism. It isn't even apocalypticism or elevation of the marginalized. It is the message that, elsewhere, is called "the gospel." Paul maintains that "God chose what is foolish in the world to shame the wise, God chose what is weak in the world to shame the strong" (1 Cor. 1:27). The expected reading of Matthew's story of the magi essentially offers a narrative depiction of this.[342] Such a depiction is scandalous. The gospel of God is always scandalous. At base level, the unexpected readings of Matthew's story represent attempts at removing the scandal, removing the gospel, by making the magi somehow worthy of God's favor.[343]

Matthew's story relates how God rejects kings (symbolized by Herod) and wise persons (symbolized by the chief priests and scribes) in order to reveal Christ to the weak and foolish magi. Readers have had a hard time hearing this text, and the difficulty has increased in direct proportion to the church's accumulation of power and wisdom. By actually turning the magi into kings and/or wise persons, readers have managed to create a meaning from this text that is almost exactly the opposite from what implied readers are expected to receive. By so doing, the scandalous message of the gospel has been successfully resisted and a divine preference for wisdom and power secured.

Theological Evaluation

I am suggesting that the fourth step of my paradigm—evaluation of biblical readings or interpretations—must be theological rather than simply exegetical. As such, it is necessarily autobiographical and subjective. It need not be *entirely* autobiographical and subjective, however.

An entirely subjective/autobiographical hermeneutic is one in which we just pick and choose among interpretations, selecting ones that are most congenial to us. I encounter this hermeneutic frequently in the church today. I hear people say, "I know the Bible says wives are supposed to submit to their husbands, but I don't think that applies to us anymore today." Why not? Is it just because you don't like what it says? Is there some rule or standard for deciding what does or does not still apply to us? Or, are we just supposed to read through the Bible and accept as authoritative the stuff we like and dismiss as irrelevant the stuff we don't like?

Such a hermeneutic actually rejects scripture as authoritative in any meaningful sense of the word. People who read the Bible in this way can only find confirmation for views they already hold, ammunition to use in ideological wars against others who think differently. They can never actually be transformed by what scripture says. I sometimes ask reputed Bible believers to identify one instance in which they have changed their beliefs, values, or lifestyle based on something that the Bible says. I am amazed at how many times they cannot think of a single example of this ever happening—yet they maintain that the Bible is authoritative for their lives. How can people claim that the Bible has authority over them if they have never had to submit to that authority? Is it just a hypothetical authority? They *would* change their beliefs, values, or lifestyle if these ever did turn out to conflict with what the Bible says (in passages still relevant for today), but as it turns out this just hasn't happened. This, I submit, is a hermeneutic with no "existential cash value."

Biblical interpreters who want to avoid such cavalier treatment of scripture often refer to some *exegetical* standard for determining not only "what the Bible means" but also "what is authoritative and true for us." The assumption may be that these two concepts are, or should be, identical. The most common such standard has been "authorial intent." What a Bible passage *means* is what the author intended it to mean, and whatever the author intended must be accepted as authoritative and true for us as well as for the original audience.

This looks good on paper. It looks good to the pious, at least, to those who want to maintain that the biblical authors were inspired by God. I am such a person, or at least I try to be, but I have discovered (as have most educated pietists) that it doesn't work. First, it doesn't work because in many cases we don't even know who the author is or which layer of tradition should be identified as authorial. I have used the example of a modern motion picture. Who is the author of such a film? The screenwriter? The director? The producer? The actors who utter the lines? Whose intention should be deemed normative for deciding what the work means? The Gospel of Matthew is a bit like that. We have sayings uttered by Jesus (in Aramaic) that were translated and preserved in the Q source (in Greek)[344] and then redacted and woven into a narrative framework (inherited from Mark) by an evangelist whom we call Matthew (though we have no idea who he or she was or what his or her real name might have been). Which intention should we try to discern when interpreting such a saying? The intention of Jesus? Or of Q? Or of Mark? Or of "Matthew"?

But, let's say we just forget all that and arbitrarily decide that the evangelist who put the Gospel into its final form is the one who speaks for God. This is what interpreters who embrace a hermeneutic of authorial intent usually do, ignoring the ironic fact that one clear aspect of that evangelist's intent is for no disciple of Jesus ever to be elevated above the Master himself (Matt. 10:24; 23:8). Be that as it may, the hermeneutic still does not work for the simple reasons that a) we cannot always (with confidence) discern the intentions of that ancient writer, and b) even when we can, those intentions often have nothing to do with us. The latter point is ultimately the most significant. A hermeneutic that privileges authorial intent grounds revelation so definitively in the past as to render its relevance inversely proportionate to the passage of time. The task of biblical interpretation becomes discernment of what God said to other people a long time ago in a far away place. The Holy Spirit becomes obsolete and the character of scripture as a *living* word is lost.

I have a friend who belongs to one of those big, generic (no name brand) churches—a nondenominational fellowship that calls itself "The New Testament Church." He tells me, "We do everything just like they did in the New Testament."[345] I doubt that this is true, but if it is, then I think it should be called "The First-Century Church." In Matthew's Gospel, Jesus tells a parable about a man giving talents to his slaves before he goes on a journey (25:14–30). Two of them use the money wisely and increase its worth. The third buries it in the ground so as to make certain he can return it to his master in the same condition in which it was entrusted to him. His approach seems to illustrate the very *mission statement* of my friend's church. Their goal will be achieved, their proudest accomplishment won, when on that great day of our Lord's return, they are able to say, "Look, here is your church exactly as you left it. Here, you have what is yours." They think he will be pleased to hear this. I'll spare you the conclusion to the parable (25:30), which I hope is metaphorical.

A hermeneutic that privileges authorial intent inevitably points in this direction. It should be repudiated above all by the pious.[346] Many such interpreters seem to recognize this intuitively but find themselves unable to say the words since they still want to maintain that the biblical authors were inspired by God. What they do, then, is affirm the hermeneutic of authorial intent in theory yet find ways to cheat on its application. There are two especially popular ways of cheating. First, some interpreters will involve themselves in all sorts of exegetical gymnastics to assert that certain authors did not really mean or intend to say what they appear to mean or intend to say. So the author of Ephesians did not really think that wives should submit to their husbands (Eph. 5:22–24); Matthew (or Jesus) did not really think it is wrong to save money for the future (Matt. 6:19); the author of Titus did not really believe that people from Crete are dishonest, vicious, and lazy (Tit. 1:12); Paul did not really think that nature itself teaches it is shameful for a man to have long hair (1 Cor. 11:14). And so on. Lesser commentaries are filled with attempts to explain away what biblical authors appear to have believed on the premise that if the biblical authors *did* believe these things, then we would be obliged to believe them also. A slightly misquoted line from Shakespeare often comes to mind: "Methinks, they do protest too much."[347]

The second way to cheat on the hermeneutic of authorial intent is to invoke a principle of *analogy.* The interpreter affirms that the author was inspired by God, but admits that this revelation of God's word was to people of a time and place other than our own and so cannot be directly applicable to us. The words of scripture are indirectly applicable, however, insofar as our situations are analogous to those addressed in the Bible. Thus, the counsel to first-century Ephesian wives may still be relevant for twenty-first century American marriages, but "submit to your husband's authority" becomes "respect your spouse's interests" in the analogous situation. The counsel to the Ephesians is not directly applicable to us because it presupposes a social context in which one of the two marriage partners (the husband) was invested with totalitarian authority. Rather than insisting that twenty-first century society should be like first-century society, we look for analogous ways to fulfill the author's intentions in the transformed world.

I have nothing against this principle of analogy; in fact, I think it is absolutely necessary and should be identified more explicitly in contexts where it is now applied surreptitiously. Nothing in our world ever corresponds *exactly* to the world of the Bible, and no word of scripture can ever be read as applicable to us without some assumption of analogy. For example, when Jesus says, "[W]hoever divorces his wife and marries another commits adultery" (Mark 10:11), he is speaking about the termination of marriages recognized by Palestinian Jewish law. The evangelist Mark's inclusion of this saying in his Gospel probably implies that the author intends for the words to apply to the termination of marriages recognized by laws of the Roman empire in general. Virtually all biblical interpreters assume (correctly, I think) that the words also apply to the termination of marriages in modern societies. But in doing this, they evoke a principle of analogy. Marriage in our world may be an obvious analogy to marriage in the biblical world, but it is an analogy nonetheless; the two concepts are not identical. Hypothetically, a scholar might argue that first-century Palestinian marriages and twenty-first-century American marriages are such radically different institutions that the termination of one is *not* analogous to the termination of the other. I would have to be persuaded of such an argument, but the point is that Christians who think Jesus spoke against divorce (by which they mean termination of marriage as we know it) are often invoking an analogy without even realizing it.

I have no problem with the principle of analogy, but those who invoke it are cheating on the hermeneutic of authorial intent. How so? The nature and extent of any analogy must be determined by *readers.* Ultimately, the author's intent is not determinative for meaning. What is determinative for meaning is the readers' perception of that intent and the readers' assessment of whether and how it is applicable to the readers' own situation. As soon as author-oriented critics begin to invoke a principle of analogy, they have entered the realm of reader-response criticism. They've left Kansas for what at first seems to be a scarier world. But perhaps it just *seems* scary because it is so unfamiliar: munchkins and witches are no worse than tornadoes, once you learn how to deal with them. Still . . . it does help to know where you are.

In my own understanding of scripture I admit once again to a "default pref-erence" for readings that concur with what appears analogous to authorial intent. But I have also discovered that this cannot be the final arbitrating stan-dard for evaluating biblical interpretations. Personally, I doubt that very many Christian interpreters of the Bible *really* allow authorial intent to be determina-tive of what they think all scripture means. The system breaks down and excep-tions intrude. The Song of Songs is allegorized,[348] as is the beatitude on those who smash the heads of Babylonian babies against the rocks (Ps. 137:9).[349] Isaiah 53 and, indeed, the entire Old Testament is interpreted in light of "the Christ event." Disciples are allowed to own two shirts (contra Matt. 10:10) and to save money for their children to go to college (contra Matt. 6:19). The Jesus of the Gospels is understood in light of the christological insight of Paul. Inter-preters who preach or teach from the scriptures inevitably find meaning in the Bible that transcends or surpasses what was in the minds of historical authors. Few Christians commend castration (either as a path to holiness [Matt. 19:12] or as a panacea for their enemies [Gal. 5:12]), think sexual desire alone is a sound basis for marriage (1 Cor. 7:8–9), fear uncovered female heads may pro-voke angels to lust after their women (1 Cor. 11:10; cf. Gen. 6:4), suppose a fit punishment for rapists would be to make them marry their victims (Deut. 22:28–29), or believe it is God's will that every human being on this planet should "be fruitful and multiply" (Gen. 1:28).[350]

For a while, some thought that narrative criticism offered a good compro-mise between the inevitable subjectivity of reader response and the failed hermeneutic of authorial intent.[351] The thought now was to privilege not the intention of a historical author but the expectations of implied readers. What-ever readers are expected to derive from their engagement with a biblical text might be deemed the authoritative and divinely inspired meaning of that text. This may have seemed promising because meaning that is so defined tends to be more general and, therefore, more "timeless" than meaning defined by the specific interests of a particular historical context: even if Matthew did polemi-cize against Pharisees as a way of denouncing the synagogue across the street, implied readers are expected to see these characters as exemplars of evil in the world and to draw conclusions not about one particular social or ethnic group but about how evil functions in every day and age.

Again I admit my preference. I like it when my own reading of scripture seems to concur with that which is expected of implied readers. It yields a sense of continuity and congruence, a communion with the text, an almost sacra-mental awareness of the Spirit at work. But ultimately, it doesn't work, not con-sistently or reliably enough to serve as the standard by which interpretations are evaluated. As I hope this book has demonstrated, the differences in defining expectations of implied readers and intentions of historical authors are of degree, not kind. I think we can achieve greater success at the former, but cer-tainty still eludes us. And, as we have seen, expected readings must often be defined with reference to the discourse setting of a narrative, to the time and place in which it was written. Thus, revelation remains, to a certain extent, grounded in the past. Matthew's implied readers are expected to regard slavery as an acceptable social institution and to view the world with an essentially unchallenged patriarchal mind-set that regards men as socially superior to women (that is, as *justifiably* more powerful than women). I cannot embrace a hermeneutic that elevates the implicit, contextually derived assumptions of biblical literature to the level of divinely revealed truth.

No, it seems that the systematic theologians have been right all along. There is no pure exegetical standard through which an objective method can discover timeless truth. Thus, the standard for truth is not the Bible per se but the gospel of Jesus Christ, and all interpretations of the Bible (expected readings and unexpected ones) must be evaluated in light of this.[352] The Bible remains authoritative because the gospel itself is derived from the Bible. Protestants recognize this as the principle of "scripture interpreting scripture." Lutherans recognize it as the principle of "a canon within the canon."[353]

Readers' Responses/Criticisms

My thinking on these matters is neither complete nor perfect. A number of people have raised questions that have prompted further thought. I share two encounters.

First Encounter: What Is the Gospel?

I shared an early draft of my magi study, focusing primarily on the question of royalty, at the annual gathering of the (Roman) Catholic Biblical Association. I used only a three-step paradigm that sought to identify, compare, and account for the unexpected reading that views the magi as kings. Still, the question of evaluation inevitably arose. In keeping with what I have previously discussed, I declared that for me such evaluation can only be offered with reference to the theological standard of "the gospel." The reading that crowns the magi as kings is to be rejected not simply because it is historically inaccurate or because it fails to agree with the implicit intent of the author or the expected response of readers but, primarily, because it compromises the gospel of Jesus Christ.

A Bible teacher, a nun, asked, "And just who gets to determine what this 'gospel' is?"

"Um . . ." I hesitated for a moment, and then answered, ". . . Martin Luther?"

Okay, that was a joke—but only partly so. As a Lutheran, I readily admit that the sixteenth-century Reformer has probably had more of an effect on my understanding of "the gospel" than anyone else. He has not had an exclusive effect, however, so perhaps the more accurate answer would have been "Mark Allan Powell." *I* determine what *I* think the gospel is, and then I apply this standard evaluatively to all ideas and perspectives, including my own.

My understanding of the gospel, based on Luther and others, is of course subject to critique. The nature of such a critique, however, is significant. Let us imagine that you have been able to follow me in the magi study right up to this final stage of evaluation. That is, let's imagine that you think my analysis of what are and are not expected readings of that story is valid. Now I am proposing that the unexpected readings that regard the magi as kings or as wise persons are to be rejected as contrary to the gospel of Jesus Christ. Even if you have followed me through the last three chapters of this book, you still might object to this evaluation. And you might do so for either of two reasons:

- You might claim the readings are *not* contrary to the gospel, but that my understanding of the gospel is limited or false. The unexpected readings of the magi story that I am so quick to reject may actualize potential implications of the Christian gospel in ways that I do not realize.
- You might claim that the gospel itself is too limited or false to serve as such a pervasive evaluative standard. Unexpected readings of the magi story may be appreciated regardless of whether they pass muster with some arbitrary sectarian dogma.

These are two different matters. The nun at the Catholic Biblical Association meeting might have challenged me on the first point, but she never would have challenged me on the second.

In response to the first objection, I would humble myself for enlightenment. Certainly, I have grown in my understanding of the gospel over the years and certainly I expect to continue growing in that understanding in whatever years I have left. Early on, I think that I equated "the gospel" with the Pauline message of "justification by grace," narrowly defined. Basically, I thought the good news revealed in and through Jesus Christ was that "God accepts us just the way we are." A lot of Lutherans think that.

Then, I encountered liberation theology. I remember a seminar I attended in college. A large African-American man had two big signs up front. One read, "Jesus Christ accepts you the way you are." The other said, "Jesus Christ will change your life." Both are biblical and both are good news, the speaker affirmed. "So why is it that you Lutherans equate the gospel with one sign and not the other? You say, 'Jesus will change my life? Well, that's nice, but the *really* good news is that he accepts me the way I am!' You get so excited that Jesus will accept you as you are that, after a while, some of us begin to wonder whether this isn't because you plan on *staying* the way you are—whether Jesus will change you or not. Now, where I come from, in the inner city, I know some folks who—if you tell them, 'Jesus accepts you the way you are'—will respond, 'Well, that's nice of him, but the fact is I don't really like being the way I am. My life isn't so good. It's nice that Jesus loves me even though I'm poor and hungry and my life is a mess, but you know what some *really* good news would be? *Really* good news would be if he'd change my life so that I don't have to be this way.'"

Later, I discovered that the best Lutheran theologians (starting with Luther) have always defined justification in ways that include sanctification *and* liberation—it's not just a matter of "Jesus accepts you the way you are," though it is that, too. And as I kept studying the Bible, I came to understand Paul's concern for justification by grace in light of his overarching eschatological vision and his regard for the righteousness of God. These, too, are part of the gospel. Historical Jesus studies helped me to see the significance of what Paul leaves out: the importance of Jesus' teaching and earthly ministry, which identify proclamation and enactment of God's reign as "the gospel of God" (Mark 1:14–15). Feminist theology and contact with international scholars helped me to rethink my traditional understanding of sacrificial atonement in light of equally biblical emphases on reconciliation.[354]

So, my understanding of the gospel is itself a dynamic standard. You may challenge me on whether I understand the gospel sufficiently, and I will hear you out. If your arguments seem sound, I will modify my views as I have many times before. Thus, "my understanding of the gospel" is not an entirely subjective standard by which I evaluate interpretations. True, it is and must be *my* understanding, but it is asserted with reference to something outside of myself—to the Bible and to communities of biblical interpreters.

But I draw a line somewhere between the two objections stated previously (p. 181). Those who offer the second do not belong to my community of interpreters, and both they and I must recognize this. Respectfully, of course. I feel no need to shake the dust off my shoes or anything so insulting. If you want to make "scientology" or "socialism" or "evangelicalism" or "the Republican party" or "what benefits Al Franken" or "the conventional wisdom of modern America" or *whatever* the evaluative standard by which you determine what is true, honorable, just, pure, pleasing, commendable, excellent, and worthy of praise (Phil. 4:8), so be it. I believe, quite stubbornly, that God acted in and through Jesus Christ so definitively that what that act revealed (which is what I call "the gospel") has set the standard by which all other standards must be judged. You can think I'm wrong, and I will think you're wrong. You can pity me, and I will pity you. But let us both save some tears for those who have no such standard at all, or—and this is always the case—who have one and don't know what it is.[355]

Encounter Number Two: The Danger of Education

This entire study began as an address that I was invited to give when I was installed into an endowed chair at my academic institution, a school that grants graduate degrees in various fields of theological study. The part about God rejecting the wise and intelligent in favor of the foolish and ignorant (now contained in chapter 8) was not fully developed, but it was present, and it prompted the Dean of our fine school to inquire why, if I believe this, I want to occupy a chair at an institution devoted to transforming foolish and ignorant people into wise and intelligent ones (not his exact words, obviously). Is scholarship a *bad* thing? And do I believe this *as a scholar*?

Well, no, I don't, but it is a worthy question, and it requires a two-part answer. First, recall that I do not reject identification of Matthew's magi as "wise persons" because I agree with Matthew's antiintellectualism but, rather, because such a conceptualization results in a story where God is shown to *favor* the wise. Worldly wisdom can of course be appreciated and valued (though Matthew's story does not appear to appreciate or value it) without possession of such wisdom being identified as a sign of God's favor—or as a quality that earns such favor. I have argued that acceptance of biblical authority does not mean that real readers must come to believe or think the way that implied readers are expected to believe or think within the world of the narrative. I feel no more compulsion to adopt the Matthean bias against scholarship than I do to embrace its patriarchal mind-set, attitude toward slavery, or belief that all kingdoms of the earth are ruled by agents of the devil.

What accepting biblical authority *does* mean for me, however, is adopting the perspective of the implied readers long enough to determine the effect that the story is expected to have. In this case, I discern that such an effect is in keeping with my understanding of the gospel, so I yield to its rhetorical power. It does transform me, changing my thinking and perhaps my life.

My description of that effect will be a poor substitute for what you might experience by so yielding yourself, and I'm not even sure if I can describe it very well. I have to resort to analogy, and the best analogy I can think of is the relationship of faith and wealth. We all know that there are faithful, rich Christians who use their money for the glory of God and for the advancement of God's purposes. We do not think that having money is necessarily a bad thing; we know that the world would be even worse than it is if everyone were poor and no one rich. Still, we realize that money is a powerful incentive to unrighteousness, and we recognize that in the Bible God seems almost invariably to favor the poor over the rich. Similarly, education itself is a good thing, and we may serve both God and humanity by increasing the quantity and quality of knowledgeable people in our world. But the accumulation of knowledge grants power—and power corrupts.

Imagine a young person who says, "This is my plan: I am going into business, and I intend to be successful. I want to make lots of money, and I intend to be very rich, much richer than most people in our society. Then, I intend to use my wealth in ways that are pleasing to God."

If someone were to say that to me, I would see red flags of warning. It's not that this couldn't happen. But I would say, "The way that you describe is fraught with peril. If your goal is to have more money than other people, the chances of your compromising your ethics to achieve that goal or of your exploiting others once you have achieved it are great indeed."

Yet people come to us regularly at the theological seminary with a similar agenda. They want to obtain a Master's degree, to be better educated than most people in our society. They want to gain specialized learning regarding matters of God and faith. They want to acquire far more knowledge in such areas than is possessed by the great majority of people in the church. Though, of course, they intend to use this education and knowledge in God-pleasing ways.

As near as I can tell, most of them do so use it. But still I warn them: You are seeking power. You are seeking to become officially recognized as an expert on matters that are important to your local religious community. You are seeking *power.* Realize this—and what it means.

It means, at least, that the way is fraught with peril. The temptations to use such knowledge abusively are great. And it *may* mean, though I am not certain, that they are deciding here and now to give up a share of their celestial reward. I'm not sure if anybody really knows what life will be like in the Great Beyond. All we have is mythological language. But what we have tells us that there will be "levels" of reward and participation in heaven. Once, I was excited that Matthew says those who teach Jesus' commandments will be "greatest in the kingdom" (5:19); now, I am quite sure that this does not mean me. The first will be last, the last first—and for Matthew, the "first" certainly include the educated. Jesus does not say anywhere (I've looked) that those who are among the first in this world can still be first in heaven, provided they use their "firstness" in God-pleasing ways. No, the first will be last, period. If there's a "low-rent district" inside those pearly gates, those who were rich on earth will occupy it. Saved by God's grace, they will rejoice to be there, knowing it is only by a supernatural miracle that they made it through the needle's eye at all. And whatever kings and Bible professors make it will be right there with them.

I have chosen to be one of the least in the kingdom. I guess I made that choice a long time ago. Perhaps I can use my education to serve those who seek knowledge, just as I use my material resources to aid those who crave bread, but I no longer have any illusions about where I do and will stand. I'm hoping for a shanty on the edge of town, a trailer even. Put me with Chris Farley in "a van down by the river." Just let me inside . . . I understand . . . the mansions are for the magi.

BONUS TRACKS

Some extras.

- *Sequels to Elisha.* This is a sermon that was preached at the Gloria
  Dei Worship Center at Trinity Lutheran Seminary on February 14,
  1996. It is basically unedited, except that I added a few explanatory
  notes and omitted some jokes that would not really work outside the
  community. They were pretty good jokes, too. The text is 2 Kings
  5:1–14, as appointed in the Revised Common Lectionary for
  Epiphany 6 (Series B). I include this sermon because the reliance on
  reader-response criticism and particularly *Wirkungsgeschichte* is quite
  evident. Normally it would not be so evident. My colleague Lynn
  Nakamura tells preachers that exegesis is like underwear—your congregation wants you to have it on but they don't really want to see it.
  Heeding her advice, I always do this sort of exegetical research (historical criticism, narrative criticism, *Wirkungsgeschichte,* reader
  response) for every sermon I preach, but I rarely refer so explicitly to
  the reading strategies themselves. I did so this time because the sermon was for seminarians and one of my objectives was to demonstrate how the strategies that I teach in the classroom affect my
  practice of pastoral ministry. It is almost a sermon about preaching.
  Metahomiletics.
- *"Oh Henry!": Another Gift of the Magi.* A little reflection on how
  ivory tower scholarship (in this case, that of Richard Trexler) might
  trickle down to benefit people for whom it probably was not
  intended, in ways that were probably not intended. Sometimes it
  happens.

Chapter Eleven
Sequels to Elisha

I always think of Elisha as "the sequel prophet." His whole life and ministry were pretty much one big sequel. He did some cool things, like making the ax head float, but he's destined always to be best remembered as the successor of another prophet, Elijah. Their names are similar, and maybe only people who read the Bible a lot know the difference. Elijah (with a "j") came first, and there's a whole series of great miracle stories in the Bible about him. The series concludes with a grand special-effects finale, with Elijah ascending up to heaven in a whirlwind accompanied by chariots of fire. If this were Hollywood, I'd think that's probably so they can bring him back next year for Elijah II, but instead they introduce a new character: Elisha (with an "sh"). The Bible says he has a double portion of the spirit of Elijah, but there are fewer stories about him and instead of ending with a big finale, the series just sort of fizzles out.

I don't mean to discount the importance of poor Elisha. Quite the contrary. I'm sure he was a very fine prophet in his own right, and it's our own fickle nature that gives him the Roger Moore treatment. I think the Elisha stories deserve a closer look, and the one that comes up in the Series B lectionary for this week is the best of the bunch. Martin Luther liked this story, and so did

Jesus, and so did one of my former professors, Nelson Trout. They had their own particular reasons for liking it, reasons that remain worthy of recall even today.

We're going to have a little adventure in reader-response criticism this morning. Reader-response criticism tells us that sometimes readers have insight into stories that even the authors might have missed. It doesn't work all the time, but it works this time. Martin Luther and Jesus both read this story and found meaning that lesser readers—people like you and me—might have missed. In fact, they found meaning that the author—that is, the Deuteronomic Historian—might have missed.

We'll take Luther first. Martin Luther thought this was a story about baptism and that the whole point was justification by grace. I suspect that interpretation would have come as a surprise to the Deuteronomic Historian, who wrote this story centuries before baptism had ever been practiced and who did not prioritize justification or grace as primary theological concerns.

Where does Luther get this? Naaman is a leper, infected with a virulent disease that might be taken as a symbol of the sin that affects every human being. We are spiritual lepers, you and I, for the image of God in which we were created has been corrupted by the Fall, and the inheritance of Adam renders us among the walking dead. Naaman would *give* anything to be healed; he would *do* anything to be healed. He takes ten talents of silver and six thousand shekels of gold; he takes horses and chariots; he gets a letter of reference from his king, the king of Syria—stating no doubt his worthiness to be healed. But that might not be enough, and Naaman still does not feel prepared to go to Elisha with his request. Instead, he goes also to Elisha's king, to the king of Israel, bearing lavish gifts, to get perhaps another reference letter. Finally . . . he arrives at the prophet's door with all his horses and chariots. But Elisha never sees the horses and the chariots. He does not read the letters of reference. He does not accept the talents of silver or shekels of gold. Elisha does not even come out of the house to meet with Naaman the leper. He just sends out a servant with the message: Leprosy, eh? Well, go wash in the Jordan, and you'll be clean.

That's where the baptism comes in. The bath in the Jordan. It's so simple. It's *too* simple. Naaman is furious, and his anger is born of pride. "I thought that *for me* he would come out! Maybe not for someone else—but for *me*—I'm the commander of the Syrian army! I've got a letter from the king! I brought silver. I brought gold! I've got *chariots!*"

And then, after he's calmed down a bit, I suppose, his servants come up, kind of timid, and say, "You know, if the prophet had asked you to perform some difficult task for him, you would have done it, wouldn't you? So—how much more—when all he said was, 'Wash and be clean.'" And there you have it: the scandal of God's grace offered to us in baptism, offensive to those whose vision of life is grounded in works-righteousness, in the desire to believe themselves worthy of what God gives freely to the undeserving—but only to the undeserving.

If Martin Luther had written an exegetical paper on this passage, he might have gotten an "F"—or at least a "Marginal," what with grade inflation. But he wasn't writing an exegetical paper; he was preaching, proclaiming the message of the text for *his* day. And even if it's not what the Deuteronomic Historian had in mind, Luther's reading is faithful to the text, for this text does indeed present God's gift of mercy as a scandal of grace, insofar as it reflects favorably on the character of the giver rather than on that of the recipient.

What *did* the author have in mind? Originally, the story of Naaman the leper appears to have been a nationalistic tale demonstrating the superiority of Israel's faith over Syrian religion. Naaman is the commander in chief of the armies of Aram—and the nations of Aram and Israel are at best competitive, at worst, enemies. Right now, they appear to be nurturing a fragile peace that the king of Israel fears could be upset by the tiniest incident.

So, against that background, how would the original audience have heard this story? The commander in chief of all the armies of Aram must come to Israel and ask a favor, first of its king, then of its prophet. He and his king must admit that in their own country the powers that be are unable to help, but that—get this!—a Hebrew slave girl has offered hope when all the Syrian priests and sorcerers could not. Not only that, but the help—when it is offered—comes in a humbling if not humiliating fashion. The Syrian commander is told that if he wants his skin to clear up he ought to take a bath! Only not in those Syrian waters—no, a real bath in the River Jordan. Seven times. No wonder Naaman is angry! "Are not Abana and Pharpar, the rivers of Damascus, better than all the waters of Israel?" he exclaims. "Could I not wash in them and be clean?" No. Sorry, you can't.

Nationalism. The whole point of the story for Israel seems to have been to provide an excuse to tell the Syrians, "Our God is better than your gods; our prophets are better than your prophets; our country is better than your country; and, for that matter, our *river* is better than your *rivers*—and the commander of your own army knows it!"

This was a very popular story until Jesus came along and ruined it. You may remember when that happened (read about it in Luke 4:14–30). It was the famous Nazareth incident, the one that led to the coining of that proverb "A prophet is not without honor except in his own hometown." The prophet who lost honor was not Elisha but Jesus. And he did so not by preaching a whole sermon on this text, but by making a casual observation. He said, "You know, there must have been a lot of lepers in Israel at the time of Elisha, but we don't hear about any of them being cleansed. It seems the only one who was healed was that guy from Syria." That's it. Just one subversive little comment, and the story is ruined. Because of course he is right. You can talk about who has the best rivers all day long; the bottom line is—in this story—*God helps a foreigner.* And not just any foreigner but the commander of enemy troops. This man Naaman keeps a conquered Israelite as a slave. And God appears to be on his side! God heals him, restores his flesh, makes him clean. "There were plenty of lepers in Israel," Jesus notes, "but none of them was cleansed."

All Jesus did that day was offer a little commonsense insight into one of the congregation's favorite Bible passages. This inspired an impromptu gathering of the board of elders at which it was decided that they would "hurl him off a cliff" (Luke 4:29). Imagine what might have happened if he had actually preached a whole sermon, if, for instance, he'd had the opportunity to update this message about Israelites and Syrians with a discussion concerning Jews and Samaritans. Or if he had launched into one of his famous "Love your enemies" homilies: "God makes the rain to fall on the good and on the bad. God makes the sun to shine on the just and the unjust alike!" (Matt. 5:45).

The effect of Jesus' comment was to *deconstruct* traditional readings of the Naaman story in a way that prepared for more explicit teaching on the universality of God's grace. As a result, the story came to mean almost the opposite of what people had wanted it to mean. The very story that had appeared to support the notion "God's on our side" now seemed to challenge that perspective.

This is the way it is with stories. Authors may think they give their stories meaning, but *readers* have the final say. But the really great thing is that this final say is never quite final, for just when we think we've got the story down, more readers come along behind us. So the story keeps taking on new meanings again and again. Such stories do not need sequels. Every reading provides a sequel of its own.

Nelson Trout was one of my professors at seminary many years ago. Later, he would become the first African-American bishop in my denomination, and before his death in 1996 he earned renown as a modern hero of the church. But I knew him years before any of this, when I was growing up. He was a friend of my parents, who were active in the Civil Rights movement, and he used to stay at our house whenever he was passing through town. He'd come to church with us, and, as a visiting ordained minister, he would often read the lessons.

Nelson had this trick of playing with his eyeglasses and pretending he couldn't read quite clearly. As it turns out, I heard Nelson read the Nazareth story from Luke's Gospel twice when I was a child, on two different occasions: once in my small Texas town and then, again, two years later, in San Antonio. He did the same thing—or almost the same thing—both times. In my home congregation, when he read the passage he said, "There were also many lepers in Israel in the time of Elisha, but none of them was cleansed except Naaman, the Communist . . . uh, wait . . . darn these bifocals! . . . not Communist, but Syrian . . . I'm sorry." Now, this was around 1962, in about the most conservative town in America, in a church where the greater part of the congregation was composed of personnel from the local military academy. Then, in San Antonio, when he read the lesson he said, ". . . none of them was cleansed except Naaman the Mexican . . . uh, wait . . . darn these bifocals!" This was in an all-white church of course. Both times Nelson's antics elicited obligatory chuckles, but I suspect there were people present who wanted to hurl him off a cliff.

Over the years, when I have read this story and many others, I've developed the habit of asking myself, "What would Nelson's bifocals see? If he were reading here . . . and now."

Chapter Twelve
"Oh, Henry!":
Another Gift of the Magi

My first parish was in southwest Texas, in the town where John Travolta and Debra Winger shot that *Urban Cowboy* movie. They filmed it while I was there, and a lot of folks turned out to watch. I didn't bother, associating Travolta with disco and . . . well, I hadn't even heard of Winger. Now, of course, I wish I'd gone.

I was only a moderately good pastor, but I was blessed to work with two highly competent senior ministers: Delmas Luedke and Henry Flathmann. It was during the latter's tenure that we had a little crisis with the Christmas program. The person in charge let a girl play one of the magi. Normally, girls were angels and boys were shepherds. This worked well because there were no necessary numbers involved: you could have twelve angels and three shepherds one year and three angels and twelve shepherds the next year, depending on how many girls and boys turned out. The angels made styrofoam halos for themselves, as well as cardboard wings with lots of glitter on them. Shepherds didn't make anything; they just brought bathrobes from home. This, too, worked well because in that place and time it could pretty much be assumed that girls were into glitter and making things while boys were into just showing up.

But then there were the magi. There were always three magi, and they were always boys, even though they had to make aluminum foil crowns and wear a lot of gaudy jewelry and bright colored, silky gowns. Sometimes girls made the crowns for them and brought jewelry and dresses that would work as gowns, and then the boys could just show up and wear what was provided. I don't think many boys would have picked being magi over shepherds if there had been a lot of choice involved, but there wasn't. Then one year we had a little eight-year-old Rosa Parks who wanted to be "one of the kings," and they let her.

It came up at church council. One member informed us that "several members" whom she represented were upset by the spectacle. Girls are not supposed to play boys' parts and vice versa. She talked on for awhile, concluding with something about "this is why there are so many homosexuals in the world" and "what kind of a message are we sending to our children?" I was about to make some ironically humorous remark about boys in purple dresses and jewelry becoming a symbol of *hetero*sexuality when, thanks be to God, Pastor Flathmann spoke first.

"The magi just represent people who love Jesus," he said. "That's all. They worship Jesus with their hearts and give him their treasures. Don't we want all of our children to do that?"

"Oh, *Henry!*" she responded, practically exploding, and everyone at the table sat up straight, startled by her tone. No one had ever talked to the pastor that way before. She called him by his first name, as though rebuking a child. She spoke with a voice that signified frustration with his stubbornness and embarrassment at his stupidity. She was exasperated—not just with him, but with a world gone mad. Yet she was inspired, recognizing it was high time someone stood up and said, "Enough is enough!"

"Oh, *Henry!*" she continued, "we've got girl acolytes . . . and girl lectors . . . and girl ushers . . . and girl preachers . . . well . . . you can't have *girl* wise men!"

Hmmm. Can't you? We have reviewed the traditions that the magi were kings or wise persons and found them wanting. What about this one? Were the magi *men?*

On the one hand, the Bible does not say that the magi are men.[356] On the other hand, readers may simply be expected to assume that these magi are men because they are expected to know that *all* magi are men. Imagine a story from the nineteenth century featuring a Presbyterian minister as a character—readers would be expected to regard the minister as a male pastor because in the world that formed the discourse setting for that narrative, all Presbyterian ministers were men. But was this the case with magi? And, even if it were, must this control interpretation of the story?

The short answer to the first question is, we just don't know. I have not found any explicitly female magi in ancient literature. But to say this is only to affirm that magi are identified as male *when their gender is specified*—and such identification is relatively rare. More often, magi are referenced generically, as they are in Matthew's Gospel. We could draw an analogy to another field for which we have more data: prophets in ancient Israel. When we read a text that refers to "a group of prophets" (e.g., 1 Sam. 10:10), are we expected to regard those prophets as men? My guess is that most modern readers do assume that such generic references to prophets are references to men, even though the gender of the prophets is not specified in the text. They do so because they think all Israelite prophets were men. But that is not quite true. The most famous prophets (Melchizedek and Samuel and Nathan and Elijah and Elisha—plus all the ones who have books named after them) have male names, but then in 2 Kings 22:14 we suddenly hear of Huldah the prophet, who was also "the wife of Shallum son of Tikvah." She is introduced casually with no special attention to her gender; there is no indication that some divine exception has been made for her inclusion among the prophetic ranks. Such a reference obviously forces us to question the assumption that regards all generic references to prophets as necessarily referring (exclusively) to male prophets.[357] In a similar fashion, we might do well to question blatant assumptions regarding the gender of magi. The database of "references to magi of known gender" is sparse; if it were larger, we might find a Huldah there.

But we must admit to another possibility. Some would argue that magi are less analogous to Israelite prophets than they are to Levitical priests.[358] No one doubts that both women and men practiced sorcery and magic in the Eastern world, but the term *magoi* may refer to a particular class of people that practiced such arts in a prescribed way. Indeed, I have indicated previously that I think this probably was the case: *magoi* were professional sorcerers employed by the government. As such, they may have been selected from among the ranks of Persian priests. The office could have been hereditary, and it could have been restricted to men. Or not. The fact is, we do not know whether all Persian priests were male,[359] whether all magi were priests (especially Persian ones), or—most important—whether any of this could be assumed to be common knowledge in the world that formed the discourse setting for Matthew's narrative.

My guess is that the gender of Matthew's magi is as ambiguous as their number. Matthew's readers may imagine three magi coming to Jerusalem, or thirty, or three hundred. Likewise, they may imagine that these magi were a mixed group of men and women or a group of all men—or, for that matter, a group of all women, if they prefer. There is nothing in the story that requires specification of number or gender, and there is no firm reason from our knowledge of the narrative's discourse setting to contend that readers would be expected to make such specifications one way or another. The narrative leaves gaps where gender and number are concerned, and I suspect that these are "rhetorical gaps"—ones that are not inadvertent but intended to facilitate the narrative's reception. In this case, such gaps enhance reader identification, inviting empathy with the magi from a wide spectrum of readers.

Now, to rephrase the second question, must our (limited) historical knowledge of magi control interpretation of the story? In fact, it has not done so. Instead, the rhetorical ambiguity of the magi's characterization has controlled interpretation. Readers have in fact done precisely what the narrative invites them to do: they have read themselves into the story and pictured the magi as being people "like them." The history of magian art and sculpture traced in

Richard Trexler's *Journey of the Magi* documents well the tendency for patrons to have themselves or loved ones displayed as magi in representations of the story.

A real gift of Trexler's study, however, lies in its exposition of a contrary but paradoxically related theme: representations of the magi also tended toward the exotic; they went out of their way to depict the magi as diverse—as different from the artwork's principal audience and as different from one another.[360] A tradition arose that encompassed medieval concern for what we might call "inclusivity." Trexler traces this tradition with regard to several factors (dress, class, cultural appearance), three of which I summarize here (parenthetical numbers indicate page references for specific quotations from Trexler's study):

- *The young magus*: One of the magi is often depicted as noticeably younger than the others in European art. Most often, such youth is indicated by the absence of a beard. In Italy, the youthful king is often blond, while the others have hair that is "somber in tone" (96). Often, the young king "wears rakishly short or tight clothes" while his companions are dressed in cloaks (96–97). In liturgical dramas, the youth of one of the three kings became a favorite element for development. Many dramas featured a dialogue or argument between the magi as to which of them should be first to adore the child. The youth would be told that he must go last because of his age, or perhaps he would volunteer to do so. This motif could then be elaborated with numerous variations: a) an actor playing an aged king would symbolically remove his beard and place it on the youth, inviting him to go first; b) the youth would be rewarded by the infant Christ for his zeal by being transformed into a bearded senior himself who could then kneel first before the child; c) the youth would refuse to give way to his elders and so (as punishment?) would miraculously become old and the elders young. Most interesting, perhaps, is the tradition that the nature of each magus's epiphany was determined by his age. Marcus Polo reports that the three magi came through the encounter with Jesus to see God in ways "that matched their own identities" (100), and he elaborates this specifically with regard to age. The old magi envisioned God as an elder, and the youthful magus envisioned God as young.
- *The black magus*: As early as the mid-thirteenth century, and in earnest a hundred years later, the European custom strongly favored presenting one of the magi as black. In some cases (mostly in Italy), a triad developed of an old white man, a white youth, and a black man. More often the black magus simply replaced the young magus; frequently, the two were combined into one exotic figure: a young, black man. Artists seemed to be especially interested in this figure, clothing him in the most elaborate (or gaudy, depending on your perspective) garb.[361] Indeed, once the idea of a black magus took hold, many painters went back and retouched older works to make sure that one of the three kings was black. "What could have been

the cause of this mania?" Trexler asks. "One possible explanation can be ruled out from the beginning. It had nothing to do with biblical exegesis" (102). What, then? Most likely, the simple, increased exposure of Europeans to blacks. Obviously, the representation may be triumphalistic, symbolizing the conversion of the African and consequent subjugation of non-Europeans to Christian authority. But such a trajectory cannot mask the fact that for centuries cultures that knew black Africans primarily through the slave trade nevertheless created and venerated figures of a black *king*, an image, if you will, of black power. The black magus, even when kneeling before Christ, does not remove his crown. He remains as much a king as the others, an apparent equal to those white monarchs whose potency is only confirmed through Christ's acceptance of their gifts. Sometimes, however, the representations may indicate subtle or subliminal awareness of the potential effect of this depiction: the black magus is sometimes shown standing apart, as though observing the worship of the other two rather than actually kneeling himself. Trexler detects a subtle "cultural criticism" in such works that presents the black magus as narcissistic and as a questionable devotee. I detect a subliminal recognition of resistance, which presents the African as hesitant regarding just what acceptance of this Western(-ized) god might mean.

- *The feminine magus*: A strong tendency can also be demonstrated for presenting one of the magi as a particularly effeminate man. Of course, this is already assumed by the depiction of a "young magus" as described above, since medieval art tended to portray youth as an intrinsically feminine phenomenon. But the trend went beyond this, sometimes in ways that require cognizance of relevant cultural codes to detect. So, Trexler notes, "by 'female' or 'effeminate qualities' I mean nothing more than what contemporaries labeled as such" (111). Such characteristics might apply to features, gestures, or stance that were regarded as fluid, delicate, or dancelike. Trexler indicates the frequent ascription of such qualities to one of the three magi. He is the expert; I take his word for it. Then he provides examples of something that is easier for the novice to discern—instances in which a magus is shown wearing what would normally be identified as female accouterments. These include not only earrings[362] and effeminate form-fitting tights but also more blatant examples of transvestism. One magus sports braided hair; another wears a bodice that is bound up beneath his breasts; still another actually wears a veil over his hair—an item that Trexler emphasizes is especially exclusive for women. Indeed, with regard to the latter work, Trexler concludes, "We have found a king who is formally gendered female" (117).

The latter instance of diversity is most significant for crafting a response to the "Oh, Henry!" lament of my former parishioner. Long before contemporary feminism raised its collective voice against contemporary patriarchy—way back in the middle of the Middle Ages—something subversive was going on. Why?

Trexler's best attempt at an explanation appeals to yet another tradition. In numerous depictions of the magi—especially those that were created for convents (nunneries)—the all-male magi are balanced in the scene by a group of women. Trexler actually calls such figures the "female magi,"[363] though they are not depicted as literal magi but as female equivalents. Thus, in one triptych, the Holy Family is shown in one panel, the adoring magi in another, and a group of worshiping female saints in the third. Along similar lines, another work depicts midwives at the nativity in a way that clearly balances the male magian figures with female ones. Yet another uses three feminine angels for the same purpose. In all of these works, the additional female figures seem to be introduced to the nativity scene primarily to balance the otherwise masculine dominance of the magi. Trexler notes, "[T]here can be little doubt that the artist and patron meant to say that the adoration of the magi showed males submitting to Jesus, but that women also did so in their own way."[364]

The more common depiction of an effeminate magus seems to have provided an alternative route to the same purpose. Rather than introducing new characters to the scene, some artists and patrons chose simply to transform the traditional ones. We have seen that the magi story held peculiar significance as a paradigm for who was included (or favored) among true worshipers of Christ. The dramatic dialogues regarding youth and age and the ambiguous portrayals of Africans attest to the value attached to whom the magi were thought to represent. And even in the Middle Ages there was widespread belief that they ought, somehow, to represent women. The artists and the patrons may have thought that "all magi were men," but even apart from questioning the legitimacy of that assumption, they did not feel constrained by it. One way of emphasizing that the magi represent women was to present one of the male magi as being "like a woman."[365] And if you had to put him in a bodice or a veil to get this point across, so be it.

Then someone just decided to go for it. Says Trexler,

> I was elated, but not surprised, when Christine Klapisch-Zuber identified a black monarch wearing earrings, who seems very much a woman. She is the third king in an adoration of an anonymous Antwerp mannerist, which is housed in Palermo. Alone on the left wing of an altar retable that she shares with Joseph on the right wing, and with Mary, the child, and the older two kings in the center field, this young monarch wears Roman military clothing complete with a sword and a dagger. Similar to the virgin's, her face is soft and her breast is full.[366]

Note the pronouns. This magus appears to have crossed the line from "effeminate male" to full-fledged female. I have examined photographs of the painting to which Trexler refers, and I concur with his assessment. This magus is not simply effeminate, or even a transvestite. She *is* a woman.

What historical or exegetical insight offered the foundation for such a move? Perhaps none. The anonymous artist seems to derive his or her inspiration from some other source. Perhaps the work does not strive to depict the historical moment or even to convey the Matthean intent so much as it seeks to convey the participatory response of one on whom the story has left its mark.

In any case, it turns out that we *can* have "girl wise men" after all. This is the gift of Trexler's *Magi*, a gift that I pass on to Pastor Henry and to all like him who have their names cast out as evil on account of the gospel, and to the once eight-year-old girl who wanted to be "one of the kings," and to all children like her who insist on their place within a community that is supposed to exist for their sake (Matt. 19:13–14).

Notes

1. Harold Bloom, *Ruin the Sacred Truths: Poetry and Beliefs from the Bible to the Present* (Cambridge, Mass.: Harvard University Press, 1989). A sample quote: "Poetry and belief, as I understand them, are antithetical modes of knowledge, but they share the peculiarity of taking place *between* truth and meaning, while being somewhat alienated both from truth and from meaning" (p. 12). Or: "Poetry and belief wander about, together and apart, in a cosmological emptiness marked by the limits of truth and of meaning. Somewhere between truth and meaning can be found piled up a terrible heap of descriptions of God" (p. 4).

2. In fact, most historical critics recognize that (good) authors usually intend for their writings to have multiple applications. An excellent historical-critical study that recognizes "levels of interpretation" intended by the author of Matthew's Gospel is R. T. France, "The Formula Quotations of Matthew 2 and the Problem of Communication," *New Testament Studies* 27 (1981): 233–51. France suggests that "Matthew was well aware of differing levels among his potential readership" (p. 250) and concludes that Matthew intends to communicate both a "'surface meaning,' which any reasonable intelligent reader might be expected to grasp, and what we might call a 'bonus' meaning accessible to those who are more 'sharp-eyed,' or better instructed in the Old Testament" (p. 241). Historical critics also recognize that a text like Matthew may actually have had multiple authors throughout its tradition history. One can speak meaningfully of what was intended by Jesus, by the author(s) of Q, or by the final redactor of Matthew—all of which views are now incorporated into the text that we call "Matthew's Gospel."

3. If you do not share my appraisal of the Bible as authoritative for *your* life, you must nevertheless recognize that far more is at stake in discussions concerning the interpretation of the Bible than concerning Homer or Virgil. Why? Because, like it or not, there are a lot of people like me around, and you must share this planet with us. How we—and you—interpret the Bible affects what we believe, how we vote, how we act, and how we relate to each other.

4. Here is something pretty cool that happened to me one time. I went to see one of my favorite rock bands, Cracker, at the Newport, a semi-grungy club across from Ohio State University. There were only about fifty people there, and I got a table all to myself. The opening act was a group nobody had ever heard of called Counting Crows. After their set, they came out and sat with the audience because they wanted to see Cracker, too. The singer and songwriter, Adam Duritz, sat with me, and we put back a pitcher and chatted during the

ballads. He said they had an album coming out called *August and Everything After.* I said I liked the title. "Why?" Well, you know, *August* means the end of summer . . . school is getting ready to start . . . there's only a little time left to relax and enjoy and then you have to get serious about life . . . so, it's like "enjoy the moment, but know it won't last." He waited awhile and then said, "Well, see, I was born in August . . . so I just meant *my whole life.*" Then he took a big draw on his mug, set it down, thought another moment, and said, "But I like what you said better."

5. This view was stated and defended quite explicitly by Krister Stendahl in his highly regarded article, "Biblical Theology," in *The Interpreter's Dictionary of the Bible* (New York: Abingdon Press, 1962), 1:418–32. Stendahl distinguished between "the meaning then" and "the meaning now." The task of biblical interpretation is description of the former only; the latter is the realm of systematic theologians and homileticians. Can literary criticism save biblical studies from being reduced to such a status? See n. 351 below.

6. As is often noted, this has been the ironic position of Protestantism, which celebrates its freedom from any magisterium while essentially deferring to a "papacy of scholars."

7. Stephen D. Moore, *Poststructuralism and the New Testament: Derrida and Foucault at the Foot of the Cross* (Minneapolis: Fortress Press, 1994), 115–16 (see esp. 116, n. 9). Cf. Mark Allan Powell, *What Is Narrative Criticism?,* Guides to Biblical Scholarship [Minneapolis: Fortress Press, 1990], 88–89). I indicated in my book that the approach of narrative criticism is sometimes embraced for what I regard as illegitimate reasons. I pointed out that two of the approach's chief characteristics are compatible with matters of Christian doctrine (focus on finished form of the text corresponds to a doctrine of canon; interpretation from the perspective of an implied reader corresponds to interest in reading from a faith perspective). My intended point was that the attraction of some Christian scholars to the approach may be due to (unacknowledged) confessional reasons rather than to stated scholarly ones. Moore missed this point, I think, because he assumed my intent was to offer an apology for narrative criticism rather than to provide a critical description of the approach and its employment within the church. It seemed to me (important words) that he assumed I agreed with the position that I merely described and then attempted to correct me by rephrasing the very point that I thought I had made myself. I felt (important words) like he was now presenting what I just might have been my book's single best insight as *his* rebuttal of *my* unperceptive (and inconsistent!) thinking. But see n. 10.

8. C. S. Rodd, "Talking Points from Books," *Expository Times* 110 (1999): 309–11, citation on p. 311; cf. Mark Allan Powell, *Jesus as a Figure in History: How Modern Historians View the Man from Galilee* (Louisville, Ky.: Westminster John Knox Press, 1998), 182–84. When I read this review, I felt (important words) that it would be hard to imagine an "impression" more diametrically opposed to what I actually say in the text of the book itself. But see n. 10.

9. See Mark Allan Powell, "Marsha's Tears: An Orphan of the Church," *Christian Century* 116, no. 9 (March 17, 1999): 312–15. The letter by Walter L. Taylor appeared in *Christian Century* 116, no. 11 (May 5, 1999): 514. For those who know me and my school, the writer is not the same person as my friend and colleague Walter F. Taylor—though the latter tends to distance himself from my "liberal" views on this topic as well. To digress momentarily, I have to wonder whether the letter-writing Taylor really believes that contemporary experience should not be a factor in ethical deliberations. Does he think that the church is wrong to consider testimonies of Christians *at all?* Or does he think

that this should be the church's policy only with regard to this one issue? Or, does he think that such testimonies should be heard but only as *one* factor in deliberations that also include consideration of scripture, tradition, reason, and much more—in which case, his view would be identical to that which I expressed in the article and I would have to wonder why he bothered to write to the magazine complaining about it. But see n. 10.

10. To check out this unlikely though hypothetically possible alternative, I submitted the three texts cited above to a committee of neutral interpreters. The results were not quite what I anticipated. Suffice to say that either a) the sort of interpretation evidenced by Moore, Rodd, and Taylor's unperceptive comments regarding my crystal-clear writing is in fact endemic to our guild; or b) my texts, despite my objections, can in fact be responsibly interpreted as meaning what these critics surmised them to mean. I tend to favor the former hypothesis, but you may decide.

11. Here and throughout this book I use first-person plural pronouns with reference to areas of understanding that I think or hope I share with the people who I think are most likely to read this book. I do not by use of such pronouns envision inclusion of the entire human race. In this instance, for example, I fail to consider numerous intelligent and perceptive people who have never been to college. The pronouns are always broadly stereotypical but never universally so.

12. To recognize that "all statements of truth" are relative is certainly not the same thing as maintaining that *truth* is intrinsically relative. Belief in God seems to imply acceptance of absolute truth, at least in an eschatological sense. But one can confess the ultimate existence of absolute truth and still acknowledge that finite understanding of this truth is perspectival and relative. Likewise, one can view the Bible as divine revelation of ultimate truth and still recognize that human understanding of this revelation will be relativized by the inevitably perspectival character of interpretation. Finally, to forestall the argumentative, I am willing to limit the applicability of the college sophomore revelation to "statements of truth within the humanities." The question of whether, for instance, *mathematical* statements (2 + 2 = 4) are relative or perspectival is not relevant to our purposes.

13. I should have said, "most varieties of modern literary criticism seek to account for the responses of readers," which would have made for a more accurate, though less rhetorically congruent sentence. Some varieties of literary criticism are author-oriented; most varieties of modern literary criticism are not.

14. On literary criticism of the Bible in general, see Mark Allan Powell, Cecile G. Gray, and Melissa C. Curtis, *The Bible and Modern Literary Criticism: A Critical Assessment and Annotated Bibliography* (Westport, Conn.: Greenwood Press, 1992).

15. The basic guide to the principles and procedures of this approach is still my *What Is Narrative Criticism?*, but—at least until I write a second edition—that volume must now be supplemented by David Rhoads, "Narrative Criticism: Practices and Prospects," in *Characterization and the Gospels: Reconceiving Narrative Criticism,* ed. David Rhoads and Kari Syreeni, Journal for the Study of the New Testament Supplement Series 184 (Sheffield: Sheffield Academic Press, 1999), 264–85.

16. Formalism sought to understand "how literature works" in an absolute or objective sense. See the sidebar discussion on page 67–69.

17. The term *postmodern* was not initially intended to imply this sense of "having moved beyond whatever the latest thing is." Originally, *modernism* referred to key elements of Western thinking born in the Renaissance and weaned in the Enlightenment. Postmodernists challenged assumptions of science and reason that were held to be self-evident and, indeed, challenged the very notion of

self-evidentiary truth. The term was corrupted to serve as a synonym for "ultra-chic, ultra-elite, ultra-faddish" when it caught on just enough to function as a marketing label. Sort of like Hootie and the Blowfish being marketed as "an *alternative* rock band." Alternative to *what*? Phil Collins, maybe. Or Barry Manilow.

18. A. K. M. Adam, *What Is Postmodern Biblical Criticism?*, Guides to Biblical Scholarship (Minneapolis: Fortress Press, 1995), 5.

19. Stephen Moore's book *Literary Criticism and the Gospels* includes a historical account of how narrative criticism came to be adopted by New Testament scholars. Basically, he describes author-oriented Bible scholars discovering formalist literary criticism (narrative criticism) without realizing that, since all truth is relative, their method only discerns one possible interpretation. Eventually, the dawn of this realization leads (or should lead) to an evolutionary abandonment of narrative criticism in favor of reader response and ultimately deconstruction. While not completely inaccurate, this account is at least tendentious and, I might add, the reverse of my personal experience. If there was an evolutionary development for me, it was from acknowledging the existential reality of deconstruction to appreciating the polyvalent interpretations of reader response to developing a narrative-critical paradigm that facilitates analysis of these. (A book that describes a journey closer to my own is Edgar McKnight's *Postmodern Use of the Bible* [Nashville: Abingdon Press, 1988]. McKnight urges postmodern readers of the Bible to adopt a reader-response, literary-formalist approach similar to what I call narrative criticism. The adoption of such an approach strikes him [and me] as a potential outcome of postmodern engagement rather than as a necessary sign that readers have not engaged.) I should note that Moore's historical sketch focuses primarily on developments within the Society of Biblical Literature, especially in the Seminar on Mark and in the Literary Aspects of the Gospels and Acts Group. I was never a part of the first group and only joined the latter some time after both Moore's book and mine (*What Is Narrative Criticism?*) had been published. Perhaps Moore portrays accurately the experiences of that one group of scholars, a group that was to prove instrumental in shaping new paradigms for biblical interpretation. I suspect, however, that these very great scholars were more in touch with dynamics of relativity (the "sophomore realization") than he allows. In any event, Moore's assessment rings true in at least one respect: in terms of the *application* of narrative criticism, the approach did begin by simply accumulating formalist observations about texts and only later began to use these as bases for understanding the polyvalent responses of diverse readers (though for some of us, at least, this had been the goal all along).

20. Failure to recognize this essential point is what torpedoes the recent essay by Petri Merenlahti and Raimo Hakola, "Reconceiving Narrative Criticism," in *Characterization and the Gospels*, ed. Rhoads and Syreeni, 13–48. The authors appear to assume that narrative criticism seeks to discern *the* correct reading of a text, which is to be set in opposition to readings obtained through other approaches, rather than *a* reading to be set alongside other interpretations. Furthermore, they view the approach as essentially author oriented, as "a peculiar combination of narrative theory and redaction-critical study of the Gospels" (p. 14). Perhaps such an understanding would have been appropriate among certain seminal narrative critics some years ago—it is true that most biblical-narrative critics were initially trained in redaction criticism and had to acquire the literary vocabulary as a second language. Even today, some narrative critics use the approach primarily for the insights it offers regarding what are really redactional or even historical concerns. Still, the narrative critics that I know would not view such an application as intrinsic to the approach itself.

In my view, Merenlahti and Hakola's essay "reconceives" a caricature of narrative criticism rather than the genuine phenomenon. This, of course, does not mean that their work is without merit—the reconceived narrative criticism that they describe can be recognized as yet one more viable reading strategy, one that indeed seems promising. But I admit that I am bothered by their apparent need to find a foil, to establish their preferred approach as the correction of and proposed replacement for a discipline that serves purposes they don't seem to appreciate. David Rhoads's aforementioned piece in this volume ("Narrative Criticism: Practices and Prospects") offers a kinder, gentler response to their essay than I am capable of producing. Rhoads is a better writer than I am and, in general, just a better human being. This will be apparent to anyone who compares his essay to my remarks here and following (pages 119–20).

21. Rhoads calls this "reception criticism." See "Narrative Criticism: Practices and Prospects," 273.

22. I provide my best example of this sort of work in chapter 2 of this book. But when at last you reach my study of the magi in chapters 7 to 10, you will find that I am a bit cursory in my application of this stage of the paradigm—in exactly the way that I bemoan as typical of our guild. I do offer some comments regarding the pervasive traditions that identify magi as either kings or as wise men, and these are easy to substantiate. It's enough for what I want to do in this study. But another study—a *better* one—would begin by conducting research on those pervasive traditions: Do such factors as gender, social-economic status, level of education, and so forth affect the likelihood of people in our modern day to regard the magi one way or another? I simply lack the resources for doing that kind of work (no doctoral students, for one thing). I do admit my study is the poorer for it.

23. I am not, of course, so naive as to think that my Christian ideology might not affect my work in the preliminary stages of analysis as well. The whole point of having an articulated, public *method* (or, better, *reading strategy*) is to show others what I do and how I do it so that if they think my foundational, totalizing, or mystifying judgments have flawed the project, they will be able to see when and where this happened and amend or dismiss my remarks accordingly. Still, my stated intention is to delay the imposition of such judgments until the end, and to the extent that I succeed with this objective, even those who do not share my values might accept what I do up to that point. They might accept my conclusions but not my evaluation of those conclusions.

24. Such discoveries are the stuff of remakes. Witness Paul Verhoeven's *Starship Troopers* in which the brave pioneers become human astronauts and the hostile Indians become giant insects. I loved it, but I did feel kind of sorry for the bugs at the end.

25. Adam, *What Is Postmodern Biblical Criticism?*, 33.

26. For what it's worth, *polyvalence* derives from the Greek root *polys* (much, many) joined with Latin *valentia* (strength, capacity). Most dictionaries list the first meaning of the term as that which applies in chemistry: an enhanced capacity of certain elements to combine their atoms (or radicals) with the atoms (or radicals) of other elements.

27. Wolfgang Iser, *The Act of Reading: A Theory of Aesthetic Response* (Baltimore: Johns Hopkins University, 1978). For page references, see the entries for "blanks" and "gaps" in the subject index.

28. Mel Brooks once told an interviewer that he was making a historical motion picture called *The Hundred Years War* that was going to be even longer than *Dances with Wolves*. How long will it be? "A hundred years. I don't want to leave anything out."

29. Actually, there may be one more clue, though it is subtle. We know that Jesus' opponents taunted and reviled him as "a glutton and a drunkard" (Matt. 11:19; Luke 7:34). This was no doubt polemical exaggeration but, still, when selecting insults, people do not usually choose to call a skinny man a "glutton." It is probably safe to infer that Jesus was a bit portly—at least enough so to be regarded as overweight (potentially gluttonous) by the standards of his day.

30. Credited to *Motion Picture Guide Annual 1994* (News America Publishing, 1994).

31. Credited to *Leonard Maltin's Video Guide 1995* (Jessie Films Ltd., 1994).

32. M. H. Abrams, *A Glossary of Literary Terms,* 4th ed. (New York: Holt, Rhinehart, and Winston, 1981), 48.

33. By *real* I do not mean *nonfictional.* Knowledge that a story relates something that actually happened ("based on a true story" in common parlance) might heighten empathy for some readers, but even then the world of the story remains distinct from that of the world in which we live.

34. There is no more reason for gender to be the dominant factor in establishing such identifications between readers and characters than for any other factor (age, education, religion, values, economic class, etc.) to be dominant. What *is* interesting (and revealing) is when any one factor such as gender is consistently the determining factor for a particular reader's empathy choices.

35. Judith Fetterly, *The Resisting Reader: A Feminist Approach to American Fiction* (Bloomington, Ind.: Indiana University Press, 1978).

36. One "other reason" might be that their social location is closer to that of Luke's original audience. Such continuity facilitates the implementation of authorial intent even apart from "careful reading."

37. With the great majority of scholars (including the usually skeptical Jesus Seminar), I believe the Good Samaritan parable can be attributed reliably to the historical Jesus. The framework of the story, however, is undoubtedly Lukan, and the tale has been translated (from Aramaic to Greek). We cannot credit Jesus with the exact wording of any phrase—including that of the question posed in 10:36.

38. To start with one relatively accessible work for each of those named, see Paul Ricoeur, *Interpretation Theory: Discourse and the Surplus of Meaning* (Fort Worth, Tex.: Texas Christian University Press, 1976); Jacques Derrida, *Of Grammatology,* trans. G. C. Spivak (Baltimore: Johns Hopkins University Press, 1976); Paul Rabinow, ed., *The Foucault Reader* (New York: Pantheon Books, 1984). Actually, for Derrida and Foucault, the best starting point by far is Moore, *Poststructuralism and the New Testament.* Moore actually does understand these guys—or at least he's convinced me that he does—and he relates their insights specifically to issues of theology and biblical interpretation.

39. Remember what Bill Clinton said in his deposition before the Grand Jury—back during that whole scandal/impeachment thing? His most quotable quote was, "It depends on what the meaning of *is* is." Well, now you can be as articulate as Clinton. When someone asks you what something means you can respond, "That depends on what *means* means." Or not.

40. Note that in this example, I am still talking about meaning as something (albeit a mood or effect) conveyed by an author (artist). Many modern art classes would focus instead on the capacity for a Pollock painting to evoke *different* moods. Of course, those paintings are polyvalent, but the existential fact that many (most) people may respond to a given work in fairly similar ways could be evidence that there is a range of "expected response" within which most (but not all) responses fall. See chapter 3 of this book. Also, to be accurate, Pollock did not actually use squirt guns all the time. He did, however, dis-

dain the palette and the brush, preferring to drip paint onto a canvas laid out on the floor or to smear it on with his hands. His goal was to be "in the painting" himself while executing each work, The same sort of philosophy informed Native American sand paintings centuries before Pollock, and other European artists were credited with founding the ideological school of abstract expressionism.

41. This is true in secular literary criticism as well. See, however, the early work of Norman Holland, a reader-response pioneer who studied the effects not of external social location but of internal psychological makeup. An example is *Five Readers Reading* (New Haven, Conn.: Yale University Press, 1975).

42. I was careful not to complicate the research by testing theologically educated laity—for instance, seminary students or persons who have earned a master's degree in religious studies but not pursued a career in ministry.

43. I tried to the best of my knowledge to follow accepted standards for conducting social-scientific surveys. For instance, I surveyed only persons who did not know me. I guaranteed anonymity. I did not tell any individual that I was also surveying another person from his or her church until after he or she had completed the project.

44. This person is apparently alluding to the ecclesiastical practice of "binding and loosing" referred to twice in Matthew's Gospel (Matt. 16:19; 18:18).

45. This person has a good memory. See Mark 7:11.

46. This person seems to be alluding to Micah 6:8 or maybe to Matthew 23:23 or Luke 11:42.

47. For those who want to look, it's Isaiah 29:13.

48. It was coming up in the lectionary on a day that I was assigned to preach. Series B, Pentecost 15 (with vss. 14–15, 21–23 also included).

49. This person seems to be alluding to Matthew 7:3–5 or Luke 6:41–42.

50. This person seems to be alluding to Matthew 23:25–26 or Luke 11:39–41.

51. This person appears to be referring to Matthew 5:18 or Luke 16:17.

52. L-35 and L-36 offer interesting temporal variants on the phenomenon of realistic empathy. L-35 identifies his or her past self with the characters in the story ("I used to be like them") and L-36 identifies his or her potential future self with the characters in the story ("I may someday be like them").

53. There is no correlation between the order in which the individual responses on the two lists are presented (C-1 and L-1 are not necessarily representatives of the same church.) Though I'm (at least) as voyeuristic as the next person, I think it best to avoid concentrating on such specific comparisons.

54. When I was a student, I took a "preaching call" out in a remote rural congregation where I proclaimed the gospel as best I could. After the service, I shook hands at the door, and one old farmer said, "Son, that was good." Piously, I looked at my feet and shrugged, "Well, it wasn't me. It was Jesus." He shook his head and drawled, "Nope. Wasn't *that* good."

55. Compare Luke 7:18–19.

56. This person appears to be alluding to biblical references such as Luke 7:34; 15:1.

57. This person appears to be referring to Luke 4:18.

58. This person may be thinking of such passages as Acts 13:44–46; 18:5–6; 28:23–28.

59. This person appears to be referring to Acts 2:37. Cf. 16:30.

60. This person appears to be recalling Luke 1:76–77. Also, the reference in his or her last sentence is apparently to Luke 4:18.

61. This person appears to be referring to the story in Acts 2.

62. This person appears to be referring to Acts 19:1–7.

63. Actually it was Diana Ross ("Ain't No Mountain High Enough," Number 1 for

three weeks in August 1970)—unless, perhaps, the writer means "I Knew You Were Waiting" by Aretha Franklin and George Michael (Number 1 for two weeks in February 1987). It has similar words ("when the mountain was high, I still believed/when the valley was low, it didn't stop me").

64. This person appears to be alluding to Luke 7:28 or Matthew 11:11.

65. As with CC-49, this person appears to be alluding to Luke 7:28 or Matthew 11:11.

66. Actually I picked it because Joel Green asked me to write on the passage for a book he was editing (see Mark Allan Powell, "Narrative Criticism," in *Hearing the New Testament: Strategies for Interpretation,* ed. Joel B. Green [Grand Rapids: Wm. B. Eerdmans Publishing Co., 1995], 239–55). Whether the Holy Spirit had anything to do with this (cf. LL-41), I can't say.

67. This person answered the question on April 16.

68. This person appears to be referring to 1 Corinthians 15:50.

69. Rod did have a minor hit with that song, as a duet with Jeff Beck (Number 48 in 1985), but it was written by Curtis "Superfly" Mayfield, whose group, the Impressions, took it to Number 14 twenty years earlier. Incidentally, Curtis's first solo hit was "Don't Worry (If There's a Hell Below, We're All Gonna Go)."

70. CC-1, CC-8–9, CC-11, CC-17–38.

71. "I": CC-23, CC-29, CC-33, CC-40–44, CC-48–50; LL-2–4, LL-6–10, LL-14–15, LL-17, LL-19–20, LL-22–23, LL-25–27, LL-29, LL-31–33, LL-35, LL-38–39, LL-41, LL-43–50.

   "me": CC-47; LL-6, LL-10, LL-13–14, LL-17–19, LL-23, LL-26–29, LL-34, LL-36–39, LL-41, LL-49.

   "my": CC-29, CC-40; LL-20, LL-23, LL-26, LL-32, LL-35.

   "we": CC-10, CC-26, CC-33, CC-38, CC-40, CC-42–43, CC-45, CC-48, CC-50; LL-5, LL-7, LL-9–13, LL-15–16, LL-18, LL-21–22, LL-30, LL-33–34, LL-37–38, LL-40–43, LL-48.

   "us": CC-8, CC-23, CC-26, CC-30, CC-37–38, CC-44, CC-46; LL-1, LL-7, LL-10–11, LL-16–18, LL-21–22, LL-24, LL-30, LL-32, LL-38, LL-40, LL-43, LL-48.

   "our": CC-40, CC-49; LL-10–12, LL-15, LL-22, LL-24–25, LL-30–31, LL-37, LL-40, LL-44, LL-48.

72. "I": C-3, C-5, C-8–10, C-12, C-14, C-16, C-19, C-22–25, C-28, C-30–31, C-41–42, C-45, C-47–48, C-50; L-1–5, L-8–9, L-11–14, L-16, L-18, L-21–22, L-24–25, L-27–30, L-32, L-35–39, L-43–49.

   "me": C-1, C-7, C-9, C-11–12, C-15, C-25, C-31, C-44; L-2, L-4–5, L-8–12, L-14–16, L-19, L-26–27, L-36–37, L-41, L-48–49.

   "my": C-1–2, C-6, C-8–9, C-14, C-16, C-23–24, C-31, C-42; L-5, L-9–10, L-16, L-25–27, L-37, L-41, L-47.

   "we": C-1, C-17–18, C-27, C-29, C-37–41, C-43, C-49; L-6–7, L-15, L-17, L-20, L-28, L-30, L-32–34, L-40, L-42.

   "us:" C-4, C-13, C-20, C-28–29, C-33, C-41, C-43, C-49; L-6–7, L-20, L-31, L-33.

   "our": C-21–22, C-28, C-30, C-34, C-41, C-43; L-2, L-14, L-42, L-44.

73. But I am cautioned by an elementary school teacher not to press this assumption too far. What has been taught with regard to literature and its reception, even at a primary level, has changed over the years. Likewise, many seminaries have revised their heavily author-oriented historical-critical programs in recent years to reflect more reader-oriented literary paradigms. But I suspect that such moves have been and will remain modest. The maintenance of historical criticism as a dominant mode of biblical interpretation seems secure. "Authorship is somewhat out of fashion at the moment," says Harold Bloom, "but like shorter skirts authorship always does return again" (*Ruin the Sacred Truths,* 3).

74. In many church bulletins, I see the sermon actually called a "Message." I understand the consumer-friendly drive to find a lively synonym for the ecclesial term, but I have to wonder who decides that "sermon" and "message" are in fact synonymous. Or, again, I note that Eugene Peterson's excellent paraphrase of the New Testament is actually titled *The Message* (Colorado Springs: NavPress, 1993). As near as I can tell, the term is thus intended to serve as a secular euphemism for "the gospel." But can the gospel be equated with a message? Is the gospel (or, for that matter, the New Testament) a point or series of points that readers are cognitively to accept or reject? Isn't the gospel, rather, an *event,* the proclamation of which (in the New Testament as well as in preaching) impacts and affects people's lives?

75. Note that I, as an author, am indeed interested in such cognitive matters as *developing an argument* and *making a point.* You, as a reader, might care less about such matters than about how this book is affecting you: Is it entertaining you, inspiring you, challenging you, putting you to sleep?

76. A. K. M. Adam says it well: "The postmodern reader recognizes that the rules of interpretation are provisional guides rather than commandments . . . they are not foundations, or natural laws, but habits and styles" (*What Is Postmodern Biblical Criticism?,* 22).

77. He has also written a book that explains several such dictums in ways that reveal their "existential cash value." See Donald G. Luck, *Why Study Theology?* (St. Louis: Chalice Press, 1999). This simple-but-not-simplistic book answers the question its title poses better than any other with which I am familiar.

78. I used the terms for the first time in an article that has provided the main substance for chapter 5 of this book: "Expected and Unexpected Readings of Matthew: What the Reader Knows," *Asbury Theological Journal* 48 (1993): 41–51. I recognize that these (or any other) labels set into play the sort of foundational binary opposition that postmodernism inevitably wants to deconstruct. I recognize this; I just don't know what to do about it, except to admit that the categories (like all categories) are artificial and perhaps, in some subliminal way, politically motivated. I certainly do not consciously intend to privilege one category over the other, though I admit that such privileging may be detected implicitly in the designations themselves. The same observations are valid with regard to other language I use ("normative way of reading"; "control group"). I have not found a way to escape the constraints of such language. Why have labels at all? Why not just appreciate diverse interpretations without attempting to classify them? My best answer, at this point, is autobiographical and existential: I find this organizational scheme (and that's all it is) useful for appreciating polyvalence among the constituencies of which I am presently a part.

79. For a recent example, see discussion of Merenlahti and Hakola that follows, pages 119–20.

80. To clarify my point here, I do not think that Reader Four's interpretation of Matthew's passion narrative is wrong in a *literary* sense (a "misunderstanding") simply because it is an unexpected reading. I do, of course, think it is wrong in other ways. It is *theologically* wrong because any interpretation that delights in the torture of a human being is morally perverse and ethically delinquent. But such an interpretation would be wrong (theologically, ethically, morally) even if it were the expected reading of the text. Thus, I embrace the dialogical understanding of scripture that affirms the paradoxical interdependence of theology and exegesis: biblically sound theology is in large part determined by exegetical interpretation of scripture, but exegetical interpretations of scripture are also evaluated in light of biblically sound theology. More on this in chapter 10.

81. Examples abound. I discuss one in chapter 11 of this book. Jesus' resistant reading of the Elisha and Naaman story effectively deconstructs the nationalistic pride that an expected reading of that text probably would elicit (Luke 4:27, cf. 2 Kings 5:1–14).

82. The term was coined by Alice Walker in *In Search of Our Mother's Gardens* (New York: Harcourt Brace Jovanovich, 1974). See Jacquelyn Grant, *White Woman's Christ and Black Woman's Jesus: Feminist Theology and Womanist Response* (Atlanta: Scholars Press, 1989); Clarice J. Martin, "Womanist Biblical Interpretation," in *Dictionary of Biblical Interpretation,* ed. John Hayes (Nashville: Abingdon Press, 1999), 2:655–58.

83. All of these have been applied to the Gospel of Mark. See Fernando Belo, *A Materialist Reading of the Gospel of Mark* (Maryknoll, N.Y.: Orbis Books, 1981); Diarmuid McGann, *The Journeying Self: The Gospel of Mark through a Jungian Perspective* (New York: Paulist Press, 1985); John P. Keenan, *The Gospel of Mark: A Mahāyāna Reading* (Maryknoll, N.Y.: Orbis Books, 1995); Jose Cádenas Pallares, *A Poor Man Called Jesus: Reflections on the Gospel of Mark* (Maryknoll, N.Y.: Orbis Books, 1986); Hisako Kinukawa, *Women and Jesus in Mark: A Japanese Feminist Perspective* (Maryknoll, N.Y.: Orbis Books, 1994). As this list indicates, Orbis is the publisher of choice for finding such materials.

84. As I understand it, deconstruction is not a method of biblical interpretation but an ironically methodological application of a philosophy that critiques the fundamental notion of "method" itself. I once attempted to describe the role of deconstruction in biblical interpretation in a now infamous paper presented to the Literary Aspects of the Gospels and Acts Group at the annual meeting of the Society of Biblical Literature. I used the Indian story of the six blind men examining an elephant as a metaphor for various biblical disciplines attempting to find "meaning." One man grabs the elephant's trunk and says, "It is like a snake"; another feels its side and says, "It is like a wall." So also biblical scholars use their methods to experience only in part what they might mistakenly take to be a totality of meaning. But then I said that those who practice deconstruction are like a seventh person who does not examine the elephant at all but listens to the stories of those who do and decides that either a) the elephant does not exist; or b) even if it does, the testimonies of those who experience it are more interesting and revealing than the beast itself. See Mark Allan Powell, "What Is 'Literary' about Literary Aspects?" in *Society of Biblical Literature 1992 Seminar Papers,* ed. Eugene H. Lovering (Atlanta: Society of Biblical Literature, 1992), 40–48. This paper was widely perceived as an attack on the legitimacy of deconstruction (the ever witty Stephen Moore opined that I was more interested in *ex*communication models than communication models) but such had not been my authorial intent. What I apparently did not say very well is that deconstruction is important to the process of interpretation precisely because it is interested in critiquing that process itself rather than in simply adding one more voice to the mix. I did indicate that deconstructors seem destined always to feel out of place and unappreciated in communities devoted to interpretation (especially objective interpretation), but I also stressed that this does not diminish their importance. I compared their presence in the guild of biblical scholars to that of an agnostic at a prayer meeting, an analogy I chose advisedly. Their presence is indeed useful to those who are discerning and patient enough to hear them out, but that helpfulness would cease the moment they were converted. I am certainly not opposed to the important role that deconstruction plays in biblical studies, but I *am* suspicious of attempts to present the guild with a tame variety of that school, a de-fanged, de-clawed deconstruction that wants to take its place

alongside other interpretive approaches as just "one more method" to be used in conjunction with other methods. That seems to have been the role envisioned for deconstruction by those who objected most strenuously to my elephant paper: "Amend the parable! Let the deconstructors be characters who describe the elephant too." Of course, if we do that, they have to become blind. I had envisioned them as the only character who could see.

85. That would be Powell, *What Is Narrative Criticism?*

86. For this reason, some scholars prefer to identify narrative criticism as a formalist, text-oriented approach to literature, akin to structuralism and rhetorical criticism. I think the approach may have begun that way, but it has developed increasingly into a mode of reader response, emphasizing, for instance, "meaning as effect" over "meaning as message." See sidebar discussion on pages 67–69.

87. I have elsewhere defined an implied reader as "one who actualizes the potential for meaning in a text, who responds to it in ways consistent with the expectations that we may ascribe to its implied author." Further, "the concept of the implied reader is a heuristic construct that allows critics to limit the subjectivity of their analysis by distinguishing between their own responses to a narrative and those that the text appears to invite." Powell, "Narrative Criticism," in *Hearing the New Testament*, 241. Compare Powell, *What Is Narrative Criticism?*, 19–21. Similarly, Jack Dean Kingsbury has defined an implied reader as "an imaginary person for whom the intention of the text always reaches its fulfillment." See *Matthew As Story*, 38. Especially influential for this notion is Wolfgang Iser, *The Act of Reading*; idem, *The Implied Reader: Patterns of Communication in Prose Fiction from Bunyan to Beckett* (Baltimore: Johns Hopkins University Press, 1974). See also Wayne C. Booth, *The Rhetoric of Fiction*, 2nd ed. (Chicago: University of Chicago Press, 1983), esp. 421–31; Seymour Chatman, *Story and Discourse: Narrative Structure in Fiction and Film* (Ithaca, N.Y.: Cornell University Press, 1978), esp. 149–50; Peter J. Rabinowitz, *Before Reading: Narrative Conventions and the Politics of Interpretation* (Ithaca, N.Y.: Cornell University Press, 1987), 15–46.

88. I define evaluative point of view as the norms, values, and general worldview that appear to be operative within a narrative. See Powell, *What Is Narrative Criticism?*, 23–24. Theoretical background for this understanding is found in Boris Uspensky, *A Poetics of Composition: The Structure of the Artistic Text and Typology of a Compositional Form* (Berkeley and Los Angeles, Calif.: University of California Press, 1973); Norman R. Petersen, "Point of View in Mark's Narrative," *Semeia* 12 (1978): 97–121. In a work such as the Gospel of Matthew, the evaluative point of view of the narrator may be regarded as normative, in that implied readers are expected to concur with the standards of judgment the narrator establishes for evaluating the events, characters, and settings that comprise the story. But, of course, real readers sometimes bring other standards of judgment to the text and evaluate it in ways that I label "unexpected."

89. It occurs to me that my use of the words "control group" could be unfortunate, in light of accusations that narrative critics want to "control" and not just understand interpretive processes. At the very least, it could provide Stephen Moore's wit with an easy (and so, perhaps, unworthy) target (cf. n. 84). But when scientists set up a control group, the purpose is not to guide, direct, or restrain any processes outside of the control group. The whole point is to control processes within the group so that it can serve as a basis for comparison with the uncontrolled processes elsewhere. Likewise, narrative criticism uses a process of "controlled interpretation" to discern expected readings that may then be contrasted with uncontrolled readings in order to understand and appreciate what may be distinctive about the latter.

90. Feminist, Marxist, Womanist, and other ideological interpretations may of course produce unexpected readings that are regarded as legitimate within the interpretive communities that embrace those ideologies. On "interpretive communities," see Stanley E. Fish, *Is There a Text in This Class? The Authority of Interpretive Communities* (Cambridge, Mass.: Harvard University Press, 1980). There is a sense in which all readers belong to some sort of interpretive community, whether this is explicitly acknowledged or not. Real readers always read from some ideological perspective.

91. Adam, *What Is Postmodern Biblical Criticism?*, 8–10. Adam notes the modernist tendency to posit totalities that exclude embarrassing counterexamples, "as when one ascribes universal human significance to *King Lear* and overlooks the numerous people to whom *Lear* is uninteresting and irrelevant" (p. 10).

92. Of course, narrative *critics* may make such judgments—and they often do—but the judgments are not made through the practice of narrative criticism itself.

93. As Robert Fowler puts it, "Readers sometimes discern implied readers that, for ethical reasons, they are unwilling to become." See Robert M. Fowler, *Let the Reader Understand: Reader-Response Criticism and the Gospel of Mark* (Minneapolis: Fortress Press, 1991), 33, n. 28. The standard work on such ethical distancing has become Fetterly, *The Resisting Reader*, but Fowler cites several others, including Wayne Booth, *The Company We Keep: An Ethics of Fiction* (Berkeley, Calif.: University of California Press, 1988), and Susan R. Suleiman, "Ideological Dissent from Works of Fiction: Toward a Rhetoric of the *roman à thèse*," *Neophilologus* 60 (1976): 162–77.

94. Perhaps I dwell on this subject because so often I hear proponents of "resistant reading" attack narrative criticism as though the approach itself is opposed to what they do. I find this ironic, since they invariably seem to practice narrative criticism themselves—if they had not somehow discerned an expected reading of the story, how would they know what to resist?

95. I repeat a line from a paper I delivered on this topic at the 1997 annual meeting of the Society of Biblical Literature (Literary Aspects of the Gospels and Acts Group): "I think that it is certainly possible to make such distinctions in the only sense that I have ever intended for them to be made, namely, as overtly heuristic categories applied within a particular community devoted to a chosen reading strategy."

96. Attention to "the text itself" was the battlecry of a now outmoded (some would say, discredited) movement in the middle third of the twentieth century. The movement was global and took on many forms (Russian Formalism, French Structuralism). In America, it seemed to crystallize around what came to be known as "the New Criticism," headquartered in Chicago in the 1940s. See the sidebar overview on pages 67–69 of this book, but keep in mind that a) my summary is necessary simplistic and b) I am anything but a dispassionate reporter.

97. This analogy was suggested to me by David T. Landry (in his oral response to the paper cited in note 111).

98. These comments with regard to putative authorial intent could also be made with reference to *genre identification*. Postmodern thinkers rightly reject the notion of any "pure genre," and my suggested alternative origins for the note in the sanctuary raise the question of whether the note would be properly identified as a "joke" in such scenarios. Genre (like implicit authorial intent and the notion of expected reading in general) is something that readers attribute to texts. Nevertheless, I would aver that most readers—given the presupposed data—would in fact identify this text as a joke, regardless of who wrote it or why.

99. On the concept of "implied authors" see Powell, *What Is Narrative Criticism?*, 5–6. I use the term in the sense given to it in Booth, *Rhetoric of Fiction*, 66–77.

100. The best example I can think of at the moment concerns the Gospel of Luke. Protestant and Roman Catholic scholars in this century have often agreed that Luke's writings espouse a form of "early catholicism." The Protestants, however, have tended to interpret this as an unfortunate corruption of the gospel that occurred in the years after Paul, while Catholic scholars point to it as exemplary of the scriptural grounding for post-Pauline developments that they evaluate positively. See the discussion and citations in Mark Allan Powell, *What Are They Saying about Acts?* (New York: Paulist Press, 1991), 62–63.

101. The classic example of this would be interpretations of Jesus' commission to Peter in Matthew 16:15–18. See Ulrich Luz, *Matthew in History: Interpretation, Influence, and Effects* (Minneapolis: Fortress Press, 1994), 57–74.

102. Rudolf Bultmann, "Is Exegesis Without Presuppositions Possible?" in *Existence and Faith* (New York: World Publishing Co., 1961), 287–96.

103. Adam, *What Is Postmodern Biblical Criticism?*, 15–16. I am aware that Adam himself does not seem to regard narrative criticism as a postmodern reading strategy. I am not sure why this is, since my experience with the approach seems to me to have almost always involved the sort of engagement that he calls "postmodern." We need not quibble over labels, of course. Perhaps I am self-deceived. But my guess (and it is only that)—based on comments he offers on p. 25 of his book—is that he has accepted Stephen Moore's account of the development of narrative criticism in biblical studies as foundational and views embarrassing counterexamples like Edgar McKnight (and me?) as anomalies (compare n. 19). Moore presents postmodern thought as coming to the attention of biblical scholars later than narrative criticism and as offering potential liberation for narrative critics, whose discipline does not sufficiently recognize relativity. McKnight presents narrative criticism as an approach to be embraced by postmodern thinkers precisely because it is useful to those who have recognized the pervasiveness of such relativity. This "chicken or egg" question is probably unresolvable, but, at any rate, most of the narrative critics I know use the approach in the "postmodern" ways described here and many would claim that they have always attempted to do so. [See "Replies," p. 237 below.]

104. Jonathan Culler, *Structuralist Poetics: Structuralism, Linguistics, and the Study of Literature* (Ithaca, N.Y.: Cornell University Press, 1975), 123–24; Fish, *Is There a Text in This Class?*, 48–49.

105. Daniel Patte speaks of Matthew's Gospel as evincing "a system of convictions," which he takes to be "truths that do not depend upon a demonstration or argument" but rather "impose themselves" in such a way that they are apparently held to be self-evident. See *The Gospel According to Matthew: A Structural Commentary on Matthew's Faith* (Philadelphia: Fortress Press, 1987).

106. Jack Dean Kingsbury, "Reflections on 'the Reader' of Matthew's Gospel," *New Testament Studies* 34 (1988): 442–60, esp. 459; idem, *Matthew as Story*, 147.

107. Many redaction critics initially denounced narrative criticism as antihistorical only to discover that, ironically, the discipline sometimes offers a more reliable approach to the accomplishment of their goals than redaction criticism itself. Definitions of authorial intent offered with reference to implied readers reconstructed from the text (to which we have access) are bound to be more accurate in some respects than ones based on reconstructions of communities of original readers whose provenance and identity remain speculative. For a sensitive and competent example of the adoption of literary-critical method by a confirmed redaction critic, see Graham Stanton, *A Gospel for a New People: Studies in Matthew* (Edinburgh: T. & T. Clark, 1992). I regard the use of

literary criticism in the pursuit of historical-critical goals as a bonus, supplemental to the furtherance of understanding texts as literature, which is a legitimate enterprise in its own right. Still, there are potential flaws in the approach being used to discern authorial intent. Narrative criticism discerns how readers are expected to respond to the narrative in its present form, without inquiring as to which elements of that form derive from various compositional stages. Thus, the results of narrative criticism are actually more of an index of the intention of the implied author, who should not be equated with any specific historical figure. For instance, the "authorial intent" that narrative criticism might be able to discern behind Matthew's Gospel is actually a composite intent, incorporating elements that probably derive from the historical Jesus, from Mark, from the redactors of the Q document, and from the evangelist whom we call Matthew.

108. In Matthean studies, the term has been especially favored by Warren Carter. See his *Matthew: Storyteller, Interpreter, Evangelist* (Peabody, Mass.: Hendrickson Publishers, 1996).

109. Rabinowitz, *Before Reading,* 15–46.

110. There are other problems, however, in applying the concept of an "authorial audience" to Matthew's Gospel. First, which stage in the work's compositional history is to be deemed normative (see n. 2)? Is the authorial audience for Matthew's Beatitudes (5:3–12) the audience that Jesus had in mind when he first said these things, or the audience that the author of Q had in mind when he incorporated the sayings into his document, or the audience that the evangelist we call Matthew had in mind when he edited Q into the present Gospel? Whichever audience we pick will beg the question, Why that one? Second, the very notion of a *written* text having an implicit *audience* is illogical; written texts have implied *readers* (see pages 85–86). [See "Replies," pp. 238–40.]

111. Interestingly, A. K. M. Adam tries to make the opposite argument with reference to another satirical document, *The Shortest Way with the Dissenters* by Daniel Defoe, which calls for members of the Low-Church party in England to be hanged. Adams notes that "the pamphlet was warmly received by High-Church opponents of Non-conformity" who apparently failed to realize they were being satirized. See "Matthew's Readers, Ideology, and Power," in *Society of Biblical Literature Seminar Papers* 33 (1994): 435–49, esp. 437–38. Still, Adam has not demonstrated that there are no expected readings but only that there are also unexpected ones. (See "Replies," p. 238.)

112. Richard A. Edwards, *Matthew's Story of Jesus* (Philadelphia: Fortress Press, 1985), 9. This is the first sentence of what I believe to be the first book to apply modern literary criticism to Matthew. I do not think it an overstatement to say that with this single sentence a new era of Matthean scholarship began.

113. Studies in Matthew that use narrative criticism include Carter, *Matthew: Storyteller, Interpreter, Evangelist;* David Howell, *Matthew's Inclusive Story,* Journal for the Study of the New Testament Supplement Series 42 (Sheffield: Sheffield Academic Press, 1990); Kingsbury, *Matthew as Story.*

114. Of historical-critical methods, only composition analysis has emphasized the understanding of a book such as Matthew's Gospel as a complete and integral work. Many forms of historical criticism have shown no interest in the book of Matthew as a whole, but have sought rather to elucidate isolated passages with regard to their origin in earlier sources or in oral tradition. Redaction criticism has emphasized literary context in a way that sometimes means interpreting a passage in light of its placement within the overall work, but redaction critics have explicitly attempted to produce unexpected readings by emphasizing discernment of the evangelist's editorial activity, that is, by calling attention to emendations and omissions that readers are not expected to

notice. The goal of redaction criticism is to understand the text from the perspective of the redactor, which means to understand it in light of information that readers are not supposed to have (on this point, see also page 101). The whole point of redaction criticism is to understand texts in ways that readers are not expected to understand them, on the apparent assumption that the way readers *are* expected to understand them is limited and superficial. But see n. 157.

115. For a reading of Matthew from the perspective of a "first-time reader," see Edwards, *Matthew's Story of Jesus.*

116. Perceptive student Sue Gaeta indicates that this is a reversal of the position I took in *What Is Narrative Criticism?* (p. 20). She appears to be correct, though I cannot recall ever actually holding the contrary position.

117. We can of course define the narrative text (the "story") to be studied as something other than "Matthew's Gospel (as a whole)." We can, if we like, decide to do a narrative-critical study of "The Parable of the Bridesmaids" found in Matthew 25:1–13, and we can treat this story as a narrative in its own right rather than as a portion of a larger work. But even then, I would argue, the implied readers of the Parable of the Bridesmaids would be conceived of as persons reading that (short) story for the first time.

118. When I say this, some people may want to throw my own words back at me from a previous discussion. Have I not insisted before on a hermeneutic with "existential cash value" and ridiculed hermeneutical concepts that deny common experience? (See pages 59, 66–70). Well, yes, but I think one part of our common experience with texts is that we are able to imagine a certain idealized response to the text that may or may not match our own. The theoretical concept of implied readers is not itself an existential reality, but our ability to conceive this construct is.

119. The more conventional literary term for this concept is "the virginal reader." For some reason, it also inspires snickers, even among presumably mature and pious seminarians.

120. This comment assumes that *my* readers are reading *this* book sequentially. They are expected to recall the illustration I used on page 76. People who have just opened the book in the middle or decided to read this chapter first may find this comment completely extraneous—an unexpected response.

121. All of this, however, is contested. One recent book argues against the notion that any of the four Gospels were written for specific communities, suggesting that they were each intended for all Christians everywhere. See Richard Bauckham, ed., *The Gospels for All Christians: Rethinking the Gospel Audiences* (Grand Rapids: Wm. B. Eerdmans Publishing Co., 1998).

122. I learned it from John Meier who, in turn, got it from Karl Rahner.

123. On the notion of "reliable narrators," see Booth, *Rhetoric of Fiction,* esp. 169–209; Powell, *What Is Narrative Criticism?,* 25–27.

124. On the concept of a reader's "repertoire," see Iser, *The Implied Reader* (see subject index for page references).

125. Chatman, *Story and Discourse,* 19–22.

126. For example, a fairly extensive recent critique is offered in David Lee, *Luke's Stories of Jesus: Theological Reading of Gospel Narrative and the Legacy of Hans Frei,* Journal for the Study of the New Testament Supplement Series 185 (Sheffield: Sheffield Academic Press, 1999). As near as I can tell, I agree with all of his criticisms, as would all the narrative critics I know, and probably Chatman himself. I'm not sure that anybody thinks, or ever has thought, that Chatman's scheme provides an objective description of some intrinsic reality. I think that most critics simply view it as a useful contrivance for talking about various things. By analogy, I strongly suspect that the linguistic classification

of words as "nouns" or "verbs" or "adjectives" is only an artificial scheme that, if pressed far enough, would turn out to be arbitrary and flawed. I keep talking about words that way anyway. As an aside, let me add that I like Lee's book and commend it, although he doesn't think much of my work. He thinks that my *What Is Narrative Criticism?* (like Chatman's *Story and Discourse*) lacks rigorous theoretical consistency. It probably does; I'm not really rigorous or consistent enough to tell. I admit that the limitations of my intelligence and the excesses of my piety lead me to prioritize "useful" over "tidy" in assessment of theoretical constructs. But I also do recognize that the adoption of *any* construct, even when it is labeled as such, is never neutral. We must always remember that, hence this note.

127. Of course, Matthew's Gospel makes it clear elsewhere that disciples of Jesus are to do good to all people, even their enemies (5:44). But the point of Matthew 25:31–46 seems to be that an especially close identification can be made between Jesus and his metaphorical siblings, who are not defined generically as "needy persons" but specifically as "persons who do God's will." The thinking could be parallel to that expressed by Paul in Galatians 6:10. But even more likely, in my opinion, is a parallel to Matthew 10:40–42. At the end of the age, members of pagan nations will have to give account for how they treated the godly people (missionaries?) who Jesus sent to them (cf. Matt. 28:19). See Stanton, *A Gospel for a New People,* 207–31.

128. *Soapdish,* 1991. *Premiere* magazine runs a regular column listing such gaffes in feature films.

129. Regarding the text (or the author) as "inerrant" is clearly distinct from regarding the narrator as "reliable." I see no contradiction in affirming the latter expectation while rejecting the former. Indeed, I am actually protecting the integrity of the reliable narrator device here by saying that, in a rare instance where an author does present a reliable narrator as providing false information, this is an error on the part of the author—one that implied readers are not expected to notice.

130. I would add that, since the expectations of implied readers are often an index of the intentions of historical authors, I think it is extremely unlikely that the author(s) of Matthew's Gospel ever intended for the work to be regarded as inerrant. The sad irony of fundamentalist interpretation is that the practitioners of such a strategy often appear to be convinced that their unexpected reading strategy is the approach that the biblical authors would have wanted readers to adopt—and they defend it specifically along those untenable lines. Most proponents of other varieties of ideological criticism are more blatant about acknowledging that they are imposing a foreign perspective on the text.

131. Some would also suggest a criterion of *recurrence.* This criterion suggests that readers are more likely to notice information that is repeated within the narrative. The problem with this criterion is that we can never say that implied readers aren't expected to notice information that is provided only once. As such, I don't find this supposed criterion very useful. At most, let me say that my argument that implied readers are not expected to notice the discrepancy between 12:40 and 27:57–28:10 would be less tenable if the "three days and three nights" information were provided more than once.

132. Iser talks about the process of "consistency building," by which implied readers are expected to try to fit everything in a narrative together into a coherent pattern. See *The Implied Reader,* 283.

133. Compare, for example, 26:21 with 26:47–49; 26:31 with 26:56; and 26:33 with 26:69–75.

134. George Steiner distinguishes between typical readers and professional readers (or "critics"). See "'Critic'/'Reader'," *New Literary History* 10 (1979): 423–52.

135. The one major exception (relevant to Matthean studies) would be Richard A. Edwards, who has now quit using the term "implied reader" altogether and speaks instead of "the Text-Connoted Reader." See his *Matthew's Narrative Portrait of Disciples: How the Text-Connoted Reader Is Informed* (Harrisburg, Penn.: Trinity Press International, 1997). Edwards tries to recapture the experience of a reader who knows nothing except what is stated in the text. I appreciate his efforts and insights, but the method just does not seem sustainable. Is it logically consistent (or, for that matter, useful [cf. n. 126]) to assume that readers do not know anything about the world outside the text and yet to assume that they know the meanings of the basic vocabulary words of which the text is composed? Aren't those words given meaning from something outside the text? How can the reader know what the word "Caesar" means without knowing that there is a Roman empire?

136. Implied readers are a fiction, an imaginary construct; original readers were actual people who lived in a particular time and place. Implied readers are not characterized by such factors as gender, ethnicity, or age. Still, implied readers must be assumed to know certain things that original readers would have known (and to believe things that they would have believed). Thus, the concept of implied readers may be informed by historical data concerning the actual, original readers, but the concept retains a theoretical integrity of its own, grounded in what is actually presupposed for the narrative. For more on distinguishing the implied readers of Matthew from the book's intended readers see Kingsbury, "Reflections on 'the Reader' of Matthew's Gospel."

137. See, for instance, Craig L. Blomberg, *Jesus and the Gospels* (Nashville: Broadman & Holman, 1997), 133–35; Robert H. Gundry, *Matthew: A Commentary on His Handbook for a Mixed Church under Persecution,* 2nd ed. (Grand Rapids: Wm. B. Eerdmans Publishing Co., 1994), 599–609. Cf. Mark Allan Powell, *Fortress Introduction to the Gospels* (Minneapolis: Fortress Press, 1998), 71–75.

138. I prefer the term "common knowledge" to "universal knowledge," which I have used in previous discussions (Powell, "Expected and Unexpected"). In part, this is because (as I have always noted), no knowledge is truly "universal," that is, free of cultural determination. If one searches, one can always find human beings (infants, the severely retarded or isolated, the insane) who, in fact, do *not* know whatever it is that we would label "universal." The categories for my previous studies were (grudgingly) derived from Philip Wheelwright's classes of symbolic speech, especially as the latter are interpreted by R. Alan Culpepper. See Wheelwright, *Metaphor and Reality* (Bloomington, Ind.: Indiana University Press, 1962), 99–110; Culpepper, *Anatomy of the Fourth Gospel: A Study in Literary Design* (Philadelphia: Fortress Press, 1983), 184. I finally decided (with some prompting from my editor) that the categories are too flawed to be serviceable and rejected them. I now use Chatman's categories (also as interpreted by Culpepper, actually), admitting that these, too, are flawed—but useful! (See note 126.)

139. This example (for Matthew's Gospel) is similar to that which I used above (page 73) for *Gulliver's Travels.* The intended, historical audience may have recognized a specific satire of Protestant/Catholic conflict in Ireland that implied readers are not expected to notice.

140. Epithets may include names and nicknames, which in this narrative would include the so-called titles for Jesus (such as "Son of God," "Son of Man," "Messiah"). The meaning of such labels may be simply assumed as a matter of common knowledge. Part of the evidence for this is that sometimes, when readers are not expected to know the meaning of an epithet, the meaning is provided within the narrative (in Matthew, see 1:21 for the narrator's explicit

explanation of the meaning of the name "Jesus," and compare 16:18, for "Peter"). Sometimes, meaning ascribed to titles or epithets may be influenced by intertextual connections to the Jewish scriptures (see pages 98–101).

141. By contrast, the implied readers of John's Gospel are not necessarily expected to understand this euphemism, since an explanation of it is provided within the narrative (John 11:11–13).

142. Fowler, *Let the Reader Understand*, 179.

143. Fowler attributes the ambiguity of the wineskin metaphor in Mark 2:21–22 (as well as many other ambiguities in Mark's Gospel) to the rhetoric of the narrator rather than to the ignorance of modern readers. Although I suspect that this judgment is too hasty even with regard to Mark's Gospel, I am all the more certain that it can not apply to Matthew's use of the same metaphor in 9:17. Even Fowler agrees that Matthew's Gospel does not display the sort of "rhetoric of indirection" that he thinks he sees in Mark (pp. 233–260). When Matthew and Mark are compared, it can be seen that numerous potential gaps and ambiguities in Mark's Gospel are closed or resolved in Matthew's. For example, the "leaven" metaphor in Matthew 16:12 is clearly defined while the same metaphor in Mark 8:15 is not.

144. For instance, William Barclay, *The Gospel of Matthew*, 2 vols., rev. ed., Daily Study Bible Series (Philadelphia: Westminster Press, 1975), 2:217.

145. It is in this light that we should consider the special problem of *anachronism*, where information from the discourse setting is referenced explicitly in the text, albeit inappropriately. Most literary critics regard anachronisms as mistakes, as impositions of the discourse setting on the story. Accordingly, implied readers are expected to notice the reference but not to notice that it is anachronistic. One of the most famous instances of anachronism in literature is Shakespeare's reference to a clock striking in the play *Julius Caesar*. Many members of this play's real audiences have known that such clocks are inappropriate for the setting of the story (ancient Rome), but the play's implied audience is not expected to consider the clock to be remarkable or out of place. Does Matthew's Gospel contain any anachronisms? The reference that Jesus makes to a "church" in 18:17 should probably be understood as such. Real readers may know that no such institution existed during the lifetime of Jesus, but the characters in the story are not the least bit puzzled by Jesus' reference to this institution. Accordingly, Matthew's implied readers are probably expected to understand these references in light of the setting presupposed for the discourse of the narrative rather than in light of that which would actually be appropriate for the story. They are to understand the word "church" (*ekklēsia*) as referring to the Christian community that came into existence after the earthly ministry of Jesus (cf. 16:18) rather than as a reference to some generic "assembly" that may have existed during his ministry.

146. Those who have read my earlier treatment on what Matthew's readers can be assumed to know ("Expected and Unexpected Readings of Matthew," 39–41) will see that I have revised if not reversed the somewhat mangled views on this particular point that were presented there.

147. William Demby, *The Catacombs* (New York: Random House, 1965).

148. Rabinowitz, *Before Reading*, 21; Booth, *Rhetoric of Fiction*, 423.

149. I note that both of our "difficult cases" call for more precise information regarding the discourse setting of Matthew's narrative than we actually possess. Other examples—the talents or the mustard seed—only require us to consider what would have been known in the Roman empire during the last half of the first century. But when we consider what readers are expected to know concerning the inscription on the coin or concerning the destruction of the temple, we need to locate the production of the narrative more precisely. We *think*

this Gospel was written around 85 C.E., but we do not know that—a number of respected and competent scholars disagree (see n. 137).

150. Sometimes *recurrence* of such references can be stressed to emphasize that knowledge concerning a given matter is presupposed. The identity of the Caesar on the coin may be said to be referenced only once, while allusions to the temple's destruction could be multiple (24:2, 15; 26:61; 27:40). I admit to a certain logic here, but do not want to convey the impression that we can assume readers are not expected to know things that are presupposed only once (e.g., the relative value of talents and denarii in 18:23–35). Quality of reference is more significant for me than quantity, though I suppose I might find the supposition that we are to know it is Tiberius on the coin more tenable if that information was alluded to elsewhere in the narrative. Compare n. 131.

151. At most, some scholars might argue that 24:16 is an obscure allusion to the flight to Pella, or (as we have indicated) that passages such as 5:17–20 are offered with Paul in mind. Even if valid, these assertions would not offer a strong enough connection for me to decide that such information is presupposed for understanding the story.

152. The only scholars who doubt that this verse alludes to Titus's invasion of the Temple in 70 C.E. are those who, for various reasons, date the composition of Matthew's Gospel earlier than this. If a post–70 date for Matthew is accepted, the connection becomes virtually inescapable.

153. I am not implying anything about the validity of investigations that seek to specify the political interests of the historical Jesus. Obviously, the original context of this saying could have given it a more exact application than Matthew's readers are expected to recognize. Historical investigations of pre–narrative traditions are intriguing and important, but they are not the stuff of narrative criticism.

154. This somewhat narrow definition suits our purposes. Some literary critics use the term "intertextuality" to include the full range of knowledge to which a work alludes—the "texts" taken up in the work may be cultural scripts or codes rather than actual documents. I prefer the narrow definition, for clarity's sake, though I am willing to allow that such "texts" can be oral rather than written. A good starting point for literary discussion of intertextuality is Peter J. Rabinowitz, "'What's Hecuba to Us?': The Audience's Experience of Literary Borrowing," in *The Reader in the Text,* ed. S. Suleiman and I. Crosman (Princeton, N.J.: Princeton University Press, 1980), 241–63.

155. So Jonathan Culler, *The Pursuit of Signs: Semiotics, Literature, Deconstruction* (Ithaca, N.Y.: Cornell University Press, 1981), 102.

156. See Robert H. Gundry, *Matthew's Use of the Old Testament,* Novum Testamentum Supplement Series 18 (Leiden: E. J. Brill, 1967), 122–27.

157. We should not think that redaction criticism has "failed" in this regard, for reading Matthew in this manner was never a goal of that method. An approach should not be denounced for failing to accomplish what it never attempted.

158. Gérard Genette uses the analogy of a palimpsest to understand this phenomenon. In ancient times, parchment manuscripts were sometimes reused, resulting in manuscripts called "palimpsests" that actually had two texts written on them, one on top of another. See Genette, *Palimpsestes: La littérature au second degré,* Collection Poétique (Paris: Seuil, 1982). Readers treat Matthew's Gospel as a palimpsest when they read it in light of knowledge gained from the other Gospels.

159. These criteria correspond to three of the seven tests for hearing intertextual echoes suggested by Richard B. Hays in *Echoes of Scripture in the Letters of Paul* (New Haven, Conn.: Yale University Press, 1989), 29–33. What I call "degree of repetition," Hays calls "volume." Two of Hays's tests (historical plausibility,

history of interpretation) strike me as too concerned with responses of real readers to be of help in determining what is expected of implied readers. And another of his tests (satisfaction) seems redundant with thematic coherence. I note that Robert L. Brawley came to similar conclusions regarding Hays's tests in "Intertextuality in John 19:28–29," a paper presented to the Literary Aspects of the Gospels and Acts Groups at the 1991 Annual Meeting of the Society of Biblical Literature. Hays also cites "recurrence," which I would sometimes allow in a limited, positive sense but do not generally find compelling (see previous nn. 131, 150, and also below, n. 160).

160. This is the only sort of instance in which I might appeal to the criterion of "recurrence": if someone wanted to argue that Matthew's implied readers are not expected to recognize an allusion to Psalm 22:18 in 27:35, I would indicate that the supposition of such an allusion is strengthened by the observation that Psalm 22 is also referenced by 27:46 ("My God, My God, why have you forsaken me?") where the degree of repetition is extremely high. But I would not use this criterion in a negative sense, to indicate that lack of recurrence makes an intertextual connection unlikely.

161. Interestingly, Leviticus 19:18 is also cited in Matthew 19:19 and 22:39.

162. E. Stauffer, *Die Botschaft Jesu. Damals und heute* (Bern: Francke, 1959), 128–32; O. Seitz, "Love Your Enemies," *New Testament Studies* 16 (1969/70): 39–54. See also the discussion by W. D. Davies in *The Setting of the Sermon on the Mount* (Cambridge, Mass.: Cambridge University Press, 1964), 245–48.

163. Matthew's narrative probably alludes to this tradition of the elders elsewhere, although the phrase itself is not used again. See 16:12; 23:2–3, 16, 18, 23; 24:20. Jesus' attitude toward this tradition is ambivalent. See Jack Dean Kingsbury, *Matthew,* 2nd ed., Proclamation Commentaries (Philadelphia: Fortress Press, 1986), 88–89.

164. Although some portions of this tradition were no doubt incorporated into such writings as the Mishna, Gemara, and Talmud, the "tradition of the elders" referred to in Matthew 15:2 was by definition an oral code, and we cannot know how faithfully it has been preserved in the later written versions.

165. Some scholars think that Matthew's readers are expected to accept the charge as accurate because 1) Matthew does not explicitly describe the persons who bring it as false witnesses (contrast Mark 14:57–58); 2) the presence of two witnesses satisfies the requirement for reliable testimony according to Deuteronomy 17:16; and, 3) the wording of the claim attributed to Jesus ("I am able to . . ." as opposed to "I will . . ." in Mark 14:58) is in keeping with something that the Matthean Jesus would say (cf. 12:6). See, for example, Donald Senior, *The Passion of Jesus in the Gospel of Matthew* (Wilmington, Del.: Michael Glazier 1985), 92–93. Other scholars think that Jesus' silent response is an indication that the charge should be regarded as false. See Kingsbury, *Matthew as Story,* 87.

166. One problem with this explanation is that Jesus' words about the temple's destruction, his own resurrection, and the building of the church were all directed to the disciples in contexts where the witnesses at the trial would not have been present. But *is* this a problem? It might explain *why* the witness' testimony is so far off the mark. The implied readers, who were present with the disciples, know what Jesus really said and are able to compare the actual sayings with the mangled report by persons who weren't there. Note that the witnesses do not claim to have been present or to have heard with their own ears the words that they allege Jesus said (26:61; cf. Mark 14:58).

167. Hays, *Echoes,* 29.

168. See Philippe Lejeune, *Le pacte autobiographique* (Paris: Seuil, 1978). The principal concern here is with stories that employ first-person narration and so are

explicitly autobiographical. But many of Lejeune's insights (heavily indebted to Roland Barthes and Gérard Genette) are applicable in a broader sense.

169. The full phrase is worth repeating: "that willing suspension of disbelief for the moment, which constitutes poetic faith." The line is from his *Bibliographia Literaria,* chapter 14.

170. Robert Fowler says, "In any reading experience, the real reader is beckoned to become the implied reader of the tale, at least while reading" (*Let the Reader Understand,* 77). Fowler is the grand master of biblical reader-response criticism. You may have noticed elsewhere in this book that he and I have had our little disagreements, but even though I am right and he is wrong on those selected points, he generally knows a lot more about this subject than I do and, most of the time, you should listen to him.

171. Actually, this is another point at which we may differentiate between "implied readers" and "intended, historical readers" (see also nn. 136, 139). I have little doubt that Matthew's intended readers were expected to ascribe a certain historical referentiality to the narrative, that is, they were expected to believe that the episodes reported in this Gospel really did occur in a manner very similar to what is described. They were expected to allow the Gospel to shape and define their view of the world in which they lived. I do not think that implied readers are expected to do this. By definition, beliefs ascribed to implied readers are ones held *by readers*—by hypothetical persons who are supposed to be reading the narrative in a particular way. The construct cannot be stretched to include assumptions about what such persons might believe when they are *not* reading the narrative. The construct of implied readers, let us once again recall, is precisely that—a construct. Implied readers do not actually exist outside the narrative and so are not able to have beliefs about any world other than that of the story.

172. In the New Testament, the Greek word *selēniazomai* is used only here (17:15) and in Matthew 4:24, where it is also linked with demonic possession. The concept of being struck malevolently by the Moon is also referred to in Psalm 121:6. Note that the word "moonstruck" has persisted in English as a nonliteral adjective describing those who are mentally unbalanced (or, by analogy, those who are unbalanced due to romantic obsession, for which it seems Venus would be the more appropriate celestial culprit). Likewise, the English word *lunacy* owes its origin to ancient attributions of insanity to lunar malevolence.

173. Note that eventually Jesus will claim that all authority—both in *heaven* and on earth—has been given to him (28:18). See also such passages as Colossians 2:10 and Galatians 4:3 for emphasis on Christ overcoming "the elemental spirits of the universe." Moon worship was an ancient problem for Israel (Deut. 4:19, 17:3; 2 Kings 23:5), and by Matthew's day the influence of Persian astrology had made the association of heavenly bodies with deities almost indisputable. What *was* disputable within Judaism and early Christianity was the status and disposition of such second-tier divinities.

174. See David Rhoads, Joanna Dewey, and Donald Michie, *Mark as Story: An Introduction to the Narrative of a Gospel,* 2nd ed. (Minneapolis: Fortress Press, 1999), 43–47.

175. I'm messing with your minds a little bit here. The "not *a,* but *b*" speech formula used in Matthew 9:13b is probably intended to emphasize inclusion of the latter element without implying necessary exclusion of the former (it's called "the idiom of relative negation"; examples appear in John 6:32; Acts 5:4; Rom. 9:11–12; 1 Cor. 1:17; 1 Thess. 4:8). Still, a preference or priority is indicated. However it is interpreted, Matthew 9:13 deconstructs the emphasis that might otherwise be blindly attributed to righteousness in Matthew's story. I suspect the issue is that there are different *kinds* of righteousness; in 5:20 Jesus'

disciples are called to evince a righteousness that "exceeds that of the scribes and Pharisees" (to whom Jesus speaks in 9:13!). I suspect this means that the righteousness of his disciples (like that of Joseph in 1:19?) is to be of a different order than that of the scribes and Pharisees and of that of the people Jesus would neglect for the sake of sinners. The righteousness of his disciples is to "exceed" the righteousness of the scribes and Pharisees not just quantitatively but qualitatively. We catch a glimpse of what the lower order of "righteousness" could entail in 23:27–28.

176. I am, of course, aware that people may adopt a vegetarian diet for many reasons, including ones that do not presuppose moral objection to the killing of animals. I am referring to an ideologically motivated vegetarian who does object to this.

177. The Greek word used in Matthew 8:6 for the servant who is ill is *pais,* which carries a note of affection and can denote a son or other member of the household (one who is "like a son"). The word used in 8:9 is *doulos,* the same term employed in Matthew 18:23–35, where it refers to one over whom the master has extreme power.

178. I anticipate the objection that such an expectation contradicts what was said previously about despising tyranny. How can implied readers be expected both to despise tyranny and to accept slavery? The very passage that I quoted to assert the first point (20:25) continues, "It shall not be so among you, but whoever wishes to be great among you must be your servant [*diakonos*], and whoever wishes to be first among you must be your slave [*doulos*]" (20:26–27). For Matthew, despising tyranny does not mean doing away with slavery; it means honoring and recognizing slaves as greater (in God's eyes) than their masters.

179. See especially Bruce J. Malina, *The New Testament World: Insights from Cultural Anthropology,* 2nd ed. (Louisville, Ky.: Westminster John Knox Press, 1993); Richard Rohrbaugh, ed., *The Social Sciences and New Testament Interpretation* (Peabody, Mass.: Hendrickson, 1996).

180. Bruce J. Malina and Jerome H. Neyrey, *Calling Jesus Names: The Social Value of Labels in Matthew* (Sonoma, Calif.: Polebridge Press, 1988); Bruce J. Malina and Richard L. Rohrbaugh, *Social-Science Commentary on the Synoptic Gospels* (Minneapolis: Fortress Press, 1992); Jerome H. Neyrey, *Honor and Shame in the Gospel of Matthew* (Louisville, Ky.: Westminster John Knox Press, 1998).

181. Neyrey, *Honor and Shame,* 18, quoting a study of George M. Foster that is not listed in his bibliography.

182. E. M. Forster, *Aspects of the Novel* (New York: Harcourt, Brace, Jovanovich, 1927), 103–18. I should warn you, however, that David Lee faults me for citing this work in a book I wrote ten years ago: "Powell continues to employ Forster's 1927 distinction between 'flat' and 'round' characters, which is a crude and now obsolete categorization" (*Luke's Stories of Jesus,* 129, n. 35). I trust that anyone who has read this far in the present volume has discerned that I do not shun what scholars deem "crude" for that reason alone. Nor do I judge the usefulness of concepts by the date when they were proposed.

183. See Kingsbury, *Matthew as Story,* 17–24.

184. I have become convinced, however, that the prejudice is not so much against *Jewish* leaders (extendable to all Jews) as it is against Jewish *leaders* (extendable to all leaders). The bias of this narrative is against *worldly power,* whether that takes the form of political clout, financial stability, or (this is the one that really gets me) education. But now we are getting ahead of ourselves. Wait till the next chapter.

185. Notably, Stephen Moore has also used this example to criticize the legitimacy of narrative criticism. He notes that another scholar, Fred Burnett, has

approached the same topic with the same approach and come up with differ- ent results (*Poststructuralism and the New Testament*, 116, n. 11). I'm not sure why this would invalidate the approach as such. Obviously, either Burnett or I or both of us might fail in our application of the approach, or (and I suspect this is the case) we might be using somewhat different approaches but calling them by the same name. Likewise, David Lee thinks that my suggestion that implied readers by definition interpret Matthew's religious leaders as exercis- ing a role within the narrative must arise from my own "sense of embarrass- ment about the text" (*Luke's Stories of Jesus*, 135, n. 49). Well, obviously, I am embarrassed by the referential meaning that has often been given to this text (who wouldn't be?), but Lee gives no indication as to why such embarrassment would be necessary to motivate an interpretation that is perfectly consistent with the approach that I am describing. This is strange, given his concern with theoretical consistency (cf. n. 126). He seems to think that I am accurate to claim that narrative criticism deals with the poetic function of texts rather than with their referential function (p. 135) but then thinks it must be embarrass- ment that leads me (as a narrative critic) to interpret this text in a poetic rather than in a referential way. An odd complaint, from a usually perceptive book.

186. Merenlahti and Hakola, "Reconceiving Narrative Criticism," 41. The response is to comments I made in *What Is Narrative Criticism?*, 64–67.

187. Perhaps it would be more accurate to say that they have a limited or narrow concept of what narrative criticism can be and of what it can seek to do. They have detected that narrative criticism, while basically a literary-critical approach, can nevertheless serve to advance historical-critical goals. This is true. See the sidebar summary on page 67–69.

188. Merenlahti and Hakola take on other narrative critical studies as well, includ- ing Jeffrey Staley's *The Print's First Kiss: A Rhetorical Investigation of the Implied Reader in the Fourth Gospel*, Society of Biblical Literature Dissertation Series 82 (Atlanta: Scholars Press, 1988). Staley explicitly labels his study as an exam- ple of "reader-response criticism"; that is, he claims to use narrative criticism to further the goals of reader-oriented criticism, not author-oriented criticism. But for Merenlahti and Hakola, "the question is whether Staley's reading of John is a reading that comes naturally" (27). And, "why is there so little evi- dence that any real readers ever experienced the text in the way Staley describes?" (27). But, the notion of implied readers is a theoretical construct; whether any real readers ever have or ever will respond to a text in the manner expected of its implied readers is irrelevant to definition of the concept. There is merit to a critic identifying how he or she construes a text's implied readers apart from any claim that this construction illustrates how real readers do or should read the text. (See "Replies," p. 237.)

189. I hope you note the distinction between what I describe as "a normative way of reading" (pages 72–74) and what Merenlahti and Hakola advocate as "*the* natural way of reading." I use the latter phrase to indicate a designated rhetor- ical strategy through which an identifiable reading can be obtained that may then be compared and contrasted with other readings obtained through other strategies. I do not believe that the interpretations gained through what I describe as a normative way of reading are intrinsically correct, much less exclusively so. (See "Replies," p. 237.)

190. One may, of course, argue that a given set of goals are not worthy of pursuit but that requires a different tack, one that Merenlahti and Hakola do not take.

191. Mark Allan Powell, *What Is Narrative Criticism?*, 101.

192. In fact, I already have. Their proposal for a "positively comprehensive approach that pays due attention to literary, ideological and historical dimen- sions of the text" (17) is not revolutionary. A great many scholars (e.g.,

Warren Carter, John Paul Heil, Jack Dean Kingsbury, Amy-Jill Levine, Graham Stanton, Mary Ann Tolbert, and Joseph Tyson) have been attempting such wholistic study for years. To a lesser extent, such was the approach I employed in my book *God with Us: A Pastoral Theology of Matthew's Gospel* (Minneapolis: Fortress Press, 1995).

193. This seemingly obvious observation was apparently so obvious that it was completely ignored (overlooked?) in modern criticism until the appearance of a landmark study by Norman Petersen. No, *not* the guy from *Cheers* (and he's really tired of hearing that). See "Point of View in Mark's Narrative."

194. I challenge the affirmation often made by narrative critics that implied readers are "a mirror image of the implied author." I suppose it would be more accurate to say that they are expected to *become* such an image. The implied author possesses knowledge, beliefs, and values from the outset that must be imparted to the implied readers throughout the reading process.

195. To be precise, Matthew's implied readers are expected to believe that the *character of Jesus* is the Messiah *in this story.* Implied readers are not expected to believe that the historical Jesus was or is the historical Messiah, any more than they are expected to believe anything else about the real, historical world. See n. 171. I'm getting tired of saying this, and I know you're getting tired of reading it, but I fear that some readers (other readers, not you) still might not be getting it.

196. Even this basic example has been challenged, in a now-famous exchange between two classic Matthean scholars, Jack Dean Kingsbury and David Hill. The latter argued that the point of view of *Jesus* (not God) is normative, and that readers come to regard God as reliable because Jesus reveals this to them. Theologically, I've got no problem with the point Hill wanted to make (what systematicians call "christology from below"), but I don't think the argument works for a literary study of Matthew's narrative. Matthew's implied readers are not expected to start out believing Jesus is reliable and, so, be willing to believe that whatever he says about God must be true. Rather, they are expected to start out believing God is reliable and so be willing to regard what God says about Jesus as true. In other words, the reliability of Jesus is something the Gospel seeks to establish, while the reliability of God is something that it assumes. But check it out for yourself: Kingsbury, "The Figure of Jesus in Matthew's Story: A Literary-Critical Probe," *Journal for the Study of the New Testament* 21 (1984): 3–36; Hill, "The Figure of Jesus in Matthew's Story: A Response to Professor Kingsbury," *Journal for the Study of the New Testament* 21 (1984): 37–52; Kingsbury, "The Figure of Jesus in Matthew's Story: A Rejoinder to David Hill," *Journal for the Study of the New Testament* 25 (1985): 61–81.

197. Neyrey, *Honor and Shame in the Gospel of Matthew*, 164–228.

198. Robert Fowler indicates that the rhetoric of Mark's Gospel functions continually to distance the reader from the disciples, who represent bad examples of what the reader ought not to be. See *Let the Reader Understand*, 70–73, 256–60. But Matthew's narrative is more complex in this regard. Sometimes readers are expected to understand what the disciples don't (just as in Mark); at other times, the disciples appear to be ahead of what would be expected for readers, such that the readers might learn from them. But much of the time, I think, the disciples in Matthew are pretty much where the implied readers are expected to be at that point in the narrative, thinking what readers are assumed to think and asking what readers are expected to ask.

199. See the traditional commentaries, and Gail R. O'Day, "Surprised by Faith: Jesus and the Canaanite Woman," *Listening* 24 (1989): 290–301; Elaine Wainwright, *Shall We Look for Another?: A Feminist Rereading of the Matthean Jesus* (Maryknoll, N.Y.: Orbis Books, 1998), 84–92.

200. I hope you will not miss the irony. Matthew's Gospel has often been read as supporting *anti-Semitism*—as indicated earlier in this chapter.

201. Such surprise is only implicit. Matthew does not actually say that Jesus was amazed by this encounter (cf. 8:10). Still, I think it possible that this incident allows a mild exception to what I said earlier about instruction in values typically being one-directional. Perhaps Matthew here portrays Jesus himself as learning something about what God is doing. Perhaps. But this element is much stronger in the Markan parallel, which I claim presents the woman as an agent of revelation to Jesus. My thoughts on that text (Mark 7:24–30) have only been published in devotional and denominational materials, but they are highly compatible with and often dependent on the insights of two of my favorite scholars, David Rhoads and Sharon H. Ringe. See Rhoads, "The Syrophoenician Woman in Mark: A Narrative-Critical Study," *Journal of the American Academy of Religion* 62 (1994): 342–75; Ringe, "A Gentile Woman's Story," in *Feminist Interpretation of the Bible,* ed. Letty M. Russell (Philadelphia: Westminster Press, 1985), 65–72.

202. I am excluding the raising of Jairus's daughter (9:18–19, 23–25) here because, like most interpreters, I read this more as a boon to the father than to the child. In any case, she obviously does not request the healing—her father intercedes for her.

203. For a sustained feminist reading of Matthew's Gospel, see Wainwright, *Shall We Look for Another?*

204. Mark Allan Powell, "Matthew," in *Harper-Collins Bible Commentary,* rev. ed., ed. James L. Mays and Beverly R. Gaventa (San Francisco: HarperSanFrancisco, 2000).

205. Keith Howard Reeves, *The Resurrection Narrative in Matthew: A Literary-Critical Examination* (Lewiston, N.Y.: Mellen Press, 1993), 55.

206. Compare my discussion of these matters with that offered in Jane Kopas, "Jesus and Women in Matthew," *Theology Today* 47 (1990): 13–21; Elizabeth Struthers Malbon, "Fallible Followers: Women and Men in the Gospel of Matthew," *Semeia* 28 (1983): 29–48; Talvikki Mattila, "Naming the Nameless: Gender and Discipleship in Matthew's Passion Narrative," in Rhoads and Syreeni, *Characterization in the Gospels,* 153–79.

207. And even this is not certain. Most interpreters assume that since there are twelve male disciples who are called "apostles" in Matthew (10:2–4) and twelve thrones, each throne will have a male, apostolic occupant. But Jesus does not actually say which of his followers will get the thrones. He merely says that the twelve thrones are for people who have followed him, which would include a larger and more diverse group (27:35). Judas, at least, seems to forfeit his throne. Who will occupy it?

208. Richard C. Trexler, *The Journey of the Magi: Meanings in History of a Christian Story* (Princeton, N.J.: Princeton University, 1997), 3.

209. Powell, *What Is Narrative Criticism?*

210. Ulrich Luz, *Matthew 1–7: A Commentary.* Continental Commentaries (Minneapolis: Augsburg Publishing House, 1989), 95–99.

211. Luz, *Matthew 1–7,* 141.

212. On the development of such traditions, particularly as they appear in drama and art, see M. Hengel and H. Merkel, "Die Magier aus dem Osten und die Flucht nach Ägypten (Mt 2) im Rahmen der antiken Religionsgeschichte und der Theologie des Matthäus," in *Orientierung an Jesus,* FS Josef Schmid; ed. P. Hoffmann (Freiburg: Herder, 1973), 139–69; Hugo Kehrer, *Die heiligen drei Könige in Literatur und Kunst,* 2 vols. (Leipzig: Seemann, 1908–09); Karl Meisen, *Die heiligen drei Könige und ihr Festtag im volkstümlichen Glauben und Brauch* (Cologne, 1949); Bruce M. Metzger, "Names for the Nameless in the New

Testament," in *Kyriakon* (FS J. Quasten; ed. P. Granfield and J. Jungmann; Münster: Aschendorf, 1970), 79–99, esp. 79–85; Moisés Mayordomo-Marín, *Den Anfang hören: leserorientierte Evangelienexegese am Beispiel von Mattäus 1–2*, Forschungen zur Religion und Literatur des Alten und Neuen Testaments 180 (Göttingen: Vandenhoeck & Ruprecht, 1998); Eberhard Nestle, "Einiges über Zahl und Namen der Weisen aus dem Morgenland," in *Marginalien und Materialien* 2 (Tübingen: Heckenhauer, 1893), 67–83; A. Schulze, "Zur Geschichte der Auslegung von Mt 2, 1–12," *Theologische Zeitschrift* 31 (1975): 150–60; C. Schoebel, *L'Histoire des Rois Mages* (Paris, 1878); Trexler, *Journey of the Magi.* Further detailed bibliographies are included in Trexler and in Hengel and Merkel.

213. In "The First Noel," the Matthean story has conquered the Lukan. The shepherds are alerted to Christ's birth not by angels but by a star—"that same star" that summons the magi "from country far."

214. Calvin called the decision that there must be three magi because there were three (types of) gifts a "childish Papist error," although it was first asserted by Origen, under no apparent pressure from a pope (See Luz, *Matthew 1–7*, 140, nn. 69–70). In the Eastern church, the number of magi is frequently twelve.

215. See chapter 12 of this book. I have questioned the necessity of this assumption before (Powell, *God with Us*, 54, n. 18).

216. Luz, *Matthew 1–7*, 141.

217. Ibid., 96–97.

218. Please notice the pun.

219. Aside from the usual commentaries, historical and redactional studies of the passage include M. Bourke, "The Literary Genus of Matthew 1–2," *Catholic Biblical Quarterly* 22 (1960): 160–75; R. E. Brown, *The Birth of the Messiah*, 2nd ed. (New York: Doubleday, 1993); J. E. Bruns, "The Magi Episode in Matthew 2," *Catholic Biblical Quarterly* 23 (1961): 51–54; C. H. Cave, "St. Matthew's Infancy Narrative," *New Testament Studies* 9 (1962/63): 382–90; J. D. Crossan, "Structure and Theology of Mt 1, 18–2, 23," *Cahiers de Joséphologie* 16 (1968): 119–35; Jean Daniélou, *The Infancy Narratives* (London: Burns & Oates, 1968); Charles Thomas Davis, "Tradition and Redaction in Matthew 1,18—2,23," *Journal of Biblical Literature* 90 (1971): 404–21; A. M. Denis, "L'adoration des mages vue par S. Matthieu," *La nouvelle revue théologique* 82 (1960): 32–39; J. D. Derrett, "Further Light on the Narratives of the Nativity," *Novum Testamentum* 17 (1975): 81–108; Albrecht Dieterich, "Die Weisen aus dem Morgenlande," *Zeitschrift für die neutestamentliche Wissenschaft und die Kunde der älteren Kirche* 3 (1902): 1–14; Morton Enslin, "The Christian Stories of the Nativity," *Journal of Biblical Literature* 39 (1940): 317–38; P. Gaechter, "Die Magierperikope (Mt 2, 1–12)," *Zeitschrift für katholische Theologie* 90 (1968): 257–94; Herman Hendrickx, *Infancy Narratives* (London: Geoffrey Chapman, 1975); A. R. C. Leaney, "The Birth Narratives in St. Luke and St. Matthew," *New Testament Studies* 8 (1961–62): 158–66; E. Nellessen, *Das Kind und seine Mutter*, Stuttgarter Bibelstudien 39 (1969); A. Paul, *L'Évangile de l'enfance Saint Matthieu* (Paris: Éditions de Cerf, 1968); E. Peretto, "Ricerche su Mt 1–2," *Marianum* 31 (1969): 140–247; H. J. Richards, "The Three Kings (Mt ii. 1–12)," *Scripture* 8 (1956): 23–28; P. Stuhlmacher, "Epiphanias. Matthäus 2, 1–12," *Göttinge Predigtmeditationen* 27 (1972): 63–70. A recent study that works with reader-response criticism on a historical level is Moisés Mayordomo-Marín, *Den Anfang hören: leserorientierte Evangelienexegese am Beispiel von Mattaüs 1–2*, Forschungen zur Religion und Literatur des Alten und Neuen Testaments 180 (Göttingen: Vandenhoeck & Ruprecht, 1998).

220. Such a recognition is certainly not unique to reader response, but is in fact inherited from traditional historical-critical exegesis. The classic work is Bultmann, "Is Exegesis Without Presuppositions Possible?"

221. Trexler, *Journey of the Magi*, 3.

222. Portions of chapters 7, 8, and 9 have appeared previously in three published articles: Mark Allan Powell, "Neither Wise Nor Powerful: Reconsidering Matthew's Magi in Light of Reader Expectations," *Trinity Seminary Review* 20 (1998): 19–32; idem, "The Magi as Kings: An Adventure in Reader-Response Criticism," *Catholic Biblical Quarterly* 62 (2000): 459–80; idem, "The magi as wise men: re-examining a basic supposition," *New Testament Studies* 46 (2000): 1–20.

223. *Sermo* 139-*PL* 39, 2018.

224. Cited in Metzger, "Names," 82. The work provides blatantly extrabiblical detail, identifying the magi specifically as Hormizdah, king of Persia; Yazdegerd, king of Saba; and Perozadh, king of Sheba. The Western tradition of names may also date from the sixth century. The earliest occurrence of the names Balthasar, Melchior, and Gaspar (= Caspar) is in the *Excerpta Latina Barbari*, a somewhat corrupt translation of a sixth-century Greek work.

225. Luz, *Matthew 1–7*, 140.

226. Luz cites a passage from the "Sermon of 1524," which has not been translated into English but can be found in the Weimar edition of D. *Martin Luthers Werke*, vol. 15, p. 409. See also the discussion in "The Gospel for the Festival of the Epiphany, Matthew 2[:1–12]," *Luther's Works*, vol. 52, ed. Hans J. Hillerbrand (Philadelphia: Fortress Press), 159–286, esp. 161. In general, Luther was even more concerned with denouncing the cult of relics concerning the supposed kings than the alleged royalty itself. In his Epiphany Sermon of 1531 (in the Weimar edition, again, vol. 34, pp. 21–32), he discouraged his congregation from going to Cologne to see the magi's remains, which he had seen himself and which, he asserted, might just as well belong to "Westphalian farmers" as to Arabian kings. The whole thing was a sham. He called on Christians to ignore the magi altogether and celebrate Jesus' baptism instead. See Trexler, *Journey of the Magi*, 158. Compare n. 307.

227. John Calvin, *A Harmony of the Gospels: Matthew, Mark, and Luke*, 3 vols. (Grand Rapids: Wm. B. Eerdmans Publishing Co., 1972), I:82.

228. Juán de Maldonado, *Commentarii in quatuor Evangelistas*, 2 vols., ed. J. Raich (Moguntiae/Kirchheim, 1874), I:25.

229. The views of a notable exception, Richard Horsley, are discussed below (pages 165–66).

230. According to Marsh-Edwards (p. 8), artists began to crown the magi in the twelfth century. See note 292.

231. See Gerhard Delling, "*magos, mageia, mageuō*," *Theological Dictionary of the New Testament* IV:356–59. Delling cites numerous references from ancient writings for each of the four meanings, and Davies and Allison add more. The latter reference is W. D. Davies and Dale C. Allison, *A Critical and Exegetical Commentary on The Gospel According to Saint Matthew*, 3 vols., International Critical Commentary (Edinburgh: T. & T. Clark, 1988), 3:228. See also Samuel K. Eddy, *The King Is Dead: Studies in the Near Eastern Resistance to Hellenism, 334–31 B.C.* (Lincoln, Nebr.: University of Nebraska Press, 1961), 65–80; E. M. Yamauchi, "The Episode of the Magi," in *Chronos, Kairos, Christos*, ed. J. Vardaman and E. M. Yamauchi (Winona Lake, Ind.: Eisenbrauns, 1989), 15–39.

232. On the Persian background, see especially J. M. Cook, *The Persian Empire* (New York: Schocken, 1983), 154–55; M. A. Dandamaev, *Persien unter den ersten Achämeniden*, trans. H. D. Pohl (Wiesbaden: Ludwig Reichert, 1976), 238–40; Eddy, *King Is Dead*; R. N. Frye, *The History of Ancient Iran* (Munich: Beck, 1984), 120–24; M. Schwartz, "The Religion of Achaemenian Iran" in *The Cambridge History of Iran 2: The Median and Achaemenian Periods*, ed. I. Gershevitch (Cambridge: Cambridge University Press, 1985), 696–97.

233. The evidence for this is empirical: millions of readers have done so.

234. The key word *anatolē* is found in the LXX as a textual variant only. The preferred LXX reading has simply "to your brightness (*tē lamprotēti sou*)."

235. The magi's gifts may also suggest intertextual allusions to a number of other passages: gold and frankincense, Sir. 50:9; myrrh and frankincense, Exod. 30:34; Song of Sol. 3:6; gold and myrrh, Song of Sol. 11:13.

236. The question may be raised whether *any* knowledge of magi could have been considered basic in the world that provided the discourse setting for Matthew's narrative. I think this question can be answered affirmatively with some confidence. The otherwise sparse characterization of the magi in Matthew suggests that the term *magoi* itself is supposed to depict them adequately for the readers. In other words, since Matthew does not tell us what "magi" are, we may assume that we are expected to know what they are.

237. Eddy, *King Is Dead*, 67 n. 7.

238. Xenophon, *Cyropaedia* 8.1.23–24.

239. Eddy (*King Is Dead*, 65) believes that magi were originally an independent tribe of priests who lived under a special law analogous to the Levitical Code. Yamauchi ("Episode") notes that later magian religion became so identified with Zoroastrianism that such writers as Plato, Plutarch, and Pliny the Elder refer to Zoroaster himself as a magus (p. 27, n. 57). Still later, the Chaldean association with astrology became prominent (p. 28). By the time of the New Testament, as Delling's article and the stories discussed here indicate, the term had come to be applied to practitioners of a variety of exotic arts.

240. Richard A. Horsley, *The Liberation of Christmas: The Infancy Narratives in Social Context* (New York: Crossroad, 1989), 53.

241. Eddy, *King Is Dead*, 65–66.

242. See Dio Cassius, *Roman History* 63.1–7; Suetonius *Nero* 13; Pliny, *Natural History* 30.6.16–17.

243. For full references and discussion, see Paul Henning, "The Murder of the Magi," *Journal of the Royal Asiatic Society* (1944): 133–44; J. Wiesehöfer, *Der Aufstand Gaumatas und die Anfänge Dareios I* (Bonn: Rudolf Habelt, 1978).

244. Herodotus, *History* III. 67, 79.

245. Aristobulus, *Anabasis* vi. 29.8–30.2; Strabo, *Geography* xv. 3.7; Eddy, *King Is Dead*, contains references to a number of other such events (see esp. 72).

246. The term *midrash* (here) refers to imaginative reconstructions of biblical scenes or episodes. Secondary literature on such stories, as relevant to the magi tale, include Brown, *Birth*, 190–96; Hendrickx, *Infancy Narratives*, 8–21, 22–36; Horsley, *Liberation*, 53–60; Yamauchi, "Episode"; Paul Winter, "Jewish Folklore in the Matthean Birth Story," *Hibbert Journal* 53 (1954): 34–42.

247. Talbab, *Sanhedrin*, 101a; *Midrash Rabbah* I. 18 on Exodus 1:22. These sources also list Balaam as Pharaoh's counselor (Talbab, *Sotah*, 11a; *Midrash Rabbah* I. 9 on Exodus 1:9). *Sepher ha-Yashar* names Jannes and Jambres (cf. 2 Tim. 3:8) as the Pharaoh's chief magi and identifies them as Balaam's sons. Philo also identifies Pharaoh's counselors as magi in *Vita Moysis I*, xvi, #92. See also Numenius of Apamea in Eusebius, *Praep. Ev.* 9.8; Tg. Ps.-J. on Exod 1:15 and Num 22.2; Sepher ha-Yashar, 61–85; Ambrosiaster, *2 Tim.* on 3.8; Strack and Billerbeck, *Kommentar*, 3.660–64. For discussion, see Brown, *Birth*, 115 n. 43; 117, n. 46; Davies and Allison, *Matthew*, 195, n. 22; 229; Hendrickx, *Infancy Narratives*, 48; Eduard Schweizer, *The Good News According to Matthew*, trans. David E. Green (Atlanta: John Knox Press, 1975), 36–37; Judith R. Baskin, *Pharaoh's Counsellors: Job, Jethro and Balaam in Rabbinic and Patristic Tradition*. Brown Judaic Studies 47 (Chico, Calif.: Scholars Press, 1983), 75–113.

248. See the *Palestinian Targum* on Numbers 22–24 and Philo, *Vita Moysis I*, L, #276.

249. This is most readily apparent in the exodus midrash, for Pharaoh's sorcerers who are here identified as magi are mere sycophants, and rather ineffectual ones at that. Balaam appears to be more independent in the book of Numbers itself but the tendency of the midrash was to accentuate his eagerness to please the king and the divine confounding of this. The denigration of Balaam in the history of tradition makes for a fascinating study in its own right. To most exegetes, Balaam actually seems reluctant to curse Israel in the book of Numbers itself (22:18, 38; 23:12, 26—though even here variant traditions may have been intertwined, cf. 22:20 to 22:31–32). Philo, however, insists that his reluctance was only feigned. This hostile view is also presupposed in the New Testament (2 Pet. 2:15–16; Jude 11; Rev. 2:14).

250. I may err on the side of caution in saying this. Many historical critics detect compositional dependence that indicates the evangelist knew some of these stories, and they assume that consequently his original readers must have known them, too. Davies and Allison go so far as to say that Matthew's text "largely derived its meaning" from such parallels (*Matthew*, 1.253; specifically, they have in mind certain Moses legends). But I have argued against the presumption that implied readers should automatically be expected to know material that was known to a real author. The historical author of Matthew's Gospel almost certainly knew the Gospel of Mark, but the narrative unfolds without any expectation that readers know this Gospel. See page 101. In the present instance, my case could be strengthened through the claim that Matthew's implied readers are expected to know the specific stories described here, but I am content to argue merely that their general impressions of magi are expected to be similar to what is found there. It is enough.

251. I am referring here to the Septuagint text of the book of Daniel. The Septuagint was the Greek translation of the Hebrew and Aramaic scriptures that served as the Bible for the Greek-speaking Jewish community in Matthew's day. The word *magos* occurs in both the Old Greek and Theodotion translations.

252. Robert H. Gundry provides me with examples of how the Matthean narrative often assimilates its wording to what is found in Daniel. Compare Matt. 13:43 to Dan. 12:3; Matt. 25:46 to Dan. 12:2; Matt. 28:3 to Dan. 7:9; Matt. 28:18 to Dan. 7:14; Matt. 28:20 to Dan. 12:13.

253. We may also note that the only other references to magi in the New Testament (Acts 13:6, 8) are in the story of Elymas Bar-Jesus, who is presented as a servant to Sergius Paulus, proconsul of Cyprus (13:6–12). A similar story is told by Josephus concerning a magus called Atomos who serves Felix the governor of Judea and uses his arts to secure the latter's marriage to Drusilla (*Antiquities* 20:142; cf. Acts 24:24–25). These magi are also servants of political rulers, though those rulers are not identified as kings. By the way, Simon in Acts 8 is not called a magus, as is often supposed, but is simply identified as a worker of magic (*mageuōn*, 8:9; cf. 8:11, *mageia*). The strong tendency in literature is to restrict the term *magos* to those who not only work magic but who do so in a professional capacity as servants of a political ruler.

254. I am grateful to Kathleen Weber who, in responding to a paper I gave at the 1997 Society of Biblical Literature meeting, articulated this position quite clearly.

255. The same point holds against Richard Horsley, who insists (citing Eddy, *King Is Dead*, 65–67) that magi were not mere sycophants but, in one instance, were actually responsible for replacing a Persian king (*Liberation of Christmas*, 54). This is interesting, but ultimately beside the point. Our concern is the *perception* of magi in the discourse setting of Matthew's narrative, as evidenced in contemporary literature. There is no indication that Pharaoh or Nebuchadnezzar would have lost any sleep worrying that their magi might overthrow

them, or that Herod had any such concerns about the magi he bosses around in Matthew's story.

256. For other biblical texts that present Satan as the ruler of earthly kingdoms, see John 12:31; 14:30; 16:11; 2 Cor. 4:4; Eph. 6:12; 1 John 5:19.

257. With the majority of interpreters, I do not read Matthew 22:15–22 as an endorsement of Roman power but merely as an acknowledgment that such power structures do exist in this world and must be recognized whether they are legitimate or not (cf. 23:2–3). There is wisdom in not giving offense to powerful rulers over matters as trivial as the disbursement of mammon (cf. 17:24–27; 10:16).

258. Matthew consistently presents the power of earthly rulers as thwarted in certain respects: Herod the king is tricked by the magi (2:16); Herod the tetrarch is coerced by Herodias (14:6–11); and Pilate is manipulated by the religious leaders and the crowd (27:20–26). In every case, the tyrants act out of fear and in every case they either fail to accomplish what they wanted to accomplish or are pressured to issue commands contrary to their own will or desire. See Dorothy Jean Weaver, "Power and Powerlessness: Matthew's Use of Irony in the Portrayal of Political Leaders," in *Treasures New and Old: Contributions to Matthean Studies,* ed. David R. Bauer and Mark Allan Powell, 179–96 (Atlanta: Scholars Press, 1996).

259. Jack Dean Kingsbury, "The Developing Conflict Between Jesus and the Jewish Leaders in Matthew's Gospel: A Literary-Critical Study," *Catholic Biblical Quarterly* 49 (1987): 57–73.

260. Historical-critical studies that dismiss these castigations as anti-Semitic polemicizing or as competitive rhetoric aimed at "the synagogue across the street" miss two key elements of Matthew's theological vision: 1) the ethnic bias that this narrative betrays is against Gentiles not Jews (see pages 124–27); and 2) the story's denunciation of worldly powers makes no ethnic distinctions. Jewish *leaders* and Gentile *rulers* alike are condemned while peasants and slaves—even Gentile ones (8:5–13; 15:21–28)—are acceptable. The primary line of opposition in this story is not between Jews and Gentiles but between the powerful and the powerless.

261. This will be true only until "the renewal of all things" (the Parousia?). When the Son of Man is finally seated on his throne, then Jesus' followers will be given thrones as well (19:28). Similarly, Matthew's narrative makes occasional reference to rulers in the past who are not regarded as tyrants: David (12:3) and Solomon (12:42)—though neither of these is identified explicitly as a royal figure—and "the queen of the South" (12:42). Such references are typical of apocalyptic thought, which usually regards the past as a more sacred time when Satan's rule was less pronounced, and the ultimate future as an ideal time when that rule will be vanquished. But the era that provides the temporal setting for Matthew's story is presented as a time in which royalty is characterized only in negative terms. Of course, Jesus himself is something of an exception, as the true eschatological king (21:5; 25:34).

262. I have done this myself. See Powell, *God with Us,* 54–55.

263. Lest I appear to go too far, let me clarify that my argument is not that the magi are not wealthy. I only indicate that, in the story, the value of their gifts is not addressed and their financial status appears to be insignificant. Matthew does not say they are wealthy or call attention to their wealth in anything like the manner adopted by most modern interpreters. But even if the magi were to be regarded as wealthy, this would not prevent them (in this narrative) from being exemplars of the marginalized. The tax collector in Matthew 9:9 is apparently pretty well-to-do, yet he is practically singled out as an example of those who are treated as outcasts by society. A case for marginalized status could probably

also be made for the wealthy woman in 26:6–13, the only character in the story other than the magi who offers a gift to Jesus.

264. Homiletical treatments from the Middle Ages often suggested the gifts (especially the gold) were used to finance the subsequent journey of the holy family to Egypt. But there is nothing to indicate this in Matthew's Gospel, where, in any case, extensive travel by those who lack gold is not problematic (10:5–9; cf. n. 265).

265. A similarly fallacious argument posits that the magi had to be wealthy and hence powerful in order to travel great distances. But in this narrative, Jesus' disciples are assumed to be able to go to all nations (28:19) and to the whole world (24:14) in spite of the fact that they have abandoned their possessions (19:27) and lack worldly power (20:25–27).

266. An examination of the tradition that the magi are wealthy could proceed along the same lines as the two traditions studied in this book (that they are royal or wise). Though Matthew does not say that the magi are wealthy, the mention of gifts opens a "gap" that has allowed readers to assume that they are. Are readers *expected* to assume this? Whether they are or aren't, the tradition of magian wealth (like those of magian royalty and magian wisdom) has certainly been exploited by interpreters. The implication that such foreign wealth rightfully belongs at Christian feet helped to fuel crusades and colonialism.

267. Once the magi were taken to be kings, this apparent lapse had to be corrected. Expansions on the story often included accounts of the gifts Mary gave to the magi—usually, the child's swaddling clothes, but sometimes a magic stone or loaf of eucharistic bread. Of course, such gifts had remarkable effects. See Trexler, *Journey of the Magi,* 37, 40.

268. We have to ask from a compositional perspective why Matthew did not simply have kings come to Bethlehem instead of magi. R. T. France's answer is that he is constrained by fact. Matthew could have come up with a story in which scriptures were fulfilled more obviously, but he uses scripture to interpret history, not create fiction. See "Formula Quotations of Matthew 2," 236. Roger Aus suggests rather ingeniously that the magi were intended to parallel those whom Herodotus describes in his story of the birth of Cyrus. See "The Magi at the Birth of Cyrus, and the Magi at Jesus' Birth in Matt. 2:1–12," in *New Perspectives on Ancient Judaism, Volume Two: Religion, Literature, and Society, in Ancient Israel, Formative Christianity, and Judaism,* ed. Jacob Neusner et al. (Lanham, Md.: University Press of America, 1987), 99–114. The parallel to scripture is maintained, since Isaiah portrays Cyrus as a messianic figure (45:1).

269. As yet. Of course, there's always the off chance that I might convince a couple. Warren Carter, who has written a commentary on Matthew for Orbis Books and who is very smart, has read my papers on this and seems to think that I am right. Everyone should buy his commentary when it comes out.

270. W. K. Lowther Clarke, *Divine Humanity: Doctrinal Essays on New Testament Problems* (New York: Macmillan Company, 1936), 41–51.

271. C. S. Mann, "Epiphany—Wise Men or Charlatans?" *Theology* 61 (1958): 495–500.

272. R. A. Rosenberg, "The Star of the Magi Reconsidered," *Biblica* 53 (1972): 105-09.

273. See H. L. Strack and P. Billerbeck, *Kommentar,* 1:77–78.

274. Cicero, *De divinatione I,* xxiii, 47; Tacitus, *Annals II,* 27–33.

275. Suetonius, *Tiberius,* 36.

276. This remains true even if, as some contend, astrology was sometimes accepted within first-century Judaism. On this, see James H. Charlesworth, "Jewish Astrology in the Talmud, Pseudepigrapha, the Dead Sea Scrolls and early Palestinian Synagogues," *Harvard Theological Review* 70 (1977): 183–200;

plus references cited in W. F. Albright and C. S. Mann, *Matthew,* Anchor Bible (Garden City, N.Y.: Doubleday, 1971), 14; Davies and Allison, *Matthew,* 1.229; Hengel, *Judaism and Hellenism,* 1.236–239. The more spectacular evidence dates from a later period—the Zodiac floor of Beth-Alpha is from the 6th century C.E. At any rate, it is entirely possible (though not necessarily logical) that Jews could have adopted some Judaized version of astrology while continuing to regard the magian version (from which their own system was no doubt derived) as false wisdom and foolishness. Many rabbinic writings condemn Gentiles as "worshipers of stars" (*b. Sanh.* 59a; *b.'Abod. Zar.* 3a; *Sipra* on Lev. 20:7), which indicates that a distinction between astrologies could have been drawn over what attitude was adopted with regard to the Zodiac. The fact is (whether it makes sense to us or not), even if Jewish writings from this period sometimes seem to approve of some type of astrology, they never approve of whatever it is that magi were thought to know or practice.

277. Trexler thinks that the author of Matthew's Gospel may have "imagined figures somewhat akin to the snake oil salesmen of the American heritage: healers who peddled occult wisdom with their goods." But for later generations of readers "to assume that the magi were intellectuals or rulers was one thing. To suggest that they might have been spice and drug merchants, as the class of magi were sometimes understood to be, was clearly unworthy" (Trexler, *Journey of the Magi,* 13).

278. To state the matter in this way exposes the artificiality of separating what readers are expected to "know" from what they are expected to "believe." Obviously, the classification of any data as knowledge is evaluative, and nothing can be "known" apart from some perspective. All knowledge is, in some sense, belief. But, please, let's not become too embroiled in an epistemological deconstruction of my tidy categories. The point is that some beliefs acquire the status of knowledge within a given community when they come to be generally recognized as truth that does not need to be argued. I think that the discernible (though fictive) community consisting of Matthew's implied author and implied readers has elevated the belief that "magi are fools" to such a level. It is considered to be a fact, something that everyone (except fools) is assumed to know.

279. I am intentionally defining our interest more narrowly than Matthew's understanding of wisdom in general, a topic on which full monographs could and have been written.

280. Note, by way of comparison, that in Luke's Gospel, Jesus' criticisms of the religious leaders frequently conclude with a summons for them to change their ways ("Go and do likewise," Luke 10:37) and sometimes with a promise of the benefit they will receive if they do so: "Do this and you will live" (Luke 10:28); "Everything will be clean for you" (Luke 11:41); "You will be repaid at the resurrection" (Luke 14:14). Nothing like this is ever found in Matthew, where Jesus makes no more effort to minister to the religious leaders than to the demons he exorcises. They are "plants that the heavenly Father did not plant," destined to be uprooted in time (Matt. 15:13). Jesus informs them that they are going to hell, and that's really all there is to it (Matt. 23:33).

281. We should note that Matthew does esteem Sophia herself highly (11:19), recognize that Solomon was a wise man favored by God (12:42), identify Jesus as one who possesses wisdom (13:54), and refer mysteriously to wise people (*sophoi*) whom Jesus will send to Israel after Easter (23:34). This all parallels what we observed earlier with regard to royalty and power (see n. 261): the royal power of God is a good thing; there were good kings once in the sacred past; Jesus can be identified in some sense as the true king; and someday (probably after the Parousia) his followers will sit on thrones. Still, *the setting of the story* is one in which God rejects both the royal and the wise.

282. Some recoil immediately at this assertion, thinking it unlikely if not impossible because the magi are presented positively in Matthew, and "ignorance" is assumed to be a negative trait. Let me be clear about this: I am not arguing against the widespread notion that the magi are presented positively in Matthew; I am, however, arguing that they are presented as "servile" and "ignorant," both of which (in this narrative) can be *positive* traits (in precisely the same way that "meek" or "poor in spirit" can be positive traits).

283. Matthew's narrative does present Jesus as king in an ironic (21:5) or eschatological (25:34, 40) sense, but the magi appear to intend the designation to be taken literally. Notably, the precise title, "king of the Jews" is used only by Gentiles. Contrast "king of Israel" in 27:42.

284. Some interpreters have tried to tie this revelation in a dream to magian wisdom, since the latter may have included dream interpretation as well as astrology. But the immediate narrative context suggests the magi's dream was similar to those of Joseph, in which God gave clear directions that required no esoteric skill to understand (1:21; 2:13). Granted, no angel of the Lord is referenced here, so I would not press the point too far in either direction. Matthew's implied readers, however, are expected to know (and to regard as authoritative scripture) the Daniel story, where magi are specifically presented as failures at dream interpretation (Daniel 2).

285. David Hill, *The Gospel of Matthew*, New Century Bible (Grand Rapids: Wm. B. Eerdmans Publishing Co., 1972), 82.

286. The very earliest reference to this story is probably found in Justin, *Dialogue* 78. His statement there that the magi came from Arabia is perhaps an attempt to strengthen the allusion to Psalm 72 since Sheba and Seba (vss. 10, 15) were located in south Arabia. See Eric F. F. Bishop, "Some Reflections on Justin Martyr and the Nativity Narratives," *Evangelical Quarterly* 39 (1967): 30–39.

287. Tertullian, *Adv. Marc.,* 3:13.

288. Here's a longer version: Tertullian disputes an argument that would present Christ as a warrior. The argument apparently applied to Christ the words of Isaiah 8:4, which Tertullian and his opponent translated "he will take up the strength of Damascus and the spoils of Samaria against the king of the Assyrians" (Modern translations render the verse such that the goods of Damascus and Samaria are taken *by* the king of Assyria). Tertullian wants to show that this scripture has already been fulfilled—in a symbolic sense—when Christ received gifts from the eastern kingdoms as a child "without fighting or armament" (the king of Assyria becomes an allegorical reference to Herod). The comment that the East considers the magi almost as kings is made in an effort to tighten the case geographically via Psalm 72. If Matthew's magi can be identified with the "kings of the Arabs" in Psalm 72:10, then the gold of Arabia (Ps. 72:15) that they present to Christ can be identified with the strength of Damascus in Isaiah 8:4 since "Damascus was formerly reckoned to Arabia."

289. Especially noteworthy in this regard are the words, "the East considers." The implication is "People in the West may not know this, but . . . ." Thus, historical ignorance is not only recognized but contextualized.

290. It is ignored in a footnote to the Oxford edition of this work: "Tertullian is the earliest writer to say that the Magi were kings." This goes beyond the translation of the text ("the Orient for the most part held the Magi for kings"), which is itself suspect. The Latin: "Nam et Magos reges habuit fere oriens." See *Tertullian. Adversus Marcionem,* ed. and trans. by Ernest Evans (Great Britain: Oxford University Press, 1972), 209.

291. Sermon 200, "On the Lord's Epiphany," as found in John E. Rotelle, ed., *The Works of Saint Augustine: A Translation for the 21st Century,* vol. III/6 (Sermons 184–229Z), trans. Edmund Hill (Brooklyn: New City Press), 83–85.

292. This may or may not be the earliest reference that identifies the magi with kings (or—to be precise—vice versa). J. C. Marsh-Edwards cites passages from St. Ephraem without giving the references in a sketchy article, "The Magi in Tradition and Art," *Irish Ecclesiastical Record* 85 (1956): 1–9. Ephraem (c. 306–393) was a contemporary of Augustine and his designations of the magi's royalty are supposedly more explicit, giving the kings' names and listing the regions they ruled. Metzger, however, is either ignorant of the reference Marsh-Edwards has found or disputes it, for he claims that the earliest literary reference to the names of the magi occurs in the sixth century ("Names," 80). Given the confusion and paucity of data, I am content to limit our examination to the Western tradition.

293. Rotelle, *Works of Augustine,* vol. III/6 (Sermons 184–229Z), 83–84.

294. Ibid., 84.

295. See Peter Brown, *Augustine of Hippo* (Berkeley, Calif.: University of California Press, 1969); Jean Bethke Eshtain, *Augustine and the Limits of Politics* (Notre Dame, Ind.: University of Notre Dame, 1995); R. A. Markus, *Saeculum: History and Society in the Theology of St. Augustine* (Cambridge: Cambridge University Press, 1970); Charles Villa-Vicencio, *Between Christ and Caesar: Classic and Contemporary Texts on Church and State* (Grand Rapids: Wm. B. Eerdmans Publishing Co., 1986), 20–23.

296. Rosemary Radford Reuther, "Augustine and Christian Political Theology," *Interpretation* 29 (1975): 252–65, esp. 261.

297. Sermons 199–205 in Rotelle, *Works of Augustine,* vol. III/6 (Sermons 184–229Z), and Sermons 373–375 in vol. III/10 (Sermons 341–400).

298. This observation is even more impressive when we note that fulfillment of prophecy is a prominent theme. Almost all the sermons treat the citation of Micah 5:2 in Matthew 2:5–6, and several discuss the apologetic value of demonstrating that Christ was born in a way that fulfilled ancient prophecies. One (Sermon 202) even discusses Isaiah 8:4 in language that is likely to be dependent on Tertullian. Still, none of these sermons, not even the one that takes the magi as models of earthly kings, makes any connection with Isaiah 60 or Psalm 72.

299. In the *Cave of Treasures* document, concern for literal fulfillment of the Old Testament reaches a peak, as the magi are identified by name with historical kings of the East. But such identifications only served to buttress interpretations that we have seen could also be asserted apart from such support. Granted that the literal identification evident in *Cave of Treasures* might not have arisen apart from the kinds of intertextual connections made by Tertullian, it would have had no reason to arise apart from the ideological shift evident in Augustine.

300. Trexler, *Journey of the Magi,* 25–27.

301. To quote Trexler, "The magi were commonly viewed as ambassadors of a monarch even if they were not said to be kings themselves" (*Journey of the Magi,* 36; see also 11, 212, n. 7). Though no longer necessary, such interpretations persisted even when historical knowledge was lost: an eleventh-century menologium shows the magi being dispatched by the king of Persia, who is identified as Cyrus the Great!

302. The tradition was less pronounced in the East. Byzantine art before the Latin conquest of 1204 rarely shows the magi as kings. The Byzantine emperor, furthermore, was represented by a star, not a magus. Trexler relates this to the different political and social organization of the East. See *Journey of the Magi,* 45–52.

303. Ibid. esp., 24–25, 31, 79.

304. Discussion of these festivals forms much of Trexler's *Journey of the Magi* and yields his most original insights. For what is described here, see especially 53–72, 86–92, 118–23, 152–85 (quoted words are on 91).

305. This was Otto IV, the same emperor who managed to usurp an arch for himself in the Cologne cathedral. See Trexler, *Journey of the Magi*, 79–85.
306. Ibid., 85.
307. *Luther's Works*, vol. 13, 199. See also vol. 36, 294; vol. 40, 96.
308. Horsley, *Liberation of Christmas*, 54. He footnotes here Eddy, *King Is Dead*, 65–67, which proposes that magi may once have been a royal class.
309. We do not have to argue with this political agenda to identify Horsley's reading as unexpected. Although Horsley provides a wealth of historical information, he shows no interest in determining what knowledge can be reasonably presupposed for Matthew's implied readers. Personally, I think Horsley exaggerates the amount of political power that can be attributed historically to magi in the first century, but even if he were right in this regard, we must reckon with the fact that stories from the discourse setting of Matthew's narrative invariably present magi as persons who lack power, as figures who invoke either sympathy or ridicule. Horsley might argue that the latter portrayal was historically inaccurate, but that would be quite beside the point. It was in any event a formidable stereotype, one that is much more likely to represent the impression Matthew's readers are assumed to bring to the text than one based on more exact knowledge of Persian governance. As we have seen, regarding the magi as kings also seems to ignore the characterization of the magi in Matthew's narrative, where they exhibit traits more closely associated with servants. And, most important, Horsley's interpretation fails to reckon with the ideological point of view concerning royalty that Matthew's implied readers are presumed to espouse. Indeed, the departure from the apocalyptic perspective is pronounced, insofar as it relocates the solution to oppression within history through a replacement of rulers rather than through their displacement at the end of time. For Horsley, the point is simply "resistance against western Imperial domination" (p. 56) instead of resistance to domination, period.
310. Compare the comment from a pre-critical commentary by J. C. Ryle, written in 1856: "Let us observe in this passage how true it is that the rulers of this world are seldom friendly to the cause of God. . . . Do we think that Christ's cause depends upon the power and patronage of princes? We are mistaken. They have seldom done much to advance the true religion; they have far more frequently been the enemies of truth. 'Do not put your trust in princes' (Psalm 146:3)." Then, in true Augustinian fashion, he adds, "There are many people like Herod. Those who are like Josiah and Edward VI of England are few." See *Matthew*, The Crossway Classic Commentaries (Wheaton, Ill.: Crossway Books, 1993), 10.
311. Surveys of some of this literature are found in U. Riedinger, *Die Heilige Schrift im Kampf der griechischen Kirche gegen die Astrologie* (Innsbruck: Wagner, 1956), 142–46, and in Lowther Clarke, *Divine Humanity.*
312. Justin, *Dialogue* 78.9.
313. Many scholars think Ignatius and Matthew were actually members of the same community—the church at Antioch. On the close social and theological relationship of the two, see John Meier, "Antioch," in *Antioch and Rome: New Testament Cradles of Catholic Christianity,* ed. Raymond E. Brown and John P. Meier (New York: Paulist Press, 1983), 11–86.
314. Ignatius, *Ephesians,* 19.2–3.
315. Augustine, Sermon 374, in Rotelle, *Works of Augustine,* vol. III/10, 324.
316. Augustine, Sermon 201, in Rotelle, *Works of Augustine,* vol. III/6, 87.
317. For other early examples, see especially Origen, *Con. Cels.* I. 60, and Tertullian, *De Idol.* 9.
318. See Trexler, *Journey of the Magi,* 27, for references and discussion.
319. See Lowther Clarke, *Divine Humanity,* 47.

320. Davies and Allison offer four reasons why the thesis for a polemic against astrology in this text fails (*Matthew*, 1.229). These are not really convincing, but at any rate, I do not claim that the text presents such a polemic. I think that Matthew's readers are assumed to regard magian wisdom (which probably included some form of astrology) as foolishness. There is no need for the narrative to polemicize against what it assumes its readers will reject.

321. Rotelle, *Works of Augustine*, vol. III/6, 99. The quote is from Sermon 204.

322. John Chrysostom, *Homily On Matt.* 6.4.

323. Albertus Magnus is said to have entertained some astrological conjectures in his interpretation of this story, and Cardinal Pierre d'Ailly actually maintained that the Incarnation was in part due to heavenly and stellar influence ("per celi et astorum virtutem"). On such "peculiar references" among medieval authorities, see Stephen M. Buhler, "Marsilio Ficino's *De stella magorum* and Renaissance Views of the Magi," *Renaissance Quarterly* 43 (1990): 348–71, esp. 360.

324. Other interpretations of the gifts abound, with sufficient material for a lengthy paper on this subject alone. The most enduring, perhaps, are those which associate the items with christological functions (for example, gold—king; incense—high priest; myrrh—physician). Myrrh is also often taken as signifying Christ's suffering, on the basis of Mark 15:23. See Luz, *Matthew 1–7*, 138.

325. The Venerable Bede, *In Matthaei Evangelium exposito*, in *Patrologia latina*, ed. J. Migne, 9–132, esp. 13–15. Ecumenicity has its limits, as Gentile wisdom is contrasted with Jewish obtusity.

326. See Buhler, "Marsilio Ficino," 360–61. Citations of the work here are from the 1928 Burke translation of Bacon, as quoted (and slightly amended) by Buhler.

327. On the idea of a separate, parallel "Gentile revelation," see also D. P. Walker, *The Ancient Theology* (Ithaca, N. Y.: Cornell University, 1972), 3–10.

328. See Buhler, "Marsilio Ficino." For an interesting contrast to Ficino, see the 1638 work of Jacques d'Auzoles Lapeyre, *L'Epiphanie, ou Pensées nouvelles à la Gloire de Dieu touchant les trois Mages* (Paris, 1638). He proposes that the three magi were in fact Melchizedek, Enoch, and Elijah (three Hebrew prophets who were thought never to have died). Thus, they could be respected as true wise men in the Judeo-Christian tradition. While avoiding association with the wrong kind of wisdom (pagan learning), they could still be celebrated as possessors of true intellectual power.

329. Trexler, *Journey of the Magi*, 189.

330. Lancelot Andrewes, *XCVI Sermons*, 2nd ed. (London, 1632), 136. Cited in Buhler, "Marsilio Ficino," 370.

331. These works are displayed and discussed in Trexler, *Journey of the Magi*, 122.

332. Voltaire, "Épiphanie," in *Questions sur l'Encyclopédie par des amanteurs* (Paris, 1771), 5.225–28. Cited by Schoebel, *L'Histoire des Rois Mages*, 98; Trexler, *Journey of the Magi*, 185.

333. To see what happens when rationalism and pietism collide, we need only sample the 1856 commentary of J. C. Ryle (*Matthew*, 8–9), a British cleric similar in some respects to Charles Spurgeon. He thought Matthew's magi were definitely wise men, but he defined wisdom in terms of the virtue of diligence. He asks us to consider "the trouble it must have cost these wise men to travel . . . the time that such a journey would occupy . . . the dangers to be encountered." The main point of the text is that it "teaches us the truth of the old saying, 'Where there is a will, there is a way.'"

334. As always, a subversive undercurrent can be detected. This time, it has tended to surface in mysticism, especially (for some reason) among female visionaries, whose contributions are once again preserved for us by the indefatigable Richard Trexler (*Journey of the Magi*, 190–93). Exemplary are Anna Katrina Emmerich (1774–1824), whose visions were recorded by the German roman-

tic poet Clemens Brentano, and Theres Neumann (1898–1962). Brentano described Emmerich's magi as fundamentally "childish" (*kindlich*), as in "Oh how stirring is the good humor and childish simplicity of these loving kings." Trexler regards these visions as "reeking with modern anti-intellectualism, in which the magi . . . are admirable precisely because they are rubes."

335. Brown, *Birth of the Messiah,* 158. Brown fills the narrative gap left by 2:2 with a tour de force no less daring than that of Ignatius or Augustine. Somehow he knows that the magi were able to "recognize the salvific import of the Davidic star" (p. 182). The text gives no indication that the magi connected the star with anything Davidic, much less salvific.

336. Davies and Allison, *Matthew,* 1.230–31. Divine revelation, then, seems to play no role. The magi found the Christ because they were smarter than other people. This entire case depends on a (barely) unstated proposition that regards Matthew's narrative has having more in common with Greco-Roman literature than Jewish literature, an interesting turn—to say the least—for Davies. Once, he thought the story paralleled the Exodus account: "the Magi from the East are led to kneel at the feet of the greater Moses . . . their power was broken at the advent of Christ, just as the sorcerers had been vanquished by Moses." See W. D. Davies, *Setting of the Sermon on the Mount,* 79. How this scholar came in the course of a quarter century to view the story as a vindication of magian wisdom rather than a vanquishing of the same would no doubt be an interesting tale. (See Replies, p. 240.)

337. Horsley, *Liberation of Christmas,* 58. He assumes that this nonnarrated act of revelation was unlike all the narrated acts of revelation in Matthew 1–2 in that it was an esoteric natural phenomenon requiring specialized academic knowledge to interpret.

338. M. Hengel and H. Merkel, "Die Magier aus dem Osten und die Flucht nach Ägypten (Mt 2) im Rahmen der antiken Religionsgeschichte und der Theologie des Matthäus," in *Orientierung an Jesus,* ed. P. Hoffmann (Freiburg: Herder, 1973), 139–69, quotations on 152, 165. Luz evaluates this remark by affirming that although "Matthew does not state directly that (the magi) are 'the intellectual elite of the Gentile world,' many of his contemporary readers in Syria and Asia Minor probably thought so" (p. 135). Why, then, would they not be depicted as such in Jewish or Christian literature of the period?

339. It's an old tradition, going back to Luther's translation in Germany ("Weise") and to the King James Version in English, which was followed by both the Revised Standard Version and the New Revised Standard Version. This reading was explicitly defended in the 1940s by R. C. H. Lenski: "They were not sorcerers, conjurers, soothsayers, or the like. Their popular designation as 'wise men' well defines what *magoi* really signifies. The narrative presents them as astronomers." See R. C. H. Lenski, *The Interpretation of St. Matthew's Gospel* (Columbus, Ohio: Wartburg, 1943), 58. Just to be certain, I sat in the R. C. H. Lenski Reading Room in the library at the institution where I teach (the same institution where he once taught), and I read Matthew 2 in English and in Greek. I could not find anything in "the narrative" that presents the magi as practicing astronomy.

340. The same point can be made internally with regard to New Testament documents. Robert Fowler demonstrates how Matthew's Gospel produces an unexpected reading of the Gospel of Mark. See *Let the Reader Understand,* 237–66.

341. Such an interpretation could perhaps be justified through a preliminary canonical judgment. If the reading is unexpected for implied readers of the book of Isaiah, it might be expected for implied readers of the Christian Bible, when the latter is understood as a book in its own right rather than as an anthology of books. But that's not the tack I usually take.

342. I have no particular interest in reconciling Paul and Matthew, who often disagree about a great many important things.

343. A bumper sticker available in Christian bookstores reads, "Wise men seek Him still." The message of the text, then, becomes moralistic ("If you are wise, you will try to find Christ") or self-congratulatory ("If you have found Christ, it is because you are wise"). In any case, the strong implication is that people who find Christ do so because they are wiser than others. It would be hard to conceive of a formulation more antithetical to the Christian gospel.

344. Most New Testament scholars believe that several sayings of Jesus were originally collected into a now lost document that they call "the Q source." Both Matthew and Luke used this collection of Jesus' sayings when writing their Gospels, which explains why they often both quote words of Jesus not found anywhere else. Whether Q was written in Greek or in Aramaic is a matter of dispute.

345. The first time he said to me, "We are just like the church in the New Testament," I responded, "Which one?" There are, of course, many churches in the New Testament and several different models for what a church can or should be like. Further, the notion that the earliest Christians got everything right but it's been downhill ever since (called "the Protestant prejudice" by some church historians) is just silly. Do we really *want* to be like "the church in the New Testament"? How about Laodicea? How about Corinth? Anyone get drunk at Communion lately?

346. This statement does not contradict my affirmations of the validity of historical-critical methods for studying scripture (pages 56, 59). I speak here not of the method itself but of the hermeneutic that some unthinkingly attach to it. The Bible may be studied in many different ways for many different reasons. But as a Christian I do reject equation of "authorial intent of scripture discerned through historical-critical scholarship" with "the inspired word of God."

347. The actual line, from Hamlet, is uttered by Queen Gertrude: "The lady doth protest too much, methinks" (Act 3, scene 2, line 230). In context, Queen Gertrude implies that the lady in question (a Queen in a play that she and Hamlet are watching) is *affirming* her commitments so strongly as to lose credibility. In our day, the line is often cited with reference to someone *objecting* so strongly as to lose credibility. In Elizabethan times, the word *protest* meant to "vow" or "solemnly swear." The popular modern applications of this quote derive from an unexpected reading (hearing?) of the play.

348. My favorite examples would concern 4:5 and 7:3, 8, in which the male speaker longs for the lovely breasts of his beloved. The history of mammophobic interpretation is impressive. Chinese pietist Watchman Nee assumes by way of 1 Thessalonians 5:8 that the desirable entities are actually "faith" and "love," which every Christian man should crave. See *Song of Songs* (Canby, Or.: Christian Literature International, 1992 [orig., 1945]), 77–78.

349. For instance, C. S. Lewis liked to think of these "babies" as sins, which are best destroyed before they get too big: When temptations first arise, act quick and "knock the little bastards' brains out." Edifying, but *not* what the psalmist intended. See *Reflections on the Psalms* (New York: Harcourt, Brace, and World, 1958), 136. Actually the entire three chapters of this book that deal with "second meanings" in scripture are worth another look now that we have (re)discovered the value of literary study of the Bible.

350. You may have noticed that every example cited here has something to do with sexual functions. This would not necessarily have to be because I am obsessed with that topic. It could just be that I wanted to have lots of examples related to a single theme. I might have picked "politics" or "money" and come up with a similar list. Though, of course, I didn't. Anyway, the author of Genesis

expects us to believe that sheep will have striped lambs if only they mate in front of poles with stripes on them (30:25–43). I didn't even mention that one.

351. I argued a decade ago that this would not work (Powell, *What Is Narrative Criticism?*, 100). Narrative criticism evades to some extent the hermeneutical chasm between "the meaning then" and "the meaning now" (cf. n. 5), but at the same time opens a new divide, between "meaning for the world of the story" and "meaning for the world of the reader." Thus, "the full task of biblical interpretation requires gifts and insights that are not provided by the exegetical discipline itself. . . . The interpreter must rely on the gift of the Spirit and on insight drawn from other fields, such as systematic theology and pastoral care."

352. Stephen Moore claims that poststructuralism finds narrative criticism intrinsically repulsive when the latter is exercised from a perspective of evangelical faith (*Poststructuralism and the New Testament*, 116). Why should this be so, when that perspective is clearly acknowledged? Even Moore seems ready to give a poststructuralist seal of approval to other (acknowledged) ideological or resistant reading strategies. I have never been able to see the logic in a position that I sometimes encounter at academic meetings devoted to biblical scholarship, namely, that which maintains the legitimacy of reading biblical texts from diverse ideological perspectives (feminist, Marxist, etc.) but denies the legitimacy of reading those texts from the perspective of evangelical Christianity. Why should the gospel of Christ be the only unacceptable philosophy?

353. The term comes from the work of Ernst Käsemann, to whom I remain indebted even while (now) considering his equation of the "canon within the canon" with the doctrine of justification by grace to be inadequate. I would define my canon within the canon as "the revelation of God in Jesus Christ," though I realize that this definition itself needs a good deal of defining. See two essays by Käsemann in *Essays on New Testament Themes*, Studies in Biblical Theology 41 (London: SCM, 1964): "Is the Gospel Objective?" 48–62, and "The Canon of the New Testament and the Unity of the Church," 95–107, and two more essays (also by Käsemann) in *New Testament Questions for Today* (Philadelphia: Fortress Press, 1969): "Paul and Early Catholicism," 236–51; "Unity and Multiplicity in the New Testament Doctrine of the Church," 252–59.

354. On this see Rita Nakashima Brock, *Journeys by Heart: A Christology of Erotic Power* (New York: Crossroad, 1988); Mary C. Grey, *Redeeming the Dream: Feminism, Redemption, and Christianity* (London: SPCK, 1989); and the womanist study, Delores S. Williams, *Sisters in the Wilderness: The Challenge of Womanist God Talk* (Maryknoll, N.Y.: Orbis Books, 1993).

355. We discover the (sometimes acknowledged) Achilles' heel of postmodernism: the claim that "there are no foundations" becomes foundational. The postmodern objection to my desire (even this late in the game) to let my understanding of the gospel of Jesus Christ be the standard by which I evaluate everything else posits no alternative but to allow "postmodernism" to be the standard by which I evaluate everything else. Ultimately, postmodernists seem to claim that postmodernism itself is the Way, the Truth, and the Life. No. I will not go there.

356. I refer of course to the Greek text of Matthew 2, not to English translations that may indeed identify them as "wise men."

357. There are other texts. Deborah is called a prophet in Judges 4:4. The Hebrew text of Isaiah 8:3 can be translated as either "the prophet's wife" or "the woman prophet" (the latter seems more likely). Joel thinks the Spirit of the Lord will cause daughters and sons alike to prophesy (Joel 2:28). The New Testament

also makes casual references to pre-Pentecost women prophets in Israel (Anna, certainly, in Luke 2:36, and probably Elizabeth in Luke 1:41–45).

358. Eddy draws such an analogy explicitly in *The King Is Dead,* 65.

359. Part of the issue here is what is meant by "Persian religion." Zoroastrianism? Or something more vague or generic (such as "astrology")? My guess is that when Matthew's narrative identifies the magi simply as coming from "the East" (as opposed to "from Persia" or "from Babylon"), it invites readers to regard them simply as representatives of some obscure paganism, the specific variety of which is irrelevant.

360. Trexler, *Journey of the Magi,* 92–118.

361. Trexler takes special note of earrings: "The Western prejudice against men who wore earrings was ancient. At least as far back as the Satyricon, Romans associated pierced ears with 'Arabians,' and in the Middle Ages, one may find mosaics of men wearing earrings burning in the Christian hell. It is not surprising that despite an extensive search, I could not find a single white king or magi servant sporting earrings" (*Journey of the Magi,* 104). Yet the black magus often has earrings, as a clear sign that he is not European.

362. See note 361. In this regard the black magus and the effeminate magus might be combined. According to Trexler, a white (i.e., European) magus *never* wears earrings even when he is otherwise effeminate, but a black (i.e., non-European) magus might wear earrings if he is also effeminate.

363. Trexler, *Journey of the Magi,* 109.

364. Ibid.

365. Ibid., 108.

366. Ibid., 117.

REPLIES

When I write things about another person that might be perceived as critical or unflattering (either of them or of their work), I think it is only courteous to send that person a copy of what I have written and give them an opportunity to respond. Accordingly, here are the unedited replies that the following individuals have offered to comments made in this book. I thank them for being willing to continue our public dialogue.

Petri Merenlahti and Raimo Hakola reply to comments on pages 119–20 and in notes 20 and 186–92

Thank you very much for giving us the opportunity to respond. We only wish to make a couple of short remarks.

First, there are the words "grossly misreading." They seem to bother you, and you refer to them several times. We must admit that we are a bit surprised at this. This is because we do not think we initiated this strong rhetoric in the first place. It rather came along when we responded to your original claim that, from the perspective of narrative criticism, (referential) readings that view Matthew's Gospel as arousing hostility for Jewish people "represent a gross example of the referential fallacy and completely miss the point of the story." We thought we were just playing the ball back.

So much for the choice of words. But then there is also our key argument. If we perhaps didn't get yours, we fear that you may not have grasped ours.

In our article, we grounded our argument on the current discussion (within narrative theory and philosophy of literature) concerning the difference of fictional and non-fictional narratives and the difference this categorization makes for the use of such heuristic concepts as the implied reader. What we actually called into question was the applicability of non-referential reading strategies to non-fictional narratives (the Gospels included) if this is to take place in the name of critical praxis.

We certainly wouldn't advocate a return to author-oriented criticism of fiction. Nor would we like to set a norm of natural reading to be followed by every reader. We only regard non-referential readings of non-fictional texts (say, weather forecasts or medical reports or accounts of the Good News of Jesus Christ) as less than adequate descriptive poetics. In fact, this does not seem to be an unusual view among the narratologists of today.

A. K. M. Adam replies to comments in n. 103

I haven't taken a stand on whether "narrative criticism" is postmodern, partly because I'm not sure that there's an intrinsic coherence to what "narrative criticism" is, and partly because (as you note) fighting over labels is usually a waste of time. If it came to labels, though, I wouldn't characterize most of your work as "postmodern"—not because Stephen Moore convinced me of anything, but because my sense is that you want to hang on to notions like "implied readers," "implied authors," "expected readings," "normative ways of reading," "linguistic competence," and so on. Your disclaimer that you're only talking about "expected" or "unexpected" readings without regard to legitimacy doesn't convince me—yet—especially since the open-endedness of who's doing the "expecting" troubles me.

A. K. M. Adam replies to comments in note 111

That article doesn't try to argue that there are no "expected" readings—a foolish enough thing to try, since "expectation" is hardly separable from most human endeavors. I'm arguing that there are no text-immanent features that constrain interpretation, such that our construction of *The Shortest Way* as a satire depends entirely on our awareness that Defoe was himself a dissenter not on any information "encoded" in *The Shortest Way*. I just don't see where knowledge that Defoe was a dissenter makes "the expected reading" that we construe *The Shortest Way* as a satire a feature of the text. I don't dispute the fact that we justifiably suppose *The Shortest Way was* a satire—I do doubt that expectation derives its currency from anything but a large number of people's agreement that we ought so to read it (not, in other words, from "the text").

Warren Carter replies to comments on pages 85–86 and in note 110

Your comments in note 110 that supposedly exemplify "problems" with the term "authorial audience" do not seem at all convincing to me. As one who uses the notion, borrowed as you indicate from Rabinowitz, I should clarify that I do not regard reading in relation to "the authorial audience" as normative in any way (see my *Matthew: Storyteller, Evangelist, Interpreter*, pp. 259–71). I do not use this strategy to establish the normative reading of a text, by which the adequacy of all other readings is to be assessed. Rather, I use it to specify an audience, one possible audience among many possible audiences. Specifying an audience is important, I think, because any act of interpretation is a matter of interaction between text and interpreters. What an audience does or does not bring to that process very much shapes the outcome. The audience could be me, or a sixteenth-century audience, or a ninth-century audience, or a first-century audience. Each will bring different experiences, knowledge, and ignorance to the text and different understandings will emerge. So I use *authorial audience* to denote an audience that by temporal and physical location shares a range of experiences and knowledge with the Gospel's author, experiences that have left some mark on aspects of the text. I think that some of this knowledge and experience can be reconstructed (guessed at?) by later interpreters who attend both to the text and to its circumstances of production. Doing so is useful for subsequent readers in that it clarifies some aspects of the text. But I don't think for one moment that these meanings thereby become normative for all subsequent readings. Subsequent readings must enter into dialogue with them. Nor do they preclude investigating (or comparing) the interaction of other audiences from other temporal and geographical locations with the text.

Further, you write that you have problems with the word "audience" in relation to a written text. Written texts have readers not audiences. But it's not quite as simple as that. As you know, the ancient world frequently accessed written texts by *hearing* them, not by seeing them (just as we might access a written speech by hearing it). Written documents were commonly read out loud to audiences who could not read. (They were often read out loud when people were "reading" them privately to themselves too). Hearing is, of course, a quite different dynamic than reading. So if one chooses to examine the interaction between the Gospel of Matthew and those for whom it is first written, it would be appropriate to be aware that they were hearing, not reading, the Gospel, and that they are thereby an audience, not readers. If one were contemplating the interaction of a modern group with the Gospel, then readers would be more appropriate.

Finally, I think your discussion of implied readers throughout overlooks a major advantage that the notion of an "authorial audience" has for engaging the Gospels. The notion of implied reader has suggested (whether rightly or wrongly is not my concern) to many an ahistorical and monolithic reading of each Gospel. Claims such as "the reader understands . . ." often seem to be general statements that applied to every reading, but which begged the question of "whose reader"? The question of "whose reader" becomes all the more pressing by conflicting claims about what implied readers were supposed to be doing at any one point in the text. The term and approach, then, has suggested to some that one ideal (text-constituted?) reading of each Gospel can be described, that this reading is not dependent on any socio-historical factors, and that this "pure" or "model" or "ideal" reading is normative for assessing all others. In effect, the "implied reader" approach masks "flesh-and-blood" readers, blinds its users to the text's socio-historical groundedness as well as to their own location, and produces (so it has been thought) an ahistorical reading.

But of course no such reading can ever exist. No act of interpretation can be separated from socio-historical contexts, whether of the text or of the interpreter. That means among other things that an interpreter's location at least gives any implied reader and resultant reading socio-historical shape, even though the method (at least as it was practiced by some) was inattentive to such dynamics.

Such concerns and debates were part of the context in which I first took up Rabinowitz's term, "authorial audience." One advantage of the notion of "authorial audience" is that it causes the interpreter to be honest and explicit (as much as historical distance will allow) about what constitutes this audience, and about one's own role in this interpretive strategy. I as interpreter constitute an "authorial audience" within clearly defined historical parameters. To do so I employ not only the text but also the larger socio-political world that impacts both text and interpretation. I choose to posit an audience limited by and familiar with the author's world. The authorial audience, then, is always a construction, but the elements of the reconstruction are acknowledged and explicit in terms of a particular socio-historical context (the author's world) as understood by me the interpreter (shaped by various other interpreters, knowledge, experience, etc.). The approach is a way of saying, "I am choosing to take into account in this interpretation the following socio-historical factors (as much as I can assess their impact given historical distance). . . ." In this sense, an authorial audience approximates a real audience (inasmuch as historical distance allows us to reconstruct the past) but is not the same as "original/intended readers" (who remain unknown to us).

Of course, one could define "implied reader" in this way, with some clear historical parameters. But then you may as well talk about "authorial audience." That in fact would be preferable for two reasons: you would bypass the ahistorical associations of "implied reader" named above, and you would avoid the anachronistic term "reader" for the Gospels, more accurately denoting the oral/aural means of interaction with the text indicated by the audience.

I could say a bunch more about various nuances and elaborations (some of which is said in my article on narrative/literary approaches to Matthew in *Journal for the Study of the New Testament* 67 [1997]: 3–27) but space has run out.

If I may add one final comment: on at least one matter we seem to be in total agreement. Your note 269 is very astute and wise!

Dale C. Allison replies to comments in note 336

As the preface to volume three of the ICC commentary makes plain, I wrote the commentary and W. D. Davies read and commented on what I produced. Thus, the comments on the magi cited by Powell are mine; Davies did not change his mind about anything and would not have written what I wrote. The presentation of the magi in Davies's *Setting* does not agree with the presentation in the ICC commentary for the same reason that the presentation in Powell's book and in that commentary are different—they are by different authors.

Index of Biblical Passages

Index of Names

Authors and Artist, Past and Present